Statistical Application Development with R and Python

Second Edition

Power of statistics using R and Python

Prabhanjan Narayanachar Tattar

BIRMINGHAM - MUMBAI

Statistical Application Development with R and Python
Second Edition

First published: July 2013

Second edition: August 2017

Production reference: 1290817

Published by Packt Publishing Ltd.
Livery Place
35 Livery Street
Birmingham B3 2PB, UK.

ISBN 978-1-78862-119-9

www.packtpub.com

Credits

Author
Prabhanjan Narayanachar Tattar

Reviewers
Dr. Ratnadip Adhikari
Ajay Ohri
Abhinav Rai

Commissioning Editor
Adarsh Ranjan

Acquisition Editor
Tushar Gupta

Content Development Editor
Snehal Kolte

Technical Editor
Dharmendra Yadav

Copy Editor
Safis Editing

Project Coordinator
Manthan Patel

Proofreader
Safis Editing

Indexer
Tejal Daruwale Soni

Graphics
Kirk D'Penha
Tania Dutta
Abhinash Sahu

Production Coordinator
Nilesh Mohite

Cover Work
Nilesh Mohite

About the Author

Prabhanjan Narayanachar Tattar has a combined twelve years of experience with R and Python software. He has also authored the books *A Course in Statistics with R*, Wiley, and *Practical Data Science Cookbook*, Packt. The author has built three packages in R titled gpk, RSADBE, and ACSWR. He has obtained a PhD (statistics) from Bangalore University under the broad area of survival snalysis and published several articles in peer-reviewed journals. During the PhD program, the author received the young Statistician honors for the IBS(IR)-GK Shukla Young Biometrician Award (2005) and the Dr. U.S. Nair Award for Young Statistician (2007) and also held a Junior and Senior Research Fellowship at CSIR-UGC.

Prabhanjan has worked in various positions in the analytical industry and nearly 10 years of experience in using statistical and machine learning techniques.

Acknowledgment

I would like to thank the readers and reviewers of the first edition and it is their constructive criticism that a second edition has been possible. The R and Python open source community deservers a huge applause for making the software so complete that it is almost akin to rubbing a magical lamp.

I continue to express my gratitude to all the people mentioned in the previous edition. My family has been at the forefront as always in extending their cooperation and whenever I am working on a book, they understand the weekends would have to be spent on the idiot box.

Profs. D. D. Pawar and V. A. Jadhav were my first two Statistics teachers and I learnt my first craft from them during 1996-99 at Department of Statistics, Science College, Nanded. Prof. Pawar had been very kind and generous towards me and invited in March 2015 to deliver some R talks from the first edition. Even 20 years later they are the flag-bearers of the subject in the Marathawada region and it is with profound love and affection that I express my gratitude to both of them. Thank you a lot, sirs.

It was a mere formal dinner meeting with Tushar Gupta in Chennai a month ago and we thought of getting the second edition. We both were convinced that if we work in sync, do parallel publication processing, we would finish this task within a month. And it has been a roller-coaster ride with Menka Bohra, Snehal Kolte, and Dharmendra Yadav that the book is a finished product in a record time. My special thanks to this wonderful Packt team.

About the Reviewers

Dr. Ratnadip Adhikari received his B.Sc degree with Mathematics Honors from Assam University, India, in 2004 and M.Sc in applied mathematics from Indian Institute of Technology, Roorkee, in 2006. After that he obtained M.Tech in Computer Science and Technology and Ph.D. in Computer Science, both from Jawaharlal Nehru University, New Delhi, India, in 2009 and 2014, respectively.

He worked as an Assistant Professor in the **Computer Science & Engineering (CSE)** Dept. of the **LNM Institute of Information Technology (LNMIIT)**, Jaipur, Rajasthan, India. At present, he works as a Senior Data Scientist at Fractal Analytics, Bangalore, India. His primary research interests include Pattern recognition, time series forecasting, data stream classification, and hybrid modeling. The research works of Dr. Adhikari has been published in various reputed international journals and at conferences. He has attended a number of conferences and workshops throughout his academic career.

Ajay Ohri is the founder of Decisionstats.com and has 14 years work experience as a data scientist. He advises multiple startups in analytics off-shoring, analytics services, and analytics education, as well as using social media to enhance buzz for analytics products. Mr. Ohri's research interests include spreading open source analytics, analyzing social media manipulation with mechanism design, simpler interfaces for cloud computing, investigating climate change and knowledge flows.

He founded Decisionstats.com in 2007 a blog which has gathered more than 100,000 views annually since past 7 years.

His other books include *R for Business Analytics* (Springer 2012) and *R for Cloud Computing* (Springer 2014), and *Python for R Users* (Wiley 2017)

Abhinav Rai has been working as a Data Scientist for nearly a decade, currently working at Microsoft. He has experience working in telecom, retail marketing, and online advertisement. His areas of interest include the evolving techniques of machine learning and the associated technologies. He is especially more interested in analyzing large and humongous datasets and likes to generate deep insights in such scenarios. Academically, he holds a double master's degree in Mathematics from Deendayal Upadhyay Gorakhpur University with an NBHM scholarship and in Computer Science from Indian Statistical Institute, rigor and sophistication is a surety with his analytical deliveries.

www.PacktPub.com

eBooks, discount offers, and more

Did you know that Packt offers eBook versions of every book published, with PDF and ePub files available? You can upgrade to the eBook version at www.PacktPub. com and as a print book customer, you are entitled to a discount on the eBook copy. Get in touch with us at customercare@packtpub.com for more details.

At www.PacktPub.com, you can also read a collection of free technical articles, sign up for a range of free newsletters and receive exclusive discounts and offers on Packt books and eBooks.

https://www.packtpub.com/mapt

Get the most in-demand software skills with Mapt. Mapt gives you full access to all Packt books and video courses, as well as industry-leading tools to help you plan your personal development and advance your career.

Why subscribe?

- Fully searchable across every book published by Packt
- Copy and paste, print, and bookmark content
- On demand and accessible via a web browser

Customer Feedback

Thanks for purchasing this Packt book. At Packt, quality is at the heart of our editorial process. To help us improve, please leave us an honest review on this book's Amazon page at https://www.amazon.com/dp/1788621190.

If you'd like to join our team of regular reviewers, you can e-mail us at customerreviews@packtpub.com. We award our regular reviewers with free eBooks and videos in exchange for their valuable feedback. Help us be relentless in improving our products!

Table of Contents

Preface

R and Python are interchangeably required languages these days for anybody engaged with data analysis. The growth of these two languages and their inter-dependency creates a natural requirement to learn them both. Thus, it was natural where the second edition of my previous title *R Statistical Application Development by Example* was headed. I thus took this opportunity to add Python as an important layer and hence you would find *Doing it in Python* spread across and throughout the book. Now, the book is useful on many fronts, those who need to learn both the languages, uses R and needs to switch to Python, and vice versa. While abstract development of ideas and algorithms have been retained in R only, standard and more commonly required data analysis technique are available in both the languages now. The only reason for not providing the Python parallel is to avoid the book from becoming too bulky.

The open source language R is fast becoming one of the preferred companions for statistics, even as the subject continues to add many friends in machine learning, data mining, and so on among its already rich scientific network. The era of mathematical theory and statistical application embeddedness is truly a remarkable one for society and R and Python has played a very pivotal role in it. This book is a humble attempt at presenting statistical models through R for any reader who has a bit of familiarity with the subject. In my experience of practicing the subject with colleagues and friends from different backgrounds, I realized that many are interested in learning the subject and applying it in their domain which enables them to take appropriate decisions in analyses, which involves uncertainty. A decade earlier my friends would have been content with being pointed to a useful reference book. Not so anymore! The work in almost every domain is done through computers and naturally they do have their data available in spreadsheets, databases, and sometimes in plain text format. The request for an appropriate statistical model is invariantly followed by a one word question software? My answer to them has always been a single letter reply R! Why? It is really a very simple decision and it has been my companion over the last seven years. In this book, this experience has been converted into detailed chapters and a cleaner breakup of model building in R.

A by-product of my interactions with colleagues and friends who are all aspiring statistical model builders has been that I have been able to pick up the trough of their learning curve of the subject. The first attempt towards fixing the hurdle has been to introduce the fundamental concepts that the beginners are most familiar with, which is data. The difference is simply in the subtleties and as such I firmly believe that introducing the subject on their turf motivates the reader for a long way in their journey. As with most statistical software, R provides modules and packages which mostly cover many of the recently invented statistical methodologies. The first five chapters of the book focus on the fundamental aspects of the subject and the R language and therefore hence cover R basics, data visualization, exploratory data analysis, and statistical inference.

The foundational aspects are illustrated using interesting examples and sets up the framework for the next five chapters. Linear and logistic regression models being at the forefront, are of paramount importance in applications. The discussion is more generic in nature and the techniques can be easily adapted across different domains. The last two chapters have been inspired by the Breiman school and hence the modern method of using classification and regression trees has been developed in detail and illustrated through a practical dataset.

What this book covers

Chapter 1, Data Characteristics, introduces the different types of data through a questionnaire and dataset. The need of statistical models is elaborated in some interesting contexts. This is followed by a brief explanation of the installation of R and Python and their related packages. Discrete and continuous random variables are discussed through introductory programs. The programs are available in both the languages and although they do not need to be followed, they are more expository in nature.

Chapter 2, Import/Export Data, begins with a concise development of R basics. Data frames, vectors, matrices, and lists are discussed with clear and simpler examples. Importing of data from external files in CSV, XLS, and other formats is elaborated next. Writing data/objects from R for other languages is considered and the chapter concludes with a dialogue on R session management. Python basics, mathematical operations, and other essential operations are explained. Reading data from different format of external file is also illustrated along with the session management required.

Chapter 3, Data Visualization, discusses efficient graphics separately for categorical and numeric datasets. This translates into techniques for bar chart, dot chart, spine and mosaic plot, and four fold plot for categorical data while histogram, box plot, and scatter plot for continuous/numeric data. A very brief introduction to ggplot2 is also provided here. Generating similar plots using both R and Python will be a treatise here.

Chapter 4, Exploratory Analysis, encompasses highly intuitive techniques for the preliminary analysis of data. The visualizing techniques of EDA such as stem-and-leaf, letter values, and the modeling techniques of resistant line, smoothing data, and median polish provide rich insight as a preliminary analysis step. This chapter is driven mainly in R only.

Chapter 5, Statistical Inference, begins with an emphasis on the likelihood function and computing the maximum likelihood estimate. Confidence intervals for parameters of interest is developed using functions defined for specific problems. The chapter also considers important statistical tests of z-test and t-test for comparison of means and chi-square tests and f-test for comparison of variances. The reader will learn how to create new R and Python functions.

Chapter 6, Linear Regression Analysis, builds a linear relationship between an output and a set of explanatory variables. The linear regression model has many underlying assumptions and such details are verified using validation techniques. A model may be affected by a single observation, or a single output value, or an explanatory variable. Statistical metrics are discussed in depth which helps remove one or more types of anomalies. Given a large number of covariates, the efficient model is developed using model selection techniques. While the stats core R package suffices, statsmodels package in Python is very useful.

Chapter 7, The Logistic Regression Model, is useful as a classification model when the output is a binary variable. Diagnostic and model validation through residuals are used which lead to an improved model. ROC curves are next discussed which helps in identifying of a better classification model. The R packages pscl and ROCR are useful while pysal and sklearn are useful in Python.

Chapter 8, Regression Models with Regularization, discusses the problem of over fitting, which arises from the use of models developed in the previous two chapters. Ridge regression significantly reduces the probability of an over fit model and the development of natural spine models also lays the basis for the models considered in the next chapter. Regularization in R is achieved using packages ridge and MASS while sklearn and statsmodels help in Python.

Chapter 9, Classification and Regression Trees, provides a tree-based regression model. The trees are initially built using raw R functions and the final trees are also reproduced using rudimentary codes leading to a clear understanding of the CART mechanism. The pruning procedure is illustrated through one of the languages and the reader should explore to find the fix in another.

Chapter 10, CART and Beyond, considers two enhancements to CART, using bagging and random forests. A consolidation of all the models from *Chapter 6, Linear Regression Analysis*, to *Chapter 10, CART and Beyond*, is also provided through a dataset. The ensemble methods is fast emerging as very effective and popular machine learning technique and doing it in both the languages will improve users confidence.

What you need for this book

You will need the following to work with the examples in this book:

- R
- Python
- RStudio

Who this book is for

If you want to have a brief understanding of the nature of data and perform advanced statistical analysis using both R and Python, then this book is what you need. No prior knowledge is required. Aspiring data scientist, R users trying to learn Python and Python users trying to learn R.

Conventions

In this book, you will find a number of text styles that distinguish between different kinds of information. Here are some examples of these styles and an explanation of their meaning.

Code words in text, database table names, folder names, filenames, file extensions, pathnames, dummy URLs, user input, and Twitter handles are shown as follows: "We can include other contexts through the use of the `include` directive."

A block of code is set as follows:

```
abline(h=0.33,lwd=3,col="red")
abline(h=0.67,lwd=3,col="red")
abline(v=0.33,lwd=3,col="green")
```

Any command-line input or output is written as follows:

```
sudo apt-get update
sudo apt-get install python3.6
```

New terms and **important words** are shown in bold. Words that you see on the screen, for example, in menus or dialog boxes, appear in the text like this: "Clicking the **Next** button moves you to the next screen."

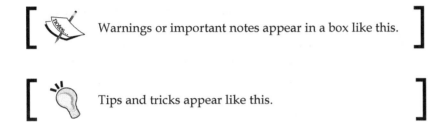

> Warnings or important notes appear in a box like this.

> Tips and tricks appear like this.

Reader feedback

Feedback from our readers is always welcome. Let us know what you think about this book—what you liked or disliked. Reader feedback is important for us as it helps us develop titles that you will really get the most out of.

To send us general feedback, simply e-mail feedback@packtpub.com, and mention the book's title in the subject of your message.

If there is a topic that you have expertise in and you are interested in either writing or contributing to a book, see our author guide at www.packtpub.com/authors.

Customer support

Now that you are the proud owner of a Packt book, we have a number of things to help you to get the most from your purchase.

Downloading the example code

You can download the example code files for this book from your account at http://www.packtpub.com. If you purchased this book elsewhere, you can visit http://www.packtpub.com/support and register to have the files e-mailed directly to you.

You can download the code files by following these steps:

1. Log in or register to our website using your e-mail address and password.
2. Hover the mouse pointer on the **SUPPORT** tab at the top.
3. Click on **Code Downloads & Errata**.
4. Enter the name of the book in the **Search** box.
5. Select the book for which you're looking to download the code files.
6. Choose from the drop-down menu where you purchased this book from.
7. Click on **Code Download**.

You can also download the code files by clicking on the **Code Files** button on the book's webpage at the Packt Publishing website. This page can be accessed by entering the book's name in the **Search** box. Please note that you need to be logged in to your Packt account.

Once the file is downloaded, please make sure that you unzip or extract the folder using the latest version of:

- WinRAR / 7-Zip for Windows
- Zipeg / iZip / UnRarX for Mac
- 7-Zip / PeaZip for Linux

The code bundle for the book is also hosted on GitHub at `https://github.com/PacktPublishing/Statistical-Application-Development-with-R-and-Python-Second-Edition`. We also have other code bundles from our rich catalog of books and videos available at `https://github.com/PacktPublishing/`. Check them out!

Errata

Although we have taken every care to ensure the accuracy of our content, mistakes do happen. If you find a mistake in one of our books—maybe a mistake in the text or the code—we would be grateful if you could report this to us. By doing so, you can save other readers from frustration and help us improve subsequent versions of this book. If you find any errata, please report them by visiting `http://www.packtpub.com/submit-errata`, selecting your book, clicking on the **Errata Submission Form** link, and entering the details of your errata. Once your errata are verified, your submission will be accepted and the errata will be uploaded to our website or added to any list of existing errata under the Errata section of that title.

To view the previously submitted errata, go to https://www.packtpub.com/books/content/support and enter the name of the book in the search field. The required information will appear under the **Errata** section.

Piracy

Piracy of copyrighted material on the Internet is an ongoing problem across all media. At Packt, we take the protection of our copyright and licenses very seriously. If you come across any illegal copies of our works in any form on the Internet, please provide us with the location address or website name immediately so that we can pursue a remedy.

Please contact us at copyright@packtpub.com with a link to the suspected pirated material.

We appreciate your help in protecting our authors and our ability to bring you valuable content.

Questions

If you have a problem with any aspect of this book, you can contact us at questions@packtpub.com, and we will do our best to address the problem.

1
Data Characteristics

Data consists of observations across different types of variables, and it is vital that any data analyst understands these intricacies at the earliest stage of exposure to statistical analysis. This chapter recognizes the importance of data and begins with a template of a dummy questionnaire and then proceeds with the nitty-gritties of the subject. We will then explain how uncertainty creeps in to the domain of computer science. The chapter closes with coverage of important families of discrete and continuous random variables.

We will cover the following topics:

- Identification of the main variable types as nominal, categorical, and continuous variables
- The uncertainty arising in many real experiments
- R installation and packages
- The mathematical form of discrete and continuous random variables and their applications

Questionnaire and its components

The goal of this section is to introduce numerous variable types at the first possible occasion. Traditionally, an introductory course begins with the elements of probability theory and then builds up the requisites leading to random variables. This convention is dropped in this book and we begin straightaway with, data. There is a primary reason for choosing this path. The approach builds on what the reader is already familiar with and then connects it with the essential framework of the subject.

It is very likely that the user is familiar with questionnaires. A questionnaire may be asked after the birth of a baby with a view to aid the hospital in the study about the experience of the mother, the health status of the baby, and the concerns of the immediate guardians of the new born. A multi-store department may instantly request the customer to fill in a short questionnaire for capturing the customer's satisfaction after the sale of a product. Customer's satisfaction following the service of their vehicle (see the detailed example discussed later) can be captured through a few queries.

The questionnaires may arise in different forms than merely on a physical paper. They may be sent via email, telephone, **short message service (SMS)**, and so on. As an example, one may receive an SMS that seeks a mandatory response in a Yes/No form. An email may arrive in an Outlook inbox, which requires the recipient to respond through a vote for any of these three options, *Will attend the meeting, Can't attend the meeting,* or *Not yet decided.*

Suppose the owner of a multi-brand car center wants to find out the satisfaction percentage of his customers. Customers bring their car to a service center for varied reasons. The owner wants to find out the satisfaction levels post the servicing of the cars and find the areas where improvement will lead to higher satisfaction among the customers. It is well known that the higher the satisfaction levels, the greater would be the customer's loyalty towards the service center. Towards this, a questionnaire is designed and then data is collected from the customers. A snippet of the questionnaire is given in the following figure, and the information given by the customers leads to different types of data characteristics.

The Customer ID and Questionnaire ID variables may be serial numbers, or randomly generated unique numbers. The purpose of such variables is unique identification of people's responses. It may be possible that there are follow-up questionnaires as well. In such cases, the Customer ID for a responder will continue to be the same, whereas the Questionnaire ID needs to change for the identification of the follow up. The values of these types of variables in general are not useful for analytical purposes.

Customer ID: **Questionnaire ID**:

  1.   Full Name (in caps):   _____
  2.   Gender: Male/ Female
  3.   Age in Years: _____
  4.   Car Model: _____
  5.   Car Manufacture (MM/YY): _____/_____
  6.   Did the workshop fix all your minor problems?   Yes   No
  7.   Did the workshop fix all your major problems?   Yes   No
  8.   What is the mileage (km/liter) of car? _____
  9.   Odometer: _____
10. Please give an overall rating of your satisfaction for the work done.
       a.   Very Poor
       b.   Poor
       c.   Average
       d.   Good
       e.   Very Good

A hypothetical questionnaire

The information of `FullName` in this survey is a beginning point to break the ice with the responder. In very exceptional cases the name may be useful for profiling purposes. For our purposes the name will simply be a text variable that is not used for analysis purposes. `Gender` is asked to know the person's gender and in quite a few cases it may be an important factor explaining the main characteristics of the survey; in this case it may be mileage. `Gender` is an example of a categorical variable.

Age in Years is a variable that captures the age of the customer. The data for this field is numeric in nature and is an example of a continuous variable.

The fourth and fifth questions help the multi-brand dealer in identifying the car model and its age. The first question here enquires about the type of the car model. The car models of the customers may vary from Volkswagen Beetle, Ford Endeavor, Toyota Corolla, Honda Civic, to Tata Nano (see the following screenshot). Though the model name is actually a noun, we make a distinction from the first question of the questionnaire in the sense that the former is a text variable while the latter leads to a categorical variable. Next, the car model may easily be identified to classify the car into one of the car categories, such as a hatchback, sedan, station wagon, or utility vehicle, and such a classifying variable may serve as one of the ordinal variable, as per the overall car size. The age of the car in months since its manufacture date may explain the mileage and odometer reading.

The sixth and seventh questions simply ask the customer if their minor/major problems were completely fixed or not. This is a binary question that takes either of the values, Yes or No. Small dents, power windows malfunctioning, a niggling noise in the cabin, music speakers low output, and other similar issues, which do not lead to good functioning of the car, may be treated as minor problems that are expected to be fixed in the car. Disc brake problems, wheel alignment, steering rattling issues, and similar problems that expose the user and co-users of the road to danger are of grave concerns as they affect the functioning of a car and are treated as major problems. Any user will expect all his issues to be resolved during a car service. An important goal of the survey is to find the service center efficiency in handling the minor and major issues of the car. The labels Yes/No may be replaced by a +1 and -1 combination, or any other label of convenience.

The eighth question, *What is the mileage (km/liter) of car?*, gives a measure of the average petrol/diesel consumption. In many practical cases, this data is provided by the belief of the customer who may simply declare it between 5 km/liter to 25 km/liter. In the case of a lower mileage, the customer may ask for a finer tune up of the engine, wheel alignment, and so on. A general belief is that if the mileage is closer to the assured mileage as marketed by the company, or some authority such as **Automotive Research Association of India (ARAI)**, the customer is more likely to be happy. An important variable is the overall kilometers done by the car up to the point of service. Vehicles have certain maintenances at the intervals of 5,000 km, 10,000 km, 20,000 km, 50,000 km, and 100,000 km. This variable may also be related to the age of the vehicle.

Let us now look at the final question of the snippet. Here, the customer is asked to rate his overall experience of the car service. A response from the customer may be sought immediately after a small test ride post the car service, or it may be through a questionnaire sent to the customer's email ID. A rating of Very Poor suggests that the workshop has served the customer miserably, whereas a rating of Very Good conveys that the customer is completely satisfied with the workshop service.

Note that there is some order in the response of the customer, in that we can grade the ranking in a certain order of Very Poor < Poor < Average < Good < Very Good. This implies that the structure of the ratings must be respected when we analyze the data of such a study. In the next section, these concepts are elaborated through a hypothetical dataset.

Customer_ID	Questionnaire_ID	Name	Gender	Age	Car_Model	Car Manufacture Year	Minor Problems	Major Problems	Mileage	Odometer	Satisfaction Rating
C6O1FAKNQXM	QC6O1FAKNQXM	J. Ram	Male	57	Beetle	Apr-11	Yes	Yes	23	18892	Good
C5H28CP1NFB	QC5H28CP1NFB	Sanjeev Joshi	Male	53	Camry	Feb-09	Yes	Yes	17	22624	Average
CY72H4JOVIX	QCY72H4JOVIX	John D	Male	20	Corolla	Dec-10	Yes	No	21	25207	Good
CH1N2O5VCD8	QCH1N2O5VCD8	Pranathi P T	Female	20	Nano	Apr-10	Yes	Yes	24	42008	Good
CV1YI0SFW7N	QCV1YI0SFW7N	Pallawi M. Daksh	Female	54	Civic	Oct-11	Yes	Yes	23	32556	Average
CXOO4WUYQAJ	QCXOO4WUYQAJ	Mohammed Khan	Male	53	Civic	Mar-12	Yes	No	14	41449	Good
CJQ2AYMI59Z	QCJQ2AYMI59Z	Anand N T	Male	65	Endeavor	Aug-11	Yes	Yes	23	28555	Good
CIZTA35PW19	QCIZTA35PW19	Arun Kumar T	Male	50	Beetle	Mar-09	Yes	No	19	36841	Very Poor
CLZXU9JOOAT	QCLZXU9JOOAT	Prakash Prabhak	Male	22	Nano	Mar-11	Yes	No	23	1755	Very Good
CXWBTOVI17G	QCXWBTOVI17G	Pramod R. K.	Male	49	Nano	Apr-11	No	No	17	2007	Good
C5YOUIZ7PLC	QC5YOUIZ7PLC	Mithun Y.	Male	37	Beetle	Jul-11	Yes	No	14	28265	Poor
CYJF269HVUO	QCYJF269HVUO	S.P. Bala	Male	42	Nano	Dec-09	Yes	Yes	23	27997	Poor
CAIE3ZDSYK9	QCAIE3ZDSYK9	Swamy J	Male	47	Camry	Jan-12	Yes	Yes	7	27491	Good
CEO9U2HDP63	QCEO9U2HDP63	Julfikar	Male	31	Endeavor	May-12	Yes	Yes	25	29527	Very Poor
CDWJ6ESYPZR	QCDWJ6ESYPZR	Chris John	Male	24	Fortuner	Aug-09	Yes	Yes	17	2702	Good
CH7XR26W9JQ	QCH7XR26W9JQ	Naveed Khan	Female	47	Civic	Oct-11	No	No	21	6903	Good
CGXATR9DQEK	QCGXATR9DQEK	Prem Kashmiri	Male	54	Camry	Mar-10	No	Yes	6	40873	Poor
CYQO5RFIPK1	QCYQO5RFIPK1	Sujana Rao	Female	32	Civic	Mar-12	Yes	No	8	48172	Very Good
CG1SZ8IDURP	QCG1SZ8IDURP	Josh K	Male	39	Endeavor	Jul-11	Yes	Yes	8	15274	Poor
CTUSRQDX396	QCTUSRQDX396	Aravind	Male	61	Fiesta	May-10	Yes	Yes	22	9934	Average

Hypothetical DataSet of a Questionnaire

Understanding the data characteristics in an R environment

A snippet of an R session is given in the following figure . Here we simply relate an R session with the survey and sample data of the previous table. The simple goal here is to get a feel/buy-in of R and not necessarily follow the R codes. The R installation process is explained in the *R installation* section. Here the user is loading the SQ R data object (SQ simply stands for sample questionnaire) in the session. The nature of the SQ object is a data.frame that stores a variety of other objects in itself. For more technical details of the data.frame function, see *The data.frame object* section of *Chapter 2, Import/Export Data*. The names of a data.frame object may be extracted using the variable.names function. The R function class helps to identify the nature of the R object. As we have a list of variables, it is useful to find all of them using the sapply function. In the following screenshot, the mentioned steps have been carried out:

```
> library(RSADBE)
> data(SQ)
> class(SQ)
[1] "data.frame"
> variable.names(SQ)
 [1] "Customer_ID"           "Questionnaire_ID"      "Name"
 [4] "Gender"                "Age"                   "Car_Model"
 [7] "Car_Manufacture_Year"  "Minor_Problems"        "Major_Problems"
[10] "Mileage"               "Odometer"              "Satisfaction_Rating"
> sapply(SQ,class)
$Customer_ID
[1] "character"
$Questionnaire_ID
[1] "character"
$Name
[1] "character"
$Gender
[1] "factor"
$Age
[1] "numeric"
$Car_Model
[1] "character"
$Car_Manufacture_Year
[1] "Date"
$Minor_Problems
[1] "factor"
$Major_Problems
[1] "factor"
$Mileage
[1] "integer"
$Odometer
[1] "integer"
$Satisfaction_Rating
[1] "ordered" "factor"
```

Understanding variable types of an R object

The variable characteristics are also on the expected lines, as they should be, and we see that the variables Customer_ID, Questionnaire_ID, and Name are character variables; Gender, Car_Model, Minor_Problems, and Major_Problems are factor variables; DoB and Car_Manufacture_Year are date variables; Mileage and Odometer are integer variables; and, finally, the variable Satisfaction_Rating is an ordered and factor variable.

In the remainder of the chapter, we will delve into more details about the nature of various data types. In a more formal language, a variable is called a **random variable (RV)** in the rest of the book, and in the statistical literature. A distinction needs to be made here. In this book, we do not focus on the important aspects of probability theory. It is assumed that the reader is familiar with probability, say at the level of Freund (2003) or Ross (2001). An RV is a function that is mapping from the probability (sample) space Ω to the real line. From the previous example, we have Odometer and Satisfaction_Rating as two examples of a random variable. In a formal language, the random variables are generally denoted by letters $X, Y, \ldots$. The distinction that is required here is that in the applications that we observe are the realizations/values of the random variables. In general, the realized values are denoted by the lower cases $x, y, \ldots$. Let us clarify this at more length.

Suppose that we denote the random variable Satisfaction_Rating by X. Here, the sample space Ω consists of the elements Very Poor, Poor, Average, Good, and Very Good. For the sake of convenience, we will denote these elements by $O_1, O_2, O_3, O_4,$ and O_5 respectively. The random variable X takes one of the values $O_1,\ldots, O_5$ with respective probabilities p1,..., p5. If the probabilities were known, we don't have to worry about statistical analysis. In simple terms, if we know the probabilities of Satisfaction_Rating RV, we can simply use it to conclude whether more customers give a Very Good rating against Poor. However, our survey data does not contain every customer who has used the car service from the workshop, and as such, we have **representative probabilities** and not **actual probabilities**. Now, we have seen 20 observations in the R session, and corresponding to each row we had some value under the Satisfaction_Rating column. Let us denote the satisfaction rating for the 20 observations by the symbols $X_1,\ldots, X_{20}$. Before we collect the data, the random variables $X_1,\ldots, X_{20}$ can assume any of the values in Ω. Post the data collection, we see that the first customer has given the rating as Good (that is, O_4), the second as Average (O_3), and so on up to the twentieth customer's rating as Average (again O_3). By convention, what is observed in the data sheet is actually $x_1,\ldots, x_{20}$, the realized values of the RVs $X_1,\ldots, X_{20}$.

Experiments with uncertainty in computer science

The common man of the previous century was skeptical about chance/randomness and attributed it to the lack of accurate instruments, and that information is not necessarily captured in many variables. The skepticism about the need for modeling for randomness in the current era continues for the common man, as he feels that the instruments are too accurate and that multi-variable information eliminates uncertainty. However, this is not the fact and we will look here at some examples that drive home this point.

In the previous section, we dealt with data arising from a questionnaire regarding the service level at a car dealer. It is natural to accept that different individuals respond in distinct ways, and further, the car being a complex assembly of different components, responds differently in near identical conditions. A question then arises as to whether we may have to really deal with such situations in computer science, which involve uncertainty. The answer is certainly affirmative and we will consider some examples in the context of computer science and engineering.

Suppose that the task is the installation of software, say R itself. At a new lab there has been an arrangement of 10 new desktops that have the same configuration. That is, the RAM, memory, the processor, operating system, and so on, are all same in the 10 different machines.

For simplicity, assume that the electricity supply and lab temperature are identical for all the machines. Do you expect that the complete R installation, as per the directions specified in the next section, will be the same in milliseconds for all the 10 installations? The runtime of an operation can be easily recorded, maybe using other software if not manually. The answer is a clear *No* as there will be minor variations of the processes active in the different desktops. Thus, we have our first experiment in the domain of computer science that involves uncertainty.

Suppose that the lab is now 2 years old. As an administrator, do you expect all the 10 machines to be working in the same identical conditions as we started with an identical configuration and environment? The question is relevant, as according to general experience, a few machines may have broken down. Despite warranty and assurance by the desktop company, the number of machines that may have broken down will not be exactly the same as those assured. Thus, we again have uncertainty.

Assume that three machines are not functioning at the end of 2 years. As an administrator, you have called the service vendor to fix the problem. For the sake of simplicity, we assume that the nature of failure of the three machines is the same, say motherboard failure on the three failed machines. Is it practical that the vendor would fix the three machines within an identical time?

Again, by experience, we know that this is very unlikely. If the reader thinks otherwise, assume that 100 identical machines were running for 2 years and 30 of them now have the motherboard issue. It is now clear that some machines may require a component replacement while others would start functioning following a repair/fix.

Let us now summarize the preceding experiments with following questions:

- What is the average installation time for the R software on identically configured computer machines?
- How many machines are likely to break down after a period of 1 year, 2 years, and 3 years?
- If a failed machine has issues related to the motherboard, what is the average service time?
- What is the fraction of failed machines that have a failed motherboard component?

The answers to these types of questions form the main objective of the Statistics subject. However, there are certain characteristics of uncertainty that are covered by the families of probability distributions. According to the underlying problem, we have discrete or continuous RVs. The important and widely useful probability distributions form the content of the rest of the chapter. We will begin with the useful discrete distributions.

Installing and setting up R

The official website of R is the **Comprehensive R Archive Network (CRAN)** at www.cran.r-project.org. At the time of writing, the most recent version of R is 3.4.1. This software is available for the three platforms: Linux, macOS X, and Windows.

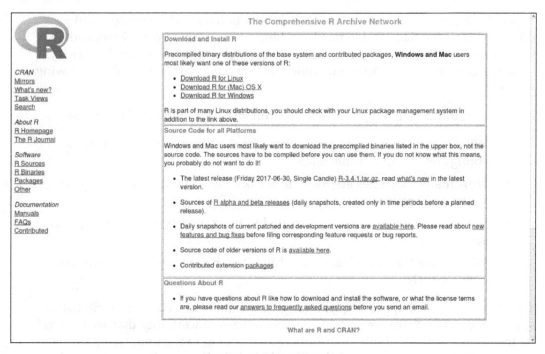

The CRAN Website (snapshot)

A Linux user may simply key in sudo apt-get install r-base in the Terminal, and post the return of the right password and privilege levels, and the R software would be installed. After the completion of the download and installation, the software is started by simply keying in R in the Terminal.

A Windows user needs to perform the following steps:

1. Firstly, click on **Download R for Windows**, as shown in the preceding screenshot.

2. Then in the **base** subdirectory click on **install R for the first time**.

3. In the new window, click on **Download R 3.4.0 for Windows** and download the .exe file to a directory of your choice.

4. The completely downloaded R-3.0.0-win.exe file can be installed as any other .exe file.

5. The R software may be invoked either from the **Start** menu, or from the icon on the desktop. The installed versions of R in Windows and Linux appears as follows:

Using R packages

The CRAN repository hosts 10,969 packages as of July 2, 2017. The packages are written and maintained by statisticians, engineers, biologists, and others. The reasons are varied and the resourcefulness is very rich and it reduces the need of writing exhaustive and new functions and programs from scratch. These additional packages can be obtained from `https://cran.r-project.org/web/packages/`. The user can click on `https://cran.rproject.org/web/packages/available_packages_by_date.html`, which will direct you to a new web package. Let us illustrate the installation of an R package named `gdata`:

- We now wish to install the `gdata` package. There are multiple ways of completing this task:

   1. Clicking on the `gdata` label leads to the web page: `https://cran.r-project.org/web/packages/gdata/index.html`.

   2. In this HTML file, we can find a lot of information about the package through Version, Depends, Imports, Published, Author, Maintainer, License, System Requirements, Installation, and CRAN checks.

   3. Furthermore, the download options may be chosen from the package source, macOS X binary, and Windows binary, depending on whether the user's OS is Unix, macOS, or Windows respectively.

   4. Finally, a package may require other packages as a prerequisite, and it may itself be a prerequisite to other packages.

This information is provided in Reverse dependencies, Reverse depends, Reverse imports, and Reverse suggests.

- Suppose that the user has Windows OS. There are two ways to install the `gdata` package:

  1. Start R, as explained earlier. At the console, execute the code `install.packages("gdata")`.

  2. A CRAN mirror window will pop-up, asking the user to select one of the available mirrors.

  3. Select one of the mirrors from the list. You may need to scroll down to locate your favorite mirror, and then hit the **Ok** button.

  4. A default setting is `dependencies=TRUE`, which will then download and install all the other required packages.

  5. Unless there are some violations, such as the dependency requirement of the R version being at least 2.3 in this case, the packages would be installed successfully.

- A second way of installing the `gdata` package is as follows:

  1. At the `gdata` web page, click on the following link: `gdata_2.18.0.zip`.

  2. This action will then attempt to download the package through the **File download** window.

  3. Choose the option **Save** and specify the path where you wish to download the package.

  4. In my case, I have chosen the `C:\Users\author\Downloads` directory.

  5. Now go to the R windows. In the menu ribbon, we have seven options in **File**, **Edit**, **View**, **Misc**, **Packages**, **Windows**, and **Help**.

  6. Yes, your guess is correct and you would have wisely selected **Packages** from the menu.

  7. Now, select the last option of **Packages** in **Install Package(s) from local zip files** and direct it to the path where you have downloaded the ZIP file.

  8. Select the `gdata_2.18.0` file and R will do the required remaining part of installing the package.

The one drawback of doing this process manually is that if there are dependencies, the user needs to ensure that all such packages have been installed before embarking on this second task of installing the R packages. However, despite this problem, it is quite useful to know this technique, as we may not be connected to the internet all the time, and we can install the packages when it is convenient.

RSADBE – the books R package

This book uses lot of datasets from the web, statistical text books, and so on. The file format of the datasets have been varied and thus to help the reader, we have put all the datasets used in the book in an R package, RSADBE, which is the abbreviation of this book's title. This package will be available from the CRAN website as well as this book's web page. Thus, whenever you are asked to run data(xyz), the dataset xyz will be available either in the RSADBE package or datasets package of R.

The book also uses many of the packages available on CRAN. The following table gives the list of packages and the reader is advised to ensure that these packages are installed before you begin reading the chapter. That is, the reader needs to ensure that, as an example, install.packages(c("qcc","ggplot2")) is run in the R session before proceeding with *Chapter 3, Data Visualization*.

Chapter number	Packages required
2	foreign, RMySQL
3	qcc, ggplot2
4	LearnEDA, aplpack
5	stats4, PASWR, PairedData
6	faraway
7	pscl, ROCR
8	ridge, DAAG
9	rpart, rattle
10	ipred, randomForest

Python installation and setup

The major change in the second edition is augmenting the book with parallel Python programs. The reader might ask the all-important one word question *Why?* A simple reason, among others, is this: R has an impressive 11,212 packages, and the quantum of impressiveness for Python's 11,4368 is left to the reader.

Of course, it is true that not all of these Python packages are related to data analytics. The number of packages is as of the date August 11, 2017. Importantly, the purpose of this book is to help the R user learn Python easily and vice versa. The main source of Python would be its website: `https://www.python.org/`:

- Version- A famous argument debated among Python users is related to the choice of version 2.7 or 3.4+. Though the 3.0 version has been available since a decade earlier from 2008, the 2.7 version is still too popular and shows no signs of fading away. We will not get into the pros and cons of using the versions and will simply use the 3.4+ version. The author has run the programs in 3.4 version Ubuntu and 3.6 version in Windows and the code ran without any problems. The users of the 2.7 version might be disappointed, though we are sure that they can easily adapt it to their machines. Thus, we are providing the code for the 3.4+ version of Python.

Ubuntu OS already has Python installed and the version that comes along with it is 2.7.13-2. The two lines of code can be run in the gnome-terminal to update Python to the 3.6 version:

```
sudo apt-get update
sudo apt-get install python3.6
```

The Windows version can be easily downloaded from `https://www.python.org/downloads/` and for making good use of the book code, the user is recommended to use the current version 3.6. The exe files don't need an explanation. The snippets of Python software after they are started in Ubuntu and Windows are given next:

Ubuntu

pranathi@pranathi-Aspire-ES1-521: ~/test

File   Edit   View   Terminal   Tabs   Help

```
Python 3.4.1 (default, Jul  3 2014, 12:30:40)
[GCC 4.8.2] on linux
Type "help", "copyright", "credits" or "license" for more information.
>>>
```

Windows

Administrator: Anaconda Prompt - python

```
(C:\Users\tprabhan\AppData\Local\Continuum\Anaconda3) C:\Users\tprabhan>python
Python 3.6.1 |Anaconda 4.4.0 (64-bit)| (default, May 11 2017, 13:25:24) [MSC v.1
900 64 bit (AMD64)] on win32
Type "help", "copyright", "credits" or "license" for more information.
>>>
```

Simple arithmetic operations are easily carried out in Python. The user can key-in 2+7 at the prompt. Important programming will be taken up soon and the user can learn them from scratch from the next chapter.

Using pip for packages

Additional packages as required need to be installed separetely. `pip` is the package manager for Python. If any software is required, we can run the following line as the Python prompt:

```
pip install package
```

The table of packages required according to the chapters is given in the following table:

Chapter number	Python Packages
2	os, numpy, pandas, pymysql, pickle
3	os, numpy, pandas, matplotlib
4	os, numpy, pandas, matplotlib
5	os, numpy, pandas, matplotlib, scipy
6	os, numpy, pandas, matplotlib, scipy
7	os, numpy, pandas, matplotlib, sklearn pylab, pysal, statsmodels
8	os, numpy, pandas, matplotlib, sklearn, pylab, statsmodels
9	os, numpy, pandas, matplotlib, sklearn
10	os, numpy, pandas, matplotlib, sklearn

IDEs for R and Python

The **Integrated Development Environment** or IDE- most users do not use the software frontend these days. IDEs are convenient for many reasons and the uninitiated reader can search for the keyword. In very simple terms, the IDE may be thought of as the showroom and the core software as the factory. The RStudio appears to be the most popular IDE for R and Jupyter Notebook for Python.

The website for RStudio is `https://www.rstudio.com/` and for Jupyter Notebook, it is `http://jupyter.org/`. The authors of the RStudio version are shown in the following screenshot:

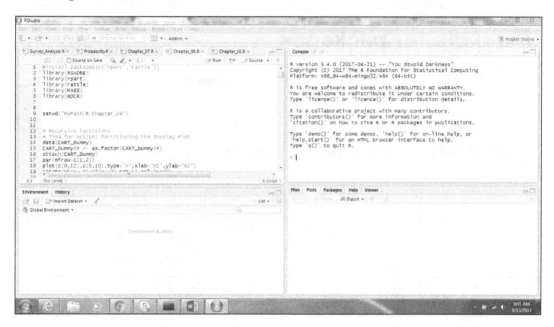

We will not delve into details on the IDEs and the role they play. It is good enough to use them. More details about the importance of IDEs can be easily obtained on the web, and especially Wikipedia. An important Python distribution is Anaconda and there are lots of funny stories about the Anaconda-Python predators and how their names fascinate the software programmers. The Anaconda distribution is available at `https://www.continuum.io/downloads` and we recommend the reader to use the same. All the Python programs are run on the Jupyter Notebook IDE. The authors of the Anaconda Prompt are shown in the following screenshot:

The code in the `jupyter notebook` has not yet run. And if you enter that on your Anaconda Prompt and hit the return key, the IDE will be started. The frontend of the `Jupyter notebook`, which will be opened in your default internet browser, looks like the following:

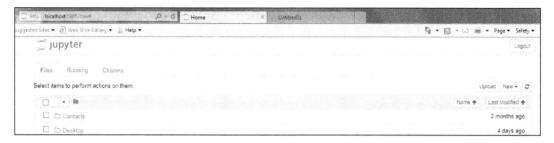

Now, an important question is the need of different IDEs for different software. Of course, it is not necessary. The R software can be integrated with the Anaconda distribution, particularly with options later in the Jupyter IDE. Towards this, we need to run the code `conda install -c r r-essentials` in the Anaconda Prompt. Now, if you click on the **New** drop-down button, you will see two options under the Notebook: one is Python 3 and the other is R. Thus, you can now run Python as well as R in the Jupyter Notebook IDE:

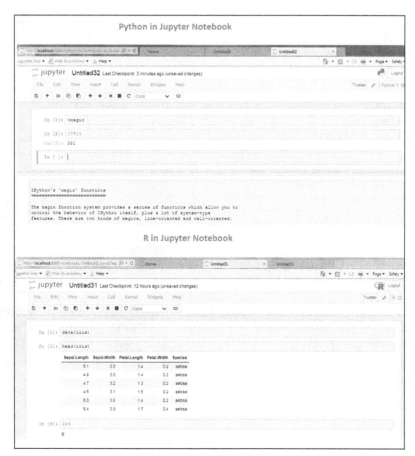

Python Idle is also another popular IDE and the Windows version looks like this:

```
Python 3.6.1 Shell                                                    [ □ ] [ □ ] [ X ]

File  Edit  Shell  Debug  Options  Window  Help
Python 3.6.1 |Anaconda 4.4.0 (64-bit)| (default, May 11 2017, 13:25:24) [MSC v.1
900 64 bit (AMD64)] on win32
Type "copyright", "credits" or "license()" for more information.
>>>
```

The companion code bundle

After the user downloads the code bundle, RPySADBE.zip, from the publisher's website, the first task is to unzip it to a local machine. We encourage the reader to download the code bundle since the R and Python code in the ebook might be in image format and it is a futile exercise to key in long programs all over again.

The folder structure in the unzipped format will consist of two folders: R and Python. Each of these chapters further consists of 10 sub-folders, one folder for each chapter. R software has a special package for itself as RSADBE available on CRAN. Thus, it does not have a Data sub-folder with the exception of *Chapter 2, Import/Export Data*. The chapter level folders for R will contain two sub-folders: Output and SRC. The SRC folder contains a file named Chapter_Number.R, which consists of all code used in the package. The Output folder contains a Microsoft Word document named Chapter_Number.doc. The reader is given an exercise to set up the Markdown settings; search for it on the web. The Chapter_Number.doc is the result of running the R file Chapter_Number.R. The graphics in the Markdown files will be different from the ones observed in the book.

Python's chapter sub-folders are of three types: Data, Output, SRC. The required **Comma Separated Values (CSV)** data files are available in the Data folder while the SRC folder consists of the Python code file, Chapter_Number.py. The output file as a consequence of running the Python file in the IDE is saved as a Chapter_Number_Title.ipynb file. In many cases, the graphics generated by either R or Python for the same purpose yields the same display.

Since the R software has been run first and the explanation with the interpretation given following it, we have given the corresponding Python program, which is different; the graphical output is not necessarily produced in the book. In such cases, the ipynb files would come in handy as they contain all the graphics. Markdown is available for Python too, but we don't pursue it though.

Here's a final word about executing the R and Python files. The author does not have access about the path of the unzipped folder. Thus, the reader needs to specify the path appropriately in the R and Python files. Most likely, the reader would have to replace `MyPath` by `/home/user/RPySADBE` or `C:/User/Documents/RPySADBE`.

We will now begin formal discussion of the essential probability distributions.

Discrete distributions

The previous section highlights the different forms of variables. The variables such as `Gender`, `Car_Model`, and `Minor_Problems` possibly take one of the finite values. These variables are particular cases of the more general class of discrete variables.

It is to be noted that the sample space Ω of a discrete variable need not be finite. As an example, the number of errors on a page may take values on the set of positive integers, $\{0, 1, 2, \ldots\}$. Suppose that a discrete random variable X can take values among $x_1, x_2, \cdots$ with respective probabilities $p_1, p_2, \cdots$, that is, $P(X = x_i) = p(x_i) = p_i$. Then, we require that the probabilities be non-zero and further that their sum be 1:

$$p_i \geq 0, i = 1, 2, \ldots, and \sum_i p_i = 1$$

where the Greek symbol $\sum$ represents summation over the index i.

The function $p(x_i)$ is called the **probability mass function (pmf)** of the discrete RV X. We will now consider formal definitions of important families of discrete variables. The engineers may refer to Bury (1999) for a detailed collection of useful statistical distributions in their field. The two most important parameters of a probability distribution are specified by **mean** and **variance** of the RV X.

In some cases, and important too, these parameters may not exist for the RV. However, we will not focus on such distributions, though we caution the reader that this does not mean that such RVs are irrelevant. Let us define these parameters for the discrete RV. The mean and variance of a discrete RV are respectively calculated as:

$$E(X) = \sum_i p_i x_i \ and \ Var(X) = \sum_i p_i (x_i - E(X))^2$$

The mean is a measure of central tendency, whereas the variance gives a measure of the spread of the RV.

The variables defined so far are more commonly known as categorical variables. Agresti (2002) defines a **categorical variable** as a measurement scale consisting of a set of categories.

Let us identify the categories for the variables listed in the previous section. The categories for the Gender variable are male and female; whereas the car category variables derived from Car_Model are hatchback, sedan, station wagon, and utility vehicles. The Minor_Problems and Major_Problems variables have common but independent categories, yes and no; and, finally, the Satisfaction_Rating variable has the categories, as seen earlier, Very Poor, Poor, Average, Good, and Very Good. The Car_Model variable is just a set of labels of the name of car and it is an example of a nominal variable.

Finally, the output of the Satistifaction_Rating variable has an implicit order in it: Very Poor < Poor < Average < Good < Very Good. It may be apparent that this difference poses subtle challenges in their analysis. These types of variables are called **ordinal variables**. We will look at another type of categorical variable that has not popped up thus far.

Practically, it is often the case that the output of a continuous variable is put in a certain bin for ease of conceptualization. A very popular example is the categorization of the income level or age. In the case of income variables, it has become apparent in one of the earlier studies that people are very conservative about revealing their income in precise numbers.

For example, the author may be shy to reveal that his monthly income is Rs. 34,892. On the other hand, it has been revealed that these very same people do not have a problem in disclosing their income as belonging to one of the following categories: < Rs. 10,000, Rs. 10,000-30,000, Rs. 30,000-50,000, and > Rs. 50,000. Thus, this information may also be coded into labels and then each of the labels may refer to any one value in an interval bin. Thus, such variables are referred as **interval variables**.

Discrete uniform distribution

A random variable X is said to be a discrete uniform random variable if it can take any one of the finite M labels with equal probability.

As the discrete uniform random variable X can assume one of the 1, 2, ..., M with equal probability, this probability is actually $1/M$. As the probability remains the same across the labels, the nomenclature *uniform* is justified. It might appear at the outset that this is not a very useful random variable. However, the reader is cautioned that this intuition is not correct. As a simple case, this variable arises in many cases where simple random sampling is needed in action. The pmf of a discrete RV is calculated as:

$$P(X = x_i) = p(x_i) = \frac{1}{M}, i = 1, 2, \dots, M$$

A simple plot of the probability distribution of a discrete uniform RV is demonstrated next:

```
> M = 10
> mylabels=1:M
> prob_labels=rep(1/M,length(mylabels))
> dotchart(prob_labels,labels=mylabels,xlim=c(.08,.12),
+ xlab="Probability")
> title("A Dot Chart for Probability of Discrete Uniform RV")
```

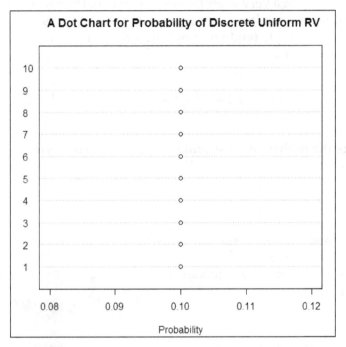

Probability distribution of a discrete uniform random variable

The R programs here are indicative and it is not absolutely necessary that you follow them here. The R programs will actually begin from the next chapter and your flow won't be affected if you do not understand certain aspects of them.

An equivalent Python program and its output is given in the following screenshot:

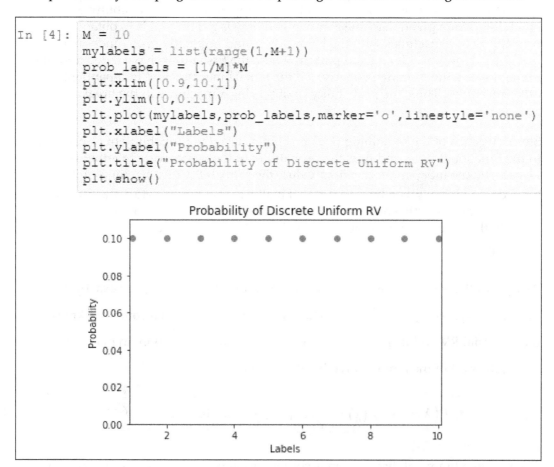

```
In [4]:  M = 10
         mylabels = list(range(1,M+1))
         prob_labels = [1/M]*M
         plt.xlim([0.9,10.1])
         plt.ylim([0,0.11])
         plt.plot(mylabels,prob_labels,marker='o',linestyle='none')
         plt.xlabel("Labels")
         plt.ylabel("Probability")
         plt.title("Probability of Discrete Uniform RV")
         plt.show()
```

Binomial distribution

Recall the second question in the *Experiments with uncertainty in computer science* section, which asks: *How many machines are likely to break down after a period of 1 year, 2 years, and 3 years?*. When the outcomes involve uncertainty, the more appropriate question that we ask is related to the probability of the number of break downs being *x*.

Consider a fixed time frame, say 2 years. To make the question more generic, we assume that we have n number of machines. Suppose that the probability of a breakdown for a given machine at any given time is p. The goal is to obtain the probability of x machines with the breakdown, and implicitly $(n\text{-}x)$ functional machines. Now consider a fixed pattern where the first x units have failed and the remaining are functioning properly. All the n machines function independently of other machines. Thus, the probability of observing x machines in the breakdown state is p^x.

Similarly, each of the remaining $(n\text{-}x)$ machines have the probability of $(1\text{-}p)$ of being in the functional state, and thus the probability of these occurring together is $(1-p)^{n-x}$. Again, by the independence axiom value, the probability of x machines with a breakdown is then given by $p^x(1-p)^{n-x}$. Finally, in the overall setup, the number of possible samples with a breakdown being x and $(n\text{-}x)$ samples being functional is actually the number of possible combinations of choosing x-out-of-n items, which is the combinatorial $\binom{n}{x}$.

As each of these samples is equally likely to occur, the probability of exactly x broken machines is given by $\binom{n}{x}p^x(1-p)^{n-x}$. The RV X obtained in such a context is known as the binomial RV and its pmf is called as the binomial distribution. In mathematical terms, the pmf of the binomial RV is calculated as:

$$P(X=x)=p(x)=\binom{n}{x}p^x(1-p)^{n-x}, x=0,1,\ldots,n, 0\le p\le1$$

The pmf of a binomial distribution is sometimes denoted by $b(x;n,p)$. Let us now look at some important properties of a binomial RV. The mean and variance of a binomial RV X are respectively calculated as:

$$E(X)=np \text{ and } Var(X)=np(1-p)$$

 As p is always a number between 0 and 1, the variance of a binomial RV is always lesser than its mean.

Example 1.3.1: Suppose $n = 10$ and $p = 0.5$. We need to obtain the probabilities $p(x)$, $x=0, 1, 2, …, 10$. The probabilities can be obtained using the built-in R function, dbinom. The function dbinom returns the probabilities of a binomial RV.

The first argument of this function may be a scalar or a vector according to the points at which we wish to know the probability. The second argument of the function needs to know the value of n, the size of the binomial distribution. The third argument of this function requires the user to specify the probability of success in p. It is natural to forget the syntax of functions and the R help system becomes very handy here. For any function, you can get details of it using ? followed by the function name. Please do not insert a space between ? and the function name. Here, you can try ?dbinom:

```
> n <- 10; p <- 0.5
> p_x <- round(dbinom(x=0:10, n, p),4)
> plot(x=0:10,p_x,xlab="x", ylab="P(X=x)")
```

The R function round fixes the accuracy of the argument up to the specified number of digits.

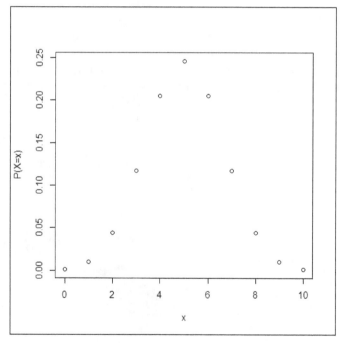

Binomial probabilities

We have used the `dbinom` function in the previous example. There are three utility facets for the binomial distribution. The three facets are p, q, and r. These three facets respectively help us in computations related to cumulative probabilities, quantiles of the distribution, and simulation of random numbers from the distribution. To use these functions, we simply augment the letters with the distribution name, `binom`, here, as `pbinom`, `qbinom`, and `rbinom`. There will be, of course, a critical change in the arguments. In fact, there are many distributions for which the quartet of d, p, q, and r are available; check `?Distributions`.

The Python code block is the following:

```
In [6]:  n = 10; p = 0.5
         from scipy.stats import binom
         p_x = binom.pmf(range(1,n+1),n,p)
         plt.plot(range(1,n+1),p_x,marker='o',linestyle='none')
         plt.show()
```

Example 1.3.2: Assume that the probability of a key failing on an 83-set keyboard (the authors, laptop keyboard has 83 keys) is 0.01. Now, we need to find the probability when at a given time there are 10, 20, and 30 non-functioning keys on this keyboard. Using the `dbinom` function, these probabilities are easy to calculate. Try to do this same problem using a scientific calculator or by writing a simple function in any language that you are comfortable with:

```
> n <- 83; p <- 0.01
> dbinom(10,n,p)
[1] 1.168e-08
> dbinom(20,n,p)
[1] 4.343e-22
> dbinom(30,n,p)
[1] 2.043e-38
> sum(dbinom(0:83,n,p))
[1] 1
```

As the probabilities of 10-30 keys failing appear too small, it is natural to believe that maybe something is going wrong. As a check, the sum clearly equals 1. Let us have a look at the problem from a different angle. For many x values, the probability $p(x)$ will be approximately zero. We may not be interested in the probability of an exact number of failures though we are interested in the probability of at least x failures occurring, that is, we are interested in the cumulative probabilities $P(X \leq x)$. The cumulative probabilities for binomial distribution are obtained in R using the `pbinom` function. The main arguments of `pbinom` include `size` (for n), `prob` (for p), and `q` (the at least x argument). For the same problem, we now look at the cumulative probabilities for various p values:

```
> n <- 83; p <- seq(0.05,0.95,0.05)
> x <- seq(0,83,5)
> i <- 1
> plot(x,pbinom(x,n,p[i]),"l",col=1,xlab="x",ylab=
+ expression(P(X<=x)))
> for(i in 2:length(p)) { points(x,pbinom(x,n,p[i]),"l",col=i)}
```

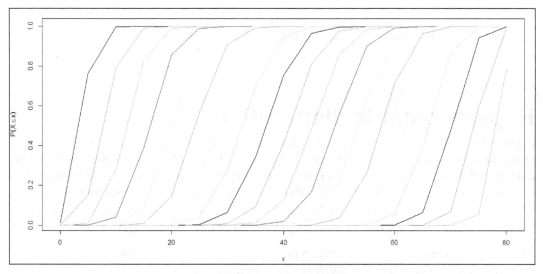

Cumulative binomial probabilities

Try to interpret the preceding figure, the parallel Python program would be the following:

```
In [8]:  n = 83; p = 0.01
         from scipy.stats import binom
         binom.pmf(10,n,p)

Out[8]:  1.1678635875854576e-08


In [9]:  binom.pmf(20,n,p)

Out[9]:  4.3427057681383424e-22


In [10]:  binom.pmf(30,n,p)

Out[10]:  2.0426109845185026e-38


In [11]:  xr = range(0,84)
          sum(binom.pmf(xr,n,p))

Out[11]:  0.99999999999997236
```

Hypergeometric distribution

A box of N = 200 pieces of 12 GB pen drives arrives at a sales center. The carton contains M = 20 defective pen drives. A random sample of n units is drawn from the carton. Let X denote the number of defective pen drives obtained from the sample of n units. The task is to obtain the probability distribution of X. The number of possible ways of obtaining the sample of size n is $\binom{N}{n}$. In this problem, we have M defective units and $N-M$ working pen drives, and x defective units can be sampled in $\binom{M}{x}$ different ways and $n-x$ good units can be obtained in $\binom{N-M}{n-x}$ distinct ways. Thus, the probability distribution of the RV X is calculated as:

$$P(X = x) = h(x; n, M, N) = \frac{\binom{M}{x}\binom{N-M}{n-x}}{\binom{N}{n}}$$

where x is an integer between $\max(0, n-N+M)$ and $\min(n,M)$. The RV is called the **hypergeometric RV** and its probability distribution is called the **hypergeometric distribution**.

Suppose that we draw a sample of $n = 10$ units. The `dhyper` function in R can be used to find the probabilities of the RV X, assuming different values:

```
> N = 200; M = 20
> n = 10
> x = 0:11
> round(dhyper(x,M,N,n),3)
 [1] 0.377 0.395 0.176 0.044 0.007 0.001 0.000 0.000 0.000 0.000 0.000
0.000
```

The equivalent Python implementation is as follows:

```
In [13]: N = 200; M = 20
         n = 10
         k = range(0,12)
         from scipy.stats import hypergeom
         np.round(hypergeom.pmf(k,N,M,n),3)

Out[13]: array([ 0.34 ,  0.397,  0.198,  0.055,  0.009,  0.001,  0.   ,  0.   ,
                 0.   ,  0.   ,  0.   ,  0.   ])
```

The mean and variance of a hypergeometric distribution are stated as follows:

$$E(X) = n\frac{M}{N}, \, and \, Var(X) = n\frac{M}{N}\frac{(N-M)}{N}\frac{(N-n)}{N-1}$$

Negative binomial distribution

Consider a variant of the problem described in the previous subsection. The 10 new desktops need to be fitted with an add-on, five megapixel external cameras, to help the students attend a certain online course. Assume that the probability of a non-defective camera unit is p. As an administrator, you keep on placing orders until you receive 10 non-defective cameras. Now, let X denote the number of orders placed for obtaining the 10 good units. We denote the required number of successes by k, which in this discussion has been $k = 10$. The goal in this unit is to obtain the probability distribution of X.

Suppose that the xth order placed results in the procurement of a kth non-defective unit. This implies that we have received $(k-1)$ non-defective units among the first $(x-1)$ orders placed, which is possible in $\binom{x-1}{k-1}$ distinct ways. At the xth order, the instant of having received the kth non-defective unit, we have k successes and $x-k$ failures. Thus, the probability distribution of the RV is calculated as:

$$P(X=k) = \binom{x-k}{k-1}(1-p)^{x-k} p^{k}, x=k, k+1,\ldots$$

Such an RV is called a **negative binomial RV** and its probability distribution as the **negative binomial distribution**. Technically, this RV has no upper bound as the next required success may never turn up. We state the mean and variance of this distribution as follows:

$$E(X) = \frac{kp}{1-p}, and\, Var(X) = \frac{kp}{(1-p)^{2}}$$

A particular and important special case of the negative binomial RV occurs for $k = 1$, which is known as the **geometric RV**. In this case, the pmf is calculated as:

$$P(X=x) = (1-p)^{x-1} p, x=0,1,2,\ldots$$

Example 1.3.3. (Baron (2007). Page 77) sequential testing: In a certain setup, the probability of an item being defective is *(1-p) = 0.05*. To complete the lab setup, 12 non-defective units are required. We need to compute the probability that at least 15 units need to be tested. Here we make use of the cumulative distribution of the negative binomial distribution pnbinom function available in R. Similar to the pbinom function, the main arguments that we require here would be size, prob, and q. This problem is solved in a single line of code:

```
> 1-pnbinom(3,size=12,0.95)
[1] 0.005467259
```

Note that we have specified 3 as the quantile point (at least x argument) as the size parameter of this experiment is 12 and we are seeking at least 15 units that translate into three more units than the size of the parameter. The `pnbinom` function computes the cumulative distribution function and the requirement is actually the complement and hence the expression in the code is `1-pnbinom`. We may equivalently solve the problem using the `dnbinom` function, which straightforwardly computes the required probability:

```
> 1-(dnbinom(3,size=12,0.95)+dnbinom(2,size=12,0.95)+dnbinom(1,
+ size=12,0.95)+dnbinom(0,size=12,0.95))
[1] 0.005467259
```

Poisson distribution

The number of accidents on a 1 km stretch of road, the total calls received during a 1-hour slot on your mobile, the number of "likes" received on a status on a social networking site in a day, and similar other cases, are some of the examples that are addressed by the Poisson RV. The probability distribution of a Poisson RV is calculated as:

$$P(X = x) = \frac{e^{-\lambda}\lambda^x}{x!}, x = 0,1,2,\ldots, \lambda > 0$$

Here, λ is the parameter of the Poisson RV with X denoting the number of events. The Poisson distribution is sometimes also referred to as the law of rare events. The mean and variance of the Poisson RV are surprisingly the same and equal λ, that is, $E(X) = Var(X) = \lambda$.

Example 1.3.4: Suppose that Santa commits errors in a software program with a mean of three errors per A4-size page. Santa's manager wants to know the probability of Santa committing 0, 5, and 20 errors per page. The R function, `dpois`, helps to determine the answer:

```
> dpois(0,lambda=3); dpois(5,lambda=3); dpois(20, lambda=3)
[1] 0.04978707
[1] 0.1008188
[1] 7.135379e-11
```

Note that Santa's probability of committing 20 errors is almost 0.The Python program is the following:

```
In [15]:  from scipy.stats import poisson
          poisson.pmf(0,3)
          poisson.pmf(5,3)
          poisson.pmf(20,3)

Out[15]:  7.1353787687771534e-11
```

We will next focus on continuous distributions.

Continuous distributions

The numeric variables in the survey, Age, Mileage, and Odometer, can take any values over a continuous interval and these are examples of continuous RVs. In the previous section, we dealt with RVs that had discrete output. In this section, we will deal with RVs that have continuous output. A distinction from the previous section needs to be pointed out explicitly.

In the case of a discrete RV, there is a positive number for the probability of an RV taking on a certain value that is determined by the pmf. In the continuous case, an RV necessarily assumes any specific value with zero probability. These technical issues cannot be discussed in this book. In the discrete case, the probabilities of certain values are specified by the pmf, and in the continuous case the probabilities, over intervals, are decided by the **probability density function**, abbreviated as **pdf**.

Suppose that we have a continuous RV X with the pdf $f(x)$ defined over the possible x values; that is, we assume that the pdf $f(x)$ is well defined over the range of the RV X, denoted by R_x. It is necessary that the integration of $f(x)$ over the range R_x is necessarily 1; that is, $\int_{R_x} f(s)\,ds = 1$. The probability that the RV X takes a value in an interval $[a, b]$ is defined by:

$$P\left(X \in [a,b]\right) = \int_a^b f\left(x\right) dx$$

In general, we are interested in the cumulative probabilities of a continuous RV, which is the probability of the event $P(X<x)$. In terms of the previous equations, this is obtained as:

$$P(X<x) = \int_{-\infty}^{x} f(s)ds$$

A special name for this probability is the **cumulative density function**. The mean and variance of a continuous RV are then defined by:

$$E(X) = \int_{R_x} x f(x)dx \, and \, Var(X) = \int_{R_x} (x-E(X))^2 f(x)dx$$

As in the previous section, we will begin with the simpler RV in uniform distribution.

Uniform distribution

A RV is said to have uniform distribution over the interval $[0,\theta], \theta > 0$ if its probability density function is given by:

$$f(x;\theta) = \frac{1}{\theta}, 0 \leq x \leq \theta, \theta > 0$$

In fact, it is not necessary to restrict our focus on the positive real line. For any two real numbers a and b, from the real line, with $b > a$, the uniform RV can be defined by:

$$f(x;a,b) = \frac{1}{b-a}, a \leq x \leq b, b > a$$

The uniform distribution has a very important role to play in simulation, as will be seen in *Chapter 6, Simulation*. As with the discrete counterpart, in the continuous case any two intervals of the same length will have an equal probability occurring. The mean and variance of a uniform RV over the interval [*a, b*] are respectively given by:

$$E(X) = \frac{a+b}{2}, Var(X) = \frac{(b-a)^2}{12}$$

Example 1.4.1. Horgan's (2008), Example 15.3: The International Journal of Circuit Theory and Applications reported in 1990 that researchers at the University of California, Berkeley, had designed a switched capacitor circuit for generating random signals whose trajectory is uniformly distributed over the unit interval [0, 1]. Suppose that we are interested in calculating the probability that the trajectory falls in the interval [0.35, 0.58]. Though the answer is straightforward, we will obtain it using the `punif` function:

```
> punif(0.58)-punif(0.35)
[1] 0.23
```

Of course, we don't need software for such simple integrals, nevertheless:

```
In [17]:  from scipy.stats import uniform
          uniform.cdf(0.58)-uniform.cdf(0.35)

Out[17]:  0.22999999999999998
```

Exponential distribution

The exponential distribution is probably one of the most important probability distributions in statistics, and more so for computer scientists. The numbers of arrivals in a queuing system, the time between two incoming calls on a mobile, the lifetime of a laptop, and so on, are some of the important applications where this distribution has a lasting utility value. The pdf of an exponential RV is specified by:

$$f(x;\lambda) = \lambda e^{-\lambda x}, x \geq 0, \lambda > 0$$

The parameter λ is sometimes referred to as the failure rate. The exponential RV enjoys a special property called the memory-less property, which conveys that:

$$P(X \geq t+s \mid X \geq s) = P(X \geq t), \textit{ for all } t, s > 0$$

The mathematical statement translates into the property that if X is an exponential RV, then its failure in the future depends on the present, and the past (age) of the RV does not matter. In simple words, this means that the probability of failure is constant in time and does not depend on the age of the system. Let us obtain the plots of a few exponential distributions:

```
> par(mfrow=c(1,2))
> curve(dexp(x,1),0,10,ylab="f(x)",xlab="x",cex.axis=1.25)
> curve(dexp(x,0.2),add=TRUE,col=2)
> curve(dexp(x,0.5),add=TRUE,col=3)
> curve(dexp(x,0.7),add=TRUE,col=4)
> curve(dexp(x,0.85),add=TRUE,col=5)
> legend(6,1,paste("Rate = ",c(1,0.2,0.5,0.7,0.85)),col=1:5,pch=
+ "___")
> curve(dexp(x,50),0,0.5,ylab="f(x)",xlab="x")
> curve(dexp(x,10),add=TRUE,col=2)
> curve(dexp(x,20),add=TRUE,col=3)
> curve(dexp(x,30),add=TRUE,col=4)
> curve(dexp(x,40),add=TRUE,col=5)
> legend(0.3,50,paste("Rate = ",c(1,0.2,0.5,0.7,0.85)),col=1:5,pch=
+ "___")
```

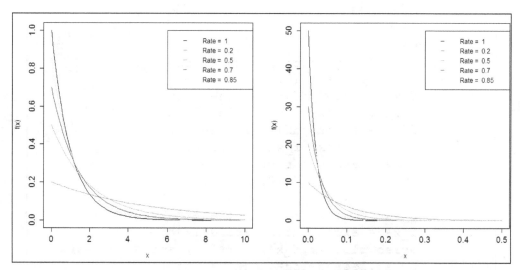

The exponential densities

The mean and variance of this exponential distribution are listed as follows:

$$E(X) = \frac{1}{\lambda} \, and \, Var(X) = \frac{1}{\lambda^2}$$

The complete Python code block is given next:

```
In [19]:  from scipy.stats import expon
          xr = np.arange(0,10.2,0.20)
          f_x = expon.pdf(xr,scale=1)
          pylab.plot(xr,f_x,'r',label='Rate=1')
          f_x1 = expon.pdf(xr,scale=1/0.2)
          pylab.plot(xr,f_x1,'g',label='Rate=0.2')
          f_x2 = expon.pdf(xr,scale=1/0.5)
          pylab.plot(xr,f_x2,'b',label='Rate=0.5')
          f_x3 = expon.pdf(xr,scale=1/0.7)
          pylab.plot(xr,f_x3,'y',label='Rate=0.7')
          f_x4 = expon.pdf(xr,scale=1/0.85)
          pylab.plot(xr,f_x4,'purple',label='Rate=0.85')
          pylab.legend(loc='upper right')
          plt.show()

In [21]:  from scipy.stats import expon
          xr = np.arange(0,0.5,0.02)
          f_x = expon.pdf(xr,scale=1/50)
          pylab.plot(xr,f_x,'r',label='Rate=50')
          f_x1 = expon.pdf(xr,scale=1/10)
          pylab.plot(xr,f_x1,'g',label='Rate=10')
          f_x2 = expon.pdf(xr,scale=1/20)
          pylab.plot(xr,f_x2,'b',label='Rate=20')
          f_x3 = expon.pdf(xr,scale=1/30)
          pylab.plot(xr,f_x3,'y',label='Rate=30')
          f_x4 = expon.pdf(xr,scale=1/40)
          pylab.plot(xr,f_x4,'purple',label='Rate=40')
          pylab.legend(loc='upper right')
          pylab.show()
```

Normal distribution

The normal distribution is in some sense an all-pervasive distribution that arises sooner or later in almost any statistical discussion. In fact, it is very likely that the reader may already be familiar with certain aspects of the normal distribution; for example, the shape of a normal distribution curve is bell-shaped. The mathematical appropriateness is probably reflected through the reason that though it has a simpler expression, its density function includes the three most famous irrational numbers $e, \sqrt{2}, and \pi$

Suppose that X is normally distributed with the mean μ and the variance σ^2. Then, the probability density function of the normal RV is given by:

$$f\left(x; \mu, \sigma^2\right) = \frac{1}{\sqrt{2\pi}\sigma} \exp\left\{-\frac{1}{2\sigma^2}(x-\mu)^2\right\}, -\infty < x < \infty, -\infty < \mu < \infty, \sigma > 0$$

If the mean is zero and the variance is 1, the normal RV is referred to as the standard normal RV, and the standard is to denote it by Z.

Example 1.4.2. Shady Normal Curves: We will again consider a standard normal random variable, which is more popularly denoted in Statistics by Z. Some of the most needed probabilities are $P(Z > 0)$ and $P(-1.96 < Z < 1.96)$. These probabilities are now shaded:

```
> par(mfrow=c(3,1))
> # Probability Z Greater than 0
> curve(dnorm(x,0,1),-4,4,xlab="z",ylab="f(z)")
> z=seq(0,4,0.02)
> lines(z,dnorm(z),type="h",col="grey")
> # 95% Coverage
> curve(dnorm(x,0,1),-4,4,xlab="z",ylab="f(z)")
> z=seq(-1.96,1.96,0.001)
> lines(z,dnorm(z),type="h",col="grey")
> # 95% Coverage
> curve(dnorm(x,0,1),-4,4,xlab="z",ylab="f(z)")
> z=seq(-2.58,2.58,0.001)
> lines(z,dnorm(z),type="h",col="grey")
```

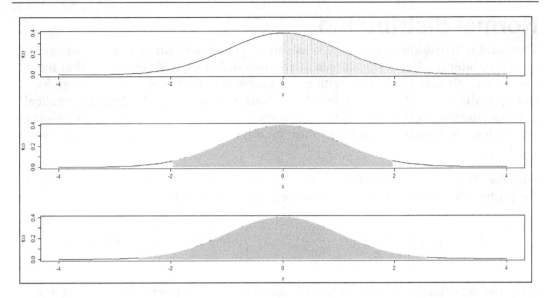

Shady normal curves

The Python program for the shady normal probabilities is given next:

```
In [23]:  from scipy.stats import norm
          xr = np.arange(-4,4.1,0.1)
          fx = norm.pdf(xr)
          pylab.plot(xr,fx)
          p1 = np.arange(0,4.02,0.02)
          pylab.fill_between(p1,norm.pdf(p1))
          pylab.show()
          xr = np.arange(-4,4.1,0.1)
          fx = norm.pdf(xr)
          pylab.plot(xr,fx)
          p2 = np.arange(-1.96,1.961,0.001)
          pylab.fill_between(p2,norm.pdf(p2))
          pylab.show()
          xr = np.arange(-4,4.1,0.1)
          fx = norm.pdf(xr)
          pylab.plot(xr,fx)
          p3 = np.arange(-2.58,2.581,0.001)
          pylab.fill_between(p3,norm.pdf(p3))
          pylab.show()
```

Summary

The reader should now be clear with the distinct nature of variables that arise in different scenarios. In R, the reader should be able to verify that the data is in the correct format. Furthermore, the important families of random variables are introduced in this chapter, which should help the reader in dealing with them when they crop up in their experiments. Computation of simple probabilities were also introduced and explained.

In the next chapter, the reader will learn how to perform the basic R computations, creating data objects, and so on. As data can seldom be constructed completely in R, we need to import data from external foreign files. The methods explained help the reader to import data in file formats such as `.csv` and `.xls`. Similar to importing, it is also important to be able to export data/output to other software. Finally, the R session management will conclude the next chapter.

2
Import/Export Data

The main goals of this chapter are to familiarize the reader with the various classes of objects in R, help the reader extract data from various popular formats, connect R with popular databases such as MySQL, and finally, the best export options of the R output. The main purpose is that the practitioner frequently has data available in a fixed format, and sometimes the dataset is available in popular database systems. This chapter helps the reader to extract data from various sources, and also recommends the export options of the R output.

We will begin by gaining a better understanding of the various formats in which R stores the data. Updated information about the import/export options is maintained on `http://cran.r-project.org/doc/manuals/R-data.html`. On the Python front, we will be using the Jupyter Notebook throughout the book. Here, we will deal with the basic operations and give indications to import the data from external sources. Python session management will be covered too. To summarize, the main learning outcomes from this chapter will be the following:

- Basic and essential computations in R and Python
- Importing data from CSV, XLS, and MySQL
- Exporting data for other software
- R and Python session management

The essential R and Python packages will be loaded at the beginning of the chapter session.

Packages and settings – R and Python

First, we load the essential R packages:

 Note: To install the required packages, you need to add a code line before loading the packages:

Syntax:

```
install.packages("Package Name")
```

1. Load the R packages `foreign`, `RMySQL`, and RSADBE:

```
> library(RSADBE)
> library(foreign)
> library(RMysSQL)
```

2. Import the Python packages as follows:

```
In [1]:  # Package(s) Import and Path Setting

In [2]:  import os
         import numpy as np
         import pandas as pd
         import pymysql as pysql
         import pymysql.cursors
         os.chdir('/home/pranathi/Documents/RPySADBE/Python/Chapter_02')
```

Note that you might have to set the working directory path as per your settings.

Understanding data.frame and other formats

Any software comes with its structure and nuances. The *Questionnaire and its component* section of *Chapter 1, Data Characteristics*, introduced various facets of data. In the current section, we will go into the details of how R works with data of different characteristics. Depending on the need, we have different formats of the data. In this section, we will begin with simpler objects and move up the ladder toward some of the more complex ones.

Constants, vectors, and matrices

R has five inbuilt objects that store certain constant values. The five objects are LETTERS, letters, month.abb, month.name, and pi. The first two objects contain the letters A-Z in upper and lower cases. The third and fourth objects have months in their abbreviated form and the complete month names. Finally, the object pi contains the value of the famous irrational number. So here, the exercise for the reader is to find the value of the irrational number e. The details about these R constant objects may be obtained using the function ?Constants or example(Constants), of course by executing these commands at the console.

There is also another class of constants in R that is very useful. These constants are called NumericConstants and include Inf for infinite numbers, NaN for not a number, and so on. The reader is encouraged to find more details and other useful constants by running ?NumericConstants. R can handle numerical, character, logical, integer, and complex kinds of vectors and it is the class of the object that characterizes the vector. Typically, we deal with vectors that may be numeric, character, and so on. A vector of desired class and the number of elements for a vector may be initiated using the vector function. The length argument declares the size of the vector, which is the number of elements for the vector, whereas mode characterizes the vector to take one of the required classes. The elements of a vector can be assigned names if required. This may be seen as follows. Each element of a vector object may be assigned a name. The R names function comes in handy for this purpose.

Arithmetic on numeric vector objects can be performed in an easier way. The operators (+, -, *, /, ^) are respectively used for (addition, subtraction, multiplication, division, and power). The characteristics of a vector object may be obtained using functions such as sum, prod, min, max, and so on. Accuracy of a vector up to certain decimals may be fixed using options in digits, round, and so on.

Now, two vectors need not have the same number of elements and we may carry the arithmetic operation between them, say addition. In a mathematical sense, two vectors of unequal length cannot be added. However, R goes ahead and performs the operations just the same. Thus, there is a necessity to understand how operations are carried out in such cases.

To begin with the simpler case, let us consider two vectors with an equal number of elements. Suppose that we have a vector $x = (1, 2, 3, ..., 9, 10)$ and $y = (11, 12, 13, ..., 19, 20)$. If we add these two vectors, $x + y$, the result is an element-wise addition of the respective elements in x and y, that is, we will get a new vector with elements 12, 14, 16, ..., 28, 30. Now, let us increase the number of elements of y from 10 to 12 with $y = (11, 12, 13, ..., 19, 20, 21, 22)$. The operation is carried out in the order that the elements of x (the smaller object one) are added element-wise added to the first 10 elements of y.

Now, R finds that there are two more elements of y in 11 and 12 that have not been touched as of now. It now picks the first two elements of x in 1 and 2 and adds them to 11 and 12. Hence, the 11 and 12 elements of the output are 11+1 =12 and 12 + 2 = 14. The warning says that longer object length is not a multiple of shorter object length, which has now been explained.

Let us have a brief peep at a few more operators related to the vectors. The operator `%%` on two objects, say x and y, returns the remainder following an integer division, and the operator `%/%` returns the integer division.

Time for action – understanding constants, vectors, and basic arithmetic

We will look at a few important and interesting examples. The reader will understand the structure of vectors in R and will also be able to perform the basic arithmetic related to their requirement:

1. Key in `LETTERS` at the R console and hit the *Enter* key.

2. Key in `letters` at the R console and hit the *Enter* key.

3. To obtain the first five and the last five alphabets, try the following code: `LETTERS[c(1:5,22:26)]` and `letters[c(1:5,22:26)]`.

4. Month names and their abbreviations are available in the `base` package and you can explore them using `?Constants` at the console.

5. Selected month names and their abbreviations can be obtained using `month.abb[c(1:3,8:10)]` and `month.name[c(1:3,8:10)]`. Also, the value of `pi` in R can be found by entering `pi` at the console.

6. To generate a vector of length 4, without specifying the class, try `vector(length=4)`. In specific classes, vector objects can be generated by declaring the "mode" values for a vector object. That is, a numeric vector (with default values of 0) is obtained by the code `vector(mode = "numeric", length=4)`. The reader can similarly generate `logical`, `complex`, `character`, and `integer` vectors by specifying them as options in the mode argument.

   The R output screenshots are available in the *What just happened* section.

7. **Creating new vector objects and name assignment**: A generated vector can be assigned to new objects using either of `=`, `<-`, or `->`. The last two assignments are in the order from the generated vector of the tail end to the new variables at the end of the arrow:

   1. First assign integer vector 1:10 to x by using `x <- 1:10`.

   2. Check the names of x by using `names(x)`.

   3. Assign the first 10 `letters` of the alphabets as names for elements of x by using `names(x) <- letters[1:10]`, and verify that the assignment is done using `names(x)`.

   4. Finally, display the numeric vector x by simply keying in x at the console.

8. **Basic arithmetic**: Create new R objects by entering `x<-1:10; y<-11:20; a<-10; b<--4;` and `c<-0.5` at the console. In a certain sense, x and y are vectors while a, b, and c are constants:

   1. Perform simple addition of numeric vectors with `x + y`.

   2. Scalar multiplication of vectors and then summing the resulting vectors is easily done by `a*x + b*y`.

   3. Verify the result `(a + b)x = ax + bx` by checking that `(a+b)*x == a*x + b*x` results in a logical vector of length 10, each having a TRUE value.

   4. Vector multiplication is carried by using `x*y`.

   5. Vector division in R is simply element-wise division of the two vectors, and does not have an interpretation in mathematics. We obtain the accuracy up to 4 digits using `round(x/y,4)`.

   6. Finally, (element-wise) exponentiation of vectors is carried out through `x^2`.

9. **Adding two unequal length vectors**: The arithmetic explained before applies to unequal length vectors in a slightly different way. Run the following operations `x=1:10; x+c(1:12)`, `length(x+c(1:12))`, `c(1:3)^c(1,2)`, and `(9:11)-c(4,6)`.

10. The integer divisor and remainder following integer division may be obtained respectively using `%/%` and `%%` operators. Key in `-3:3 %% 2`, `-3:3 %% 3`, and `-3:3 %% c(2,3)` to find remainders between the sequence -3, -2, ..., 2, 3 and 2, 3, and `c(2,3)`. Replace the operator `%%` by using `%/%` to find the integer divisors.

All the codes are available in *Chapter 2, Import/Export Data* R file located in the folder `R/Chapter_02/SRC` of the companion code bundle.

What just happened?

We split the output into multiple screenshots for ease of explanation:

```
> LETTERS
 [1] "A" "B" "C" "D" "E" "F" "G" "H" "I" "J" "K" "L" "M" "N"
[15] "O" "P" "Q" "R" "S" "T" "U" "V" "W" "X" "Y" "Z"
> letters
 [1] "a" "b" "c" "d" "e" "f" "g" "h" "i" "j" "k" "l" "m" "n"
[15] "o" "p" "q" "r" "s" "t" "u" "v" "w" "x" "y" "z"
> LETTERS[c(1:5,22:26)]
 [1] "A" "B" "C" "D" "E" "V" "W" "X" "Y" "Z"
> letters[c(1:5,22:26)]
 [1] "a" "b" "c" "d" "e" "v" "w" "x" "y" "z"
> ?Constants
starting httpd help server ... done
> month.abb[c(1:3,8:10)]
[1] "Jan" "Feb" "Mar" "Aug" "Sep" "Oct"
> month.name[c(1:3,8:10)]
[1] "January"   "February"  "March"     "August"
[5] "September" "October"
> pi
[1] 3.142
> vector(length=4)
[1] FALSE FALSE FALSE FALSE
> vector(mode="numeric",length=4)
[1] 0 0 0 0
> vector(mode="logical",length=4)
[1] FALSE FALSE FALSE FALSE
> vector(mode="complex",length=4)
[1] 0+0i 0+0i 0+0i 0+0i
> vector(mode="character",length=4)
[1] "" "" "" ""
> vector(mode="integer",length=4)
[1] 0 0 0 0
```

Introducing constants and vectors functioning in R

LETTERS is a character vector available in R that consists of the 26 uppercase letters of the English language, whereas letters contains the alphabet in lowercase letters. We have used the integer vector c(1:5,22:26) in the index to extract the first and last five elements of both the character vectors. When the ?Constants command is executed, R pops out an HTML file in your default internet browser and opens a page with the link http://my_IP/library/base/html/Constants.html. The reader can find more details about Constants from the base package on this web page.

Months, as in January-December, are available in the character vector month.name, whereas the popular abbreviated forms of the months are available in the character vector month.abb. Finally, the numeric object pi contains the value of pi up to the first three decimals only.

Next, we consider the generation of various types of vector using the R vector function. Now, the code vector(mode="numeric",length=4) creates a numeric vector with default values of 0 and a required length of four. Similarly, the other vectors are created.

```
> x=1:10 # Creating two simple integer vectors
> y=11:20
> a=10
> b=-4 # Creating constants
> x + y # Adding two vectors
 [1] 12 14 16 18 20 22 24 26 28 30
> a*x + b*y # Further simple vector operations
 [1] -34 -28 -22 -16 -10  -4   2   8  14  20
> sum((a+b)*x == a*x + b*x)
[1] 10
> x*y # Elementwise multiplication of two vectors
 [1]  11  24  39  56  75  96 119 144 171 200
> round(x/y,4) # round helps to get accuracy
 [1] 0.0909 0.1667 0.2308 0.2857 0.3333 0.3750 0.4118 0.4444
 [9] 0.4737 0.5000
> x^2 # Squaring a vector
 [1]   1   4   9  16  25  36  49  64  81 100
> x+c(1:12) # Adding a vector to x with more elements
 [1]  2  4  6  8 10 12 14 16 18 20 12 14
Warning message:
In x + c(1:12) :
  longer object length is not a multiple of shorter object length
> length(x+c(1:12)) # Verifying the no. of elements of previous action
[1] 12
Warning message:
In x + c(1:12) :
  longer object length is not a multiple of shorter object length
> c(1:3)^c(1,2) # What you expect?
[1] 1 4 3
Warning message:
In c(1:3)^c(1, 2) :
  longer object length is not a multiple of shorter object length
> (9:11)-c(4,6) # Check your expectations
[1] 5 4 7
Warning message:
In (9:11) - c(4, 6) :
  longer object length is not a multiple of shorter object length
```

Vector arithmetic in R

An integer vector object is created by the code x = 1:10. We could have alternatively used options such as x<- 1:10 or 1:10 -> x. The final result is of course the same. The choice of the assignment operator — find more details by running ?assignOps at the R console — <- is far more popular in the R community and it can be used during any part of R programming. However, this book uses the = assignment, which is generally used at the top-level of programming. By default, there won't be any names assigned for either vectors or matrices. Thus, the output is NULL. names is a function in R that is useful for assigning appropriate names.

Our task is to assign the first 10 lowercase letters of the alphabet to the vector x. Hence, we have the code names(x) <- letters[1:10]. We verify if the names have been properly assigned and then changed on the display of x following the assignment of the names using names(x) and x.

Next, we create two integer vectors in x and y, and two objects a and b, which may be treated as scalars. Now, x + y; a*x + b*y; sum((a+b)*x == a*x + b*x) performs three different tasks. First, it performs addition of vectors and returns the result of element-wise addition of the two vectors leading to the answer 12, 14, …, 28, 30. Second, we are verifying the result of scalar multiplication of vectors, and third, the result of (a + b)x = ax + bx.

In the next round of R codes, we ran x*y; round(x/y,4); x^2. Similar to the addition operator, the * operator performs element-wise multiplication for the two vectors. Thus, we get the output as 11, 24, …, 171, 200. In the next line, recall that ; executes the code on the next line/operation; first, the element-wise division is carried out. For the resulting vector (a numeric one), the round function gives the accuracy up to four digits as specified there. Finally, x^2 gives us the square of each element of x. Here, 2 can be replaced by any other real number.

For the last code of the line, we repeat some of the earlier operations with the minor difference that the two vectors are not of the same length. As predicted earlier, R issues a warning that the length of the longer vector is not a multiple of the length of the shorter vector. Thus, for the operation x+c(1:12);, first all the elements of x (which is the shorter length vector here) are added with the first 10 elements of 1:12. Then the last two elements of 1:12 at 11 and 12 need to be added with elements from x, and for this purpose.

R picks the first two elements of x. If the longer length vector is a multiple of the shorter one, the entire elements of the shorter vector are repeatedly added over in cycles. The remaining results as a consequence of running c(1:3)^c(1,2); (9:11)-c(4,6) are left to the reader for interpretation.

Let us look at the output after the R codes for the integer and remainder between two objects are carried out:

```
> -3:3 # The Sequence
[1] -3 -2 -1  0  1  2  3
> -3:3 %% 2 # Remainder post division by 2
[1] 1 0 1 0 1 0 1
> -3:3 %% 3 # Remainder post division by 3
[1] 0 1 2 0 1 2 0
> -3:3 %% c(2,3)  # What do you expect?
[1] 1 1 1 0 1 2 1
Warning message:
In -3:3%%c(2, 3) :
  longer object length is not a multiple of shorter object length
> -3:3 %/% 2 # Integer divisor by 2
[1] -2 -1 -1  0  0  1  1
> -3:3 %/% 3 # Integer divisor by 3
[1] -1 -1 -1  0  0  0  1
> -3:3 %/% c(2,3) # Expectations?
[1] -2 -1 -1  0  0  0  1
Warning message:
In -3:3%/%c(2, 3) :
  longer object length is not a multiple of shorter object length
```

Integer divisor and remainder operations

In the segment `-3:3 %% 2`, we are first creating a sequence -3, -2, ..., 2, 3 and then we are asking for the remainder if we divide each of them by 2. Clearly, the remainder for any integer if divided by 2 is either 0 or 1, and for a sequence of consecutive integers, we expect an alternate sequence of 0s and 1s, which is the output in this case. Check the expected result for `-3:3 %% 3`. Now, for the operation `-3:3 %% c(2,3)`, first look at the complete sequence `-3:3` as -3, -2, -1, 0, 1, 2, 3. Here, the elements -3, -1, 1, and 3 are divided by 2 and the remainders are returned, whereas -2, 0, and 2 are divided by 3 and the remainders are returned. The operator `%/%` returns the integer divisor and the interpretation of the results is left to the reader. Please refer to the previous screenshot for the results.

We will now replicate some of the analysis in Python. In the code bundle, access the folder `Chapter_02` and go to the `Output` folder and, using the Anaconda Prompt for Windows or the gnome-terminal on Ubuntu, run the following line to explore the output of an already ran Python session:

```
jupyter notebook RPySADBE_Chapter_02.ipynb
```

to explore the output of an already ran Python session. Note that an `.ipynb` file generally is the output file of a ran session in Jupyter Notebook. Alternatively, you can explore the code in the folder `Chapter_02/SRC` and open the file `Chapter_02.py` in your choice of Python editor.

Doing it in Python

We will now illustrate carrying out elementary and essential operations in the next block of codes:

1. Simple arithmetic is easily performed in Python:

```
In [3]:  # Simple Operations

In [4]:  x = 8
         y = 15
         a = 10
         b = -4
         a,b=10,-4 # equivalently
         x + y

Out[4]:  23
```

Commenting in a cell is easily done and we see it here. Long commenting will be dealt with later. We created units x, y, a, and b. Note the equivalent way of assignments and that it is not possible in R.

2. A simple verification of the BODMAS rule is in order:

```
In [5]:  a*x + b*y

Out[5]:  20

In [6]:  (a+b)*x == a*x + b*x

Out[6]:  True

In [7]:  x*y

Out[7]:  120

In [8]:  round(x/y,4)

Out[8]:  0.5333

In [9]:  x**2

Out[9]:  64
```

Differencing, rounding, and square operations are carried out and the natural result is obtained.

3. Vector creation is possible with the numpy package. We create two vectors, x and y, and perform the usual analysis:

```
In [10]:  # Python Vectors

In [11]:  x = np.array([1,4,3])
          y = np.array([2,9,14])
          x+y
Out[11]:  array([ 3, 13, 17])

In [12]:  x-y
Out[12]:  array([ -1,  -5, -11])

In [13]:  x*y
Out[13]:  array([ 2, 36, 42])

In [14]:  x/y
Out[14]:  array([ 0.5       ,  0.44444444,  0.21428571])
```

If you perform an incompatible operation, an error will be the thrown by the software:

```
In [15]:  x-[1,2,3,4]

ValueError                                Traceback (most recent call last)
<ipython-input-15-d2eb8d2f1fcd> in <module>()
----> 1 x-[1,2,3,4]

ValueError: operands could not be broadcast together with shapes (3,) (4,)
```

4. The dot product between two vectors and the norm of a vector is obtained using the dot and sqrt functions from the numpy package:

```
In [16]:  np.dot(x,y)

Out[16]:  80

In [17]:  np.sqrt((x*x).sum())

Out[17]:  5.0990195135927845

In [18]:  # Equivalently
          np.sqrt(sum(x*x))

Out[18]:  5.0990195135927845
```

Numpy is one of the most important Python packages. In the next segment of the section, we deal with matrix computations. We now look at the matrix objects. Similar to the vector function in R, we have matrix as a function, which creates matrix objects. A matrix is an array of numbers with a certain number of rows and columns. By default, the elements of a matrix are generated as NA, that is, not available.

Let *r* be the number of rows and c the number of columns. The order of the matrix is then *r* x *c*. A vector object of length rc in R can be converted into a matrix by the code matrix(vector, nrow=r, ncol=c, byrow=TRUE). The rows and columns of a matrix may be assigned names using the dimnames option in the matrix function.

The mathematics of matrices in R is preserved in relation to the matrix arithmetic. Suppose we have two matrices, A and B, with respective dimensions, m x n and n x o. The cross-product, A x B is then a matrix of order m x o, which is obtained in R by the operation A %*% B. We are also often interested in the determinant of a square matrix, the number of rows being equal to the number of columns, and this is obtained in R using the det function on the matrix, say det(A). Finally, we also more often require the computation of the inverse of a square matrix.

The first temptation is to obtain the same by using A^{-1}. This will give a wrong answer as this leads to an element-wise reciprocal and not the inverse of a matrix. The solve function in R, if executed on a square matrix, gives the inverse of a matrix. Fine! Let us now do these operations using R.

Time for action – matrix computations

We will see the basic matrix computations in the forthcoming steps. The matrix computations, such as the cross-product of matrices, transpose, and inverse, will be illustrated:

1. Generate a 2 x 2 matrix with default values using `matrix(nrow=2, ncol=2)`.

2. Create a matrix from the `1:4` vector by running `matrix(1:4,nrow=2,ncol=2, byrow="TRUE")`.

3. Assign row and column names for the preceding matrix by using the option `dimnames`, that is, by running `A <- matrix(data=1:4, nrow=2, ncol=2, byrow=TRUE, dimnames = list(c("R_1", "R_2"),c("C_1", "C_2")))` at the R console.

4. Find the properties of the preceding matrices by the commands `nrow`, `ncol`, and `dimnames`, and a few more, with `dim(A)`; `nrow(A)`; `ncol(A)`; and `dimnames(A)`.

5. Create two matrices, X and Y, of order 3 * 4 and 4 * 3 and obtain their cross-product with the code `X <- matrix(c(1:12),nrow=3,ncol=4)`; `Y = matrix(13:24, nrow=4)` and `X %*% Y`.

6. The transposition of a matrix is obtained using the `t` function, `t(X)`.

7. Create a new matrix `A <- matrix(data=c(13,24,34,23,67,32, 45,23,11), nrow=3)` and find its determinant and inverse by using `det(A)` and `solve(A)` respectively.

The R code for the preceding action list is given in the following code snippet:

```
matrix(nrow=2,ncol=2)
matrix(1:4,nrow=2,ncol=2, byrow="TRUE")
A <- matrix(data=1:4, nrow=2, ncol=2, byrow=TRUE, dimnames =
list(c("R_1", "R_2"),c("C_1", "C_2")))
dim(A); nrow(A); ncol(A); dimnames(A)
X <- matrix(c(1:12),nrow=3,ncol=4)
Y <- matrix(13:24, nrow=4)
X %*% Y
t(Y)
A <- matrix(data=c(13,24,34,23,67,32,45,23,11),nrow=3)
det(A)
solve(A)
```

Note the use of a semicolon (;) in line five of the preceding code. The result of this usage is that the code separated by the semicolon is executed as if it was entered on a new line. Execute the preceding code in your R console. The output of the R codes is given in the following screenshot:

```
> matrix(nrow=2,ncol=2) # An empty matrix
     [,1] [,2]
[1,]   NA   NA
[2,]   NA   NA
> matrix(1:4,nrow=2,ncol=2) # An improved one?
     [,1] [,2]
[1,]    1    3
[2,]    2    4
> A <- matrix(data=1:4, nrow=2, ncol=2, byrow=T, dimnames =
+ list(c("R_1", "R_2"),c("C_1", "C_2"))) # A better one?
> dim(A); nrow(A); ncol(A); dimnames(A) # Matrix structure
[1] 2 2
[1] 2
[1] 2
[[1]]
[1] "R_1" "R_2"
[[2]]
[1] "C_1" "C_2"
> X <- matrix(c(1:12),nrow=3,ncol=4); Y <- matrix(13:24, nrow=4)
> X %*% Y # Cross-product of two matrices
     [,1] [,2] [,3]
[1,]  334  422  510
[2,]  392  496  600
[3,]  450  570  690
> t(Y) # Transpose of a matrix
     [,1] [,2] [,3] [,4]
[1,]   13   14   15   16
[2,]   17   18   19   20
[3,]   21   22   23   24
> A <- matrix(data=c(13,24,34,23,67,32,45,23,11),nrow=3)
> det(A) # Determinant of a matrix
[1] -56023
> solve(A) # Inverse of a matrix
            [,1]        [,2]        [,3]
[1,] -1.785e-05 -0.021188  0.044375
[2,] -9.246e-03  0.024758 -0.013941
[3,]  2.695e-02 -0.006533 -0.005694
```

Matrix computations in R

What just happened?

You were able to create matrices in R and learned the basic operations. Remember all the times that `solve` and not `(^-1)` gives the inverse of a matrix. It is now seen that matrix computations in R are really easy to carry out.

The parameters `nrow` and `ncol` are used to specify the dimensions of a matrix. Data for a matrix can be specified through the `data` argument. The first two lines of code in the previous screenshot create a bare-bones matrix. Using the `dimnames` argument, we have created a more elegant matrix and assigned the matrix to a matrix object named A.

We next focus on the `list` object. It has already been used earlier to specify the `dimnames` of a matrix.

Doing it in Python

Matrix computations can be performed using the various options:

1. We create two matrices using the `array` function and carry out the transpose and cross-product operations:

```
In [19]:  # Python Matrix

In [20]:  X = np.array([[10,20,30],[5,16,28],[8,2,19]])
          Y = np.array([4,5,9])
          X+45

Out[20]:  array([[55, 65, 75],
                 [50, 61, 73],
                 [53, 47, 64]])

In [21]:  np.transpose(X)

Out[21]:  array([[10,  5,  8],
                 [20, 16,  2],
                 [30, 28, 19]])

In [22]:  np.cross(X,Y)

Out[22]:  array([[ 30,  30, -30],
                 [  4,  67, -39],
                 [-77,   4,  32]])
```

2. The inverse of a matrix is obtained by using the `linalg.inv` function:

```
In [23]:  np.cross(np.linalg.inv(np.cross(np.transpose(X),X)),np.cross(np.transpose(X),Y))
Out[23]:  array([[ 0.04380446,  0.19653758,  0.37267192],
                 [-0.30138658, -0.06915852,  0.79140376],
                 [-0.51307144, -0.40652873,  0.04435901]])
```

The list object

In the preceding subsection, we saw different kinds of objects such as constants, vectors, and matrices. Sometimes, it is required that we pool them together in a single object. The framework for this task is provided by the `list` object. From the online source `http://cran.r-project.org/doc/manuals/R-intro.html#Lists-and-data-frames`, we define a list as "An R `list` is an object consisting of an ordered collection of objects known as its **components**". Basically, various types of objects can be brought under a single umbrella using the `list` function. Let us create `list`, which contains a character vector, an integer vector, and a matrix. We don't deal with the list objects of Python that are quite different from their R counterparts.

Time for action – creating a list object

Here, we will have a first look at the creation of list objects, which can contain in them objects of different classes:

1. Create a character vector containing the first six capital `letters` with `A <- LETTERS[1:6]`. Create an integer vector of the first 10 integers, 1-10, with `B <- 1:10`, and a matrix with `C <- matrix(1:6,nrow=2)`.

2. Create a list that has the three objects created in the previous steps as its components with `Z <- list(A = A, B = B, C = C)`.

 Asterisked sections won't be having a parallel Python implementation. The reason for this might be varied. Sometimes, the same named function in Python may have an entirely different purpose. Other times, the parallel Python function might not exist or might be too complex.

3. Ensure that the class of `Z`, and its three components in `A`, `B`, and `C` are indeed retained as follows: `class(Z); class(Z$A); class(Z$B);` and `class(Z$C)`.

The consolidated R codes are given next, which the reader has to enter at the R console:

```
A <- LETTERS[1:6]; B <- 1:10; C <- matrix(1:6,nrow=2)
Z <- list(A = A, B = B, C = C)
Z
class(Z); class(Z$A); class(Z$B); class(Z$C)
```

```
> A <- LETTERS[1:6]; B <- 1:10; C <- matrix(1:6,nrow=2)
> Z <- list(A = A, B = B, C = C)
> Z
$A
[1] "A" "B" "C" "D" "E" "F"
$B
 [1]  1  2  3  4  5  6  7  8  9 10
$C
     [,1] [,2] [,3]
[1,]    1    3    5
[2,]    2    4    6
> class(Z); class(Z$A); class(Z$B); class(Z$C)
[1] "list"
[1] "character"
[1] "integer"
[1] "matrix"
```

Creating and understanding a list object

What just happened?

Different classes of objects can be easily brought under a single umbrella and their structures are also preserved within that newly created list object. Especially, here we put a character vector, an integer vector, and a matrix under a single list object. Next, we check for the class of the z object and find the answer to be list as it should be. A new extraction tool has been introduced in the dollar symbol, $, which needs an explanation.

Elements/objects from a list vector can be extracted using the $ option along similar lines as the [and [[extracting tools. In our example, Z$A extracts the A object from the Z list, and we use the class function wrapper on Z$A to find its class. It is then confirmed that the classes of A, B, and C are preserved under the list object. More details about the extraction tools may be obtained by running ?Extract at the R console.

Yes, you have successfully created your first list object. This utility is particularly useful when building big programs and when we need certain actions within a single object.

The data.frame object

In the figure *Understanding variable types of an R object* of *Chapter 1, Data Characteristics*, we saw that when the `class` function is applied on the `SQ` object, the output resulted in `data.frame`. The details about this function can be obtained by executing `?data.frame` at the R console. The first noticeable aspect is `data.frame {base}`, which means that this function is in the `base` library. Furthermore, the description says: "This function creates data frames, tightly-coupled collections of variables, which share many of the properties of matrices and of lists, used as the fundamental data structure by most of R's modeling software". This description is seen to be correct as in the same figure we have different numeric, character, and factor variables contained in the same `data.frame` object. Thus, we know that a `data.frame` object can contain different kinds of variables.

A data frame can contain different types of objects. That is, we can create two different classes of vectors and bind them together in a single data frame. A data frame can also be updated with new vectors and existing components can also be dropped from it. As with vectors and matrices, we can assign names to a data frame as is convenient for us.

Time for action – creating a data.frame object

Here, we create `data.frame` from vectors. New objects are then added to an existing data frame and some preliminary manipulations are demonstrated:

1. Create a numeric and character vector of length 3 each with `x <- c(2,3,4); y <- LETTERS[1:3]`.

2. Create a new data frame with `df1<-data.frame(x,y)`.

3. Verify the variable names of the data frame, the classes of the components, and display the variables distinctly with `variable.names(df1); sapply(df1, class); df1$x; df1$y`.

4. Add a new numeric vector to `df1` with `df1$z <- c(pi,sqrt(2), 2.71828)` and verify the changes in `df1` by entering `df1` at the console.

5. Nullify the x component of `df1` and verify the change.

6. Bring back the original x values with `df1$x <- x`.

7. Add a fourth observation with `df1[4,]<- list(y=LETTERS[2], z=3,x=5)` and then remove the second observation with `df1 <- df1[-2,]` and verify the change again.

8. Find the row names (or the observation names) of the data frame object by using `row.names(df1)`.

9. Obtain the column names (which should be actually x, y, and z) with `colnames(df1)`. Change the row and column names using `row.names(df1)<- 1:3; colnames(df1)=LETTERS[1:3]` and display the final form of the data frame.

The following is the consolidated code, which you have to enter in the R console:

```
# The data.frame object
x <-c(2,3,4); y <- LETTERS[1:3]
df1 <- data.frame(x,y)
variable.names(df1)
sapply(df1,class)
df1$x
df1$y
df1$z <- c(pi,sqrt(2), 2.71828)
df1
df1$x <- NULL
df1
df1$x <- x
df1[4,] <- list(y=LETTERS[2],z=3,x=5)
df1 <- df1[-2,]
df1
row.names(df1)
dim(df1)
colnames(df1)
row.names(df1) <- 1:3
colnames(df1) <- LETTERS[1:3]
df1
```

On running the preceding code in R, you will see the output as shown in the following screenshot:

```
> x <- c(2,3,4); y <- LETTERS[1:3]
> df1 <- data.frame(x,y) # Bringing together x and y
> variable.names(df1) # Names of df1
[1] "x" "y"
> sapply(df1,class) # Check classes
        x         y
"numeric"  "factor"
> df1$x; df1$y # Check for correctness
[1] 2 3 4
[1] A B C
Levels: A B C
> df1$z <- c(pi,sqrt(2), 2.71828); df1 # Some manipulation
  x y     z
1 2 A 3.142
2 3 B 1.414
3 4 C 2.718
> df1$x <- NULL; df1 # More manipulation
  y     z
1 A 3.142
2 B 1.414
3 C 2.718
> df1$x <- x # Restoring x
> df1[4,]<- list(y=LETTERS[2],z=3,x=5) # Adding a 4th object
> df1 <- df1[-2,]; df1 # Deleting y
  y     z x
1 A 3.142 2
3 C 2.718 4
4 B 3.000 5
> row.names(df1); dim(df1) # Confirm!
[1] "1" "3" "4"
[1] 3 3
> colnames(df1)
[1] "y" "z" "x"
> row.names(df1)<- 1:3; colnames(df1)<-LETTERS[1:3]
> df1 # Final form
  A     B C
1 A 3.142 2
2 C 2.718 4
3 B 3.000 5
```

Understanding a data.frame object

Let us now look at a larger data.frame object. iris is a very famous dataset and we will use it to check on some very useful tools for data display:

1. Load the iris data from the datasets package with data(iris).

2. Check the first 10 observations of the dataset with head(iris,10).

3. A compact display of a data.frame object is obtained with the str function in the following way: str(iris).

4. Using the $ extractor tool, inspect the different Species in the iris data in the following way: iris$Species.

5. We are asked to get the first 10 observations with the Sepal.Length and Petal.Length variables only. Now, we use the [extractor in the following way: iris[1:10,c("Sepal.Length","Petal.Length")].

```
> data(iris)
> head(iris,n=10)
   Sepal.Length Sepal.Width Petal.Length Petal.Width Species
1          5.1         3.5          1.4         0.2  setosa
2          4.9         3.0          1.4         0.2  setosa

9          4.4         2.9          1.4         0.2  setosa
10         4.9         3.1          1.5         0.1  setosa
> str(iris)
'data.frame':   150 obs. of  5 variables:
 $ Sepal.Length: num  5.1 4.9 4.7 4.6 5 5.4 4.6 5 4.4 4.9 ...
 $ Sepal.Width : num  3.5 3 3.2 3.1 3.6 3.9 3.4 3.4 2.9 3.1 ...
 $ Petal.Length: num  1.4 1.4 1.3 1.5 1.4 1.7 1.4 1.5 1.4 1.5 ...
 $ Petal.Width : num  0.2 0.2 0.2 0.2 0.2 0.4 0.3 0.2 0.2 0.1 ...
 $ Species     : Factor w/ 3 levels "setosa","versicolor",..: 1 1 1 1 1 1 1 1 1 1 ...
> iris$Species
  [1] setosa     setosa     setosa     setosa     setosa     setosa     setosa
  [8] setosa     setosa     setosa     setosa     setosa     setosa     setosa

 [92] versicolor versicolor versicolor versicolor versicolor versicolor versicolor
 [99] versicolor versicolor virginica  virginica  virginica  virginica  virginica

[141] virginica  virginica  virginica  virginica  virginica  virginica  virginica
[148] virginica  virginica  virginica
Levels: setosa versicolor virginica
> iris[1:10,c("Sepal.Length","Petal.Length")]
   Sepal.Length Petal.Length
1          5.1          1.4
2          4.9          1.4

10         4.9          1.5
```

Different ways of extracting objects from a data.frame object

What just happened?

A data frame may be a complex structure. Here, we first created two vectors of the same length with different structures, one being an integer and the other one a character vector. Using the `data.frame` function, we created a new object `df1`, which contains both the vectors. The variable names of `df1` are then verified with the `variable.names` function.

After verifying that the names are indeed as expected, we verify that the variable classes are preserved with the application of two functions `sapply` and `class`. `lapply` is a useful utility in R that applies a function over a list or vector and `sapply` is a more friendly version of `lapply`. In our particular example earlier, we need R to return us the classes of variables from the `df1` data frame.

Have a go hero

As an exercise, explain the rest of the R code that you have executed here yourself.

We have thus seen how to create a data frame, add and remove components, observations, change the component names, and so on.

The table object

Data displayed in a table format is easy to understand. We will begin with the famous `Titanic` dataset as it is very unlikely that the reader would not have heard about it. That the gigantic ship sinks at the end, that there are many beautiful movies about it, novels, documentaries, and many more, makes this dataset a very interesting example. It is known that the ship had some survivors post its unfortunate and premature end. The ship had children, women, and different classes of passenger onboard. This dataset is shipped (again) in the `datasets` package along with the software. The dataset relates to the passengers survival after the tragedy.

The `Titanic` dataset has four variables: `Class`, `Sex`, `Age`, and `Survived`. For each combination of the values for the four variables, we have a count of that combination. The `Class` variable is specified at four levels of `1st`, `2nd`, `3rd`, and `Crew` class. The gender is specified for the passengers and the age classification is as either `Child` or `Adult`. It is also known through the `Survived` variable whether the onboard passengers survived the clash of the ship with the iceberg. Thus, we have 4 x 2 x 2 x 2 = 32 different combinations according to the `Age`, `Sex`, `Class`, and `Survived` statuses.

The following screenshot gives a display of the dataset in two formats. On the right-hand side we can see the dataset in a spreadsheet style, while the left-hand side displays the frequencies according to a combinatorial group. The question is how we create table displays as on the left side of the screenshot. The present section addresses this aspect of table creation.

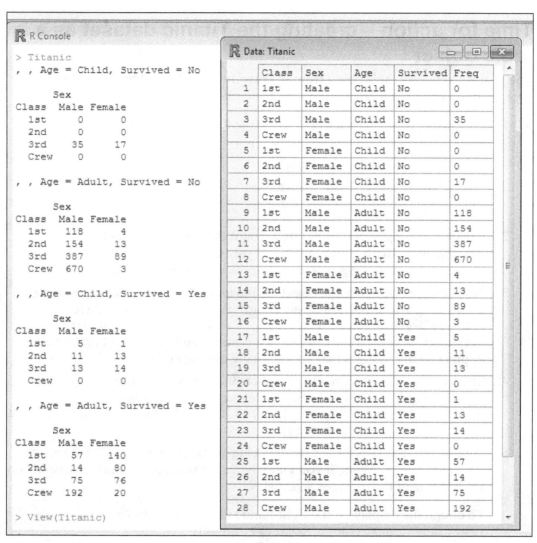

Two different views of the Titanic dataset

The left-side display of the screenshot is obtained by simply keying in `Titanic` at the R console, and the data format on the right-hand side is obtained by running `View(Titanic)` at the console. In general, we have a dataset available on the right-hand side. Hence, we will pretend that we have the dataset available in the latter format.

Time for action – creating the Titanic dataset as a table object

The goal is to create a table object from the raw dataset. We will be using the `expand.grid` and `xtabs` function toward the end:

1. First create four character vectors for the four types of variables:

   ```
   Class.Level <- c("1st","2nd","3rd", "Crew")

   Sex.Level <- c("Male", "Female")

   Age.Level <- c("Child", "Adult")

   Survived.Level <- c("No", "Yes")
   ```

2. Create a list object that takes into account the variable names and their possible levels with `Data.Level = list(Class = Class.Level, Sex = Sex.Level, Age = Age.Level, Survived = Survived.Level)`.

3. Now, create a `data.frame` object for the levels of the four variables using the `expand.grid` function by entering `T.Table = expand.grid(Class = Class.Level, Sex = Sex.Level, Age = Age.Level, Survived = Survived.Level)` at the console. It is instructive to view the `T.Table` and appreciate the changes that are occurring during at the step.

4. The `Titanic` dataset is ready except for the frequency count at each combinatorial level. Specify the counts with `T.freq = c(0,0,35,0,0,0,17,0, 118, 154,387,670,4,13,89,3, 5,11, 13,0,1,13,14,0,57,14,75,192,140,80,76,20)`.

5. Augment `T.Table` with `T.freq` by using `T.Table = cbind(T.Table, count=T.freq)`. Again, if you view the `T.Table`, you will find the display on the left side of the previous screenshot.

   To obtain the display on the right-hand side, enter `xtabs(count~ Class + Sex + Age + Survived , data = T.Table)`.

The complete R code is given next, which needs to be compiled in the software:

```
# The Table object
Class.Level <- c("1st","2nd","3rd", "Crew")
Sex.Level <- c("Male", "Female")
Age.Level <- c("Child", "Adult")
Survived.Level <- c("No", "Yes")
Data.Level <- list(Class = Class.Level, Sex = Sex.Level,
                   Age = Age.Level, Survived = Survived.Level)
T.Table <- expand.grid(Class = Class.Level, Sex =
                          Sex.Level, Age = Age.Level,
                       Survived = Survived.Level)
T.freq <- c(0,0,35,0,0,0,17,0,118,154,387,670,4,13,89,3,
            5,11, 13,0,1,13,14,0,57,14,75,192,140,80, 76,20)
T.Table <- cbind(T.Table, count=T.freq)
xtabs(count~ Class + Sex + Age + Survived , data = T.Table)
```

What just happened?

In practice, we may often have data in frequency format. It will be seen in later chapters that the table object is required for carrying out statistical analysis. To translate frequency format data into a table object, we first defined four variables through Class.Level, Sex.Level, Age.Level, and Survived.Level:

- For the required table object, these have been specified through the list object Data.Level.

- The function expand.grid creates all possible combinations of the factors of the four variables.

- The table of all possible combinations is then stored in the T.Table object.

- Next, the frequencies are assigned through the T.freq integer vector.

- Finally, the xtabs function creates the count according to the various levels of the variables and the result is a table object, which is the same as Titanic!

Have a go hero

UCBAdmissions is one of the benchmark datasets in statistics. It is available in the datasets package and it has data on the admission counts of six departments. The admissions data shows that there is a favored bias toward admitting male candidates over females and it led to an allegation against the University of California, Berkeley. The details of this problem may be found on the web at http://www.unc.edu/~nielsen/soci708/cdocs/Berkeley_admissions_bias.pdf. Information about the dataset is obtained with ?UCBAdmissions. Identify all the variables, and their classes, and regenerate the entire table from the raw codes.

Using utils and the foreign packages

Data is generally available in an external file. The types of external files are certainly varied and it is important to learn which of them may be imported into R. The probable spreadsheet files may exist in a **comma separated variable (CSV)** format, **XLS** or **XLSX** (Microsoft Excel) form, or ODS (OpenOffice/LibreOffice Calc) ones. There are more possible formats but we restrict our attention to these described previously. A snapshot of two files, `Employ.dat` and `SCV.csv`, in gedit and MS Excel are given in the following screenshot. The brief characteristics of the two files are summarized in the following list:

- The first row lists the names of the variables of the dataset

- Each observation begins on a new line

- In the DAT file, the delimiter is a tab ($\backslash$t), whereas for the CSV file, it is a comma (,)

- All three columns of the DAT file are numeric in nature

- The first five columns of the CSV file are numeric while the last column is character

- Overall, both the files have a well-defined structure going for them

The screenshot underlies the theme that, when the external files have a well-defined structure, it is vital that we make the most of the structure when importing it in R:

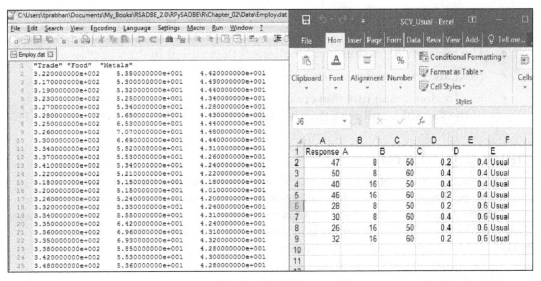

Snapshot of the two spreadsheet files

The core function for importing files into R is the `read.table` function from the `utils` package, shipped with R core. The first argument of this function is the filename; see the following screenshot. We can use `header=TRUE` to specify that the header names are the variable names of the columns. The separator option `sep` needs to be properly specified. For example, for the `Employ` dataset, it is a tab `\t`, whereas for the CSV file, it is a comma `,`. Frequently, each row may also have a name. For example, the customer name in a survey dataset, or serial number, and so on. This can be specified through `row.names`. The row names may or may not be present in the external file. That is, either the row names or the column names need not be part of the file from which we are importing the data:

```
read.table(file, header = FALSE, sep = "", quote = "\"'",
           dec = ".", row.names, col.names,
           as.is = !stringsAsFactors,
           na.strings = "NA", colClasses = NA, nrows = -1,
           skip = 0, check.names = TRUE, fill = !blank.lines.skip,
           strip.white = FALSE, blank.lines.skip = TRUE,
           comment.char = "#",
           allowEscapes = FALSE, flush = FALSE,
           stringsAsFactors = default.stringsAsFactors(),
           fileEncoding = "", encoding = "unknown", text)
```

The read.table syntax

In many files, there may be missing observations. Such data can be appropriately imported by specifying the missing values in `na.strings`. The missing values may be represented by blank cells, periods, and so on. The reader may find more details about the other options in the `read.table` function. We note that `read.csv`, `read.delim`, and so on are other variants of the `read.table` function. An Excel file of the type XLS or XLSX may be imported into R with the use of the `read.xls` function from the `gdata` package.

Let us begin with importing simpler data files into R:

- **Example 2.2.1. Reading from a DAT file**: The datasets analyzed in Ryan (2007) are available on the web at `ftp://ftp.wiley.com/public/sci_tech_med/engineering_statistics/`. Download the file `engineering_statistics.zip` and unzip the contents to the working directory of the R session. The problem is described in Exercise 1.82 of Ryan. The monthly data on the number of employees over a period of five years for three Wisconsin industries in wholesale and retail trade, food and kindred products, and fabricated metals is available in the file `Employ.dat`. The task is to import this dataset into the R session. Note that the three variables, namely the number of employees in the three industries, are numeric in their characteristics. This characteristic should be retained in our session too.

A useful practice is to actually open the source file and check the nature of the data in it. For example, the reader should question how he will interpret the number `3.220000000e+002` specified in the original DAT file. In the *Time for action – importing data from external files* section, we will use the `read.table` function to import this data file.

- **Example 2.2.2. Reading from a** `.csv` **file**: Ryan (2007) uses a dataset analyzed by Gupta (1997). In this case study related to antibiotic suspension products, the `response` variable is **Separated Clear Volume** whose smaller value indicates better quality. This experiment hosts five variables, each at two different levels, that is that each of the five variables is a factor variable, and the goal of the experiment is to determinate the best combination of these factors that yield the minimum value for the `response` variable.

  Now, sometimes the required dataset may be available in various CSV files. In such cases, we first read them from the various destinations and then combine them to obtain a single metafile. A trick is the usage of the `merge` function. Suppose that the preceding dataset is divided into two datasets, `SCV_Usual.csv` and `SCV_Modified.csv`, according to the variable `E`. We read them in two separate data objects and then merge them into a single object.

  We will carry out the importing of these files in the next Time for action section.

- **Example 2.2.3. Reading files using the** `foreign` **package**: SPSS, SAS, STATA, and so on, are some of the very popular statistical software. Each of the software has their own file structure for the datasets. The `foreign` package, which is shipped along with the R software, helps to read datasets used in these software. The **rootstock dataset** is a very popular dataset in the area of *multivariate statistics* and it is available on the web at `http://www.stata-press.com/data/r10/rootstock.dta`. Essentially, the dataset is available for the STATA software. We will now see how R reads this dataset.

Let us get set for the action using the R software.

Time for action – importing data from external files

The external files may be imported into R using the right functions available in it. Here, we will use the `read.table`, `read.csv`, and `read.sta` functions to drive home the point:

1. Verify that you have the necessary files, `Employ.dat`, `SCV.csv`, `SCV_Usual.csv`, and `SCV_Modified.csv` in the working directory by using `list.files()`.

2. If the files are not available in the list displayed, find your working directory by using `getwd()` and then copy the files to the working directory. Alternatively, you can set the working directory to the folder where the files are with `setwd("C:/my_files_are_here")`.

3. Read the data in `Employ.dat` with the code `employ <- read.table("Employ.dat", header=TRUE)`.

4. View the data with `View(employ)` and ensure that the data file has been properly imported into R.

5. Check that the class of `employ` and its variables have been imported in the correct format with `class(employ); sapply(employ,class)`.

6. Import the Separated Clear Volume data from the `SCV.csv` file using the code `SCV <- read.csv("SCV.csv",header=TRUE)`.

7. Run `sapply(SCV, class)`. You will find that the variables A-D are of the numeric class. Convert the class of variable A to factor with either `class(SCV$A) <- 'factor'` or `SCV$A <- as.factor(SCV$A)`.

8. Repeat the preceding step for variables B-D.

9. The data in the `SCV.csv` file is split into two files by the E variable values and is available in `SCV_Usual.csv` and `SCV_Modified.csv`. Import the data into these two files using the appropriate modifications in step 6 and label the respective R data frame objects as `SCV_Usual` and `SCV_Modified`.

10. Combine the data from the two latest objects with `SCV_Combined <- merge(SCV_Usual,SCV_Modified,by.y=c("Response","A","B","C","D","E"),all.x=TRUE,all.y=TRUE)`.

11. Initialize the library package `foreign` with `library(foreign)`.

12. Tell R where on the web the dataset is available by using `rootstock.url <-`
    `http://www.stata-press.com/data/r10/rootstock.dta`.

 An internet connection is required to perform this step.

13. Use the `read.dta` function from the `foreign` package to import the dataset
    from the web into R: `rootstock=read.dta(rootstock.url)`.

The necessary R codes are given next in a consolidated format:

```
# Time for Action: Importing Data from External Files
employ <- read.table("Data/Employ.dat",header=TRUE)
view(employ)
class(employ)
sapply(employ,class)
SCV <- read.csv("Data/SCV.csv",header=TRUE)
sapply(SCV, class)
SCV$A <- as.factor(SCV$A)
SCV$B <- as.factor(SCV$B)
SCV$C <- as.factor(SCV$C)
SCV$D <- as.factor(SCV$D)
SCV
SCV_Usual <- read.csv("Data/SCV_Usual.csv",header=TRUE,sep=",")
SCV_Modified <- read.csv("Data/SCV_Modified.csv",header=TRUE)
SCV_Combined <- merge(SCV_Usual,SCV_Modified,by.y=c("Response",
"A","B","C","D","E"),all.x=TRUE,all.y=TRUE)
SCV_Combined
library(foreign)
rootstock.url <- "http://www.stata-press.com/data/r10/rootstock.dta"
rootstock <- read.dta(rootstock.url)
rootstock
```

What just happened?

Functions from the `utils` package help the R users in importing data from various
external files. The screenshot, edited in a graphics tool, as a consequence of running
the previous code, is given as follows:

```
> employ=read.table("Employ.dat",header=TRUE)
> View(employ)
> class(employ)
[1] "data.frame"
> sapply(employ,class)
    Trade        Food      Metals
"numeric" "numeric" "numeric"
> SCV = read.csv("SCV.csv",header=TRUE)
> SCV
  Response  A  B   C   D       E
1       47  8 50 0.2 0.4   Usual
2       42  8 50 0.4 0.4 Modified

16      33 16 60 0.4 0.6 Modified
> SCV_Usual = read.csv("SCV_Usual.csv",header=TRUE,sep=",")
> SCV_Modified = read.csv("SCV_Modified.csv",header=TRUE)
> SCV_Combined = merge(SCV_Usual,SCV_Modified,by.y=c("Response",
+ "A","B","C","D","E"),all.x=TRUE,all.y=TRUE)
> SCV_Combined
  Response  A  B   C   D       E
1       23  8 50 0.4 0.6 Modified
2       26 16 50 0.4 0.6   Usual

16      51  8 60 0.2 0.4 Modified
> library(foreign)
> rootstock.url <- "http://www.stata-press.com/data/r10/rootstock.dta"
> rootstock=read.dta(rootstock.url)
> rootstock
  rootstock   y1    y2    y3    y4
1         1 1.11 2.569 3.58 0.760
2         1 1.19 2.928 3.75 0.821

47        6 1.13 3.064 3.63 0.707
48        6 1.11 2.469 3.95 0.952
```

Importing data from external files

The read.table function succeeded in importing the data from the Employ.dat file. The utils function View confirms that the data has been imported with the desired classes. The function read.csv has been used to import data from the SCV.csv, SCV_ Usual.csv, and SCV_Modified.csv files. The merge function combined the data in the usual way and modified objects and created a new object, which is the same as the one obtained using the SCV.csv file.

Next, we used the function read.sta from the foreign package to complete the reading of a STATA file, which is available on the web.

You learned how to import data in many different formats into R. The preceding program shows how to change the classes of variables within the object itself. You also learned how to merge multiple data objects.

Doing it in Python

The pandas package is very useful to import CSV files. The CSV files are in the Data folder:

1. Import the data using the function read_csv from the pandas package:

```
In [24]:  # Importing CSV Files and Merging

In [25]:  SCV = pd.read_csv("Data/SCV.csv")
          SCV.shape
          print SCV

              Response    A    B     C     D           E
          0         47    8   50   0.2   0.4       Usual
          1         42    8   50   0.4   0.4    Modified
          2         50    8   60   0.4   0.4       Usual
          3         51    8   60   0.2   0.4    Modified
          4         40   16   50   0.4   0.4       Usual
          5         44   16   50   0.2   0.4    Modified
          6         46   16   60   0.2   0.4       Usual
          7         40   16   60   0.4   0.4    Modified
          8         28    8   50   0.2   0.6       Usual
          9         23    8   50   0.4   0.6    Modified
          10        30    8   60   0.4   0.6       Usual
          11        38    8   60   0.2   0.6    Modified
          12        26   16   50   0.4   0.6       Usual
          13        31   16   50   0.2   0.6    Modified
          14        32   16   60   0.2   0.6       Usual
          15        33   16   60   0.4   0.6    Modified
```

The displayed result is not on an expected line and this is because only the recent line output is displayed. If you still wish to obtain the output of SCV. shape, run it in a new cell.

2. Combining different data objects is easily possible and it is demonstrated next:

```
In [26]:  SCV_M = pd.read_csv("Data/SCV_Modified.csv")
          SCV_U = pd.read_csv("Data/SCV_Usual.csv")
          comb_scv = [SCV_M, SCV_U]
          SCV_Combined = pd.concat(comb_scv)
          SCV_Combined
```

Out[26]:

	Response	A	B	C	D	E
0	42	8	50	0.4	0.4	Modified
1	51	8	60	0.2	0.4	Modified
2	44	16	50	0.2	0.4	Modified
3	40	16	60	0.4	0.4	Modified
4	23	8	50	0.4	0.6	Modified
5	38	8	60	0.2	0.6	Modified
6	31	16	50	0.2	0.6	Modified
7	33	16	60	0.4	0.6	Modified
0	47	8	50	0.2	0.4	Usual
1	50	8	60	0.4	0.4	Usual
2	40	16	50	0.4	0.4	Usual
3	46	16	60	0.2	0.4	Usual
4	28	8	50	0.2	0.6	Usual
5	30	8	60	0.4	0.6	Usual
6	26	16	50	0.4	0.6	Usual
7	32	16	60	0.2	0.6	Usual

Importing data from MySQL

Data will be often available in **databases** (**DBs**) such as SQL, MySQL, and so on. To emphasize the importance of DBs is beyond the scope of this section and we will be content with importing data from a DBs. The right-hand side of the following screenshot shows a snippet of the test DBs in MySQL. This DBs has a single table in IO_Time and it has two variables, No_of_IO and CPU_Time. The IO_Time has 10 observations, and we will be using this dataset for many concepts later in the book. The goal of this section is to show how to import this table into R.

An R package RMySQL is available from CRAN, which can be installed easily for Linux users. Unfortunately for Windows users, the package is not available in a readily implementable installation, in the sense that install.packages("RMySQL") won't work for them. The best help for Windows users is available at http://www.r-bloggers.com/installing-the-rmysql-package-on-windows-7/, though some of the code there is a bit outdated. However, the problem is certainly solvable!

The program and illustration here works neatly for Linux users and the following screenshot is performed on an Ubuntu 12.04 platform. Though simple installation of R and MySQL generally does not help in installing the RMySQL package, running sudo apt-get install libmysqlclient-dev first and then install.packages("RMySQL") helps! If you still get an error, make a note that the downloaded package is saved in the /tmp/RtmpeLu7CG/downloaded_packages folder of the local machine with the name RMySQL_0.x.x.tar.gz. The user then moves to that directory and executes sudo R CMD INSTALL RMySQL_0.x.x.tar.gz. We are now set to use the RMySQL package:

Importing data from MySQL

Note that at the Ubuntu 12.04 Terminal, we begin R with `R -q`. This suppresses the general details we get about the R software:

1. First invoke the library with `library(RMySQL)`.

2. Set up the DB driver with `d <- dbDriver("MySQL")`.

3. Specify the DB connector with `con <- dbConnect(d,dbname='test')`.

4. Then run your query to fetch the `IO_Time` table from MySQL with `io_data <- dbGetQuerry(con,'select * from IO_Time')`.

5. Finally, verify that the data has been properly imported into R with `io_data`. The right-hand side of the previous screenshot confirms that the data has been correctly imported into R.

Doing it in Python

The `pandas` package is very useful to import `.csv` files. The CSV files are in the `Data` folder.

Import the data using the function `read_csv` from the `pandas` package:

```
In [27]: # Connecting with MySQL

In [28]: connection = pysql.connect(host="localhost",user='root',password='          ',
                       db='test',cursorclass=pymysql.cursors.DictCursor)
         cur = connection.cursor()
         cur.execute("SELECT * FROM IO_Time")
         print(cur.description)
         for row in cur:
             print(row)
         cur.close()
         connection.close()

         (('No_of_IO', 3, None, 9, 9, 0, True), ('CPU_Time', 4, None, 12, 12, 31, True))
         {'No_of_IO': 1, 'CPU_Time': 0.092}
         {'No_of_IO': 2, 'CPU_Time': 0.134}
         {'No_of_IO': 3, 'CPU_Time': 0.165}
         {'No_of_IO': 4, 'CPU_Time': 0.211}
         {'No_of_IO': 5, 'CPU_Time': 0.242}
         {'No_of_IO': 6, 'CPU_Time': 0.302}
         {'No_of_IO': 7, 'CPU_Time': 0.357}
         {'No_of_IO': 8, 'CPU_Time': 0.401}
         {'No_of_IO': 9, 'CPU_Time': 0.405}
         {'No_of_IO': 10, 'CPU_Time': 0.442}
```

Thus, it is possible to connect Python with DBs such as MySQL. Note that the query can be complex and it is advised to create text strings of it first and then pass it as an argument to the function `execute`.

Exporting data/graphs

In the previous section, we learned how to import data from external files. Now, there will be many instances where we would be keen to export data from R into suitable `foreign` files. The need may arise in automated systems, reporting, and so on, where the other software requires making good use of the R output.

Exporting R objects

The basic R function that exports data is `write.table`, which is not surprising as we saw the utility of the `read.table` function. The following screenshot gives a snippet of the `write.table` function. While reading, we assign the imported file to an R object, and when exporting, we first specify the R object and then mention the filename. By default, R assigns row names while exporting the object. If there are no row names, R will simply choose a serial number beginning with `1`. If the user does not need such row names, they need to specify `row.names = FALSE` in the program:

```
write.table(x, file = "", append = FALSE, quote = TRUE, sep = " ",
            eol = "\n", na = "NA", dec = ".", row.names = TRUE,
            col.names = TRUE, qmethod = c("escape", "double"),
            fileEncoding = "")
```

Exporting data using the write.table function

Example 2.3.1. Exporting the `Titanic` data: In the *Two different views of the Titanic dataset* figure, we saw the `Titanic` dataset in two formats. It is the display of the right side of the figure that we would like to export in a `.csv` format. We will use the `write.csv` function for this purpose:

```
> write.csv(Titanic,"Titanic.csv",row.names=FALSE)
```

The `Titanic.csv` file will be exported to the current working directory. The reader can open the CSV file in either Excel or LibreOffice Calc and confirm that it is in the desired format.

The other write/export options are also available in the `foreign` package. The `write.xport`, `write.systat`, `write.dta`, and `write.arff` functions are useful if the destination software are respectively SAS, SYSTAT, STATA, and Weka.

Exporting graphs

In *Chapter 3, Data Visualization*, we will be generating a lot of graphs. Here, we will explain how to save the graphs in a desired format.

In the next screenshot, we have a graph generated by execution of the code plot(sin, -pi, 2*pi) at the terminal. This line of code generates the sine wave over the interval [-π, 2π].

Time for action – exporting a graph

Exporting of graphs will be explored here:

1. Plot the sin function over the range [-π, 2π] by running plot(sin, -pi, 2*pi).

2. A new window pops up with the title **R Graphics Device 2 (ACTIVE)**.

3. In the menu bar, go to **File | Save as | Png**:

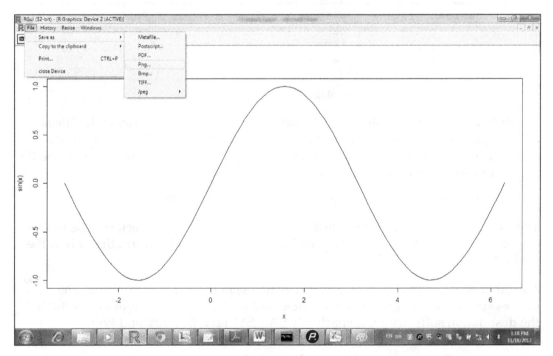

Saving graphs

4. Save the file as sin_plot.png, or any other name felt appropriate by you.

What just happened?

A file named `sin_plot.png` would have been created in the directory as specified by you in the preceding step 4.

The Unix user does not have the luxury of saving the graph in the previously mentioned way. The user has different options of saving a file. Suppose we wish to save the file when running R in a Linux environment. The `grDevices` library gives different ways of saving a graph. Here, the user can use the `pdf`, `jpeg`, `bmp`, `png`, and a few more functions to save the graph. An example is given in the following code:

```
> jpeg("My_File.jpeg")
>  plot(sin, -pi, 2*pi)
> dev.off()
null device
          1
> ?jpeg
> ?pdf
```

Here, we first invoke the required device and specify the filename to save the output; the path directory may be specified as well, along with the filename. Then, we plot the function and finally close the device with `dev.off`. Fortunately, this technique works on both Linux and Windows platforms.

Managing R sessions

We will close the chapter with a discussion of managing the R session. In many ways, this section is similar to what we do at a dining table after we have finished dinner. Now, there are quite a few aspects about saving the R session. We will first explain how to save the R codes executed during a session.

Time for action – session management

Managing a session is very important. Any well-developed software gives multiple options of managing a technical session and we will explore some of the methods available in R:

1. You have decided to stop the R session! At this moment, we would like to save all the R code executed at the console:

    1. In the **File** menu, we have an option in **Save History**. Basically, it is the action **File | Save History…**.

    2. After selecting the option, as with the previous section, we can save the history of that R session in a new text file.

3. Save the history with the filename `testhist`. Basically, R saves it as a `RHISTORY` file that may be easily viewed/modified through any text editor. The reader may also save the R history in any appropriate directory which is the destination.

2. Now, you want to reload the history `testhist` at the beginning of a new R session. The direction is **File | Load History...**, and choose the `testhist` file.

3. In an R session, you would have created many objects with different characteristics. All of them can be saved in an `.Rdata` file with **File | Save Workspace...**. In a new session, this workspace can be loaded with **File | Load Workspace...**:

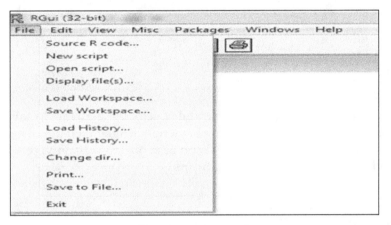

R session management

4. Another way of saving the R codes (history and workspace) is when we close the session either with **File | Exit**, or by clicking on the **X** of the R window, a window will pop up as displayed in the previous screenshot. If you click on **Yes**, R will append the `RHISTORY` file in the working directory with the codes executed in the current session and will also save the workspace.

5. If you want to save only certain objects from the current list, you can use the `save` function. As an example, if you wish to save object x, run `save(x,file="x.Rdata")`. In a later session, you can reinstate the object x with `load("x.Rdata")`.

However, the libraries that were invoked in the previous session are not available again. They again need to be explicitly invoked using the `library()` function. Thus, the reader should be careful about this fact:

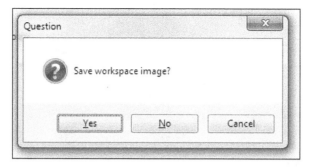

Saving the R session

What just happened?

The session history is very important, and also the objects created during a session. As the user goes deeper into the subject, it is soon realized that it is not possible to complete all the tasks in a single session. Hence, it is vital to manage the sessions properly. You learned how to save code history, workspaces, and so on.

Doing it in Python

We will work here on managing a Python session. We will consider the two tasks: saving the complete session and saving certain objects:

1. The Jupyter Notebook session can be saved as in any what-you-see-is-what-you-get software:

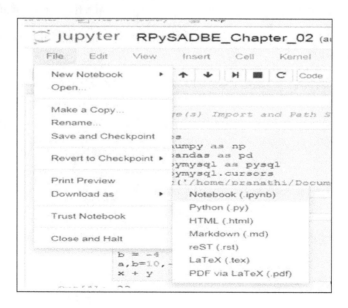

2. Python in-session objects can be saved by using the `pickle` package:

```
In [1]:  x = 10

In [2]:  import pickle

In [3]:  pickle.dump(x,open("tu.tu","wb"))

In [4]:  # Assume a new session

In [5]:  isitx = pickle.load(open("tu.tu","rb"))

In [6]:  x==isitx

Out[6]:  True
```

Here, we simply started with an object x = 10. After loading the `pickle` package, we used the `pickle.dump` function and asked Python to save x as a `tu.tu` object by writing the contents of x to it, and hence the option of `"wb"` in the `open` arguments.

Pop quiz

You have two matrices $A = \begin{bmatrix} 1 & 2 & 3 \\ 6 & 5 & 0 \end{bmatrix}$ and $B = \begin{bmatrix} 2 & 1 \\ 9 & -12 \\ 1 & 6 \end{bmatrix}$. Obtain the cross-product AB and find the inverse of AB. Next, find (BTAT) then the transpose of its inverse. What will be your observation?

Summary

In this chapter, we learned how to carry out the essential computations. We also learned how to import data from various foreign formats and then to export R objects and output suitable for other software. We also saw how to effectively manage an R session.

Now that we know how to create R and Python data objects, the next step is the visualization of such data. In the spirit of *Chapter 1, Data Characteristics*, we consider graph generation according to the nature of the data. Thus, we will see specialized graphs for data related to discrete as well as continuous random variables. There is also a distinction made for graphs required for univariate and multivariate data.

The next chapter must be pleasing on the eyes! Special emphasis is made on visualization techniques related to categorical data, which includes bar charts, dot charts, and spine plots. Multivariate data visualization is more than mere 3D plots and the R methods, such as pairs plots will be useful and will be taken there.

3
Data Visualization

Data is possibly best understood, wherever plausible, if it is displayed in a reasonable manner. Chen et. al. (2008) have compiled articles where many scientists of data visualization give a deeper, historical and modern trend of data display. Data visualization may be as historical as data itself. It emerges across all the dimensions of science, history, and every stream of life where data is captured. The reader may especially go through the rich history of data visualization in the article of Friendly (2008) from Chen et. al. (2008). The aesthetics of visualization have been described elegantly in Tufte (2001). The current chapter will have a deep impact on the rest of the book, and this chapter aims to provide the guidance and specialized graphics in the appropriate context in the rest of the book.

This chapter provides the necessary stimulus for understanding the gist that discrete and continuous data need appropriate tools, and that validation may be seen through the distinct characteristics of such plots. Furthermore, this chapter is closely related to *Chapter 4*, *Exploratory Analysis*, and many visualization techniques here indeed are exploratory in nature. Thus, the current chapter and the next complement mutually.

It has been observed that, in many preliminary courses and texts, a lot of emphasis is on the type of the plots, such as histograms, boxplots, and so on, which are most suitable for data arising for continuous variables. Thus, we need to make a distinction among the plots for discrete and continuous variable data, and towards this, we first begin with techniques that give more insight on visualization of discrete variable data.

In R there are four main frameworks for producing graphics: basic graphs, grids, lattice, and `ggplot2`. In the current chapter, the first three are used mostly and there is a brief peek to `ggplot2` at the end. Python graphics are generated using the `matplotlib` library.

This chapter will mainly cover the details on effective data visualization:

- Visualization of categorical data using bar chart, dot chart, spine and mosaic plots, and the pie chart and its variants
- Visualization of continuous data using boxplot, histogram, scatter plot and its variant, and the Pareto chart
- A very brief introduction to the rich school of ggplot2

Packages and settings – R and Python

First, we load the essential R packages:

1. Load the R packages lattice, qcc, ggplot2, and RSADBE:

```
> library(lattice)
> library(qcc)

  __   _  ___  ___
 / _  |/ _/ __|    Quality Control Charts and
| (_| | (_| (__    Statistical Process Control
 \__  |\__\___|
     |_|           version 2.7
Type 'citation("qcc")' for citing this R package in publications.
Warning message:
package 'qcc' was built under R version 3.4.1
> library(ggplot2)
> library(RSADBE)
```

2. The packages required for Python session are os, matplotlib, pandas, and numpy, and they are imported in the following:

```
In [1]:  # Package(s), Import, and Path Setting

In [2]:  import os
         os.chdir("MyPath/Python/Chapter_03/")
         import matplotlib.pyplot as plt
         import pandas as pd
         import numpy as np
```

Visualization techniques for categorical data

In *Chapter 1, Data Characteristics*, we came across many variables whose outcomes are categorical in nature. Gender, Car_Model, Minor_Problems, Major_Problems, and Satisfaction_Rating are examples of categorical data. In a software product development cycle, various issues or bugs are raised at different severity levels such as Minor and Show Stopper. Visualization methods for the categorical data require special attention and techniques, and the goal of this section is to aid the reader with some useful graphical tools.

In this section, we will mainly focus on the dataset related to bugs, which are of primary concern for any software engineer. The source of the datasets is http://bug.inf.usi.ch/ and the reader is advised to check the website before proceeding further in this section. We will begin with the software system Eclipse JDT Core, and the details for this system may be found at http://www.eclipse.org/jdt/core/index.php. The files for download are available at http://bug.inf.usi.ch/download.php.

Bar chart

It is very likely that the reader may be familiar with bar charts, though they may not be aware of categorical variables. Typically, in a bar chart one draws the bars proportional to the frequency of the category. An illustration will begin with the dataset Severity_Counts related to the Eclipse JDT Core software system. The reader may also explore the built-in examples in R.

Going through the built-in examples of R

Bar charts may be obtained using two options. The function barplot, from the graphics library, is one way of obtaining bar charts. The built-in examples for this plot function may be reviewed with example(barplot). The second option is to load the package lattice and then use the example(barchart) function. The sixth plot, after you click for the sixth time on the prompt, is actually an example of the barchart function.

The main purpose of this example is to help the reader get flair of the bar charts that may be obtained using R. It happens that many times that we have a specific variant of a plot in our mind and find it difficult to recollect it. Hence, it is suggested that you explore the variety of bar charts you can produce using R. Of course, there are a lot more possibilities than the mere samples given by example().

Example 3.1.2. Bar charts for the bug metrics dataset: The software system Eclipse JDT Core has 997 different class environments related to the development. The bug identified on each occasion is classified by its severity as Bugs, NonTrivial, Major, Critical, and High. We need to plot the frequency of the severity level, and also require the frequencies to be highlighted by **Before** and **After** release of the software to be neatly reflected in the graph. The required data is available in the RSADBE package in the Severity_Counts object.

Example 3.1.3. Bar charts for the bug metrics of the five pieces of software: In the previous example, we had considered the frequencies only on the JDT software. Now, it will be a tedious exercise if we need to have five different bar plots for different software. The frequency table for the five pieces of software is given in the Bug_Metrics_Software dataset of the RSADBE package.

Software	BA_Ind	Bugs	NonTrivial Bugs	Major Bugs	Critical Bugs	High Priority Bugs
JDT	Before	11,605	10,119	1,135	432	459
	After	374	17	35	10	3
PDE	Before	5,803	4,191	362	100	96
	After	341	14	57	6	0
Equinox	Before	325	1,393	156	71	14
	After	244	3	4	1	0
Lucene	Before	1,714	1,714	0	0	0
	After	97	0	0	0	0
Mylyn	Before	14,577	6,80-+6	592	235	8,804
	After	340	187	18	3	36

It would be nice if we could simply display the frequency table across only two graphs. This is achieved using the option beside in the `barplot` function. The data from the preceding table is copied from an XLS/CSV file, and then we execute the first line of the following R program in the Time for action – bar charts in R section.

Let us begin the action and visualize the bar charts.

Time for action – bar charts in R

Different forms of bar charts will be displayed with datasets. The type of bar chart will also depend on the problem (and data) on hand. Following are the steps for loading datasets:

1. Enter `example(barplot)` in the console and hit the **Return** key.

2. A new window pops up with the heading **Click or hit Enter for next page**. Click (and pause between the clicks) your way until it stops changing.

3. Load the `lattice` package with `library(lattice)`.

4. Try `example(barchart)` at the console. The sixth plot is an example of the bar chart.

5. Load the dataset on severity counts for the JDT software from the RSADBE package with `data(Severity_Counts)`. Also, check for this data.

    A view of this object is given in the screenshot in step 7. We have five severities of bugs: general bugs (**Bugs**), non-trivial bugs (**NT.Bugs**), major bugs (**Major.Bugs**), critical bugs (**Critical**), and high priority bugs (**H.Priority**). For the JDT software, these bugs are counted before and after release, and these are marked in the object with suffixes BR and AR. We need to understand this count data and as a first step, we use the bar plots for the purpose.

6. To obtain the `barchart` for the severity-wise comparison before and after release of the JDT software, run the following R code:

    ```
    barchart(Severity_Counts,xlab="Bug Count",xlim=c(0,12000),
    col=rep(c(2,3),5))
    ```

The `barchart` function is available from the `lattice` package. The range for the count is specified with `xlim=c(0,12000)`. Here, the argument `col=rep(c(2,3),5)` is used to tell R that we need two colors for **BR** and **AR** and that this should be repeated five times for the five severity levels of the bugs.

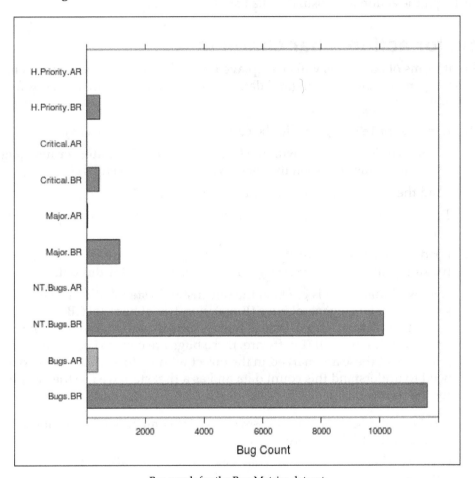

Bar graph for the Bug Metrics dataset

7. An alternative method is to use the `barplot` function from the `graphics` package:

```
barplot(Severity_Counts,xlab="Bug Count",xlim=c(0,12000), horiz
=TRUE,col=rep(c(2,3),5))
```

Here, we use the argument `horiz = TRUE` to get a horizontal display of the bar plot. A word of caution here is that the argument `horizontal = TRUE` in `barchart` of the `lattice` package works very differently.

We will now focus on `Bug_Metrics_Software`, which has the bug count data for all five pieces of software: JDT, PDE, Equinox, Lucene, and Mylyn.

```
> Severity_Counts
      Bugs.BR        Bugs.AR     NT.Bugs.BR      NT.Bugs.AR        Major.BR
        11605            374          10119              17            1135
      Major.AR    Critical.BR    Critical.AR H.Priority.BR H.Priority.AR
           35            432             10             459               3
> Bug_Metrics_Software
, , BA_Ind = Before

          Bugs
Software    Bugs NT.Bugs Major Critical H.Priority
   JDT     11605   10119  1135      432        459
   PDE      5803    4191   362      100         96
   Equinox   325    1393   156       71         14
   Lucene   1714    1714     0        0          0
   Mylyn   14577    6806   592      235       8804

, , BA_Ind = After

          Bugs
Software    Bugs NT.Bugs Major Critical H.Priority
   JDT       374      17    35       10          3
   PDE       341      14    57        6          0
   Equinox   244       3     4        1          0
   Lucene     97       0     0        0          0
   Mylyn     340     187    18        3         36
```

View of Severity_Counts and Bug_Metrics_Software

8. Load the dataset related to all five pieces of software with: `data(Bug_Metrics_Software)`.

9. To obtain the bar plots for before and after release of the software on the same window, run `par(mfrow=c(1,2))`.

   What is the `par` function? It is a function frequently used to set the parameters of a graph. Let us consider a simple example. Recollect that when you tried the code `example(dotchart)`, R would ask you to **Click or hit Enter for next page** and post the click or Enter action, and then the next graph will be displayed. However, this prompt did not turn up when you ran `barplot(Severity_Counts,xlab="Bug Count",xlim=c(0,12000), horiz =TRUE,col=rep(c(2,3),5))`.

   Now, let us try using `par`, which will ask us to first click or hit *Enter* so that we get the bar plot. First run `par(ask=TRUE)`, and then follow it with the bar plot code. You will now be asked to either click to hit *Enter*. Find more details of the `par` function with `?par`. Let us now get into the `mfrow` argument. The default plot options display the output on one device and on the next one, the former will be replaced with the new one. We require the bar plots of before and after release count to be displayed in the same window. The option, `mfrow = c(1,2)`, ensures that both the bar plots are displayed in the same window with one row and two columns.

10. To obtain the bar plot of bug frequencies before release where each `software bug frequencies are placed side-by-side for each type of the bug severity, run the following:

```
barplot(Bug_Metrics_Software[,,1],beside=TRUE,col = c("lightblue",
"mistyrose", "lightcyan", "lavender", "cornsilk"),legend = c("JDT"
,"PDE","Equinox","Lucene", "Mylyn"))
title(main = "Before Release Bug Frequency", font.main = 4)
```

Here, the code `Bug_Metrics_Software[,,1]` ensures that only before release are considered. The option `beside = TRUE` ensures that the columns are displayed as juxtaposed bars; otherwise, the frequencies will be distributed in a single bar with areas proportional to the frequency of each software. The option `col = c("lightblue", …)` assigns the respective colors for the software. Finally, the title command is used to designate an appropriate title for the bar plot.

11. Similarly, to obtain the bar plot for after release bug frequency, run the following:

```
barplot(Bug_Metrics_Software[,,2],beside=TRUE,col = c("lightblue",
"mistyrose", "lightcyan", "lavender", "cornsilk"),legend = c("JDT"
,"PDE","Equinox","Lucene", "Mylyn"))

title(main = "After Release Bug Frequency",font.main = 4)
```

The reader can extend the code interpretation for the before release to the after release bug frequencies.

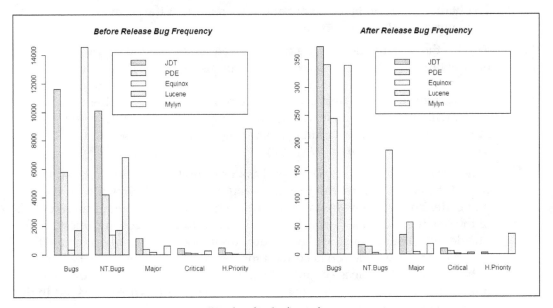

Bar plots for the five software

First, notice that the scale on the y axis for before and after release bug frequencies is drastically different. In fact, pre-release bug frequencies are in thousands while post-release are in hundreds. This clearly shows that the engineers have put a lot of effort into ensuring that the released products have the fewest possible bugs. However, the comparison of bug counts is not fair, since the frequency scales of the bar plots in the preceding figure are entirely different.

Though we don't expect the results to be different under any case, it is still appropriate that the frequency scales remain the same for both before and after release bar plots. A common suggestion is to plot the diagrams with the same range on the y axes (or x axes), or take an appropriate transformation such as logarithm. In our problem, neither of them will work, and we resort to another variant of the bar chart from the `lattice` package.

Now, we will use the `formula` structure for the `barchart` function and bring the **BR** and **AR** on the same graph.

12. Run the following code in the R console:
    ```
    barchart(Software~Freq|Bugs,groups=BA_Ind, data= as.data.
    frame(Bug_Metrics_Software),col=c(2,3))
    ```

    The formula `Software~Freq|Bugs` requires that we obtain the bar chart for the software count `Freq` according to the severity of `Bugs`. We further specify that each of the bar charts be further grouped according to `BA_Ind`. This will result in the following:

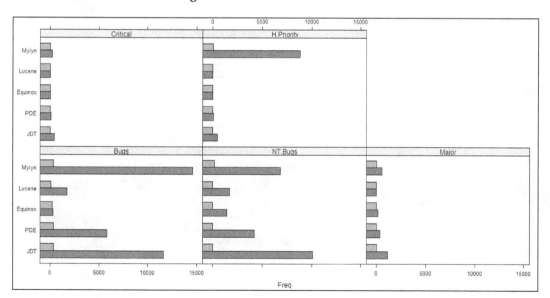

Bar chart for Before and After Release bug counts on the same scale

To find the colors available in R, try colors() in the console and you will find the names of 657 colors.

What just happened?

The barplot and barchart were the two functions we used to obtain the bar charts. For common recurring factors, **AR** and **BR** here, the colors can be correctly specified through the rep function. The argument beside=TRUE helped us to keep the bars for various software together for the different bug types. We also saw how to use the formula structure of the lattice package. We saw the diversity of bar charts and learned how to create effective bar charts depending on the purpose of the day.

Doing it in Python

The data for severity counts is available in the Data folder of the Chapter 03 folder of the code bundle. We will import it using the pandas package and then carry out appropriate conversions to obtain the bar chart for the severity counts:

1. First, import the data using the read_csv function from the pandas package. The bug type would be stored in a new object BT, their respective frequency in BFreq, and we obtain the number of bars required in Ypos:

```
sc_data = pd.read_csv("Data/SC.csv",delimiter=',')
BT = sc_data.Bug_Type
BFreq = sc_data.Frequency
Ypos = np.arange(len(BT))
```

2. Now, we can obtain the barplot using the barh function from the matplotlib library:

```
plt.barh(Ypos,BFreq,align='center',alpha=0.5)
plt.yticks(Ypos, BT)
plt.xlabel('Severity Counts')
plt.title('Bar graph for the Bug Metrics dataset')
plt.show()
```

The result of running the preceding codes in Python is the following :

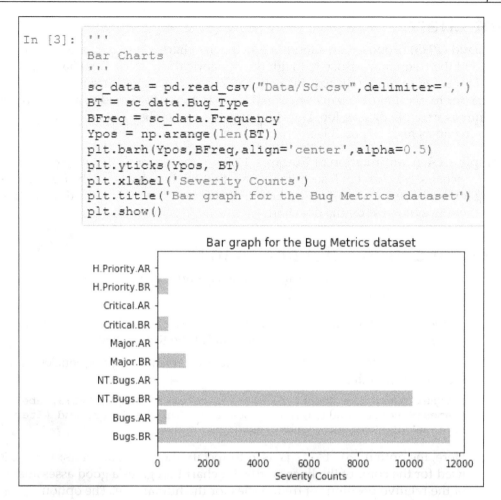

```
In [3]:  '''
         Bar Charts
         '''
         sc_data = pd.read_csv("Data/SC.csv",delimiter=',')
         BT = sc_data.Bug_Type
         BFreq = sc_data.Frequency
         Ypos = np.arange(len(BT))
         plt.barh(Ypos,BFreq,align='center',alpha=0.5)
         plt.yticks(Ypos, BT)
         plt.xlabel('Severity Counts')
         plt.title('Bar graph for the Bug Metrics dataset')
         plt.show()
```

Have a go hero

Here's a task for you:

- Explore the option stack=TRUE in the barchart(Software~Freq|Bugs,gr oups= BA_Ind,...). Also, observe that Freq for bars in the preceding figure begin a little earlier than 0. Reobtain the plots by specifying the range for Freq with xlim=c(0,15000).

- Extend the bar chart as illustrated in R for Python!

Dot chart

Cleveland (1993) proposed an alternative to the bar chart where dots are used to represent the frequency associated with the categorical variables. Dot charts are useful for small to moderate size datasets. Dot charts are also an alternative to the pie chart; refer to *The default examples* section. Dot charts may be varied to accommodate continuous variable dataset too. Dot charts are known to obey Tukey's principle of achieving an as high as possible *information-to-ink* ratio.

Example 3.1.4. (**Continuation of Example 3.1.2**): In the screenshot in step 6 in the *Time for action – bar charts in R* section, we saw that the bar charts for the frequencies of bug after release are almost non-existent. This is overcome using the dot chart; see the following action list on the dot chart.

Time for action – dot charts in R

The `dotchart` function from the `graphics` package and `dotplot` from the `lattice` package will be used to obtain the dot charts:

1. To view the default examples of dot charts, enter `example(dotplot);` `example(dotchart);` in the console and hit the **Return** key.

2. To obtain the dot chart of the before and after release bug frequencies, run the following code:

    ```
    dotchart(Severity_Counts,col=15:16,lcolor="black",pch=2:3,labels
    =names(Severity_Counts),main="Dot Plot for the Before and After
    Release Bug Frequency",cex=1.5)
    ```

    Here, the option `col=15:16` is used to specify the choice of colors; `lcolor` is used for the color of the lines on the dot chart that gives a good assessment of the relative positions of frequencies for the human eye. The option `pch=2:3` picks up circles and squares for indicating the positions of after and before frequencies. The options `labels` and `main` are trivial to understand, whereas `cex` magnifies the size of all labels by 1.5 times. On execution of the preceding R code, we get a graph as displayed in the following screenshot:

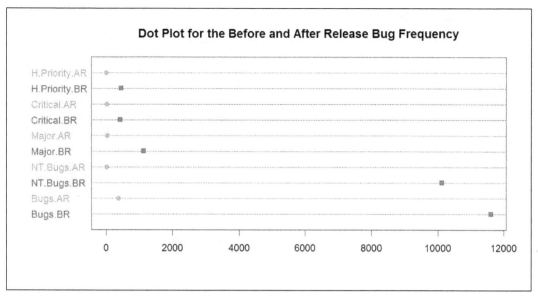

Dot chart for the Bug Metrics dataset

3. The dot plot can be easily extended for all five pieces of software as we did with the bar charts:

```
par(mfrow=c(1,2))
barplot(Bug_Metrics_Software[,,1],
        beside=TRUE,col = c("lightblue", "mistyrose", "lightcyan",
                            "lavender", "cornsilk"),
        legend = c("JDT","PDE","Equinox","Lucene", "Mylyn"))
title(main = "Before Release Bug Frequency", font.main = 4)
barplot(Bug_Metrics_Software[,,2],
        beside=TRUE,col = c("lightblue", "mistyrose", "lightcyan",
                            "lavender", "cornsilk"),
        legend = c("JDT","PDE","Equinox","Lucene", "Mylyn"))
title(main = "After Release Bug Frequency",font.main = 4)
```

The following output shows the dot plot output graph:

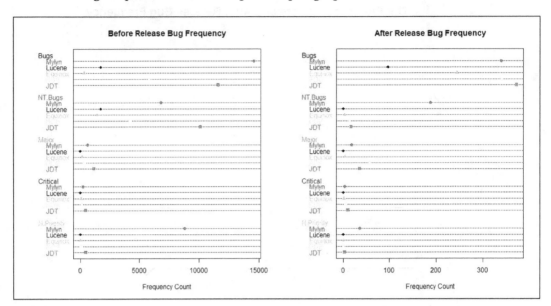

Dot charts for the five software bug frequency

For a matrix input in `barchart`, the `gcolor` option gets the same color each column. Note that though the class of `Bug_Metrics_Software` is both `xtabs` and `table`, the class of `Bug_Metrics_Software[,,1]` is a matrix, and hence we create a dot chart of it. This means that the R code `dotchart(Bug_Metrics_Software)` leads to errors! The dot chart is able to display the bug frequency in a better way as compared to the bar chart.

What just happened?

Two different ways of obtaining the dot plot were seen, and a host of other options were also clearly indicated in the current section.

Doing it in Python

For the dot chart, the major process remains the same as in the Python example of bar chart. Here, we now change the `plot` function to obtain the dot chart:

- Using the `plot` function with a slight tweak of options gives the dot chart:

```
plt.plot(BFreq,Ypos,'o')
plt.yticks(Ypos, BT)
plt.xlabel('Severity Counts')
plt.title('Dot Chart for the Bug Metrics dataset')
plt.show()
```

The final result is as follows:

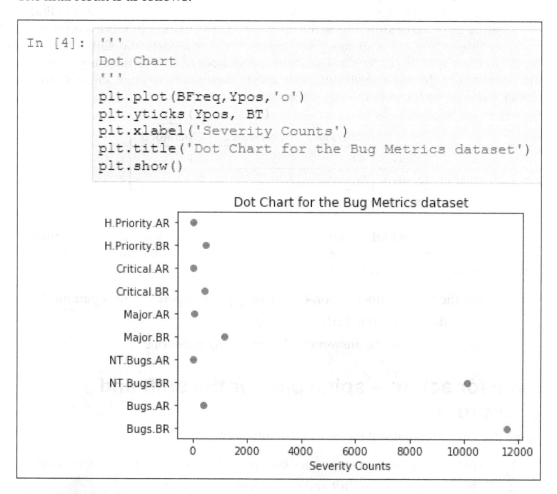

```
In [4]:  '''
         Dot Chart
         '''
         plt.plot(BFreq,Ypos,'o')
         plt.yticks Ypos, BT)
         plt.xlabel('Severity Counts')
         plt.title('Dot Chart for the Bug Metrics dataset')
         plt.show()
```

Spine and mosaic plots

In the bar plot, the length (height) of the bar varies, while the width for each bar is kept the same. In a spine/mosaic plot the height is kept constant for the categories and the width varies in accordance with the frequency. The advantages of a spine/ mosaic plot become apparent when we have frequencies tabulated for several variables via a contingency table. The spline plot is a particular case of the mosaic plot. We will first consider an example for understanding the spine plot.

Example 3.1.5. Visualizing Shift and Operator Data (Page 487, Ryan, 2007): In a manufacturing factory, operators are rotated across shifts and it is a concern to find out whether the time of shift affects the operator's performance. In this experiment, there are three operators who, in a given month, work in a particular shift. Over a period of three months, data is collected for the number of non-conforming parts an operator obtains during a given shift. The data is obtained from Page 487 of Ryan (2007) and is reproduced in the following table:

	Operator 1	Operator 2	Operator 3
Shift 1	40	35	28
Shift 2	26	40	22
Shift 3	52	46	49

We will obtain a spline plot towards an understanding of the spread of the number of non-conforming units an operator does during the shifts in the forthcoming action time. Let us ask the following questions:

- Does the total number of non-conforming parts depend on the operators?
- Does it depend on the shift?
- Can we visualize the answers to the preceding questions?

Time for action – spine plot for the shift and operator data

Spine plots are drawn using the `spineplot` function:

1. Explore the default examples for the spine plot with `example(spineplot)`.
2. Enter the data for the shift and operator example with:

    ```
    ShiftOperator <- matrix(c(40, 35, 28, 26, 40, 22, 52, 46, 49),nro
    w=3,dimnames=list(c("Shift 1", "Shift 2", "Shift 3"), c("Operator
    1", "Opereator 2", "Operator 3")),byrow=TRUE)
    ```

3. Find the number of non-conforming parts of the operators with the `colSums` function:

    ```
    > colSums(ShiftOperator)
     Operator 1 Opereator2  Operator 3
            118        121          99
    ```

    The non-conforming parts for operators 1 and 2 are close enough, and it is lesser by about 20 percent for the third operator.

4. Find the number of non-conforming parts according to the shifts using the `rowSums` function:

```
> rowSums(ShiftOperator)
Shift 1 Shift 2 Shift 3
    103      88     147
```

`Shift 3` appears to have about 50 percent more non-conforming parts in comparison with `shifts 1` and `2`. Let us look out for the `spineplot.` function.

5. Obtain the spine plot for the `ShiftOperator` data with `spineplot(ShiftOperator)`.

Now, we will attempt to make the spine plot a bit more interpretable. Under the absence of any external influence, we would expect the shifts and operators to have near equal number of non-conforming objects.

6. Thus, on the overall x and y axes, we plot lines at approximately one-third and check if we get approximate equal regions/squares:

```
abline(h=0.33,lwd=3,col="red")
abline(h=0.67,lwd=3,col="red")
abline(v=0.33,lwd=3,col="green")
abline(v=0.67,lwd=3,col="green")
```

The output in the graphics device window will be as follows:

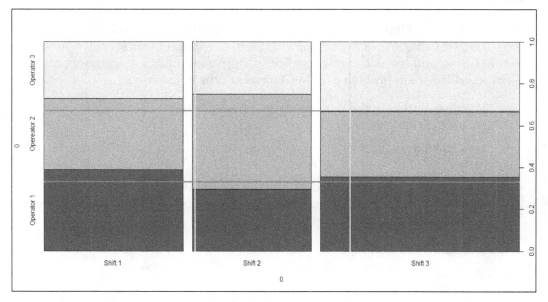

Spine plot for the ShiftOperator problem

It appears from the partition induced by the red lines that all the operators have nearly equal numbers of non-conforming parts. However, the spine chart shows that most of the non-conforming parts occur during `Shift 3`.

What just happened?

Data summaries were used to understand the behavior of the problem, and the spine plot helped in clear identification of Shift 3 as a major source of the non-conforming units manufactured. The use of the `abline` function was particularly more insightful for this dataset and needs to be explored whenever there is a scope for it.

Spine plot is a special case of the mosaic plot. Friendly (2001) has pioneered the concept of mosaic plots and *Chapter 4, Exploratory Analysis*, is an excellent reference for the same. For a simple understanding of the construction of a mosaic plot, the reader can go through slides 7-12 at `http://www.stat.auckland.ac.nz/~ihaka/120/Lectures/lecture17.pdf`. As explained there, suppose that there are three categorical variables, each with two levels. Then, the mosaic plot begins with a square and divides it into two parts with each part having an area proportional to the frequency of the two levels of the first categorical variable. Next, each of the preceding two parts is divided into two parts each according to the predefined frequency of the two levels of the second categorical variable. Note that we now have four divisions of the total area. Finally, each of the four areas is further divided into two more parts, each with an area reflecting the predefined frequency of the two levels of the third categorical variable.

Example 3.1.6. The Titanic dataset: In the *The table object* section in *Chapter 2, Import/Export Data*, we came across the `Titanic` dataset. The dataset was seen in two different forms, and we also constructed the data from scratch. Let us now continue the example. The main problems in this dataset are the following:

- The distribution of the passengers by `Class`and then spread of `Survived` across `Class`.
- The distribution of the passengers by `Sex` and its distribution across the survivors.
- The distribution by `Age` followed by the survivors among them. We now want to visualize the distribution of `Survived` first by `Class`, then by `Sex`, and finally by the `Age` group.

Let us see the detailed action.

Time for action – mosaic plot for the Titanic dataset

The goal here is to understand the survival percentages of the Titanic ship with respect to Class of the crew, Sex, and Age. We use first xtabs and prop.table to gain the insight for each of these variables, and then visualize the overall picture using mosaicplot:

1. Get the frequencies of Class for the Titanic dataset with xtabs(Freq~Class,data=Titanic).

2. Obtain the Survived proportions across Class with prop.table(xtabs(Freq~Class+Survived,data=Titanic),margin=1).

3. Repeat the preceding two steps for Sex: xtabs(Freq~Sex,data=Titanic) and prop.table(xtabs(Freq~Sex+Survived,data=Titanic),margin=1).

4. Repeat this exercise for Age: xtabs(Freq~Age,data=Titanic) and prop.table(xtabs(Freq~Age+Survived,data=Titanic), margin=1).

5. Obtain the mosaic plot for the dataset with mosaicplot(Titanic,col=c("red","green")).

The entire output is given in the following figure:

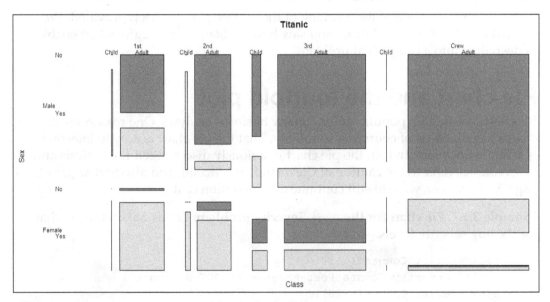

Mosaic plot for the Titanic dataset

The preceding output shows that the people travelling in higher class survived better than the lower class ones. The analysis also shows that females were given more priority over males when the rescue system was in action. Finally, it may be seen that children were given priority over adults.

The mosaic plot division process proceeds as follows:

1. First, it divides the region into four parts, with the regions proportional to the frequencies of various **Class**; that is, the width of the regions are proportionate to the **Class** frequencies.

2. Each of the four regions is further divided using the predefined frequencies of the **Sex** categories. Now, we have eight regions.

3. Next, each of these regions is divided using the predefined frequencies of the **Age** group leading to 16 distinct regions.

4. Finally, each of the regions is divided into two parts according to the **Survived** status.

    The **Yes** regions of **Child** for the first two classes are larger than the **No** regions. The third **Class** has more non-survivors than survivors, and this appears to be true across **Age** and **Gender**. Note that there are no children among the **Crew** class. The rest of the regions' interpretation is left to the reader.

What just happened?

A clear demystification of the working of the mosaic plot has been provided. We applied it to the `Titanic` dataset and saw how it obtains clear regions that enable it to deep dive into a categorical problem.

Pie chart and the fourfold plot

Pie charts are hugely popular among many business analysts. One reason for the pie chart's popularity is of course its simplicity. That the pie chart is easy to interpret is actually not a fact. In fact, the pie chart is seriously discouraged for analysis and observations; refer to the caution of Cleveland and McGill, and also Sarkar (2008), page 57. However, we will still continue an illustration of it.

Example 3.1.7. Pie chart for the `Bugs` **Severity problem**: Let us obtain the pie chart for the bug severity levels:

```
> pie(Severity_Counts[1:5])
> title("Severity Counts Post-Release of JDT Software")
> pie(Severity_Counts[6:10])
> title("Severity Counts Pre-Release of JDT Software")
```

Can you find the drawback of the pie chart?

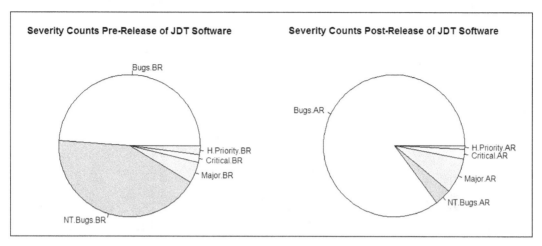

Pie chart for the Before and After Bug Counts (output edited)

The main drawback of the pie chart stems from the fact that humans have a problem in deciphering relative areas. A common recommendation is the use of a bar chart or a dot chart instead of the pie chart, as the problem of judging relative areas does not exist when comparing linear measures.

The fourfold plot is a novel way of visualizing a $2 \times 2 \times k$ contingency table. In this method, we obtain k plots for each 2×2 frequency table. Here, the cell frequency of each of the four cells is represented by a quarter circle whose radius is proportional to the square root of the frequency. In contrast to the pie chart where the radius is constant and area is varied by the perimeter, the radius in a fourfold plot is varied to represent the cell.

Example 3.1.8. The fourfold plot for the `UCBAdmissions` **dataset:** An in-built R function that generates the required plot is `fourfoldplot`. The R code and its resultant screenshots are displayed as follows:

```
> fourfoldplot(UCBAdmissions,mfrow=c(2,3),space=0.4)
```

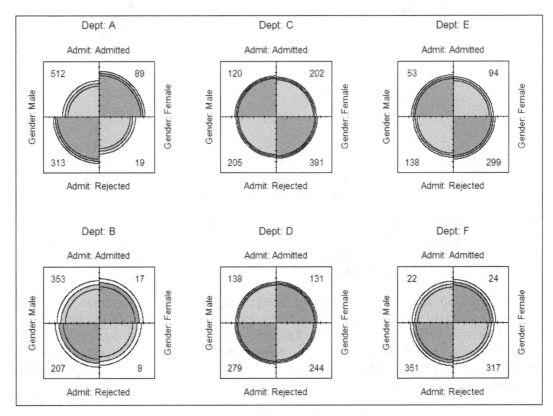

The fourfold plot of the UCBAdmissions dataset

In this section, we focused on graphical techniques for categorical data. In many texts, the graphical methods begin with tools that are more appropriate for data arising for continuous variables. Such tools have many shortcomings if applied to categorical data. Thus, we have taken a different approach where the categorical data gets the right tools, which it truly deserves. In the next section, we deal with tools that are seemingly more appropriate for data related to continuous variables.

Visualization techniques for continuous variable data

Continuous variables have a different structure and, hence, we need specialized methods for displaying them. Fortunately, many popular graphical techniques are suited very well for continuous variables. As the continuous variables can arise from different phenomena, we consider many techniques in this section. The graphical methods discussed in this section may also be considered as a part of the next chapter on exploratory analysis.

Boxplot

The boxplot is based on five points: minimum, lower quartile, median, upper quartile, and maximum. The median forms the thick line near the middle of the box, and the lower and upper quartiles complete the box. The lower and upper quartiles along with the median, which is the second quartile, divide the data into four regions, with each containing equal number of observations. The median is the middle-most value among the data sorted in the increasing (decreasing) order of magnitude. On similar lines, the lower quartile may be interpreted as the median of observations between the minimum and median data values. These concepts are dealt with in more detail in *Chapter 4, Exploratory Analysis*. The boxplot is generally used for two purposes: understanding the data spread and identifying the outliers. For this first purpose, we set the range value at zero, which will extend the whiskers to the extremes at minimum and maximum, and give the overall distribution of the data.

If the purpose of boxplot is to identify outliers, we extend the whiskers in a way that accommodates tolerance limits to enable us to capture the outliers. Thus, the whiskers are extended 1.5 times the default value, the **interquartile range (IQR)**, which is the difference between the third and first quartiles from the median. The default setting of a boxplot is the identification of the outliers. If any point is found beyond the whiskers, such observations may be marked as outliers. The boxplot is also sometimes called a **box-and-whisker plot**, and it is the whiskers that are obtained by drawing lines from the box, ends to the minimum and maximum points. We will begin with an example of a boxplot.

Example 3.2.1. example (boxplot): For a quick tutorial on the various options of the `boxplot` function, the user may run the following code at the R console. Also, the reader is advised to explore the `bwplot` function from the `lattice` package. Try `example(boxplot)` and `example(bwplot)` from the respective `graphics` and `lattice` packages.

Example 3.2.2. Boxplot for the resistivity data: Gunst (2002) has 16 independent observations from eight pairs on resistivity of a wire. There are two processes under which these observations are equally distributed. We would like to see if resistivity of the wires depends on the processes and which of the process leads to a higher resistivity. A numerical comparison based on the summary function will be first carried out, and then we will visualize the two processes through boxplot to conclude whether the effects are the same, and if not which process leads to higher resistivity.

Example 3.2.3. The Michelson-Morley experiment: This is a famous physics experiment in the late nineteenth century, which helped in proving the non-existence of ether. If the ether existed, one would expect a shift of about four percent in the speed of light. The speed of light is measured 20 times in five different experiments. We will use this dataset for two purposes: is the drift of four percent evidenced in the data, and setting the whiskers at the extremes. The first one is a statistical issue and the latter is a software setting.

For the preceding three examples, we will now read the required data into R and then look at the necessary summary functions, and finally visualize them using the boxplots.

Time for action – using the boxplot

Boxplots will be obtained here using the function boxplot from the graphics package as well as bwplot from the lattice package:

1. Check the variety of boxplot with example(boxplot) from the graphics package and example(bwplot) for the variants in the lattice package.

2. The resistivity data from the RSADBE package contains two processes' information that we need to compare. Load it into the current session with data(resistivity).

3. Obtain the summary of the two processes with the following:

```
> summary(resistivity)
        Process.1 Process.2
Min.       0.138     0.142
1st Qu.    0.140     0.144
Median     0.142     0.146
Mean       0.142     0.146
3rd Qu.    0.143     0.148
Max.       0.146     0.150
```

Clearly, Process 2 has approximately 0.004 higher resistivity as compared to Process 1 across all the essential summaries. Let us check if the boxplot captures the same.

4. Obtain the `boxplot` for the two processes with `boxplot(resistivity, range=0)`.

   The argument `range=0` is to ensure that the whiskers are extended to the minimum and maximum data values. The boxplot diagram (on the left-hand side of the following figure) clearly shows that `Process.2` has higher resistivity in comparison with `Process.1`. Next, we will consider the `bwplot` function from the `lattice` package. A slightly different rearrangement of the resistivity data frame will be required, in that we will specify all the resistivity values in a single column and their corresponding processes in another column.

   An important option for boxplots is that of notch, which is especially useful for comparison of medians. The top and bottom notches for a set of observations are defined at the points median $\pm 1.57(IQR)/n^{1/2}$ If notches of two boxplots do not overlap, it can be concluded that the medians of the groups are significantly different. Such an option can be specified in both boxplot and `bwplot` functions.

5. Convert resistivity to another useful form that will help the application of the `bwplot` function with `resistivity2 <- data.frame(rep(names( re sistivity),each=8),c(resistivity[,1],resistivity[,2]))`. Assign variable names to the new data frame with `names(resistivity2)<- c("Process","Resistivity")`.

6. Run the `bwplot` function on `resistivity2` with `bwplot(Resistivity~Process, data=resistivity2,notch=TRUE)`.

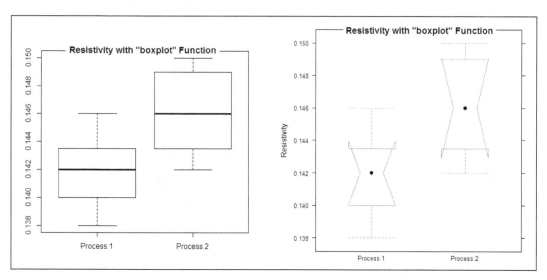

Boxplots for resistivity data with boxplot, bwplot, and notches

The notches are overlapping and hence, we can't conclude from the boxplot that the resistivity medians are very different from each other.

With the data on speed of light from the `morley` dataset, we have an important goal of identifying outliers. Towards this purpose the whiskers are extended 1.5 times the default value, the **interquartile range (IQR)**, from the median.

7. Create a boxplot with whiskers that enables identification of the outliers beyond the 1.5 IQR of the median with the following:

   ```
   boxplot(Speed~Expt,data=morley,main = "Whiskers at Lower-  and
   Upper- Confidence Limits")
   ```

8. Add the line that helps to identify the presence of ether with `abline(
   h=792.458,lty=3)`.

   The resulting diagram is as follows:

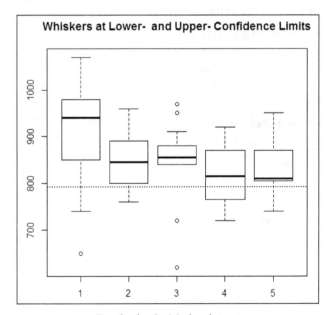

Boxplot for the Morley dataset

It may be seen from the preceding diagram that experiment **1** has one outlier, while experiment **3** has three outlier values. Since the line is well below the median of the experiment values (speed actually), we conclude that there is no experimental evidence for the existence of ether.

What just happened?

Varieties of boxplots have been elaborated in this section. The boxplot has also been put into action to identify the presence of outliers in a given dataset.

Doing it in Python

Boxplots are available in Python with a host of options. Here, we will obtain the boxplots and the notched boxplots too:

1. Import the `resistivity` data from the CSV file and subset the data for the two processes 1 and 2 in objects P1 and P2. Plot the `boxplot` using the desired function and following program:

```
resistivity = pd.read_csv("Data\Resistivity.csv",delimiter=',')
P1 = resistivity['Process.1']
P2 = resistivity['Process.2']
resistivity.boxplot(column=['Process.1','Process.2'])
plt.show()
```

2. The notched boxplots can be easily obtained by using the option `notch = True`:

```
resistivity.boxplot(column=['Process.1','Process.2'],notch=True)
plt.show()
```

3. Multiple boxplots by factor/category/group information in another data cell can be obtained as follows:

```
morley = pd.read_csv("Data\Morley.csv",delimiter=',')
morley.boxplot(column='Speed',by='Expt')
plt.show()
```

The resulting code and output is given in the following figure:

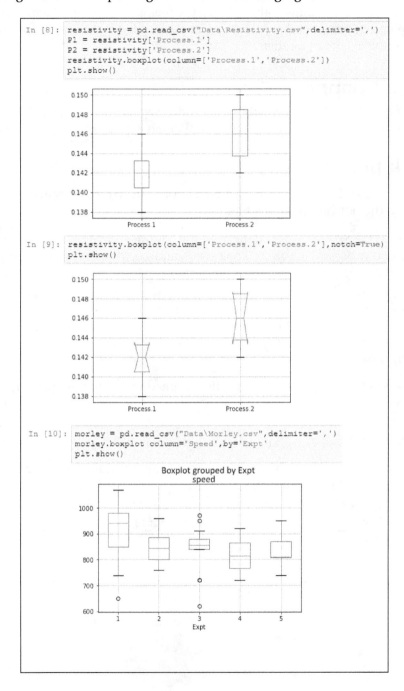

The flexibility provided in Python is sufficient to produce a variety of boxplots.

Histogram

Histograms are one of the earliest graphical techniques and undoubtedly one of the most versatile and adaptive graphs whose relevance is legitimate as it as ever was. The invention of histograms is a credit to the great statistician Karl Pearson. Its strength is also in its simplicity. In this technique, a variable is divided over intervals and the height of an interval is determined by the frequency of the observations falling in that interval. In the case of an unbalanced division of the range of the variable values, histograms are especially very informative in revealing the shape of the probability distribution of the variable. We will see more about these points in the following examples.

The construction of a histogram is explained with the famous dataset of Galton, where an attempt has been made for understanding the relationship between the heights of a child and parent. In this dataset, there are 928 pairs of observation of the height of the child and parent. Let us have a brief peek at the dataset:

```
> data(galton) > names(galton)
[1] "child"  "parent"
> dim(galton)
[1] 928    2
> head(galton)
child parent
1   61.7    70.5
2   61.7    68.5
3   61.7    65.5
4   61.7    64.5
5   61.7    64.0
6   62.2    67.5
> sapply(galton,range)
      child parent
[1,]   61.7     64
[2,]   73.7     73
> summary(galton)
     child           parent
 Min.   :61.7    Min.   :64.0
 1st Qu.:66.2    1st Qu.:67.5
 Median :68.2    Median :68.5
 Mean   :68.1    Mean   :68.3
 3rd Qu.:70.2    3rd Qu.:69.5
 Max.   :73.7    Max.   :73.0
```

We need to cover all the 928 observations in the intervals, also known as **bins**, which need to cover the range of the variable. The natural question is: how does one decide on the number of intervals and the width of these intervals? If the bin width, denoted by h, is known, the number of bins, denoted by k, can be determined by:

$$k = \left\lceil \frac{\max_i x_i - \min_i x_i}{h} \right\rceil$$

Here, the argument [ ] denotes the ceiling of the number. Similarly, if the number of bins k is known, the width is determined by $h = \left\lceil (\max_i x_i - \min_i x_i)/k \right\rceil$.

There are many guidelines for these problems. The three options available for the `hist` function in R are formulas given by Sturges, Scott, and Freedman-Diaconis, the details of which may be obtained by running `?nclass.Sturges`, or `?nclass.FD` and `?nclass.scott` in the R console. The default setting runs the Sturges option. The Sturges formula for the number of bins is given by:

$$k = \left\lceil \log_2 n + 1 \right\rceil$$

This formula works well when the underlying distribution is approximately distributed as a normal distribution. The Scott's normal reference rule for the bin width, using the sample standard deviation $\hat{\sigma}$ is:

$$h = \frac{3.5\hat{\sigma}}{\sqrt[3]{n}}$$

Finally, the Freedman-Diaconis rule for the bin width is given by:

$$h = \frac{2IQR}{\sqrt[3]{n}}$$

We will construct a few histograms describing the problems through their examples and their R setup in the *Time for action – understanding the effectiveness of histogram* section.

Example 3.2.4. The default examples: To get a first preview on the generation of histograms, we suggest that the reader goes through the built-in examples; try `example(hist)` and `example(histogram)`.

Example 3.2.5. The Galton dataset: We will obtain histograms for the height of child and parent from the Galton dataset. We will use the Freedman-Diaconis and Sturges choice of bin widths.

Example 3.2.6. Octane rating of gasoline blends: An experiment is conducted where the octane rating of gasoline blends can be obtained using two methods. Two samples are available for testing each type of blend, and Snee (1981) obtains 32 different blends over an appropriate spectrum of the target octane ratings. We obtain histograms for the ratings under the two different methods.

Example 3.2.7. Histogram with a dummy dataset: A dummy dataset has been created by the author. Here, we need to obtain histograms for the two samples in the `Samplez` data from the `RSADBE` package.

Time for action – understanding the effectiveness of histograms

Histograms are obtained using `hist` and `histogram` functions. The choice of bin widths is also discussed:

1. Have a buy-in of the R capability of the histograms through `example(hist)` and `example(histogram)` for the respective `histogram` functions from the `graphics` and `lattice` packages.

2. Invoke the graphics editor with `par(mfrow=c(2,2))`.

3. Create the histogram for the height of `Child` and `Parent` from the `galton` dataset seen in the earlier part of the section for the `Freedman-Diaconis` and `Sturges` choice of bin widths:

```
data(galton)
par(mfrow=c(2,2))
hist(galton$parent,breaks="FD",xlab="Height of Parent",
     main="Histogram for Parent Height with Freedman-Diaconis Breaks",
     xlim=c(60,75))
hist(galton$parent,xlab="Height of Parent",
     main="Histogram for Parent Height with Sturges Breaks",
     xlim=c(60,75))
hist(galton$child,breaks="FD",xlab="Height of Child",
     main="Histogram for Child Height with Freedman-Diaconis Breaks",
     xlim=c(60,75))
hist(galton$child,xlab="Height of Child",
     main="Histogram for Child Height with Sturges Breaks",
     xlim=c(60,75))
```

Consequently, we get the following diagram:

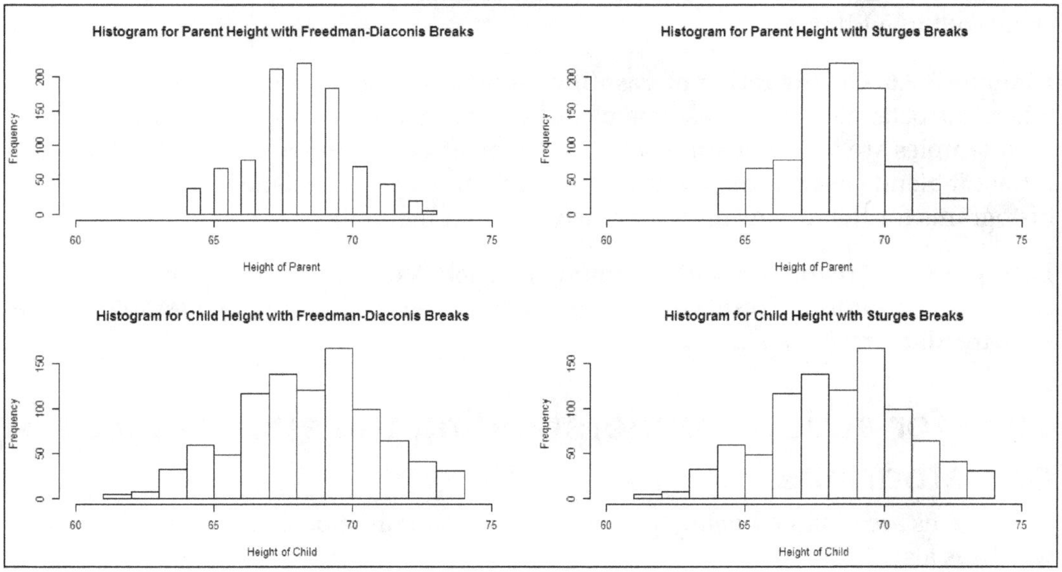

Histograms for the Galton dataset

Note that a few people may not like histogram for the height of parent for the Freedman-Diaconis choice of bin width.

4. For the experiment mentioned in *Example 3.2.9. Octane rating of gasoline blends*, first load the data in to R with `data(octane)`.

5. Invoke the graphics editor for the ratings under the two methods with `par(mfrow=c(2,2))`.

6. Create the histograms for the ratings under the two methods for the Sturges choice of bin widths with:

```
hist(octane$Method_1,xlab="Ratings Under Method I",
    main="Histogram of Octane Ratings for Method I",col="mistyrose")
hist(octane$Method_2,xlab="Ratings Under Method II",
    main="Histogram of Octane Ratings for Method II",col=" cornsilk")
```

The resulting histogram plot will be the first row of the next figure.

A visual inspection suggests that, under `Method_I`, the mean rating is around 90 while, under `Method_II`, it is approximately 95. Moreover, the `Method_II` ratings look more symmetric than the `Method_I` ratings.

7. Load the required data here with `data(Samplez)`.

8. Create the histogram for the two samples under the `Samplez` data frame with:

```
data(Samplez)
hist(Samplez$Sample_1,xlab="Sample 1",main="Histogram: Sample 1",
      col="magenta")
hist(Samplez$Sample_2,xlab="Sample 2",main="Histogram: Sample 2",
      col="snow")
```

We obtain the following histogram plot:

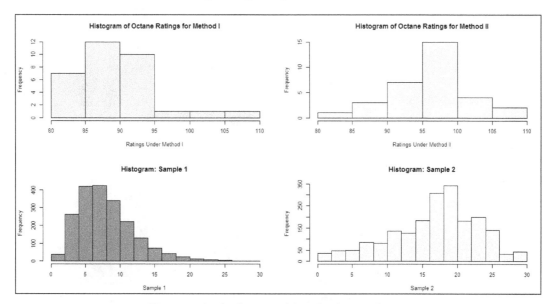

Histogram for the Octane and Samples dummy dataset

The lack of symmetry is very apparent in the second row display of the preceding diagram. It is very clear from the preceding diagram that the left histogram exhibits an example of a positive skewed distribution for `Sample_1`, while the right histogram for `Sample_2` shows that the distribution is a negatively skewed distribution.

What just happened?

Histograms have traditionally provided a lot of insight into the understanding of the distribution of variables. In this section, we dived deep into the intricacies of their construction, especially, related to the options of bin widths. We also saw how the different nature of variables is clearly brought out by their histogram.

The Python implementation of histogram is taken up in the next sub-section.

Doing it in Python

We will use the following dataset here: Galton, Samplez, and Octane.

1. The preliminary analysis of the Galton dataset is performed in the following diagram. We first import the data with the read_csv function, and then look at essential summaries:

```
Galton = pd.read_csv("Data/Galton.csv",delimiter=',')
Galton.shape
Galton.head(10)
Galton.quantile([0,0.25,0.5,0.75,1])
Galton.mean()
Galton.median()
```

The summary output of the dataset is:

```
In [11]:  Galton = pd.read_csv("Data/Galton.csv",delimiter=',')
          Galton.shape

Out[11]:  (928, 2)

In [12]:  Galton.head(10)

Out[12]:
              child  parent
          0   61.7   70.5
          1   61.7   68.5
          2   61.7   65.5
          3   61.7   64.5
          4   61.7   64.0
          5   62.2   67.5
          6   62.2   67.5
          7   62.2   67.5
          8   62.2   66.5
          9   62.2   66.5

In [13]:  Galton.quantile([0,0.25,0.5,0.75,1])

Out[13]:
                 child  parent
          0.00   61.7   64.0
          0.25   66.2   67.5
          0.50   68.2   68.5
          0.75   70.2   69.5
          1.00   73.7   73.0

In [14]:  Galton.mean

Out[14]:  child     68.08847
          parent    68.30819
          dtype: float64
```

2. The histograms are easily obtained from the `matplotlib` infrastructure and
    we also explore the two methods of setting up the bins:

```
plt.subplot(1,2,1)
plt.hist(Galton['parent'],bins='fd')
plt.xlim(60,75)
plt.title("Height of Parent")
plt.subplot(1,2,2)
plt.hist(Galton['child'],bins='fd')
plt.xlim(60,75)
plt.title("Height of Child")
plt.show()
```

The Python session is shown next:

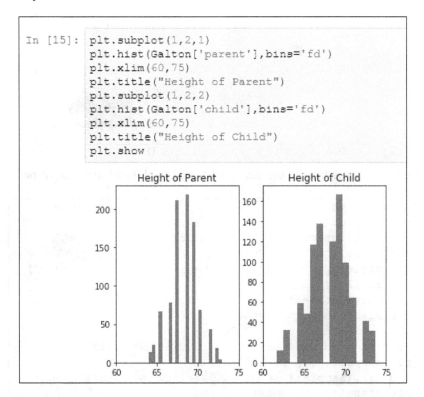

```
In [15]: plt.subplot(1,2,1)
         plt.hist(Galton['parent'],bins='fd')
         plt.xlim(60,75)
         plt.title("Height of Parent")
         plt.subplot(1,2,2)
         plt.hist(Galton['child'],bins='fd')
         plt.xlim(60,75)
         plt.title("Height of Child")
         plt.show
```

Since the Freedman-Diaconis choice does not give a good histogram, we will
look at the `sturges` method alternative.

3. The `sturges` method is stated in the following:

```
In [16]: plt.subplot(1,2,1)
         plt.hist(Galton['parent'],bins='sturges')
         plt.xlim(60,75)
         plt.title("Height of Parent")
         plt.subplot(1,2,2)
         plt.hist(Galton['child'],bins='sturges')
         plt.xlim(60,75)
         plt.title("Height of Child")
         plt.show
```

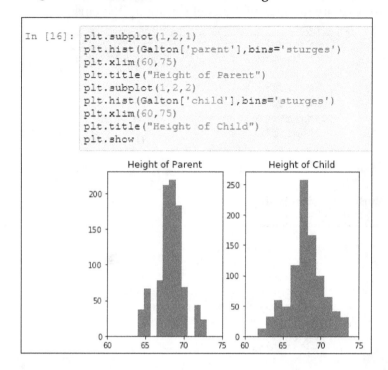

4. The histograms for the `Octane` and `Samplez` dataset are drawn next:

```
Octane = pd.read_csv("Data/Octane.csv",delimiter=',')
plt.subplot(2,2,1)
plt.hist(Octane['Method_1'],color="magenta")
plt.xlabel("Ratings Under Method I")
plt.title("Histogram of Octane Ratings for Method I")
plt.subplot(2,2,2)
plt.hist(Octane['Method_2'],color="cyan")
plt.xlabel("Ratings Under Method II")
plt.title("Histogram of Octane Ratings for Method II")
Samplez = pd.read_csv("Data/Samplez.csv",delimiter=',')
plt.subplot(2,2,3)
plt.hist(Samplez['Sample_1'],color="magenta")
plt.xlabel("Sample 1")
plt.title("Histogram of Sample 1")
plt.subplot(2,2,4)
plt.hist(Samplez['Sample_2'],color="cyan")
plt.xlabel("Sample 2")
plt.title("Histogram of Sample 2")
plt.show()
```

The output of the preceding program is as follows:

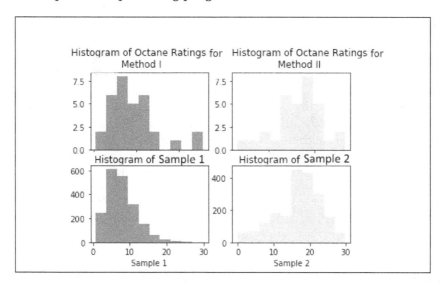

Have a go hero

The previous histogram titles are obviously messy. One of the ways is to use \n in the title string option. However, that leads to another problem. What is your solution?

Scatter plot

In the previous subsection, we used histograms to understand the nature of the variables. For multiple variables, we need multiple histograms. However, we need different tools to understand the relationship between two or more variables. A simple, yet effective, technique is the scatter plot. When we have two variables, the scatter plot simply draws the two variables across the two axes. The scatter plot is powerful in reflecting the relationship between the variables as it reveals if there is a linear/nonlinear relationship. If the relationship is linear, we may get an insight if there is a positive or negative relationship among the variables, and so forth.

Example 3.2.8. The drain current versus the ground-to-source voltage: Montgomery and Runger (2003) report an article from IEEE (Exercise 11.64) about an experiment where the drain current is measured against the ground-to-source voltage. In the scatter plot, the drain current values are plotted against each level of the ground-to-source voltage. The former value is measured in milli-amperes and the later in volts. The R function `plot` is used for understanding the relationship. We will soon visualize the relationship between the current values against the level of the ground-to-source voltage. This data is available as DCD in the RSADBE package.

The scatter plot is very flexible when we need to understand the relationship between more than two variables. In the next example, we will extend the scatter plot to multiple variables.

Example 3.2.9. The Gasoline mileage performance data: The mileage of a car depends on various factors; in fact, it is a very complex problem. In the next table, the various variables $x1$ to $x11$, which are believed to have an influence on the mileage of the car, are described. We need a plot that explains the inter-relationships between the variables and the mileage. The exercise of repeating the `plot` function may be done 11 times, though most people may struggle to recollect the influence of first plot when they are looking at the sixth or maybe the seventh plot. The `pairs` function returns a matrix of scatter plot that is really useful. Let us visualize the matrix of scatter plots:

```
> data(Gasoline)
> pairs(Gasoline) # Output suppressed
```

It may be seen that this matrix of scatter plot is a symmetric plot in the sense that the upper and lower triangle of this matrix are simply copies of each other (transposed copies, actually). We can be more effective in representing the data in the matrix of scatter plots by specifying additional parameters. Even as we study the inter-relationships, it is important to understand the variable distribution itself. Since the diagonal elements are just indicating the name of the variable, we can instead replace them with their histograms.

Furthermore, if we can give the measure of the relationship between two variables, say correlation coefficient, we can be more effective. In fact, we do a step better by displaying the correlation coefficient by increased the font size according to its stronger value. We first define the necessary functions and then use the `pairs` function.

Variable Notation	Variable Description	Variable Notation	Variable Description
Y	Miles/gallon	$x6$	Carburetor (barrels)
$x1$	Displacement (cubic inches)	$x7$	No. of transmission speeds
$x2$	Horsepower (foot-pounds)	$x8$	Overall length (inches)
$x3$	Torque (foot-pounds)	$x9$	Width (inches)
$x4$	Compression ratio	$x10$	Weight (pounds)
$x5$	Rear axle ratio	$x11$	Type of transmission (A-automatic, M-manual)

Time for action – plot and pairs R functions

The scatter plot and its important multivariate extension with pairs will be considered in detail now:

1. Consider the data `data(DCD)`.

    Use the options `xlab` and `ylab` to specify the right labels for the axes. We specify `xlim` and `ylim` to get a good overview of the relationship.

2. Obtain the scatter plot for *Example 3.2.8. The Drain current versus the ground-to-source voltage* using `plot(DCD$Drain_Current, DCD$GTS_Voltage,type="b",xlim=c(1,2.2),ylim=c(0.6,2.4),xlab="Current Drain", ylab="Voltage")`.

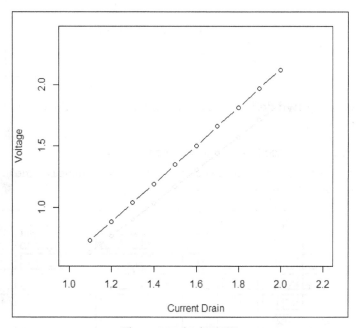

The scatter plot for DCD

We can easily see from the preceding scatter plot that as the ground-to-source voltage increases, there is an appropriate increase in the drain current. This is an indication of a positive relationship between the two variables. However, the lab assistant now comes to you and says that the measurement error of the instrument has actually led to 15 percent higher recordings of the ground-to-source voltage. Now, instead of dropping the entire diagram, we may simply prefer to add the corrected figures to the existing one. The `points` option helps us to add the new, corrected data points to the figure.

3. Now, obtain the correct `GTS_Voltage` readings with `DCD$GTS_Voltage/1.15` and add them to the existing plot with `points(DCD$Drain_Current,DCD$GTS_Voltage/1.15,type="b",col="green")`.

4. We first create two functions, `panel.hist` and `panel.cor`, defined as follows:

```
panel.hist <- function(x, ...)  {
  usr<- par("usr"); on.exit(par(usr))
  par(usr = c(usr[1:2], 0, 1.5) )
  h <- hist(x, plot = FALSE)
  breaks<- h$breaks; nB<- length(breaks)
  y <- h$counts;
  y <- y/max(y)
  rect(breaks[-nB], 0, breaks[-1], y, col="cyan", ...)
    }
panel.cor <- function(x, y, digits=2, prefix="", cex.cor, ...)  {
  usr<- par("usr"); on.exit(par(usr))
  par(usr = c(0, 1, 0, 1))
  r <- abs(cor(x,y,use="complete.obs"))
  txt<- format(c(r, 0.123456789), digits=digits)[1]
  txt<- paste(prefix, txt, sep="")
  if(missing(cex.cor)) cex.cor<- 0.8/strwidth(txt)
  text(0.5, 0.5, txt, cex = cex.cor * r)
    }
```

The preceding two defined functions are taken from the code of `example(pairs)`.

5. It is time to put these two functions into action:

```
pairs(Gasoline,diag.panel=panel.hist,lower.panel=panel.
smooth,upper.panel=panel.cor)
```

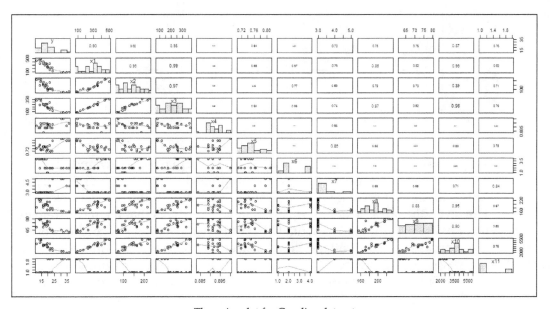

The pairs plot for Gasoline dataset

In the upper triangle of the display, we can see that the mileage has strong association with the displacement, horsepower, torque, number of transmission speeds, the overall length, width, weight, and the type of transmission. We can say a bit more too.

The first three variables x1 to x3 relate to the engine characteristics, and there is a strong association within these three variables. Similarly, there is a strong association between x8 to x10 and, together, they form the vehicle's dimension. Also, we have done a bit more than simply obtaining the scatter plots in the lower triangle of the display. A smooth approximation of the relationship between the variables is provided here.

6. Finally, we resort to the usual trick by looking at the capabilities of the plot and pairs functions with example(plot), example(pairs), and example(xyplot).

We have seen how multi-variables may be visualized. In the next subsection, we will explore more about the important Pareto chart.

What just happened?

Starting with a simple scatter plot and its effectiveness, we went at great length in the extension to the pairs function. The pairs function has been greatly explored using the panel.hist and panel.cor functions for truly understanding the relationships between a set of multiple variables.

Doing it in Python

The matrix of scatter plot in Python is obtained by using the scatter_matrix function.

The matrix of scatterplot is obtained by using the scatter_matrix function from the pandas package. The program and resulting output is given, as follows:

```
Gasoline = pd.read_csv("Data/Gasoline.csv",delimiter=',')
Gasoline2 = Gasoline
del Gasoline2['x11']
from pandas.plotting import scatter_matrix
scatter_matrix(Gasoline2)
plt.show()
```

The output is as follows:

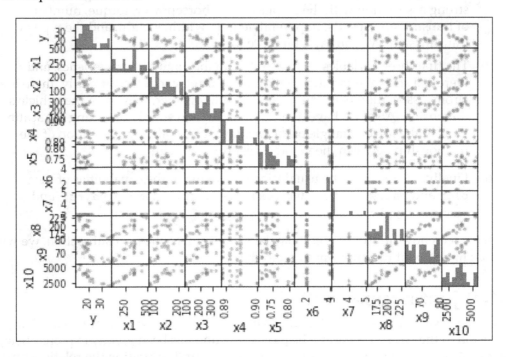

Have a go hero

Improvise the display of matrix of scatter plots.

Pareto chart

The Pareto rule, also known as the 80-20 rule or the law of vital few, says that approximately 80 percent of the defects are due to 20 percent of the causes. It is important as it can identify 20 percent vital causes whose elimination annihilates 80 percent of the defects. The qcc package contains the function pareto.chart, which helps in generating the Pareto chart. We will give a simple illustration of this chart.

The Pareto chart is a display of the cause frequencies along two axes. Suppose that we have 10 causes C1 to C10 that have occurred with defect counts 5, 23, 7, 41, 19, 4, 3, 4, 2, and 1. Causes 2, 4, and 5 have high frequencies (dominating?) and other causes look a bit feeble. Now, let us sort these causes by decreasing the order and obtain their cumulative frequencies. We will also obtain their cumulative percentages:

```
> Cause_Freq <- c(5, 23, 7, 41, 19, 4, 3, 4, 2, 1)
> names(Cause_Freq) <- paste("C",1:10,sep="")
> Cause_Freq_Dec <- sort(Cause_Freq,dec=TRUE)
```

```
> Cause_Freq_Cumsum <- cumsum(Cause_Freq_Dec)
> Cause_Freq_Cumsum_Perc <- Cause_Freq_Cumsum/sum(Cause_Freq)
> cbind(Cause_Freq_Dec,Cause_Freq_Cumsum,Cause_Freq_Cumsum_Perc)
    Cause_Freq_Dec Cause_Freq_Cumsum Cause_Freq_Cumsum_Perc
C4              41                41                 0.3761
C2              23                64                 0.5872
C5              19                83                 0.7615
C3               7                90                 0.8257
C1               5                95                 0.8716
C6               4                99                 0.9083
C8               4               103                 0.9450
C7               3               106                 0.9725
C9               2               108                 0.9908
C10              1               109                 1.0000
```

This appears to be a simple trick, and yet it is very effective in revealing that causes 2, 4, and 5 are contributing more than 75 percent of the defects. A Pareto chart completes the preceding table with bar chart in a decreasing count of the causes with a left vertical axis for the frequencies and a cumulative curve on the right vertical axis. We will see the Pareto chart in action for the next example.

Example 3.2.10. The Pareto chart for incomplete applications: A simple step-by-step illustration of Pareto chart is available on the web at http://personnel.ky.gov/nr/rdonlyres/d04b5458-97eb-4a02-bde1-99fc31490151/0/paretochart.pdf. The reader can go through the clear steps mentioned in the document.

In the example from the preceding web document, a bank that issues credit cards rejects application forms if they are deemed incomplete. An application form may be incomplete if information is not provided in one or more of the details sought in the form.

For example, an application can't be processed further if the customer/applicant has not provided address, has, illegible handwriting, their signature is missing, or the customer is an existing credit card holder among other reasons. The concern of the manager of the credit card wing is to ensure that the rejections for incomplete applications should decline, since a cost is incurred on issuing the form that is generally not charged for. The manager wants to focus on certain reasons that may be leading to the rejection of the forms.

Here, we consider the frequency of the different causes that lead to the rejection of the applications:

```
>library(qcc)
>Reject_Freq <- c(9,22,15,40,8)
>names(Reject_Freq) <- c("No Addr.", "Illegible", "Curr. Customer",
"No Sign.", "Other")
```

```
>Reject_Freq
      No Addr.    Illegible   Curr.CustomerNo Sign.        Other
            9    22                 15         40         8
>options(digits=2)
>pareto.chart(Reject_Freq)
Pareto chart analysis for Reject_Freq
Frequency Cum.Freq.Percentage Cum.Percent.
  No Sign.            40.0       40.0        42.6         42.6
  Illegible           22.0       62.0        23.4         66.0
  Curr. Customer      15.0       77.0        16.0         81.9
  No Addr.             9.0       86.0         9.6         91.5
  Other                8.0       94.0         8.5        100.0
```

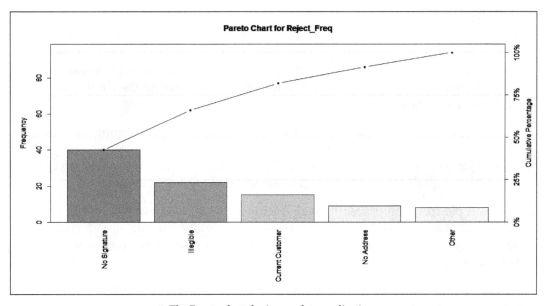

The Pareto chart for incomplete applications

In the screenshot given in step 5 of the *Time for action – plot and pairs R functions* section, the frequency of the five reasons of rejections is represented by bars as in a bar plot with the distinction of being displayed in a decreasing magnitude of frequency. The frequency of the reasons is indicated on the left vertical axis. At the mid-point of each bar, the cumulative frequency up to that reason is indicated, and the reference for this count is the right vertical axis. Thus, we can see that more than 75 percent of the rejections are due to the three causes **No Signature**, **Illegible**, and **Current Customer**. This is the main strength of a Pareto chart.

A brief peek at ggplot2

Tufte (2001) and Wilkinson (2005) emphasize the aesthetics of graphics a lot. There is indeed more to graphics than mere mathematics, and the subtle changes/corrections in a display may lead to an improved, enhanced, and pleasing feeling on the eye diagrams. Wilkinson emphasizes on what he calls *grammar of graphics*, and an R adaptation of it is given by Wickham (2009).

Thus far, we have used various functions, such as `barchart`, `dotchart`, `spineplot`, `fourfoldplot`, `boxplot`, `plot`, and so on. The grammar of graphics emphasizes that a statistical graphic is a mapping from data to aesthetic attributes of geometric objects. The aesthetics aspect consist of color, shape, and size, while the geometric objects are composed of points, lines, and bars. A detailed discussion of these aspects is unfortunately not feasible in this book, and we will satisfy ourselves with a quick introduction to the grammar of graphics. To begin with, we will simply consider the `qplot` function from the `ggplot2` package.

Time for action – qplot

Here, we fill first use the `qplot` function for obtaining various kinds of plots. To keep the story short, we are using the earlier datasets only and hence, a reproduction of the similar plots using `qplot` won't be displayed. The reader is encouraged to check `?qplot` and its examples:

1. Load the library with `library(ggplot2)`.

2. Rearrange the resistivity dataset in a different format and obtain the boxplots:

```
test <- data.frame(rep(c("R1","R2"),each=8),c(resistivity[,1],
                                               resistivity[,2]))
names(test) <- c("RES","VALUE")
qplot(factor(RES),VALUE,data=test,geom="boxplot")
```

The `gplot` function needs to be explicitly specified that RES is a factor variable and according to its levels; we need to obtain the boxplot for the resistivity values.

3. For the `Gasoline` dataset, we would like to obtain a boxplot of the mileage accordingly as the gear system could be manual or automatic. Thus, the `qplot` can be put to action with `qplot(factor(x11),y,data=Gasoline,geom= "boxplot")`.

4. A histogram is also one of the geometric aspects of `ggplot2`, and we next obtain the histogram for the height of child with `qplot(child,data=galton,geom="histogram", binwidth = 2,xlim=c(60,75),xlab="Height of Child", ylab="Frequency")`.

5. The scatter plot for the height of parent against child is fetched with `qplot(parent,child,data=galton,xlab="Height of Parent", ylab="Height of Child", main="Height of Parent Vs Child")`.

What just happened?

The `qplot` under the argument of `geom` allows a good family of graphics under a single function. This is particularly advantageous for us to perform a host of tricks under a single umbrella.

Of course, there is the all more important `ggplot` function from the `ggplot2` library, which is the primary reason for the flexibility of grammar of graphics. We will close the chapter with a very brief exposition to it. The main strength of `ggplot` stems from the fact that you can build a plot layer by layer. We will illustrate this with a simple example.

Time for action – ggplot

`ggplot`, `aes`, and `layer` will be put in action to explore the power of grammar of graphics. The steps for illustrating `ggplot` on the scatterplot are:

1. Load the library with `library(ggplot2)`.

2. Using the `aes` and `ggplot` functions, first create a `ggplot` object with `galton_gg <- ggplot(galton,aes(child,parent))` and find the most recent creation in R by running `galton_gg`. You will get an error, and the graphics device will show a blank screen.

3. Create a scatter plot by adding a layer to `galton_gg` with `galton_gg <- galton_gg + layer(geom="point")`, and then run `galton_gg` to check for changes. Yes, you will get a scatter plot of the height of child versus parent.

4. The labels of the axes are not satisfactory and we need better ones. The strength of `ggplot` is that you can continue to add layers to it with varied options. In fact, you can change the `xlim` and `ylim` on an existing plot and check each time the difference in the plot. Run the following code in a step-by-step manner and appreciate the strength of the grammar:

```
galton_gg <- galton_gg + xlim(60,75)
galton_gg
galton_gg <- galton_gg + ylim(60,75)
galton_gg
galton_gg<-galton_gg+ylab("Height of Parent")+xlab("Height ofChild")
galton_gg
galton_gg <- galton_gg + ggtitle("Height of Parent Vs Child")
galton_gg
```

What just happened?

The layer-by-layer approach of ggplot is very useful and we have seen an illustration of it on the scatter plot for the Galton dataset. In fact, the reach of ggplot is much richer than our simple illustration, of course, and the interested reader may refer to Wickham (2009) for more details.

Pop quiz

If you run par(list(cex.lab=2,ask=TRUE)) followed by barplot(Severity_Counts,xlab="Bug Count",xlim=c(0,12000), horiz =TRUE, col=rep(c(2,3),5)), what do you expect R to do?

Summary

In this chapter, we have visualized different types of graphs for different types of variables. We have also explored how to gain insights into data through the graphs. It is important to realize that, without a clear understanding of the data structure, the plots are meaningless if they are generated without exercising enough caution. The GIGO adage is very true and no rich visualization technique helps overcome this problem.

In the previous chapter, we learned the important methods of importing/exporting data, and visualized the data in different forms. Now that we have an understanding and visual insight of the data, we need to take the next step, namely quantitative analysis of the data. There are roughly two streams of analysis: exploratory and confirmative analysis. It is the former analysis technique that forms the center of the next chapter. As an instance, the scatter plot reveals whether there is a positive, negative, or no association between the two variables. If the association is not zero, the numeric answer of the positive or negative relationship is then required. Techniques such as these and extensions form the core of the next chapter.

4
Exploratory Analysis

Tukey (1977) in his benchmark book *Exploratory Data Analysis*, abbreviated popularly as EDA, explains the best about the best methods as:

> *We do not guarantee to introduce you to the best tools, particularly since we are not sure that there can be unique bests.*

The goal of this chapter is to emphasize on Exploratory Data Analysis (EDA) and its strength.

In the previous chapter, we have seen visualization techniques for data of different characteristics. Analytical insight is also important and this chapter considers EDA techniques. Furthermore, the more popular measures include the mean, standard error, and so on. It has been proved many times that mean has several drawbacks; one being that it is very sensitive to outliers/extremes. Thus, in exploratory analysis the focus is on measures that are robust to the extremes. Many techniques considered in this chapter are discussed in more detail by Velleman and Hoaglin (1981), and an e-book has been kindly made available at `http://dspace.library.cornell.edu/handle/1813/62`.

In the first section, we will have a peek at the often used measures for exploratory analysis. Unfortunately, we can't do most of the EDA analysis in Python as we do them in R and have to restrict ourselves with some quantitative summaries only. The main things we will learn from this chapter are listed as follows:

- Summary statistics based on median and its variants, which are robust to outliers
- Visualization techniques in stem-and-leaf, letter values, and `bagplot`
- First regression model in resistant line and refined methods in smoothing data and median polish

Packages and settings – R and Python

The R package `LearnEDA` is not available anymore and we need to work around it. To get over that problem, the three required functions `lval`, `rline`, and `han` are saved in a `LearnEDA_Functions.R` file and it is loaded as a `source` file:

1. First set the working directory:

   ```
   setwd("MyPath/R/Chapter_04")
   ```

2. Install the R packages `aplpack` and `vcd` in the usual way, and run the following codes to set up the required packages:

   ```
   library(RSADBE)
   library(aplpack)
   library(vcd)
   source("SRC/LearnEDA_Functions.R")
   ```

   We have the usual Python packages as a pre-requisite.

3. Import the required Python packages as follows:

   ```
   In [2]:   import os
             os.chdir("MyPath/Python/Chapter_04")
             import pandas as pd
             import matplotlib.pyplot as plt
             import numpy as np
   ```

We are now set to carry out the desired analyses.

Essential summary statistics

We have seen useful summary statistics of mean and variance in the *Discrete distributions* and *Continuous distributions* sections of *Chapter 1, Data Characteristics*. The concepts therein have their own utility value. The drawback of such statistical metrics is that they are very sensitive to outliers, in the sense that a single observation may completely distort the entire story.

In this section, we will discuss some exploratory analysis metrics that are intuitive and more robust than the metrics such as mean and variance. We'll be learning the following metrics:

- Percentiles
- Quantiles

- Median
- Hinges
- Interquartile range

Percentiles, quantiles, and median

For a given dataset and a number $0 < k < 1$, the $100k\%$ percentile divides the dataset into two partitions with $100k\%$ of the values below it and $100(1-k)\%$ of the values above it. The fraction k is referred as a quantile. In Statistics, **quantiles** are used more often than **percentiles**. The difference being that the quantiles vary over the unit interval $(0, 1)$, whereas 100 times the quantiles gives us the percentiles. It is important to note that the minimum (maximum) is the 0% (100%) percentile.

The **median** is the fiftieth percentile, which divides the data values into two equal parts with itself being the mid-point of these parts. The lower and upper quartiles are respectively the 25% and 75% percentiles. The standard notation for the lower, mid (median), and upper quartiles respectively are *Q1*, *Q2*, and *Q3*. By extension, *Q0* and *Q5* respectively denote the minimum and maximum quantities in a dataset.

Example 4.1.1. Rahul Dravid – The Wall: The game of cricket is hugely popular in India and many cricketers have given a lot of goose bumps to its followers. Sachin Tendulkar, Anil Kumble, Javagal Srinath, Saurav Ganguly, Rahul Dravid, and VVS Laxman are some of the iconic names across the world. The six players mentioned here have especially played a huge role in taking India to the number one position in the test cricket rankings, and it is widely believed that Rahul Dravid has been the backbone of this success. A century is credited to a cricketer on scoring 100 or more runs in a single innings. He has scored 36 test centuries across the globe, quite a handful of them were so resolute in nature that it earned him the nickname *The Wall*, and we will seek some percentiles/quantiles for these scores soon.

Next, we will focus on a statistic, which is similar to quantiles.

Hinges

The nomenclature of the concept of hinges is basically from the hinges seen on a door. For a door's frame, the mid-hinge is at the middle of the height of the frame, whereas the lower and upper hinges are respectively observed at the middle from the mid-hinge to bottom and top of the frame. In exploratory analysis, the hinges are defined by arranging the data in an increasing order, and to start the median is identified as the mid-hinge. The lower hinge for the (ordered) data is defined as the middle-most observation from the minimum to the median. The upper hinge is defined similarly for the upper part of the data.

On the first occasion, it may appear that the lower and upper hinges are the same as lower and upper quantiles. Consider the data as the first 10 integers. Here, the median is *5.5* as the average of two middle-most numbers *5* and *6*. Using the quantile function on *1:10*, it may be checked that here $Q_1 = 3.25$ and $Q_3 = 7.75$. The lower hinge is the middlemost number between *1* to the median *5.5* which turns out as *3*, and the upper hinge as *8*. Thus, it may be seen that the hinges are different from the quartiles.

An extension of the concept of the hinges will be seen in the *Letter Values* section. We will next look at exploratory measures of dispersion.

Interquartile range

Range, the difference between the minimum and maximum of the data values, is one measure of the spread of the variable. This measure is susceptible to the extreme points. The **interquartile range (IQR)** is defined as the difference between the upper and lower quartile, that is:

$$IQR = Q_3 - Q_1$$

The R function IQR calculates the *IQR* for a given numeric object. All the concepts theoretically described up to this point will be put into action.

Time for action – the essential summary statistics for The Wall dataset

We will understand the summary measures for EDA through the data on centuries scored by Rahul Dravid in test matches:

1. Load the useful EDA package: library(LearnEDA).

2. Load the dataset TheWALL from the RSADBE package: data(TheWALL).

3. Obtain the quantiles of the centuries with quantile(TheWALL$Score), and the difference between the quantiles using the diff function diff(quantile(TheWALL$Score)). The output is as follows:

```
> quantile(TheWALL$Score)
   0%    25%    50%    75%   100%
100.0 111.8 140.0 165.8 270.0
> diff(quantile(TheWALL$Score))
  25%    50%    75%   100%
11.75  28.25  25.75 104.25
```

As we are considering Rahul Dravid's centuries only, the beginning point is *100*. The median of his centuries is *140.0,* where the first and third quartiles are respectively *111.8* and *165.8*. The median of the centuries is *140* runs, which can be interpreted as having a 50 percent chance of The Wall reaching *140* runs if he scores a century. The highest ever score of Dravid is of course *270*. Interpret the difference between the quantiles.

4. We perform corresponding preparation in Python (Jupyter notebook actually) as follows:

```
In [3]:  TW = pd.read_csv("Data/TheWALL.csv",delimiter=',')
         TW['Score'].quantile([0,0.25,0.5,0.75,1])

Out[3]:  0.00     100.00
         0.25     111.75
         0.50     140.00
         0.75     165.75
         1.00     270.00
         Name: Score, dtype: float64

In [4]:  np.diff TW['Score'].quantile([0,0.25,0.5,0.75,1])

Out[4]:  array([ 11.75,    28.25,    25.75,   104.25])
```

5. The percentiles of Dravid's centuries can be obtained by using the quantile function again: `quantile(TheWALL$Score,seq(0,1,.1))`, here `seq(0,1,.1)` creates a vector which incrementally increases 0.1 beginning with 0 until 1, and the inter-difference between the percentiles with `diff(qu antile(TheWALL$Score,seq(0,1,.1)))`:

```
>quantile(TheWALL$Score,seq(0,1,.1))
   0%    10%    20%    30%    40%    50%    60%    70%    80%    90%   100%
100.0 103.5 111.0 116.0 128.0 140.0 146.0 154.0 180.0 208.5 270.0
> diff(quantile(TheWALL$Score,seq(0,1,.1)))
 10%   20%   30%   40%   50%   60%   70%   80%   90%  100%
3.5   7.5   5.0  12.0  12.0   6.0   8.0  26.0  28.5  61.5
```

The Wall is also known for his resolve of performing well in away Test matches. Let us verify that using the data on the centuries score.

6. The analysis repeated in Python is as follows:

```
In [5]:  TW['Score'].quantile(np.arange(0,1.1,.1))
Out[5]:  0.0    100.0
         0.1    103.5
         0.2    111.0
         0.3    116.0
         0.4    128.0
         0.5    140.0
         0.6    146.0
         0.7    154.0
         0.8    180.0
         0.9    208.5
         1.0    270.0
         Name: Score, dtype: float64

In [6]:  np.diff TW['Score'].quantile(np.arange(0,1.1,.1))
Out[6]:  array([ 3.5,   7.5,   5. ,  12. ,  12. ,   6. ,   8. ,  26. ,  28.5,  61.5])
```

7. The `Home` and `Away` number of centuries is obtained using the `table` function. Furthermore, we obtain a boxplot of the home and away centuries:

```
> table(HA_Ind)
HA_Ind
Away Home
  21   15
```

The R function table returns frequencies of the various categories for a categorical variable. In fact, it is more versatile in obtaining frequencies for more than one categorical variable. The Wall is also known for his resolve of performing well in away Test matches. This is partly confirmed by the fact that *21* of his *36* centuries came in away tests. However, the boxplot says otherwise:

```
>boxplot(Score~HA_Ind,data=TheWALL)
```

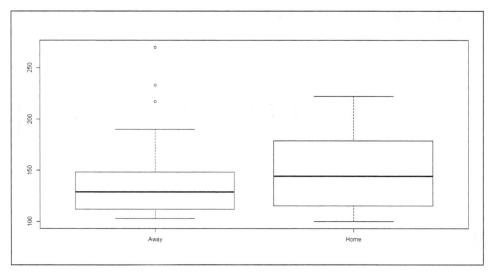

Box plot for Home/Away centuries of The Wall

It may be tempting for The Wall's fans to believe that if they remove the outliers of scores above *200*, the result may say that his performance of **Away** test centuries is better/equal to **Home** ones. However, this is not the case, which may be verified as follows.

8. Generate the boxplot for centuries whose score is less than 200 with `boxplot(Score~HA_Ind,subset=(Score<200),data=TheWALL)`.

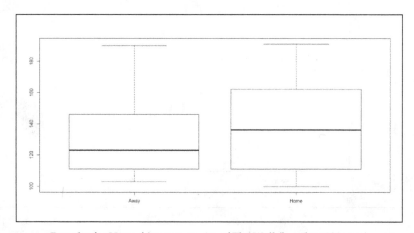

Box plot for Home/Away centuries of The Wall (less than 200 runs)

What do you conclude from the preceding figure?

9. Python does similar analysis as follows:

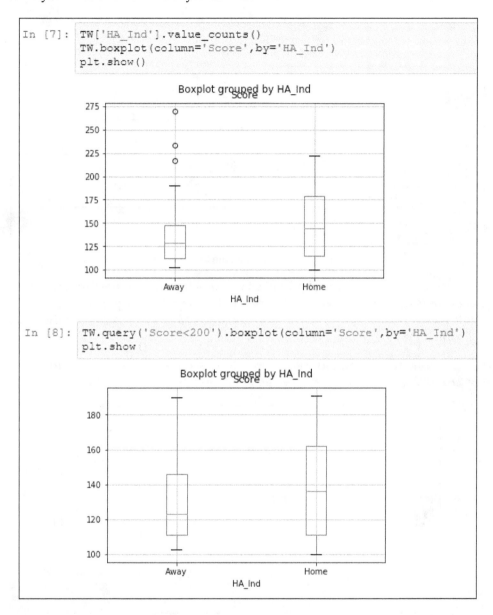

```
In [7]: TW['HA_Ind'].value_counts()
        TW.boxplot(column='Score',by='HA_Ind')
        plt.show()
```

Boxplot grouped by HA_Ind

```
In [8]: TW.query('Score<200').boxplot(column='Score',by='HA_Ind')
        plt.show
```

Boxplot grouped by HA_Ind

10. The `fivenum` summary for the centuries is:

```
>fivenum(TheWALL$Score)
[1] 100.0 111.5 140.0 169.5 270.0
```

The `fivenum` function returns minimum, lower-hinge, median, upper-hinge, and maximum for the input data. The numbers `111.5` and `169.5` are lower- and upper-hinges, and it may be seen that they are certainly different values than lower- and upper-quartiles of `111.5` and `169.5`. Thus far, we focused on measures of location and let us now look at some measures of dispersion.

The `range` function in R actually returns the minimum and maximum value of the data frame. Thus, to obtain the range as a measure of spread, we get that using `diff(range())`. We use the `IQR` function to obtain the interquartile range.

11. Using `range`, `diff`, and `IQR` functions, obtain the spread of Dravid's centuries as follows:

```
> range(TheWALL$Score)
[1] 100 270
> diff(range(TheWALL$Score))
[1] 170
> IQR(TheWALL$Score)
[1] 54
>IQR(TheWALL$Score[TheWALL$HA_Ind=="Away"])
[1] 36
> IQR(TheWALL$Score[TheWALL$HA_Ind=="Home"])
[1] 63.5
```

Here, we are extracting the home centuries from `Score` using the logic that consider only those elements of `Score` when `HA_Ind` is **Home**.

What just happened?

The data summaries in the EDA framework are slightly different. Here, we first used the `quantile` function to obtain quartiles and the deciles (10 percent difference) of a numeric variable. The `diff` function has been used to find the difference between the consecutive elements of a vector. The `boxplot` function has been used to compare the home and away test centuries, which led to the conclusion that the median score of Dravid's centuries at home is higher than the away centuries. The restriction of the test centuries under *200* runs further confirmed in particular, that Dravid's centuries at home have higher median value than those in away series, and in general that median is robust to outliers.

The IQR function gives us the interquartile range for a vector, and the fivenum function gives us the hinges. Though intuitively it appears that hinges and quartiles are similar, it is not always true. In this section, you learned the usage of functions, such as quantile, fivenum, IQR, and so on. On the Python front, we used new functions such as query to subset a dataset. As mentioned earlier in the chapter, we will not pursue Python development in the rest of the chapter.

We will now move to the main techniques of exploratory analysis.

Techniques for exploratory analysis

We will be studying the following techniques:

- The stem-and-leaf plot
- Letter values
- Data re-expression
- Bagplot—a bivariate boxplot
- Resistant line
- Smoothing data
- Median polish

The stem-and-leaf plot

The stem-and-leaf plot is considered as one of the seven important tools of **Statistical Process Control** (**SPC**); refer to Montgomery (2005). It is a bit similar in nature to the histogram plot.

The stem-and-leaf plot is an effective method of displaying data in a (partial) tree form. Here, each datum is split into two parts: the stem part and the leaf part. In general, the last digit of a datum forms the leaf part; the rest form the stem. Now, consider a datum 235. If the split criteria is the units place, the stem and leaf parts here will be respectively 23 and 5; if it is tens, then 2 and 3; and finally if it is hundreds, it will be 0 and 2. The left-hand side of the split datum is called the **leading digits** and the right-hand side the **trailing digits**.

In the next step, all the possible leading digits are arranged in an increasing order. This includes even those stems for which we may not have data for the leaf part, which ensures that the final stem-and-leaf plot truly depicts the distribution of the data. All possible leading digits are called **stems**. The leaves are then displayed to the right-hand side of the stems, and for each stem the leaves are again arranged in an increasing order.

Example 4.2.1. A simple illustration: Consider data of eight elements as *12, 22, 42, 13, 27, 46, 25,* and *52*. The leading digits for this data are *1, 2, 4,* and *5*. On inserting *3,* the leading digits complete the required stems to be *1* to *5*. The leaves for stem *1* are *2* and *3*. The unordered leaves for stem *2* are *2, 7,* and *5*. The display leaves for stem *2* are then *2, 5,* and *7*. There are no leaves for stem *3*. Similarly, the leaves for stems *4* and *5* respectively are the sets *{2, 6}* and *{2}* only. The `stem` function in R will be used for generating the stem-and-leaf plots.

Example 4.2.2. Octane rating of gasoline blends: (continued from the *Visualization techniques for continuous variable data* section of *Chapter 3, Data Visualization*): In the earlier study, we used the histogram for understanding the `octane` ratings under two different methods. We will use the `stem` function in the forthcoming *Time for action – the stem function in play* section for displaying the `octane` ratings under `Method_1` and `Method_2`.

Tukey (1977), being the benchmark book for EDA, produces the stem-and-leaf plot in a slightly different style. For example, the stem plots for `Method_1` and `Method_2` are better understood if we can put both the stem and leaf sides adjacent to each other instead of one below the other. It is possible to achieve this using the `stem.leaf.backback` function from the `aplpack` package.

Time for action – the stem function in play

The R function `stem` from the `base` package and `stem.leaf.backback` from `aplpack` is fundamental to our purpose of creating the stem-and-leaf plots. We will illustrate these two functions for the examples discussed earlier:

1. As mentioned in *Example 4.2.1. Octane Rating of Gasoline Blends,* first create the x vector, `x=c(12,22,42, 13,27,46,25,52)`.

2. Obtain the stem-and-leaf plot with:

```
> stem(x)
  The decimal point is 1 digit(s) to the right of the |
  1 | 23
  2 | 257
  3 |
  4 | 26
  5 | 2
```

To obtain the median from the stem display we proceed as follows. Remove one point each from either side of the display. First we remove 52 and 12, and then remove 46 and 13. The trick is to proceed until we are left with either one point, or two. In the former case, the remaining point is the median, and in the latter case, we simply take the average. Finally, we are left with 25 and 27 and hence, their average 26 is the median of x.

We will now look at the `octane` dataset.

3. Obtain the stem plots for both the methods: `data(octane)`, `stem(octane$Method_1,scale=2)`, and `stem(octane$Method_2, scale=2)`.

   The output will be similar to the following screenshot:

```
> data(octane)
> stem(octane$Method_1,scale=2)          > stem(octane$Method_2,scale=2)

  The decimal point is at the |            The decimal point is at the |

    80 | 44                                   82 | 3
    82 | 18                                   84 | 9
    84 | 78029                                86 |
    86 | 2584779                              88 | 82
    88 | 13                                   90 |
    90 | 02273447                             92 | 38569
    92 | 47                                   94 | 1737
    94 | 7                                    96 | 350445
    96 |                                      98 | 4614578
    98 | 0                                   100 | 239
   100 |                                     102 | 1
   102 |                                     104 |
   104 | 05                                  106 | 26
```

The stem plot for the octane dataset (R output edited)

Of course, the preceding screenshot has been edited. To generate such a back-to-back display, we need a different function.

4. Using the `stem.leaf.backback` function from `aplpack`, and the code `library(aplpack)` and `stem.leaf.backback(Method_1, Method_2,back.to.back=FALSE, m=5)`, we get the output in the desired format.

```
> library(aplpack)
> stem.leaf.backback(octane$Method_1,octane$Method_2,back.to.back=FALSE,m=5)

  1 | 2: represents 12, leaf unit: 1
        octane$Method_1   octane$Method_2

   8* |01            2  |
    t |33            4  |3             1
    f |44555         9  |5             2
    s |6667777      16  |
   8. |89           (2) |89            4
   9* |00001111     14  |
    t |23            6  |22333         9
    f |4             4  |4455         13
    s |                 |667777       (6)
   9. |8             3  |8899999      13
  10* |                 |011           6
    t |                 |3             3
    f |55            2  |
    s |                 |66            2
  10. |                 |
  11* |                 |

n:       32               32
```

Tukey's stem plot for octane data

The preceding screenshot has many unexplained and mysterious symbols! Prof. J. W. Tukey has taken a very pragmatic approach when developing EDA. The reader is strongly suggested to read Tukey (1977), as this brief chapter barely does justice to it.

Note that 18 of the 32 observations for Method_1 are in the range **80.4** to **89.3**. Now, if we have stems as **8, 9,** and **10**, the spread at stem **8** will be **18**, which will not give a meaningful understanding of the data. The stems can have substems, or be stretched out, and for which a very novel solution is provided by Prof. Tukey. For very high frequency stems, the solution is to squeeze out five more stems. For stem **8** here, we have the trailing digits at **0, 1, 2, ..., 9**. Now, adopt a scheme of tagging lines which leads towards a clear reading of the stem-and-leaf display. Tukey suggests using * for zero and one, **t** for two and three, **f** for four and five, **s** for six and seven, and a period (.) for eight and nine.

Truly ingenious! Thus, if you are planning to write about stem-and-leaf in your local language, you may not require *, **t**, **f**, **s**, .! Go back to the preceding screenshot and now it will look much more beautiful.

Following the leaf part for each method, we are given cumulative frequencies from the top and the bottom too. Why? Now, we know that the stem-and-leaf display has increasing values from the top and decreasing values from the bottom.

In this particular example, we have **n:32** observations. Thus, in a sorted order, we know that the median is a value between the sixteenth and seventeenth sorted observation. The cumulative frequencies when it exceeds 16 from either direction, leads to the median. This is indicated by **(2)** for `Method_1` and **(6)** for `Method_2`. Can you now make an approximate guess of the median values? Obviously, depending on the dataset, we may require m = 5, 1, or 2.

We have used the argument `back.to.back=FALSE` to ensure that the two stem-and-leafs can be seen independently. Now, it is fairly easy to compare these two displays by setting `back.to.back=TRUE`, in which case the stem line will be common for both the methods and thus, we can simply compare their leaf distributions. That is, you need to run `stem.leaf.backback(octane$Method_1,octane$Method_2,back.to.back=TRUE, m=5)` and investigate the results.

We can clearly see that the median for `Method_2` is higher than that of `Method_1`.

What just happened?

Using the basic `stem` function and `stem.leaf.backback` from the `aplpack`, we got two efficient exploratory displays of the datasets. The latter function can be used to compare two stem-and-leaf displays. Stems can be further squeezed to reveal more information with the options of *m* as *1, 2,* and *5*.

We will next look at the EDA technique that extends the scope of hinges.

Letter values

The median, quartiles, and the extremes (maximum and minimum) indicate how the data is spread over the range of the data. These values can be used to examine two or more samples. There is another way of understanding the data offered by letter values. This small journey begins with the use of a concept called **depth**, which measures the minimum position of the datum in the ordered sample from either of the extremes. Thus, the extremes have a depth of *1*, the second largest and smallest datum have a depth of *2*, and so on.

Now, consider a sample data of size *n*, assumed to be an odd number for convenience sake. Then, the depth of the median is *(n + 1)/2*. The depth of a datum is denoted by *d*, and for the median it is indicated by *d(M)*. Since the hinges, lower and upper, do the same to the divided samples (by median), the depth of the hinges is given by $d(H) = ([d(M)]+1)/2$.

Here, $[\ ]$ denotes the integer part of the argument. As hinges, including the mid-hinge which is the median, divide the data into four equal parts, we can define eights as the values that divide the data into eight equal parts. The eights are denoted by E. The depth of eights is given by the formula $d(E) = \left(\left[d(H)\right]+1\right)/2$. It may be seen that the depth of the median, hinges, and eights of the datum depends on the sample size.

Using the eights, we can further carry out the division of the data for obtaining the sixteenths, and then thirty seconds, and so on. The process of division should continue until we end up with the extremes where we cannot further proceed with the division any longer. The letter values continue the search until we end at the extremes.

The process of the division is well understood when we augment the lower and upper values for the hinges, the eights, the sixteenths, the thirty seconds, and so on. The difference between the lower and upper values of these metrics, a concept similar to mid-range, is also useful for understanding the data. The R function `lval` from the `LearnEDA` package gives the letter values for the data.

Example 4.3.1. Octane rating of gasoline blends. continued: We will now obtain the letter values for the `octane` dataset:

```
>library(LearnEDA)
>lval(octane$Method_1)
depth      lo     hi    mids  spreads
M   16.5 88.00   88.0 88.000    0.00
H    8.5 85.55   91.4 88.475    5.85
E    4.5 84.25   94.2 89.225    9.95
D    2.5 82.25  101.5 91.875   19.25
C    1.0 80.40  105.5 92.950   25.10
> lval(octane$Method_2)
depth      lo     hi    mids  spreads
M   16.5 97.20   97.20 97.200   0.00
H    8.5 93.75   99.60 96.675   5.85
E    4.5 90.75  101.60 96.175  10.85
D    2.5 87.35  104.65 96.000  17.30
C    1.0 83.30  106.60 94.950  23.30
```

The letter values, (look at the `lo` and `hi` in the preceding code), clearly shows that the corresponding values for `Method_1` are always lower than those under `Method_2`. Particularly, note that the lower hinge of `Method_2` is greater than the higher hinge of `Method_1`. However, the spread under both the methods are very identical.

Data re-expression

The presence of an outlier or overspread of the data may lead to an incomplete picture of the graphical display and hence, statistical inference may be inappropriate in these scenarios. In many such scenarios, re-expression of the data on another scale may be more useful, refer to *Chapter 3, The problem of scale*, Tukey (1977). Here, we list the scenarios from Tukey where the data re-expression may help circumvent the limitations cited in the beginning.

The first scenario where re-expression is useful is when the variables assume non-negative values, that is the variables never assume a value lesser than zero. Examples of such variables are age, height, power, area, and so on. A rule of thumb for the application of re-expression is when the ratio of the largest to the smallest value in the data is very large, say 100. This is one reason that in most regression analysis variables such as age are almost always re-expressed on the logarithmic scale.

The second scenario explained by Tukey is about variables such as balance and profit-and-loss. If there is a deposit to an account, the balance increases, and if there is a withdrawal it decreases. Thus, the variables can assume positive as well as negative values. Since re-expression of these variables like balance rarely helps; re-expression of the amount or quantity before subtraction helps on some occasions.

Fraction and percentage counts form the third scenario where re-expression of the data is useful, though one needs special techniques. The scenarios mentioned are indicative and not exhaustive. We will now look at the data re-expression techniques that are useful.

Example 4.4.1. Re-expression for the power of 62 hydroelectric stations: We need to understand the distribution of the ultimate power in megawatts of 62 hydroelectric stations and power stations of the Corps of Engineers. The data for our illustration has actually been regenerated from the exhibit 3 of Tukey (1977). First, we simply look at the stem-and-leaf display of the original data on the power of 62 hydroelectric stations. We use the `stem.leaf` function from the `aplpack` package:

```
> hydroelectric = c(14,18,28,26,36,30,30,34,30,43,45,54,52,60,68, + 68
,61,75,76,70,76,86,90,96,100,100,100,100,100,100,110,112,
+ 118,110,124,130,135,135,130,175,165,140,250,280,204,200,270,
+ 40,320,330,468,400,518,540,595,600,810,810,1728,1400,1743,2700)
>stem.leaf(hydroelectric,unit=1)
1 | 2: represents 12
leaf unit: 1
n: 62
    2      1 | 48
    4      2 | 68
    9      3 | 00046
```

```
      ...
     24        9 | 06
     30       10 | 000000
     (4)      11 | 0028
     28       12 | 4
     27       13 | 0055
     23       14 | 0
              15 |
     22       16 | 5
     21       17 | 5
              18 |
              19 |
     20       20 | 04
              21 |
              24 |
      ...

      7       60 | 0
  HI: 810 810 1400 1728 1743 2700
```

The data begins with values as low as 14, and grows modestly to hundreds, such as 100, 135, and so on. Furthermore, the data grows until five hundred and then literally explodes into thousands running up to 2700. If all the leading digits must be mandatorily displayed, we have 270 leading digits. With an average of 35 lines per page, the output requires approximately eight pages, and between the last two values of 1743 and 2700, we will have roughly 100 empty leading digits. The stem. leaf function has already removed all the leading digits after the hydroelectric plant producing 600 megawatts.

Let us look at the ratio of the largest to smallest value, which is as follows:

```
>max(hydroelectric)/min(hydroelectric)
[1] 192.8571
```

By the rule of thumb, it is an indication that a data re-expression is in order. Thus, we take the log transformation (with base 10) and obtain the stem-and-leaf display for the transformed data:

```
>stem.leaf(round(log(hydroelectric,10),2),unit=0.01)
1 | 2: represents 0.12
leaf unit: 0.01
n: 62
     1       11 | 5
     2       12 | 6
             13 |
```

```
   ...
   24      19 |  358
  (11)     20 |  0000044579
   27      21 |  11335
   22      22 |  24
   20      23 |  110
   ...
           30 |
    4      31 |  5
    3      32 |  44
 HI:  3.43
```

The compactness of the stem-and-leaf display for the transformed data is indeed more useful, and we can further see that the leading digits are just about 30. Also, the display is more elegant and comprehensible.

Have a go hero

The stem-and-leaf plot is considered a particular case of the histogram from a certain point of view. You can attempt to understand the hydroelectric distribution using histograms too. First obtain the histogram of the hydroelectric variable, and then repeat the exercise on its logarithmic re-expression.

Bagplot – a bivariate boxplot

In *Chapter 3, Data Visualization*, we saw the effectiveness of boxplots. For independent variables, we can simply draw separate boxplots for the variables and visualize the distribution. However, when there is dependency between two variables, distinct boxplots lose the dependency among the two variables. Thus, we need to see if there is a way to visualize the data through a boxplot. The answer to the question is provided by bagplot or **bivariate boxplot**.

The bagplot characteristic is described in the following steps:

- The depth median, denoted by * in the bagplot, is the point with highest half space depth.
- The depth median is surrounded by a polygon, called **bag**, which covers $n/2$ observations with the largest depth.
- The bag is then magnified by a factor of 3 that gives the **fence**. The fence is not plotted since it will drive the attention away from the data.
- The observations between the bag and fence are covered by a **loop**.
- Points outside the fence are flagged as outliers.

For technical details of the bagplot, refer to the paper (http://venus.unive.it/romanaz/ada2/bagplot.pdf) by Rousseeuw, Ruts, and Tukey (1999).

Example 4.5.1. Bagplot for the gasoline mileage problem: The pairs plot of the gasoline mileage problem in *Example 3.2.9. Octane rating of gasoline blends* gave a good visualization insight in understanding the nature of the data. Now, we will modify that plot and replace the upper panel with the bagplot for a cleaner comparison of the bagplot with the scatter plot. However, in the original dataset, variables *x4*, *x5*, and *x11* are factors that we remove from the bagplot study. The bagplot function is available in the aplpack package. We first define panel.bagplot, and then generate the matrix of the scatter plot with the bagplot produced in the upper matrix display.

Time for action – the bagplot display for multivariate datasets

The following are the steps to be performed:

1. Load the aplpack package with library(aplpack).

2. Check the default examples of the bagplot function with example(bagplot).

3. Create the panel.bagplot function with:

```
panel.bagplot <- function(x,y)

{

require(aplpack)

bagplot(x,y,verbose=FALSE,create.plot = TRUE,add=TRUE)

}
```

Here, the panel.bagplot function is defined to enable us obtain the bagplot for the upper panel region of the pairs function.

4. Apply the panl.bagplot function within the pairs function on the Gasoline dataset: pairs(Gasoline[-19,-c(1,4,5,13)],upper.panel =panel.bagplot).

We obtain the following display:

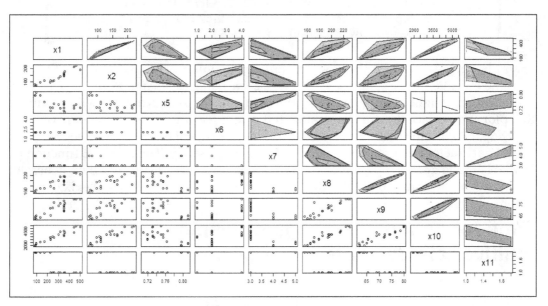

Bagplot for the Gasoline dataset

What just happened?

We created the `panel.bagplot` function and augmented it in the pairs function for effective display of the multivariate dataset. The `bagplot` is an important EDA tool towards getting exploratory insight in the important case of multivariate datasets.

Resistant line

In *Example 3.2.3. The Michelson-Morley experiment* of *Chapter 3, Data Visualization*, we visualized data through the scatter plot, which indicates possible relationships between the dependent variable (y) and independent variable (x). The scatter plot or the x-y plot is again an EDA technique. However, we would like more a quantitative model that explains the interrelationship in a more precise manner. The traditional approach will be taken in *Chapter 7, Logistic Regression Model*. In this section, we will take an EDA approach for building our first regression model.

Consider a pair of n observations: $(x_1, y_1), (x_2, y_2), ..., (x_n, y_n)$. We can easily visualize the data using the scatter plot. We need to obtain a model of the form $y = a + bx$, where a is the intercept term while b is the slope. This model is an attempt to explain the relationship between the variables x and y. Basically, we need to obtain the values of the slope and intercept from the data.

In most real data, a single line will not pass through all the n pairs of observations. In fact, it is even a difficult task for the determined line to pass through even a very few observations. As a simple task, we may choose any two observations and determine the slope and intercept. However, the difficulty lies in the choice of the two points. We will now explain how the resistant line that determines the two required terms.

The scatter plot (part A of the next screenshot) is divided into three regions, using *x*-values, where each region has approximately same number of data points, refer to part B of the next screenshot:

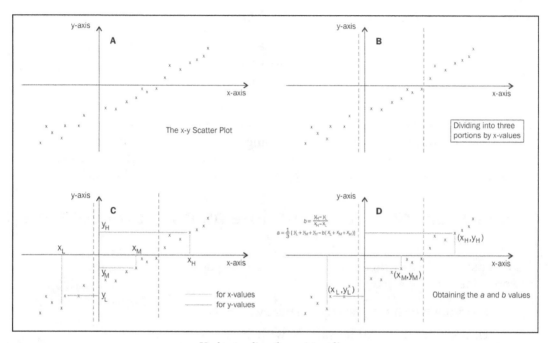

Understanding the resistant line

The three regions, from the left-hand to right-hand side, are called the lower, middle, and upper regions. Note that the *y* values are distributed among the three regions corresponding to their *x* values. Hence, there is a possibility of some y-values of lower regions to be higher than a few values in the higher regions. Within each region, we find the medians of the *x* and *y* values independently.

That is, for the lower region, the median *xL* is determined by the y-values falling in this region, and similarly, the median *xL* is determined by the x-values of the region. Similarly, the medians *xM*, *xH*, *yM*, and *yH* are determined, refer to part C of the following screenshot. Using these median values, we now form three pairs: *(xL, yL)*, *(xM, yM)*, and *(xH, yH)*. Note that these pairs need not be one of the data points.

To determine the slope *b*, two points suffice. The resistant line theory determines the slope by using the two pairs of points *(xL, yL)* and *(xH, yH)*. Thus, we obtain the following:

$$b = \frac{y_H - y_L}{x_H - x_L}$$

For obtaining the intercept value a, we use all the three pairs of medians. The value of a is determined using $a = \frac{1}{3}\left[y_L + y_M + y_H - b\left(x_L + x_M + x_H\right)\right]$.

Note that the median properties are what exactly make the solutions resistant enough. As an example, the lower and upper median would not be affected by the outliers (at the extreme ends).We will use the `rline` function from the `LearnEDA` package.

Example 4.6.1. Resistant line for the IO-CPU time: The CPU time is known to depend on the number of IO processes running at any given point of time. A simple dataset is available at `http://www.cs.gmu.edu/~menasce/cs700/files/SimpleRegression.pdf`. We aim at fitting a resistant line for this dataset.

Time for action – resistant line as a first regression model

We will use the `rline` function from the `LearnEDA` package for fitting the resistant line on a dataset:

1. Load the `LearnEDA` package: `library(LearnEDA)`.
2. Understand the default example with `example(rline)`.
3. Load the dataset `data(IO_Time)`.
4. Create the `IO_rline` resistant line for `CPU_Time` as the output and `No_of_IO` as the input with `IO_rline <- rline(IO_Time$No_of_IO, IO_Time$CPU_Time,iter=10)` for 10 iterations.
5. Find the slope and intercept with `IO_rline$a` and `IO_rline$b`. The output will then be:

   ```
   >IO_rline$a
   [1]  0.2707
   >IO_rline$b
   [1]  0.03913
   ```

6. Obtain the scatter plot of `CPU_Time` against `No_of_IO` with `plot(IO_Time$No_of_IO, IO_Time$CPU_Time)`.

7. Add the resistant line on the generated scatter plot with `abline(a= IO_rline$a,b=IO_rline$b)`.

8. Finally, give a title to the plot: `title("Resistant Line for the IO-CPU Time")`.

We then get the following figure:

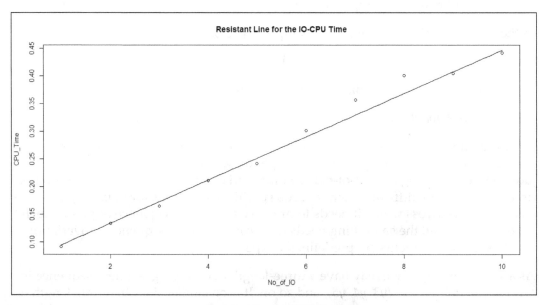

Resistant line for CPU_Time

What just happened?

The `rline` function from the `LearnEdA` package fits a resistant line given the input and output vectors. It calculated the slope and intercept terms that are driven by medians. The main advantage of the `rline` fit is that the model is not susceptible to outliers. We can see from the preceding figure that the resistant line model, IO_rline, provides a very good fit for the dataset. Well! You have created your first exploratory regression model.

Smoothing data

In the *Resistant line* section, we constructed our first regression model for the relationship between two variables. In some instances, the x-values are so systematic that their values are almost redundant, and yet we need to understand the behavior of the y-values with respect to them.

Consider the case where the *x*-values are equally spaced; the shares price (*y*) at the end of day (*x*) is an example where the difference between two consecutive *x*-values is exactly one. Here, we are more interested in smoothing the data along the *y*-values, as one expects more variation in their direction. Time series data is a very good example of this type. In the time series data, we typically have $x_n + 1 = x_n + 1$, and hence we can precisely define the data in a compact form by y_t, $t = 1, 2, \ldots$ .The general model may then be specified by $y_t = a + bt + \varepsilon, t = 1, 2, \ldots$

In the standard EDA notation, this is simply expressed as:

data = fit + residual

In the context of time series data, the model is succinctly expressed as:

data = smooth + rough

The fundamental concept of the smoothing data technique makes use of the running medians. In a free hand curve, we can simply draw a smooth curve using our judgment by ignoring the out-of-curve points and complete the picture. A computer finds this task only difficult when it needs specific instructions for obtaining the smooth points across which it needs to draw a curve. For a sequence of points, such as the sequence *yt*, the smoothing needs to be carried over a sequence of overlapping segments. Such segments are predefined of specific length.

As a simple example, we may have a three-length overlapping segment sequence in *{y1, y2, y3}*, *{y2, y3, y4}*, *{y3, y4, y5}*, and so on. It is on similar lines that four-length or five-length overlapping segment sequences may be defined as required. It is within each segment that smoothing needs to be carried out. Two popular choices are *mean* and *median*. Of course, in exploratory analysis our natural choice is the median. Note that median of the segment *{y1, y2, y3}* may be any of *y1, y2,* or *y3* values.

The general smoothing techniques, such as loess, are nonparametric techniques and require a good expertise on the subject. The ideas discussed here are mainly driven by median as the core technique.

A three-moving median cannot correct for more than two consecutive outliers, and similarly, a five-moving median for three consecutive outliers, and so on. A solution, or work around in an engineer's language, for this is to continue the smoothing of the sequence obtained in the previous iteration until there is no further change in the smoothness part.

We may also consider a moving median of span 4. Here, the median is the average of the two mid-points. However, considering that the x values are integers, the four-moving medians actually do not correspond to any of the time points t. Using the simplicity principle, it is easily possible to re-center the points at t by taking a two-moving median of the values obtained in the step of a four-moving median.

A notation for the first iteration in EDA is simply the number 3, or 5 and 7 as used. The notation for repeated smoothing is denoted by 3R where R stands for repetitions. For a four-moving median re-centered by a two-moving median, the notation will be 42. On many occasions, a smoother operation giving more refinement than 42 may be desired. It is on such occasions that we may use the running weighted average, which gives different weights to the points under a span. Here, each point is replaced by a weighted average of the neighboring points. A popular choice of weights for a running weighted average of 3 is (¼, ½, ¼), and this smoothing process is referred to as **hanning**. The hanning process is denoted by H.

Since the running median smoothens the data sequence a bit more than appropriate and hence removes interesting patterns, patterns can be recovered from the residuals which in this context are called **rough**. This is achieved by smoothing the rough sequence and adding them back to the smooth sequence. This operation is called **reroughing**.

Velleman and Hoaglin (1984) point out that the smoothing process that performs better in general is **4253H**. That is, here we first begin with running median of 4 that is re-centered by 2. The re-smoothing is then done by 5 followed by 3, and the outliers are removed by *H*. Finally, re-roughing is carried out by smoothing the roughs and then adding them to the smoothed sequence. This full cycle is denoted by 4253H, twice. Unfortunately, we are not aware of any R function or package that implements the 4253H smoother. The options available in the LearnEDA package are 3RSS and 3RSSH.

We have not explained what the smoothers 3RSS and 3RSSH are. The 3R smoothing chops off peaks and valleys and leaves behind mesas and dales two points long. What does this mean? Mesa refers to an area of high land with a flat top and two or more steep cliff-like sides, whereas dale refers to a valley. To overcome this problem, a special splitting is used at each two-point mesa and dale where the data is split into three pieces: a two-point flat segment, the smooth data to the left of the two points, and the smooth sequence to their right.

Now, let y_f-1, y_f refer to the two-point flat segment, and y_f+1, y_f+2, ... refer to the smooth sequence to the left of these two-point flat segments. Then the S technique predicts the value of y_f-1 if it were on the straight line formed by y_f+1 and y_f+2. A simple is to obtain y_f-1 as $3y_f$+1 – $2y_f$+2. The y_f value is obtained as the median of the predicted y_f-1, y_f+1, and y_f+2. After removing all the mesas and dales, we again repeat the 3R cycle. Thus, we have the notation 3RSS and the reader can now easily connect what 3RSSH means. Now, we will obtain the 3RSS for the cow temperature dataset of Velleman and Hoaglin.

Example 4.7.1. Smoothing data for the cow temperature: The temperature of a cow is measured at 6:30 a.m. for 75 consecutive days. We will use the smooth function from the base package and the han function from the LearnEDA package to achieve the required smoothing sequence. We will build the necessary R program in the forthcoming action list.

Time for action – smoothening the cow temperature data

First we use the smooth function from the stats package on the cow temperature dataset. Next, we will use the han function from LearnEDA:

1. Load the cow temperature data in R by data(CT).

2. Plot the time series data using the plot.ts function: plot.ts(CT$Temperatu re,col="red",pch=1).

3. Create a 3RSS object for the cow temperature data using the smooth function and the kind option: CT_3RSS <- smooth(CT$Temperature,kind="3RSS").

4. Han the preceding 3RSS object using the han function from the LearnEDA package: CT_3RSSH <- han(smooth(CT$Temperature,kind="3RSS")).

5. Impose a line of the 3RSS data points with points(1:nrow(CT),CT_3RSS,co l="blue",pch=2,"l").

6. Impose a line of the hanned 3RSS data points with points(1:nrow(CT),CT_ 3RSSH,col="green",pch=3,"l").

7. Add a meaningful legend to the plot: legend(20,90,c("Original","3RSS" ,"3RSSH"),col=c("red","blue","green"),pch="___").

We get a useful smoothened plot of the cow temperature data as follows:

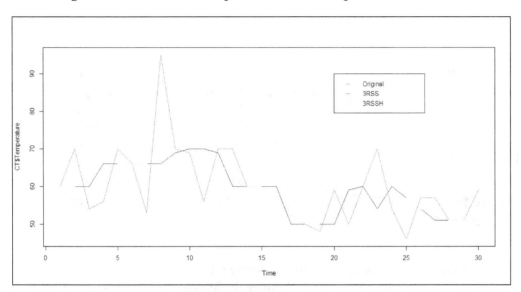

Smoothening cow temperature data

The original plot shows a lot of variation for the cow temperature measurements. The edges of the 3RSS smoother shows many sharp edges in comparison with the 3RSSH smoother, though it is itself a lot smoother than the original display. The plot further indicates that there has been a lot of decrease in the cow temperature measurements from the fifteenth day of observation. This is confirmed by all three displays.

What just happened?

The discussion of the smoothing function looked very promising in the theoretical development. We took a real dataset and saw its time series plot. Then we plotted two versions of the smoothening process and found both to be very smooth over the original plot.

Median polish

In *Example 4.6.1. Resistant line for the IO-CPU time*, we had IO as the only independent variable that explained the variations of the CPU time. In many practical problems, the dependent variable depends on more than one independent variable. In such cases, we need to factor the effect of such independent variables using a single model. When we have two independent variables, median polish helps in building a robust model. A data display in which the rows and columns hold different factors of two variables is called a two-way table. Here, the table entries are values of the independent variables.

An appropriate model for the two-way table is given by:

$$y_{ij} = \alpha + \beta_i + y_j + \varepsilon_{ij}$$

Here, α is the intercept term, β_i denotes the effect of the *i*-th row, y_j the effect of the jth column, and ε_{ij} is the error term. All the parameters are unknown. We need to find the unknown parameters through the EDA approach. The basic idea is to use row-medians and column-medians for obtaining the row- and column-effect, and then find the basic intercept term. Any unexplained part of the data is considered the residual.

Time for action – the median polish algorithm

The median polish algorithm (refer to `http://www-rohan.sdsu.edu/~babailey/stat696/medpolishalg.html`) is given next:

1. Obtain the row medians of the two-way table and upend it to the right-hand side of the data matrix. From each element of every row, subtract the respective row median.

2. Find the median of the row median and record it as the initial grand effect value. Also, subtract the initial grand effect value from each row median.

3. For the original data columns in the previously upended matrix, obtain the column median and append it with the previous matrix at the bottom. As in step 1, subtract from each column element their corresponding column median.

4. For the bottom row of column medians in the previous table, obtain the median, and then add the obtained value to the initial grand effect value. Next, subtract the modified grand effect median value from each of the column medians.

5. Iterate steps 1-4 until the changes in row or column median is insignificant.

We use the `medpolish` function from the `stats` library for the computations involved in median polish. For more details about the model, you can refer to *Chapter 8, Velleman and Hoaglin (1984)*.

Example 4.8.1. Male death rates: The dataset related to the male death rate per 1000 by the cause of death and the average amount of tobacco smoked daily is available on page 221 of Velleman and Hoaglin (1984). Here, the row effect is due to the cause of death, whereas the column constitutes the amount of tobacco smoked (in grams). We are interested in modeling the effect of these two variables on the male death rates in the region:

```
> data(MDR)
> MDR2 <- as.matrix(MDR[,2:5])
>rownames(MDR2) <- c("Lung", "UR","Sto","CaR","Prost","Other_
Lung","Pul_TB","CB","RD_Other", "CT","Other_
Cardio","CH","PU","Viol","Other_Dis")
> MDR_medpol <- medpolish(MDR2)
1 : 8.38
2 : 8.17
Final: 8.1625
>MDR_medpol$row
         Lung          UR        StoCaR        Prost    Other_
LungPul_TB          CB       RD_Other           CT Other_Cardio
      0.1200     -0.4500      -0.2800      -0.0125      -0.3050
0.2050        -0.3900        -0.2050        0.0000       4.0750
1.6875
          CH          PU         Viol     Other_Dis
      1.4725     -0.4325       0.0950        0.9650
>MDR_medpol$col
     G0     G14     G24     G25
-0.0950  0.0075 -0.0050  0.1350
>MDR_medpol$overall
[1] 0.545
>MDR_medpol$residuals
                 G0      G14         G24      G25
Lung         -0.5000  -0.2025  2.000000e-01   0.8600
UR            0.0000   0.0275  0.000000e+00  -0.0200
Sto           0.2400   0.0875 -1.600000e-01  -0.0900
CaR           0.0025   0.0000 -1.575000e-01   0.0725
Prost         0.4050   0.0125 -1.500000e-02  -0.0350
Other_Lung   -0.0150  -0.0375  1.500000e-02   0.1350
Pul_TB       -0.0600  -0.0025  3.000000e-02   0.0000
CB           -0.1250  -0.0575  5.500000e-02   0.2450
RD_Other      0.2400  -0.0025  1.387779e-17  -0.2800
CT           -0.3050   0.0125 -1.500000e-02   1.2350
Other_Cardio  0.0925  -0.0900  2.425000e-01  -0.1175
CH            0.0875  -0.0850 -1.525000e-01   0.1775
PU           -0.0175   0.0200  5.250000e-02  -0.0275
Viol         -0.1250   0.1725 -1.850000e-01   0.1250
Other_Dis     0.0350   0.2925 -3.500000e-02  -0.0750
```

What just happened?

The output associated with MDR_medpol$row gives the row effect, while MDR_medpol$col gives the column effect. The negative value of **-0.0950** for the non-consumers of tobacco shows that the male death rate is lesser for this group, whereas the positive values of **0.0075** and **0.1350** for the group under 14 grams and above 25 grams respectively is an indication that tobacco consumers are more prone to death.

Have a go hero

For the variables G0 and G25 in the MDR2 matrix object, obtain a back-to-back stem-leaf display.

Summary

Median and its variants form the core measures of EDA and you would have got a hang of it by the first section. The visualization techniques of EDA also compose more than just the stem-and-leaf plot, letter values, and bagplot. As EDA is basically about your attitude and approach, it is important to realize that you can (and should) use any method that is instinctive and appropriate for the data on hand. We have also built our first regression model in the resistant line and seen how robust it is to the outliers. Smoothing data and median polish are also advanced EDA techniques that the reader is acquainted with from their respective sections.

EDA is exploratory in nature and its findings may need further statistical validations. The next chapter on statistical inference addresses what Tukey calls, confirmatory analysis. Especially, we look at techniques that give good point estimates of the unknown parameters. This is then backed with further techniques such as goodness-of-fit and confidence intervals for the probability distribution and the parameters respectively. Post the estimation method it is a requirement to verify whether the parameters meet certain specified levels. This problem is addressed through hypotheses testing in the next chapter.

5
Statistical Inference

In the previous chapter, we came across numerous tools that gave first insights of exploratory evidence into the distribution of datasets through visual techniques as well as quantitative methods. The next step is the translation of these exploratory results to confirmatory ones and the topics of the current chapter pursue this goal. In the *Discrete distributions* and *Continuous distributions* sections of *Chapter 1, Data Characteristics*, we came across many important families of probability distribution. In practical scenarios, we have data on hand and the goal is to infer about the unknown parameters of the probability distributions.

This chapter focuses on one method of inference for the parameters using the **maximum likelihood estimator (MLE)**. Another way of approaching this problem is by fitting a probability distribution for the data. The MLE is a point estimate of the unknown parameter that needs to be supplemented with a range of possible values. This is achieved through confidence intervals. Finally, the chapter concludes with the important topic of hypothesis testing. The reader will learn the following things after being through this chapter:

- Visualizing the likelihood function and identifying the MLE
- Fitting the most plausible statistical distribution for a dataset
- Confidence intervals for the estimated parameters
- Hypothesis testing of the parameters of a statistical distribution

Using exploratory techniques, we had our first exposition with the understanding of a dataset. As an example in the octane dataset we found that the median of Method_2 was larger than that of Method_1. As explained in the previous chapter, we need to confirm whatever exploratory findings we had with a dataset. Recall that the histograms and stem-and-leaf displays suggest a normal distribution. A question that arises then is how do we assert the center values, typically the mean, of a normal distribution and how do we conclude that the average of the Method_2 procedure exceeds that of Method_1. The former question is answered by estimation techniques and the latter with testing hypotheses. A middle path is setting up confidence intervals. This forms the core of statistical inference. Most of the analysis is performed using both the software, R as well as Python. Finding MLEs and fitting distribution are the two tasks that are left out in Python.

Packages and settings – R and Python

We set up the paths and packages to start with. The Python session is available as a Chapter_05_Statistical_Inference.ipynb file in the Output folder, Python/Chapter_05, of the code bundle. The user will try to reproduce the programs using C05.R and Chapter_05.py files:

1. First set the working directory:

    ```
    setwd("MyPath/R/Chapter_05")
    ```

2. We need PASWR and PairedData packages and hence we load them now:

    ```
    > library(RSADBE)
    > library(stats4)
    > library(PASWR)
    > library(PairedData)
    > setwd("MyPath/R/Chapter05")
    ```

3. The required packages and path in Python is set up as follows:

    ```
    In [2]:  import os
             os.chdir("MyPath/Python/Chapter_05")
             import pandas as pd
             import matplotlib.pyplot as plt
             import numpy as np
             from scipy.stats import binom,poisson,norm,t
             import scipy.stats as st
    ```

The required setup is complete and we now are all set for the action.

Maximum likelihood estimator

Let us consider the discrete probability distributions as seen in the *Discrete distributions* section of *Chapter 1, Data Characteristics*. We saw that a binomial distribution is characterized by the parameters in n and p, the poisson distribution by λ, and so on. Here, the parameters completely determine the probabilities of the x values. However, when the parameters are unknown, which is the case in almost all practical problems, we collect data for the random experiment and try to infer about the parameters. This is essentially *inductive reasoning* and the subject of statistics is essentially inductive driven as opposed to the deductive reasoning of mathematics. This forms the core difference between the two beautiful subjects. Assume that we have n observations $X_1, X_2,..., X_n$ from an unknown probability distribution $f(x,\theta)$, where θ may be a scalar or a vector whose values are not known. Let us consider a few important definitions that form the core of statistical inference.

Random sample: If the observations $X_1, X_2,..., X_n$ are independent of each other, we say that it forms a random sample from $f(x,\theta)$. A technical consequence of the observations forming a random sample is that their joint probability density (mass) function can be written as a product of the individual density (mass) function. If the unknown parameter θ is the same for all the n observations we say that we have an **independent and identical distributed (iid)** sample.

Let X denote the score of Rahul Dravid in a century innings, and let Xi denote the runs scored in the ith century, $i = 1, 2, ..., 36$. The assumption of independence is then appropriate for all the values of X_i. Consider the problem of the R software installation on 10 different computers of the same configuration. Let X denote the time it takes for the software to install the software. Here, again, it may be easily seen that the installation time on the 10 machines, $X_1, ..., X_{10}$, are identical (same configuration of the computers) and independent. We will use the vector notation here to represent a sample of size n, $X = (X_1, X_2,..., X_n)$ for the random variables, and denote the realized values of random variable with the small case $x = (x_1, x_2,..., x_n)$ with x_i representing the realized value of random variable X_i. All the required tools are now ready, which enable us to define the likelihood function.

Likelihood function: Let $f(x,\theta)$ be the joint **probability mass function (pmf)** (or **probability distribution function** also known as pdf) for an iid sample of n observations of X. Here, the pmf and pdf respectively correspond to the discrete and continuous random variables. The likelihood function is then defined by:

$$L(\theta\,|\,x) = f(x\,|\,\theta) = \Pi_{i=1}^n f(x\,|\,\theta)$$

Of course, the reader may be amused about the difference between a likelihood function and a pmf (or pdf). The pmf is to be seen as a function of x given that the parameters are known, whereas in the likelihood function we look at a function where the parameters are unknown with x being known.

This distinction is vital as we are looking for a tool where we do not know the parameters. The likelihood function may be interpreted as the probability function of θ conditioned on the value of x and this is the main reason for identifying that value of θ, say $\hat{\theta}$, which leads to the maximum of $L(\theta|x)$, that is, $L(\hat{\theta}|x) \geq L(\theta|x)$. Let us visualize the likelihood function for some important families of probability distribution. The importance of visualizing the `likelihood` function is emphasized in *Chapter 7* of Tattar, et. al. (2013) and *Chapters 1-4* of Pawitan (2001).

Visualizing the likelihood function

We had seen a few plots of the pmf/pdf in the *Discrete distributions* and *Continuous distributions* sections of *Chapter 1, Data Characteristics*. Recall that we were plotting the pmf/pdf over the range of x. In those examples, we had assumed certain values for the parameters of the distributions. For the problems of statistical inference, we typically do not know the parameter values. Thus, the likelihood functions are plotted against the plausible parameter values θ. What does this mean? For example, the pmf for a binomial distribution is plotted for x values ranging from 0 to n. However, the `likelihood` function needs to be plotted against p values ranging over the unit interval [0, 1].

Example 5.1.1. The likelihood function of a binomial distribution: A box of electronic chips is known to contain a certain number of defective chips. Suppose we take a random sample of n chips from the box and make a note of the number of non-defective chips. The probability of a non-defective chip is p, and that being defective is $1-p$. Let X be a random variable, which takes value 1 if the chip is non-defective and 0 if it is defective. Then $X \sim b(1,p)$, where p is not known. Define $t_x = \sum_{i=1}^{n} x_i$. Then the `likelihood` function is given by:

$$L(p\,|\,t_x,n) = \binom{n}{t_x} p^{t_x} (1-p)^{n-t_x}$$

Suppose that the observed value of x is 7, that is, we have 7 successes out of 10 trials. Now, the purpose of the `likelihood` inference is to understand the probability distribution of p given the data t_x. This gives us an idea about the most plausible of p and hence it is worthwhile to visualize the `likelihood` function $L(p\,|\,t_x,n)$.

Example 5.1.2. The likelihood function of a poisson distribution: The number of accidents at a particular traffic signal of a city, the number of flight arrivals during a specific time interval at an airport, and so on are some of the scenarios where assumption of a poisson distribution is appropriate to explain the numbers. Now, let us consider a sample from poisson distribution. Suppose that the number of flight arrivals at an airport during the duration of an hour follows a poisson distribution with an unknown rate λ. Suppose that we have the number of arrivals over 10 distinct hours as 1, 2, 2, 1, 0, 2, 3, 1, 2, and 4. Using this data, we need to infer about λ. Towards this we will first plot the likelihood function. The likelihood function for a random sample of size n is given by:

$$L(\lambda \mid x) = \frac{e^{-n\lambda} \lambda^{\sum_{i=1}^{n} x_i}}{\Pi_{i=1}^{n} x_i!}$$

Before we consider an R program for visualizing the `likelihood` function for the samples from binomial and poisson distribution, let us look at the `likelihood` function for a sample from the normal distribution.

Example 5.1.3. The likelihood function of a normal distribution: The `CPU_Time` variable from `IO_Time` may be assumed to follow a normal distribution. For this problem, we will simulate $n = 25$ observations from a normal distribution, for more details about the simulation, refer to the next chapter. Though we simulate the n observations with mean as 10 and standard deviation as 2, we will pretend that we do not actually know the mean value with the assumption that the standard deviation is known to be 2. The likelihood function for a sample from normal distribution with known standard deviation is given by:

$$L(\mu \mid x, \sigma) = \frac{1}{\left(\sqrt{2\pi}\sigma\right)^n} e^{-\frac{1}{2\sigma^2} \sum_{i=1}^{n} (x_i - \mu)^2}$$

In our particular example, it is:

$$L(\mu \mid x, 2) = \frac{1}{\left(2\sqrt{2\pi}\right)^n} exp\left\{ -\frac{1}{2^3} \sum_{i=1}^{n} (x_i - \mu)^2 \right\}$$

It is time for action!

Time for action – visualizing the likelihood function

We will now visualize the `likelihood` function for the binomial, poisson, and normal distributions discussed before:

1. Initialize the graphics windows for the three samples using:
    `par(mfrow= c(1,3))`.

2. Declare the number of trials n and the number of success x by:
    `n <- 10; x <- 7`.

3. Set the sequence of p values with `p_seq <- seq(0,1,0.01)`.

    For `p_seq`, obtain the probabilities for $n = 10$ and $x = 7$ by using the `dbinom` function: `dbinom(x=7,size=n,prob=p_seq)`.

4. Next, obtain the `likelihood` function plot by running `plot(p_seq, dbinom( x=7,size=n,prob=p_seq), xlab="p", ylab="Binomial Likelihood Function", "l")`.

5. Enter the data for the poisson random sample into R using `x <- c(1,2,2,1, 0,2,3,1,2,4)` and the number of observations by `n <- length(x)`.

6. Declare the sequence of possible λ values through `lambda_seq <- seq(0,5,0.1)`.

7. Plot the `likelihood` function for the poisson distribution with `plot( lambda_seq, dpois(x=sum(x),lambda=n*lambda_seq)…)`.

We are generating random observations from a normal distribution using the `rnorm` function. Each run of the `rnorm` function results in different values and hence to ensure that you are able to reproduce the exact output as produced here, we will set the initial seed for random generation tool with `set.seed(123)`:

1. For generation of random numbers, fix the seed value with `set.seed(123)`. This is to simply ensure that we obtain the same result.

2. Simulate 25 observations from the normal distribution with mean 10 and standard deviation 2 using `n<-25; xn <- rnorm(n,mean=10,sd=2)`.

3. Consider the following range of μ values `mu_seq <- seq(9,11,0.05)`.

4. Plot the normal `likelihood` function with `plot(mu_seq,dnorm(x= mean(xn), mean=mu_seq,sd=2) )`.

The detailed code for the preceding action is now provided:

```
# Time for Action: Visualizing the Likelihood Function
par(mfrow=c(1,3))
# # Visualizing the Likelihood Function of a Binomial Distribution.
```

```
n <- 10; x <- 7
p_seq <- seq(0,1,0.01)
plot(p_seq, dbinom(x=7,size=n,prob=p_seq), xlab="p", ylab="Binomial
Likelihood Function", "l")
# Visualizing the Likelihood Function of a Poisson Distribution.
x <- c(1, 2, 2, 1, 0, 2, 3, 1, 2, 4); n = length(x)
lambda_seq <- seq(0,5,0.1)
plot(lambda_seq,dpois(x=sum(x),lambda=n*lambda_seq),
xlab=expression(lambda),ylab="Poisson Likelihood Function", "l")
# Visualizing the Likelihood Function of a Normal Distribution.
set.seed(123)
n <- 25; xn <- rnorm(n,mean=10,sd=2)
mu_seq <- seq(9,11,0.05)
plot(mu_seq,dnorm(x=mean(xn),mean=mu_seq,sd=2),"l",
xlab=expression(mu),ylab="Normal Likelihood Function")
```

Run the preceding code in your R session.

You will find an identical copy of the next plot on your computer screen too. What does the plot tells us? The likelihood function for the binomial distribution has very small values up to 0.4, and then it gradually peaks up to 0.7 and then declines sharply. This means that the values in the neighborhood of 0.7 are more likely to be the true value of p than the points away from it.

Similarly, the `likelihood` function plot for the poisson distribution says that λ values less than 1 and greater than 3 are very unlikely to be the true value of the actual λ. The peak of the likelihood function appears at a value a little less than 2. The interpretation for the normal likelihood function is left as an exercise for the reader.

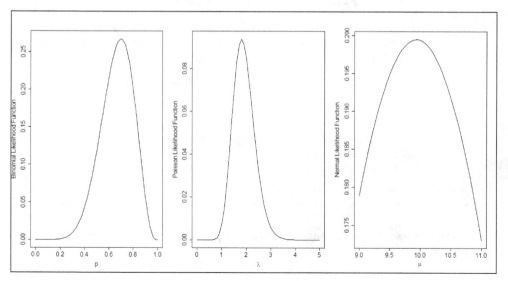

Some likelihood functions

What just happened?

We took our first step in the problem of estimation of parameters. Visualization of the `likelihood` function is a very important aspect and is often overlooked in many introductory textbooks. Moreover, and as it is natural, we did it in R!

Doing it in Python

The main functions we need related to the probability distributions, density, as well as `mass` functions are available in the `scipy.stats` package. The `likelihood` functions are then calculated for the plausible range of the parameter values. The graphics options of `xlabel`, `title`, and `subplot` are used to enhance the visualization experience:

1. Using the `binom.pmf` function from the `scipy.stats` package, we calculate the value of the `likelihood` function over a range of plausible p values and given x. The `subplot` function is invoked for creating multiple graphs in a single window:

```
In [4]:  n = 10; x = 7
         p_seq = np.arange(0,1.01,0.01)
         lik_p = binom.pmf(x,n,p_seq)
         plt.subplot(1,3,1)
         plt.plot(p_seq,lik_p)
         plt.xlabel("p")
         plt.title("Binomial Likelihood Function")

Out[4]:  <matplotlib.text.Text at 0xa8e04e0>
```

2. We use the `poisson.pmf` function to compute and visualize the `poisson` `likelihood` function:

```
In [6]:  xp = [1,2,2,1,0,2,3,1,2,4]
         lam_seq = np.arange(0,5.1,0.1)
         plt.subplot(1,3,2)
         plt.plot(lam_seq,poisson.pmf(sum(xp),len(xp)*lam_seq))
         plt.xlabel('$\lambda$')
         plt.title("Poisson Likelihood Function")

Out[6]:  <matplotlib.text.Text at 0xa958588>
```

Note the use of mathematical symbol in the LaTeX style in the `plt.xlabel` line.

3. For the normal `likelihood` function, we first simulate n = 25 observations from the normal distribution using the `random.normal` function and pretend as if we don't know the parameters and sketch the `likelihood` function in the usual way.

```
In [8]:  n = 25
         nx = np.random.normal(10,2,n)
         mu_seq = np.arange(8,12.05,0.05)
         plt.subplot(1,3,3)
         plt.plot(mu_seq,norm.pdf(np.mean(nx),mu_seq,2))
         plt.xlabel('$\mu$')
         plt.title("Normal Likelihood Function")
         plt.show()
```

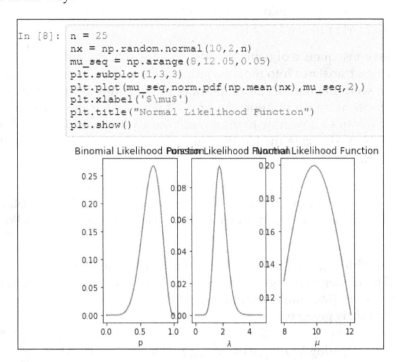

Finding the maximum likelihood estimator

The `likelihood` function plot indicates the plausibility of the data generating mechanism for different values of the parameters. Naturally, the value of the parameter for which the `likelihood` function has highest value is the most likely value of the parameter. This forms the crux of maximum likelihood estimation.

The value of θ that leads to the maximum value of the `likelihood` function $L(\theta|x)$ is referred to as the maximum likelihood estimate, abbreviated as MLE.

For the reader familiar with numerical optimization, it is not a surprise that calculus is useful for finding the optimum value of a function. However, we will not indulge in mathematics more than what is required here. We will note some finer aspects of numerical optimization.

For an independent sample of size n, the likelihood function is a product of n functions and it is very likely that we may very soon end up in the mathematical world of intractable functions. To a large extent, we can circumvent this problem by resorting to the logarithm of the function, which then transforms the problem of optimizing the product of functions to sum of functions. That is, we will focus on optimizing $\log L(\theta|x)$ instead of $L(\theta|x)$.

An important consequence of using the logarithm is that the maximization of a product function translates into that of a sum function since $log(ab) = log(a) + log(b)$. It may also be seen that the maximum point of the likelihood function is preserved under the logarithm transformation since for $a > b$, $log(a) > log(b)$. Furthermore, many numerical techniques know how to minimize a function rather than maximize it. Thus, instead of maximizing the log-likelihood function $\log L(\theta|x)$, we will minimize $-\log L(\theta|x)$ in R.

In the R package `stats4` we are provided a `mle` function, which returns the MLE. There are a host of probability distributions for which it is possible to obtain the MLE. We will continue the illustrations for the examples considered earlier in the chapter.

Example 5.1.4. Finding the MLE of a binomial distribution (continuation of *Example 5.1.1*): The negative log-likelihood function of binomial distribution, sans the constant values, (the combinatorial term is excluded since its value is independent of p), is given by:

$$-\log L\left(p\,|\,t_x, n\right) = -t_x \log p - \left(n - t_x\right)\log\left(1 - p\right)$$

The maximum likelihood estimator of p, differentiating the preceding equation with respect to p and equating the result to zero and then solving for the equation, is given by the sample proportion:

$$\hat{p} = \frac{t_x}{n}$$

An estimator of a parameter is denoted by accentuation the parameter with a hat. Though this is very easy to compute, we will resort to the useful function `mle`.

Example 5.1.5. MLE of a poisson distribution (continuation of *Example 5.1.2*): The negative `log-likelihood` function is given by:

$$-\log L\left(\lambda \mid x\right) = n\lambda - \sum_{i=1}^{n} x_i \log \lambda$$

The MLE for λ admits a closed form, which can be obtained from calculus arguments, and it is given by:

$$\hat{\lambda} = \frac{\sum_{i=1}^{n} x_i}{n}$$

To obtain the MLE, we need to write exclusive code for the negative log-likelihood function. For the normal distribution, we will use the `mle` function. There is another method of finding the MLE other than the `mle` function available in the `stats4` package. We will consider it next. The R codes will be given in the forthcoming action.

Using the fitdistr function

In the previous examples, we needed to explicitly specify the negative log-likelihood function. The `fitdistr` function from the `MASS` package can be used to obtain the unknown parameters of a probability distribution, for a list of the probability functions for which it applies see `?fitdistr`, and the fact that it uses the maximum likelihood fitting complements our approach in this section.

Example 5.1.6. MLEs for poisson and normal distributions: In the next section, we will use the `fitdistr` function from the `MASS` package for obtaining the MLEs in the *Example 5.1.2* and *Example 5.1.3* sections. In fact, using the function, we get the answers readily without the need to specify the negative log-likelihood explicitly.

Time for action – finding the MLE using mle and fitdistr functions

The `mle` function from the `stats4` package will be used for obtaining the MLE from popular distributions such as binomial, normal, and so on. The `fitdistr` function will be used too, which fits the distributions using the MLEs:

1. Load the library package `stats4` with `library(stats4)`.
2. Specify the number of success in a vector format and the number of observations with `x<-rep(c(0,1),c(3,7)); n <- length(x)`.

3. Define the negative `log-likelihood` function with a function:

```
binomial_nll <- function(prob) -sum(dbinom(x,size=1,prob,log=TRUE))
```

The code works as follows. The `dbinom` function is invoked from the `stats` package and the option `log=TRUE` is exercised to indicate that we need log of the probability (actually likelihood) values. The `dbinom` function returns a vector of probabilities for all the values of x. The sum, multiplied by -1, now returns us the value of negative `log-likelihood`.

4. Now, enter `fit_binom <- mle(binomial_nll,start=list(prob=0.5),nobs=n)` on the R console. Now, `mle` as a function optimizes the `binomial_nll` function defined in the previous step. Initial values, a guess or a legitimate value, are specified for the `start` option, and we also declare the number of observations available for this problem.

5. `summary(fit_binom)` will give details of the `mle` function applied on `binomial_nll`. The output is displayed in the following diagram.

6. Specify the data for the poisson distribution problem in `x <- c(1,2,2,1,0, 2,3,1,2,4); n <- length(x)`.

7. Define the negative `log-likelihood` function on parallel lines of binomial distribution:

```
pois_nll <- function(lambda) -sum(dpois(x,lambda,log=TRUE))
```

8. Explore different options of the `mle` function by specifying the method, a guess of the least and most values of the parameter, and the initial value as the median of the observations:

```
fit_poisson <- mle(pois_nll,start=list(lambda=median(x)),nobs=n,
method = "Brent", lower = 0, upper = 10)
```

9. Get the answer by entering `summary(fit_poisson)`.

10. Define the negative `log-likelihood` function for the normal distribution by:

```
normal_nll <- function(mean) -sum(dnorm(xn,mean,sd=2,log=TRUE))
```

11. Find the MLE of the normal distribution with `fit_normal <- mle(normal_nll,start=list(mean=8),nobs=n)`.

12. Get the final answer with `summary(fit_normal)`.

13. Load the MASS package: `library(MASS)`.

14. Fit the *x* vector with a poisson distribution by running:

```
fitdistr( x,"poisson") in R.
```

15. Fit the *xn* vector with a normal distribution by running:
    `fitdistr(xn,"normal")`.

```
> library(stats4)
> x <- rep(c(0,1),c(3,7)); n <- NROW(x)
> binomial_nll <- function(prob)-sum(dbinom(x,size=1,prob,log=TRUE))
> fit_binom <- mle(binomial_nll,start=list(prob=0.5),nobs=n)
> summary(fit_binom)
Maximum likelihood estimation
Call:
mle(minuslogl = binomial_nll, start = list(prob = 0.5), nobs = n)
Coefficients:
     Estimate Std. Error
prob      0.7     0.1449
-2 log L: 12.22
> x <- c(1, 2, 2, 1, 0, 2, 3, 1, 2, 4); n = length(x)
> pois_nll <- function(lambda) -sum(dpois(x,lambda,log=TRUE))
> fit_poisson <- mle(pois_nll,start=list(lambda=median(x)),nobs=n,
+ method = "Brent", lower = 0, upper = 10)
> summary(fit_poisson)
Maximum likelihood estimation
Call:
mle(minuslogl = pois_nll, start = list(lambda = median(x)), method = "Brent",
    nobs = n, lower = 0, upper = 10)
Coefficients:
      Estimate Std. Error
[1,]       1.8     0.4243
-2 log L: 30.32
> n <- length(xn)
> normal_nll <- function(mean) -sum(dnorm(xn,mean,sd=2,log=TRUE))
> fit_normal <- mle(normal_nll,start=list(mean=8),nobs=n)
> summary(fit_normal)
Maximum likelihood estimation
Call:
mle(minuslogl = normal_nll, start = list(mean = 8), nobs = n)
Coefficients:
      Estimate Std. Error
mean     9.933        0.4
-2 log L: 102.1
```

Finding the MLE and related summaries

What just happened?

You have explored the possibility of finding the MLEs for many standard distributions using `mle` from the `stats4` package and `fitdistr` from the `MASS` package. The main key in obtaining the MLE is the right construction of the `log-likelihood` function.

Confidence intervals

The MLE is a point estimate and as such, on its own, it is almost of no practical use. It would be more appropriate to give coverage of parameter points, which is most likely to contain the true unknown parameter. A general practice is to specify the coverage of the points through an interval and then consider specific intervals that have a specified probability. A formal definition is in order.

A confidence interval for a population parameter is an interval that is predicted to contain the parameter with a certain probability.

The common choice is to obtain either 95 percent or 99 percent confidence intervals. It is common to specify the coverage of the confidence through a significance level α, more about this in the next section, which is a small number closer to 0. The 95 percent and 99 percent confidence intervals then correspond to $100(1-\alpha)$ percent intervals with respective α equal to 0.05 and 0.01. In general, a $100(1-\alpha)$ percent confidence interval says that if the experiment is performed many times over, we expect the result to fall in the confidence interval $100(1-\alpha)$ percent times.

Example 5.2.1. Confidence interval for binomial proportion: Consider n Bernoulli trials $X_1,...,X_n$ with the probability of success being p. We saw earlier that the MLE of p is:

$$\hat{p} = \frac{t_x}{n}$$

where $t_x = \sum_{i=1}^{n} x_i$. Theoretically, the expected value of $\hat{p}$ is p and its standard deviation is $\sqrt{p(1-p)/n}$. An estimate of the standard deviation is $\sqrt{\hat{p}(1-\hat{p})/n}$. For large n and when both np and $np(1-p)$ are greater than 5, using a normal approximation, by virtue of the central limit theorem, a $100(1-\alpha)$ percent confidence interval for p is given by:

$$\left(\hat{p} - z_{\alpha/2}\sqrt{\frac{\hat{p}(1-\hat{p})}{n}}, \hat{p} + z_{\alpha/2}\sqrt{\frac{\hat{p}(1-\hat{p})}{n}} \right)$$

where $Z_{\alpha/2}$ is the $\alpha/2$ quantile of the standard normal distribution. The confidence intervals obtained by using the normal approximation are not reliable when the p value is near 0 or 1. Thus, if the lower confidence limit follows below 0, or the upper confidence limit exceeds, we will adapt the convention of taking them as 0 and 1, respectively.

Example 5.2.2. Confidence interval for normal mean with known variance:
Consider a random sample of size n from a normal distribution with unknown mean μ and known standard deviation σ. It may be shown that the MLE of mean μ is the sample mean $\bar{X} = \sum_{i=1}^{n} X_i / n$ and that the distribution of $\bar{X}$ is again normal with mean μ and standard deviation $\sigma / \sqrt{n}$. Then, the $100(1-\alpha)$ percent confidence interval is given by:

$$\left(\bar{X} - z_{\alpha/2} \frac{\sigma}{\sqrt{n}}, \bar{X} + z_{\alpha/2} \frac{\sigma}{\sqrt{n}} \right)$$

where $Z_{\alpha/2}$ is the $\alpha/2$ quantile of the standard normal distribution. The width of the preceding confidence interval is $2z_{\alpha/2} \, \sigma / \sqrt{n}$. Thus, when the sample size is increased by four times, the width will decrease by half.

xample 5.2.3. Confidence interval for normal mean with unknown variance: We continue with a sample of size n. When the variance is not known, the steps become very different. Since the variance is not known, we replace it by the sample variance:

$$S^2 = \frac{1}{n-1} \sum_{i=1}^{n} \left(X_i - \bar{X} \right)^2$$

The denominator is n - 1 since we have already estimated μ using the n observations. To develop the confidence interval for μ, consider the following statistic:

$$T = \frac{\bar{X} - \mu}{\sqrt{S^2 / n}}$$

This new statistic T has a *t-distribution* with n - 1 *degrees of freedom*. The $100(1-\alpha)$ percent confidence interval for μ is then given by the following interval:

$$\left(\bar{X} - t_{n-1,\alpha/2} \frac{S}{\sqrt{n}}, \bar{X} + t_{n-1,\alpha/2} \frac{S}{\sqrt{n}} \right)$$

where $t_{n-1,\alpha/2}$ is the $\alpha/2$ quantile of a t random variable with $n-1$ degrees of freedom.

We will create functions for obtaining the confidence intervals for the preceding three examples. Many statistical tests in R return confidence intervals at desired levels. However, we will be encountering these tests in the last section of this chapter, and hence up to that point we will contain ourselves to defined functions and applications.

Time for action – confidence intervals

We will create functions that will enable us to obtain confidence intervals of desired size:

1. Create a function for obtaining the confidence intervals of the proportion from a binomial distribution with the following function:

    ```
    binom_CI = function(x, n, alpha)   {
      phat = x/n
      ll=phat-qnorm(alpha/2,lower.tail=FALSE)*sqrt(phat*(1-phat)/n)
      ul=phat+qnorm(alpha/2,lower.tail=FALSE)*sqrt(phat*(1-phat)/n)
      return(paste("The ", 100*(1-alpha),"% Confidence Interval for
    Binomial Proportion is (", round(ll,4),",", round(ul,4),")",
    sep=''))
                  }
    ```

    The arguments of the functions are x, n, and alpha. That is, the user of the function needs to specify the x number of success out of the n Bernoulli trials, and the significance level α. First, we obtain the MLE $\hat{p}$ of the proportion p by calculating phat = x/n. To obtain the value of $Z_{\alpha/2}$, we use the qnorm quantile function qnorm(alpha/2,lower.tail= FALSE). The quantity $\sqrt{\hat{p}(1-\hat{p})/n}$ is computed with sqrt(phat*(1-phat)/n). The rest of the code for ll and ul is self-explanatory. We use the paste function to get the output in a convenient format along with the return function.

2. Consider the data in *Example 5.2.1* where we have $x = 7$, and $n = 10$. Suppose that we require 95 percent and 99 percent confidence intervals. The respective α values for these confidence intervals are 0.05 and 0.01. Let us execute the binom_CI function on this data. That is, we need to run binom_CI(x=7,n=10,alpha =0.05) and binom_CI(x=7,n=10,alpha=0.01) at the R console. The output will be as shown in the next screenshot.

    Thus, (0.416, 0.984) is the 95 percent confidence interval for p and (0.3267, 1.0733) is the 99 percent confidence interval for it. Since the upper confidence limit exceeds 1, we will use (0.3267, 1) as the 99 percent confidence interval for p.

3. We first give the function for construction of confidence intervals for the mean μ of a normal distribution when the standard deviation is known:

```
normal_CI_ksd = function(x,sigma,alpha)   {
  xbar = mean(x)
  n = length(x)
  ll = xbar-qnorm(alpha/2,lower.tail=FALSE)*sigma/sqrt(n)
  ul = xbar+qnorm(alpha/2,lower.tail=FALSE)*sigma/sqrt(n)
  return(paste("The ", 100*(1-alpha),"% Confidence Interval for
the Normal mean is (", round(ll,4),",",round(ul,4),")",sep=''))
      }
```

The function `normal_CI_ksd` works differently from the earlier binomial one. Here, we provide the entire data to the function and specify the known value of standard deviation and the significance level. First, we obtain the MLE $\overline{X}$ of the mean μ with `xbar = mean(x)`. The R code `qnorm(alpha/2,lower.tail=FALSE)` is used to obtain $Z_{\alpha/2}$. Next, $\sigma/\sqrt{n}$ is computed by `sigma/sqrt(n)`. The code for `ll` and `ul` is straightforward to comprehend. The `return` and `paste` have the same purpose as in the previous example. Compile the code for the `normal_CI_ksd` function.

4. Let us see a few examples, a continuation of *Example 5.1.3*, for obtaining the confidence interval for the mean of a normal distribution with the standard deviation known. To obtain the 95 percent and 99 percent confidence interval for the `xn` data, where the standard deviation was known to be 2, run `normal_CI_ksd(x=xn,sigma=2,alpha=0.05)` and `normal_CI_ksd(x=xn,sigma=2,alpha=0.01)` at the R console. The output is consolidated in the next screenshot.

Thus, the 95 percent confidence interval for μ is (`9.1494, 10.7173`) and the 99 percent confidence interval is (`8.903, 10.9637`).

5. Create a function `normal_CI_uksd` for obtaining the confidence intervals for μ of a normal distribution when the standard deviation is unknown:

```
normal_CI_uksd = function(x,alpha)   {
  xbar = mean(x); s = sd(x)
  n = length(x)
  ll = xbar-qt(alpha/2,n-1,lower.tail=FALSE)*s/sqrt(n)
  ul = xbar+qt(alpha/2,n-1,lower.tail=FALSE)*s/sqrt(n)
  return(paste("The ", 100*(1-alpha),"% Confidence Interval for
the Normal mean is (", round(ll,4),",",round(ul,4),")",sep=''))
      }
```

We have an additional computation here in comparison with the earlier function. Since the standard deviation is unknown, we estimate it with `s = sd(x)`. Furthermore, we need to obtain the quantile from *t*-distribution with `n-1` degrees of freedom, and hence we have `qt(alpha/2,n-1,lower.tail=FALSE)` for the computation of $t_{n-1,\alpha/2}$. The rest of the details follow the previous function.

6. Let us obtain confidence intervals, 95 percent and 99 percent, for the vector `xn` under the assumption that the variance is not known. The codes for achieving the results are given in `normal_CI_uksd(x=xn,alpha=0.05)` and `normal_CI_uksd(x=xn,alpha=0.01)`.

Thus, the 95 percent confidence interval for the mean is (9.1518, 10.7419) and the 99 percent confidence interval is (8.8742, 10.9925).

```
> binom_CI <- function(x, n, alpha){
+ phat = x/n
+ ll = phat - qnorm(alpha/2,lower.tail=FALSE)*sqrt(phat*(1-phat)/n)
+ ul = phat + qnorm(alpha/2,lower.tail=FALSE)*sqrt(phat*(1-phat)/n)
+ return(paste("The ", 100*(1-alpha),"% Confidence Interval for Binomial
+ Proportion is (", round(ll,4),",",round(ul,4),")",sep='')) }
> binom_CI(x=7,n=10,alpha=0.01)
[1] "The 99% Confidence Interval for Binomial Proportion is (0.3267,1.0733)"
> normal_CI_ksd <- function(x,sigma,alpha){
+ xbar = mean(x)
+ n = length(x)
+ ll = xbar-qnorm(alpha/2,lower.tail=FALSE)*sigma/sqrt(n)
+ ul = xbar+qnorm(alpha/2,lower.tail=FALSE)*sigma/sqrt(n)
+ return(paste("The ", 100*(1-alpha),"% Confidence Interval for the
+ Normal mean is (", round(ll,4),",",round(ul,4),")",sep='')} }
> normal_CI_ksd(x=xn,sigma=2,alpha=0.05)
[1] "The 95% Confidence Interval for the Normal mean is (9.1494,10.7173)"
> normal_CI_ksd(x=xn,sigma=2,alpha=0.01)
[1] "The 99% Confidence Interval for the Normal mean is (8.903,10.9637)"
> normal_CI_uksd <- function(x,alpha){
+ xbar = mean(x); s = sd(x)
+ n = length(x)
+ ll = xbar-qt(alpha/2,n-1,lower.tail=FALSE)*s/sqrt(n)
+ ul = xbar+qt(alpha/2,n-1,lower.tail=FALSE)*s/sqrt(n)
+ return(paste("The ", 100*(1-alpha),"% Confidence Interval for the
+ Normal mean is (", round(ll,4),",",round(ul,4),")",sep=''))}
> normal_CI_uksd(x=xn,alpha=0.05)
[1] "The 95% Confidence Interval for the Normal mean is (9.1518,10.7149)"
> normal_CI_uksd(x=xn,alpha=0.01)
[1] "The 99% Confidence Interval for the Normal mean is (8.8742,10.9925)"
```

Confidence intervals: Some raw programs

What just happened?

We created special functions for obtaining the confidence intervals and executed them for three different cases. However, our framework is quite generic in nature and with a bit of care and caution, it may be easily extended to other distributions too.

Doing it in Python

We now define three new functions in Python `binom_CI`, `normal_CI_ksd`, and `normal_CI_uksd`, and then use them to obtain the confidence intervals of desired level:

1. The `def` function of Python is handy to set up new functions. Here, `binom_CI` takes `x`, `n`, and `alpha` as three arguments where the first two are values of binomial distribution while `alpha` is the significance level. The function returns the lower and upper confidence limits:

```
In [10]:  def binom_CI(x,n,alpha):
              phat = x/n
              ll=phat-norm.ppf(1-alpha/2)*np.sqrt(phat*(1-phat)/n)
              ul=phat+norm.ppf(1-alpha/2)*np.sqrt(phat*(1-phat)/n)
              print("Binomial Lower Confidence Limit: ",max(0,ll))
              print("Binomial Upper Confidence Limit: ",min(1,ul))
          binom_CI(x=7,n=10,alpha=0.01)

          Binomial Lower Confidence Limit:  0.326726871284
          Binomial Upper Confidence Limit:  1
```

Note the small improvisation of this Python function with its counterpart in R!

2. If the variance is known, the function `normal_CI_ksd` will return us the desired confidence interval:

```
In [11]:  def normal_CI_ksd(x,sigma,alpha):
              xbar = np.mean(x)
              n = len(x)
              ll = xbar - norm.ppf(1-alpha/2)*sigma/np.sqrt(n)
              ul = xbar + norm.ppf(1-alpha/2)*sigma/np.sqrt(n)
              print("Normal Lower Confidence Limit: ",ll)
              print("Normal Upper Confidence Limit: ",ul)
          n=25
          nx = np.random.normal(10,2,n)
          normal_CI_ksd(nx,2,0.05)

          Normal Lower Confidence Limit:  8.99580732593
          Normal Upper Confidence Limit:  10.5637785136
```

After defining the function, we simulate some random observations from normal distribution and pretending that the mean is unknown, for a specified variance, we obtain the required confidence interval.

3. The `normal_CI_ksd` needs an important modification in the estimation of standard deviation when it is unknown. The changes are carried out in the `normal_CI_uksd` function:

```
In [12]: def normal_CI_uksd(x,alpha):
             xbar = np.mean(x); n = len(x)
             xsd = np.std(x)*np.sqrt(n/(n-1))
             ll = xbar - t.ppf(1-alpha/2,n-1)*xsd/np.sqrt(n)
             ul = xbar + t.ppf(1-alpha/2,n-1)*xsd/np.sqrt(n)
             print("Normal Lower Confidence Limit: ",ll)
             print("Normal Upper Confidence Limit: ",ul)
         nx = np.random.normal(10,2,n)
         normal_CI_uksd(nx,0.05)

         Normal Lower Confidence Limit:  9.6983574143
         Normal Upper Confidence Limit:  11.4359105478
```

We next move to the important problem of testing statistical hypotheses.

Hypothesis testing

Best consumed before six months from date of manufacture, Two years warranty, Expiry date: June 20, 2015, and so on, are some of the likely assurances, which readers would have easily come across. An analyst will have to arrive at such statements using the related data. Let us first define a hypothesis:

- **Hypothesis**: A hypothesis is an assertion about the unknown parameter of the probability distribution. For the quote of this section, denoting the least time (in months) until which an eatery will not be losing its good taste by θ, the hypothesis of interest will be $H_0 : \theta \geq 6$. It is common to denote the hypothesis of interest by H_0 and it is called the **null hypothesis**. We want to test the null hypothesis against the **alternative hypothesis** that the consumption time is well before six months' time, which in symbols is denoted by $H_1 : \theta < 6$. We will begin with some important definitions followed by related examples.

- **Test statistic**: A statistic that is a function of the random sample is called a test statistic.

For an observation X following a binomial distribution $b(n, p)$, the test statistic for p will be X/n, whereas for a random sample from the normal distribution, the test statistic may be mean $\bar{X} = \sum_{i=1}^{n} X_i / n$ or the sample variance $S^2 = \sum_{i=1}^{n} (X_i - \bar{X})^2 / (n-1)$ depending on whether the testing problem is for μ or σ^2. The statistical solution to reject (or not) the null hypothesis depends on the value of test statistic. This leads us to the next definition.

- **Critical region**: The set of values of the test statistic that leads to the rejection of the null hypothesis is known as the critical region.

We have made various kinds of assumptions for the random experiments. Naturally, depending on the type of the probability family, binomial, normal, and so on, we will have an appropriate testing tool. Let us look at the very popular tests arising in statistics.

Binomial test

A binomial random variable X, distribution represented by $b(n, p)$, is characterized by two parameters n and p. Typically, n represents the number of trials and is known in most cases and it is the probability of success p that one is generally interested in the hypotheses related to it.

For example, a LCD panel manufacturer would like to test if the number of defectives is at most four percent. The panel manufacturer has randomly inspected 893 LCDs and found 39 to be defective. Here the hypotheses testing problem would be $H_0 : p \leq 0.04$ vs $H_1 : p > 0.04$.

A doctor would like to test whether the proportion of people in a drought-affected area having a viral infection such as pneumonia is 0.2, that is, $H_0 : p = 0.2$ vs $H_1 : p \neq 0.2$. The drought-affected area may encompass a huge geographical area and as such it becomes really difficult to carry out a census over a very short period of a day or two. Thus the doctor selects the second-eldest member of a family and inspects 119 households for pneumonia. He records that 28 out of 119 inspected people are suffering from pneumonia. Using this information, we need to help the doctor in testing the hypothesis of interest for him. In general, the hypothesis-testing problems for the binomial distribution will be the likes of $H_0 : p \leq p_0$ vs $H_1 : p > p_0$, $H_0 : p \geq p_0$ vs $H_1 : p < p_0$, or $H_0 : p = p_0$ vs $H_1 : p \neq p_0$.

Let us see how the `binom.test` function in R helps in testing hypotheses problems related to the binomial distribution.

Time for action – testing probability of success

We will use the R function binom.test for testing hypotheses problems related to *p*. This function takes as arguments n number of trials, x number of successes, p as the probability of interest, and alternative as one of greater, less, or greater:

1. Discover the details related to binom.test using ?binom.test, and then run example(binom.test) and ensure that you understand the default example.

2. For the LCD panel manufacturer, we have n = 893 and x = 39. The null hypothesis occurs at p = 0.04. Enter this data first in R with the following code:

    ```
    n_lcd <- 893; x_lcd <- 39; p_lcd <- 0.04
    ```

3. The alternative hypothesis is that the proportion of success p is greater than 0.04, which is listed to the binom.test function with the option alternative="greater", and hence the complete binom.test function for the LCD panel is delivered by:

    ```
    binom.test(n=n_lcd,x=x_lcd,p=p_lcd,alternative="greater")
    ```

    The output, following diagram, shows that the estimated probability of success is 0.04367, which is certainly greater than 0.04. However, the p-value = 0.3103 indicates that we do not have enough evidence in the data to reject the null hypothesis $H_0 : p \leq 0.04$. Note that the binom.test also gives us a 95 percent confidence interval for p as (0.033, 1.000) and since the hypothesized probability lies in this interval we arrive at the same conclusion. This confidence interval is recommended over the one developed in the previous section, and in particular we don't have to worry about the confidence limits either being lesser than 0 or greater than one. Also, you may obtain any confidence interval of your choice $100(1-\alpha)$ percent CI with the argument conf.int.

4. For the doctors problem, we have the data as:

    ```
    n_doc <- 119; x_doc <- 28; p_doc <- 0.2
    ```

5. We need to test the null hypothesis against a two-sided alternative hypothesis and though this is the default setting of the binom.test, it is a good practice to specify it explicitly, at least until the expertise is felt by the user:

    ```
    binom.test(n=n_doc,x=x_doc,p=p_doc,alternative="two.sided")
    ```

The estimated probability of success, actually a patient's probability of having the viral infection, is 0.3193. Since the p-value associated with the test is p-value = 0.001888, we reject the null hypothesis that $H_0 : p = 0.2$. All the output is given in the following screenshot. The 95 percent confidence interval is (0.2369, 0.4110), again given by the binom.test, which does not contain the hypothesized value of 0.2 and hence we can reject the null hypothesis based on the confidence interval.

```
> n_lcd <- 893; x_lcd <- 39; p_lcd <- 0.04
> binom.test(n=n_lcd,x=x_lcd,p=p_lcd,alternative="greater")
        Exact binomial test
data:  x_lcd and n_lcd
number of successes = 39, number of trials = 893, p-value = 0.3103
alternative hypothesis: true probability of success is greater than 0.04
95 percent confidence interval:
 0.033 1.000
sample estimates:
probability of success
             0.04367
> n_doc <- 119; x_doc <- 38; p_doc <- 0.2
> binom.test(n=n_doc,x=x_doc,p=p_doc,alternative="two.sided")
        Exact binomial test
data:  x_doc and n_doc
number of successes = 38, number of trials = 119, p-value = 0.001888
alternative hypothesis: true probability of success is not equal to 0.2
95 percent confidence interval:
 0.2369 0.4110
sample estimates:
probability of success
             0.3193
```

Binomial tests for probability of success

What just happened?

Binomial distribution arises in a large number of proportionality test problems. In this section, we used the binom.test for testing problems related to the probability of success. We also note that the confidence intervals for p are given as a side-product of the application of the binom.test. The confidence intervals are also given as a by-product of the application of the binom.test.

Tests of proportions and the chi-square test

In *Chapter 3, Data Visualization*, we came across the `Titanic` and `UCBAdmissions` datasets. For the `Titanic` dataset, we may like to test if the `Survived` proportion across the `Class` is the same for the two `Sex` groups. Similarly, for the `UCBAdmissions` dataset we may wish to know if the proportion of the `Admitted` candidates for the `Male` and `Female` group is the same across the six `Dept`. Thus, there is a need to generalize the `binom.test` function to a group of proportions. In this problem, we may have k-proportions and the probability vector is specified by $p = (p_1, \ldots, p_k)$. The hypothesis problem may be specified as testing the null hypothesis $H_0 : p = p_0$ against the alternative hypothesis $H_1 : p \neq p_0$. Equivalently, in the vector form the problem is testing $H_0 : (p_1, \ldots, p_k) = (p_{01}, \ldots, p_{0k})$ against $H_1 : (p_1, \ldots, p_k) \neq (p_{01}, \ldots, p_{0k})$. The R extension of `binom.test` is given in `prop.test`.

Time for action – testing proportions

We will use the `prop.test` R function here for testing equality of proportions for the count data problems:

1. Load the required dataset with `data(UCBAdmissions)`. For the `UCBAdmissions` dataset, first obtain the `Admitted` and `Rejected` frequencies for both the genders across the six departments with:

   ```
   UCBA.Dept <- ftable(UCBAdmissions, row.vars="Dept", col.vars =
   c("Gender", "Admit"))
   ```

2. Calculate the `Admitted` proportions for `Female` across the six departments with:

   ```
   p_female <- prop.table(UCBA.Dept[,3:4],margin=1)[,1]
   ```

   Check `p_female`!

3. Test whether the proportions across the departments for `Male` matches with `Female` using the `prop.test`:

   ```
   prop.test(UCBA.Dept[,1:2],p=p_female)
   ```

   The proportions are not equal across the `Gender` as p-value < 2.2e-16 rejects the null hypothesis that they are equal.

4. Next, we want to investigate whether the `Male` and `Female` survivors, proportions is the same in the `Titanic` dataset. The approach is similar to the `UCBAdmissions` problem; run the following code:

   ```
   T.Class <- ftable(Titanic, row.vars="Class", col.vars = c("Sex",
   "Survived"))
   ```

5. Compute the `Female` survivor proportions across the four classes with `p_female <- prop.table(T.Class[,3:4],margin=1)[,1]`. Note that this new variable `p_female` will overwrite the same named variable from the earlier steps.

6. Display `p_female` and then carry out the comparison across the two genders:

   `prop.test(T.Class[,1:2],p=p_female)`

   The `p-value < 2.2e-16` clearly shows that the survivor proportions are not the same across the genders.

```
> UCBA.Dept <- ftable(UCBAdmissions, row.vars="Dept", col.vars = c("Gender", "Admit"))
> p_female <- prop.table(UCBA.Dept[,3:4],margin=1)[,1]
> p_female
[1] 0.82407 0.68000 0.34064 0.34933 0.23919 0.07038
> prop.test(UCBA.Dept[,1:2],p=p_female)
        6-sample test for given proportions without continuity correction
data:  UCBA.Dept[, 1:2], null probabilities p_female
X-squared = 246, df = 6, p-value < 2.2e-16
alternative hypothesis: two.sided
null values:
 prop 1  prop 2  prop 3  prop 4  prop 5  prop 6
0.82407 0.68000 0.34064 0.34933 0.23919 0.07038
sample estimates:
 prop 1  prop 2  prop 3  prop 4  prop 5  prop 6
0.62061 0.63036 0.36923 0.33094 0.27749 0.05898
> T.Class <- ftable(Titanic, row.vars="Class", col.vars = c("Sex", "Survived"))
> p_female <- prop.table(T.Class[,3:4],margin=1)[,1]
> prop.test(T.Class[,1:2],p=p_female)
        4-sample test for given proportions without continuity correction
data:  T.Class[, 1:2], null probabilities p_female
X-squared = 6900, df = 4, p-value < 2.2e-16
alternative hypothesis: two.sided
null values:
 prop 1  prop 2  prop 3  prop 4
0.02759 0.12264 0.54082 0.13043
sample estimates:
prop 1 prop 2 prop 3 prop 4
0.6556 0.8603 0.8275 0.7773
Warning message:
In prop.test(T.Class[, 1:2], p = p_female) :
  Chi-squared approximation may be incorrect
```

Prop.test in action

Indeed, there is more complexity to the two datasets than mere proportions for the two genders. The webpage `http://www-stat.stanford. edu/~sabatti/Stat48` has detailed analysis of the `UCBAdmissions` dataset and here we will simply apply the chi-square test to check if the admission percentage within each department is independent of the gender.

7. The data for the admission/rejection for each department is extractable through the third index in the array, that is, `UCBAdmissions[,,i]` across the six departments. Now, we apply the `chisq.test` to check if the admission procedure is independent of the gender by running `chisq.test( UCBAdmissions[,,i])` six times. The result has been edited in a foreign text editor and then a screenshot of it is provided next.

It appears that the `Dept` = A admits more males than the fair gender.

```
> chisq.test(UCBAdmissions[,,1])
        Pearson's Chi-squared test with Yates' continuity correction
data:  UCBAdmissions[, , 1]
X-squared = 16.37, df = 1, p-value = 5.205e-05
> chisq.test(UCBAdmissions[,,2])
        Pearson's Chi-squared test with Yates' continuity correction
data:  UCBAdmissions[, , 2]
X-squared = 0.0851, df = 1, p-value = 0.7705
> chisq.test(UCBAdmissions[,,3])
        Pearson's Chi-squared test with Yates' continuity correction
data:  UCBAdmissions[, , 3]
X-squared = 0.6332, df = 1, p-value = 0.4262
> chisq.test(UCBAdmissions[,,4])
        Pearson's Chi-squared test with Yates' continuity correction
data:  UCBAdmissions[, , 4]
X-squared = 0.2216, df = 1, p-value = 0.6378
> chisq.test(UCBAdmissions[,,5])
        Pearson's Chi-squared test with Yates' continuity correction
data:  UCBAdmissions[, , 5]
X-squared = 0.808, df = 1, p-value = 0.3687
> chisq.test(UCBAdmissions[,,6])
        Pearson's Chi-squared test with Yates' continuity correction
data:  UCBAdmissions[, , 6]
X-squared = 0.2182, df = 1, p-value = 0.6404
```

Chi-square tests for the UCBAdmissions problem

What just happened?

We used `prop.test` and `chisq.test` for respectively testing proportions and independence of attributes. Functions such as `ftable` and `prop.table` and arguments such as `row.vars`, `col.vars`, and `margin` were useful to get the data in the right format for the analyses' purpose.

We will now look at an important family of tests for the normal distribution.

Tests based on normal distribution – one sample

The normal distribution pops up in many instances of statistical analysis. In fact Whittaker and Robinson have quoted on the popularity of normal distribution as follows:

Everybody believes in the exponential law of errors [that is, the normal distribution]: the experimenters, because they think it can be proved by mathematics; and the mathematicians, because they believe it has been established by observation.

We will not make an attempt to find out whether the experimenters are correct or the mathematicians, well, at least not in this section.

In general we will be dealing with either one-sample or two-sample tests. In the one-sample problem we have a random sample of size n from $N\left(\mu,\sigma^2\right)$ in $\left(X_1,X_2,...,X_n\right)$. The hypotheses testing problem may be related to either or both of the parameters $\left(\mu,\sigma^2\right)$. The interesting and most frequent hypotheses testing problems for the normal distribution are listed here:

- Testing for mean with known variance σ^2:
    - $H_0:\mu<\mu_0$ vs $H_1:\mu\geq\mu_0$
    - $H_0:\mu>\mu_0$ vs $H_1:\mu\leq\mu_0$
    - $H_0:\mu=\mu_0$ vs $H_1:\mu\neq\mu_0$

- Testing for mean with unknown variance σ^2: the same set of hypotheses problems as the preceding point

- Testing for the variance with unknown mean:
    - $H_0:\sigma>\sigma_0$ vs $H_1:\sigma\leq\sigma_0$
    - $H_0:\sigma<\sigma_0$ vs $H_1:\sigma\geq\sigma_0$
    - $H_0:\sigma=\sigma_0$ vs $H_1:\sigma\neq\sigma_0$

In the case of known variance, the hypotheses testing problem for the mean is based on the Z statistic given by:

$$Z=\frac{\bar{X}-\mu_0}{\sigma/\sqrt{n}}$$

where $\bar{X} = \sum_{i=1}^{n} X_i / n$. The test procedure, known as **Z-test**, for the hypotheses testing problem $H_0 : \mu < \mu_0$ vs $H_1 : \mu \geq \mu_0$ is to reject the null hypothesis at α -level of significance $H_0 : \mu > \mu_0$ if $\bar{X} > z_\alpha \sigma / \sqrt{n} + \mu_0$, where z_α is the α percentile of a standard normal distribution. For the hypotheses testing problem $H_0 : \mu > \mu_0$ vs $H_1 : \mu \leq \mu_0$, the critical/reject region is $\bar{X} < z_\alpha \sigma / \sqrt{n} + \mu_0$. Finally, for the testing problem of $H_0 : \mu = \mu_0$ vs $H_1 : \mu \neq \mu_0$, we reject the null hypothesis if:

$$\frac{|X - \mu|}{\sigma / \sqrt{n}} \geq z_{\alpha/2}$$

An R function $z.test$ is available in the PASWR package, which carries out the Z-test for each type of the hypotheses testing problem. Now, we consider the case when the variance σ^2 is not known. In this case, we first find an estimate of the variance using $S^2 = \sum_{i=1}^{n}(X_i - \bar{X})^2 / (n-1)$. The test procedure is based on the well-known t-statistic:

$$t = \frac{\bar{X} - \mu}{\sqrt{S^2 / n}}$$

The test procedure based on the t-statistic is highly popular as the t-test or student's t-test, and its implementation is there in R with the $t.test$ function in the base package. The distribution of the t-statistic, under the null hypothesis, is the t-distribution with (n-1) degrees of freedom. The rationale behind the application of the t-test for the various types of hypotheses remains the same as the Z-test.

- For the hypotheses testing problem concerning the variance σ^2 of the normal distribution, we need to first compute the sample variance using $S^2 = \sum_{i=1}^{n}(X_i - \bar{X})^2 / (n-1)$ and define the chi-square statistic:

$$\chi^2 = \frac{(n-1)S^2}{\sigma_0^2}$$

Under the null hypothesis, the chi-square statistic is distributed as a chi-square random variable with $n-1$ degrees of freedom. In the case of known mean, which is seldom the case, the test procedure is based on the test statistic $\chi^2 = \sum_{i=1}^{n}(X_i - \mu)^2 / \sigma_0^2$, which follows a chi-square random variable with n degrees of freedom. For the hypotheses problem $H_0 : \sigma > \sigma_0$ vs $H_1 : \sigma \le \sigma_0$, the test procedure is to reject $H_0 : \sigma > \sigma_0$ if $X^2 < X_{1-\alpha}^2$. Similarly, for the hypotheses problem $H_0 : \sigma < \sigma_0$ vs $H_1 : \sigma \ge \sigma_0$, the procedure is to reject $H_0 : \sigma < \sigma_0$ if $X^2 > \chi_\alpha^2$, and finally for the problem $H_0 : \sigma = \sigma_0$ vs $H_1 : \sigma \ne \sigma_0$, the test procedure rejects $H_0 : \sigma = \sigma_0$ if either $X^2 < \chi_{1-\alpha/2}^2$ or $X^2 < \chi_{\alpha/2}^2$.

Test examples. Let us consider some situations when the preceding set of hypotheses arises in a natural way:

- A certain chemical experiment requires that the solution used as a reactant has a pH level greater than 8.4. It is known that the manufacturing process gives measurements that follow a normal distribution with a standard deviation of 0.05. The 10 random observations are 8.30, 8.42, 8.44, 8.32, 8.43, 8.41, 8.42, 8.46, 8.37, and 8.42. Here, the hypotheses testing problem of interest is $H_0 : \mu > 8.4$ vs $H_1 : \mu \le 8.4$. This problem is adopted from page 408 of Ross (2010).

- Following a series of complaints that his companies, LCD panels never last more than a year, the manufacturer wants to test if his LCD panels indeed fail within a year. Using historical data, he knows the standard deviation of the panel life due to the manufacturing process is two years. A random sample of 15 units from a freshly manufactured lot gives their lifetimes as 13.37, 10.96, 12.06, 13.82, 12.96, 10.47, 10.55, 16.28, 12.94, 11.43, 14.51, 12.63, 13.50, 11.50, and 12.87. You need to help the manufacturer validate his hypothesis.

- Freund and Wilson (2003). Suppose that the mean weight of peanuts put in jars is the required 8 oz. The variance of the weights is known to be 0.03, and the observed weights for 16 jars is 8.08, 7.71, 7.89, 7.72, 8.00, 7.90, 7.77, 7.81, 8.33, 7.67, 7.79, 7.79, 7.94, 7.84, 8.17, and 7.87. Here, we are interested in testing $H_0 : \mu > 8.0$ vs $H_1 : \mu \ne 8.0$.

- New managers have been appointed at respective places in the preceding bullets. As a consequence, the new managers are not aware about the standard deviation for the processes under their control. As an analyst, help them!

- Suppose that the variance in the first example is not known and that it is a critical requirement that the variance be lesser than 7, that is, the null hypothesis is $H_0 : \sigma^2 < 7$ while the alternative is $H_1 : \sigma^2 \geq 7$.

- Suppose that the variance test needs to be carried out for the third method, that is, the hypotheses testing problem is then $H_0 : \sigma^2 = 0.03$ vs $H_1 : \sigma^2 \neq 0.03$.

We will perform the necessary tests for all these problems.

Time for action – testing one-sample hypotheses

We will require R packages PASWR and PairedData here. The R functions such as t.test, z.test, and var.test will be useful for testing one-sample hypotheses problems related to a random sample from normal distributions:

1. Load the library library(PASWR).

2. Enter the data for pH in R by:

   ```
   pH_Data <-c(8.30,8.42,8.44,8.32,8.43,8.41,8.42,8.46,8.37,8.42)
   ```

3. Specify the known variance of pH in pH_sigma <- 0.05.

4. Use z.test from the PASWR library to test the hypotheses described in the first example with:

   ```
   z.test(x=pH_Data,alternative="less",sigma.x=pH_sigma,mu=8.4)
   ```

   The data is specified in the x option, the type of the hypotheses problem is specified by stating the form of the alternative hypothesis, the known variance is fed through the sigma.x option, and finally the mu option is used to specify the value of the mean under the null hypothesis. The output of the complete R program is collected in the forthcoming two screenshots.

   The p-value is 0.4748, which means that we do not have enough evidence to reject the null hypothesis $H_0 : \mu > 8.4$ and hence we conclude that mean pH value is above 8.4.

5. Get the data of the LCD panel in your session with:

   ```
   LCD_Data <- c(13.37, 10.96, 12.06, 13.82, 12.96, 10.47,
   10.55, 16.28, 12.94, 11.43, 14.51, 12.63, 13.50, 11.50, 12.87)
   ```

6. Specify the known variance LCD_sigma <- 2 and run the z.test with:

   ```
   z.test(x=LCD_Data,alternative="greater",sigma.x=LCD_sigma,mu=12)
   ```

   The p-value is seen to be 0.1018 and hence, we again do not have enough data evidence to reject the null hypothesis that the average mean lifetime of the LCD panel is at least a year.

7. The complete program for the third problem can be given as follows:

```
peanuts <- c(8.08, 7.71, 7.89, 7.72, 8.00, 7.90, 7.77,
7.81, 8.33, 7.67, 7.79, 7.79, 7.94, 7.84, 8.17, 7.87)
peanuts_sigma <- 0.03
z.test(x=peanuts,sigma.x=peanuts_sigma,mu=8.0)
```

Since the p-value associated with this test `2.2e-16`, it is very close to zero, we reject the null hypothesis $H_0 : \mu = 8.0$.

8. If the variance(s) are not known and a test of the sample means is required, we need to move from the `z.test` (in the PASWR library) to the `t.test` (in the base library):

```
t.test(x=pH_Data,alternative="less",mu=8.4)
t.test(x=LCD_Data,alternative="greater",mu=12)
t.test(x=peanuts,mu=8.0)
```

If the variance is not known, the conclusions for the problems related to pH and peanuts do not change. However, the conclusion changes for the LCD panel problem and here the null hypothesis is rejected as the p-value is `0.06414`.

For the problem of testing variances related to the one-sample problem, the initial idea of the author was to write raw R codes as there did not seem to be a function, package, and so on, which readily gives the answers. However, a more appropriate search at `google.com` revealed that an R package titled `PairedData`, and created by Stephane Champely did certainly have a function `var.test`, not to be confused with the same named function in the `stats` library, which is appropriate for testing problems related to the variance of a normal distribution.

The problem is that the routine method of fetching the package by `install.packages("PairedData")` gives a warning message, namely, package `PairedData` is not available (for R version 2.15.1). This is the classic case of "so near, yet so far...".

However, a deeper dive will lead us to `http://cran.r-project.org/src/contrib/Archive/PairedData/`. This web page shows the various versions of the `PairedData` package. The Linux user should have no problem in using it, though the other OS users can't be helped right away. The Linux user needs to first download one of the zipped files, say `PairedData_1.0.0.tar.gz`, to a specific directory and with the path of GNOME Terminal in that directory execute `R CMD INSTALL PairedData_1.0.0.tar.gz`.

Now, we are ready to carry out the tests related to the variance of a normal distribution. The Windows user need not be discouraged with this scenario, and the important function `var1.test` is made available in the RSADBE package of the book. A more recent check at the cran website reveals that the `PairedData` package is again available for all OS platforms since April 18, 2013.

```
> library(PASWR)
> pH_Data <- c(8.30, 8.42, 8.44, 8.32, 8.43, 8.41, 8.42,
+ 8.46, 8.37, 8.42)
> pH_sigma <- 0.05
> z.test(x=pH_Data,alternative="less",sigma.x=pH_sigma,mu=8.4)
          One-sample z-Test
data:  pH_Data
z = -0.0632, p-value = 0.4748
alternative hypothesis: true mean is less than 8.4
95 percent confidence interval:
  -Inf 8.425
sample estimates:
mean of x
    8.399
> LCD_Data <- c(13.37, 10.96, 12.06, 13.82, 12.96, 10.47,
+ 10.55, 16.28, 12.94, 11.43, 14.51, 12.63, 13.50, 11.50, 12.87)
> LCD_sigma <- 2
> z.test(x=LCD_Data,alternative="greater",sigma.x=LCD_sigma,mu=12)
          One-sample z-Test
data:  LCD_Data
z = 1.272, p-value = 0.1018
alternative hypothesis: true mean is greater than 12
95 percent confidence interval:
 11.81   Inf
sample estimates:
mean of x
    12.66
> peanuts = c(8.08, 7.71, 7.89, 7.72, 8.00, 7.90, 7.77,
+ 7.81, 8.33, 7.67, 7.79, 7.79, 7.94, 7.84, 8.17, 7.87)
> peanuts_sigma <- 0.03
> z.test(x=peanuts,sigma.x=peanuts_sigma,mu=8.0)
          One-sample z-Test
data:  peanuts
z = -14.33, p-value < 2.2e-16
alternative hypothesis: true mean is not equal to 8
95 percent confidence interval:
 7.878 7.907
sample estimates:
mean of x
    7.893
```

```
> t.test(x=pH_Data,alternative="less",mu=8.4)
          One Sample t-test
data:  pH_Data
t = -0.0604, df = 9, p-value = 0.4766
alternative hypothesis: true mean is less than 8.4
95 percent confidence interval:
  -Inf 8.429
sample estimates:
mean of x
    8.399
> t.test(x=LCD_Data,alternative="greater",mu=12)
          One Sample t-test
data:  LCD_Data
t = 1.617, df = 14, p-value = 0.06414
alternative hypothesis: true mean is greater than 12
95 percent confidence interval:
 11.94   Inf
sample estimates:
mean of x
    12.66
> t.test(x=peanuts,alternative="two.sided",mu=8.0)
          One Sample t-test
data:  peanuts
t = -2.414, df = 15, p-value = 0.02904
alternative hypothesis: true mean is not equal to 8
95 percent confidence interval:
 7.798 7.987
sample estimates:
mean of x
    7.893
```

z.test and t.test for one-sample problem

9. Load the required library with `library(PairedData)`.

10. Carry out the two testing problems in the fifth problem with:

    ```
    var.test(x=pH_Data,alternative="greater",ratio=7)
    var.test(x=peanuts,alternative="two.sided",ratio=0.03)
    ```

11. It may be seen from the next screenshot that the data does not lead to rejection of the null hypotheses. For the Windows user, the alternative is to use the `var1.test` function from the RSADBE package. That is, you need to run:

    ```
    var1.test(x=pH_Data,alternative="greater",ratio=7)
    var1.test(x=peanuts,alternative="two.sided",ratio=0.03)
    ```

You'll get the same results:

```
> library(PairedData)
> var.test(x=pH_Data,alternative="greater",ratio=7)

        One-sample variance test

data:  x
X-squared = 0.0035, df = 9, p-value = 1
alternative hypothesis: true variance is greater than 7
95 percent confidence interval:
 0.001459308            Inf
sample estimates:
   variance
0.002743333

> var.test(x=peanuts,alternative="two.sided",ratio=0.03)

        One-sample variance test

data:  x
X-squared = 15.87, df = 15, p-value = 0.7815
alternative hypothesis: true variance is not equal to 0.03
95 percent confidence interval:
 0.01732004 0.07602835
sample estimates:
variance
 0.03174
```

var.test from the PairedData library

What just happened?

The tests z.test, t.test, and var.test (from the PairedData library) have been used for the testing hypotheses problems under varying degrees of problems.

Have a go hero

Consider the testing problem $H_0 : \sigma = \sigma_0$ vs $H_1 : \sigma \neq \sigma_0$. The test statistic for this hypothesis testing problem is given by:

$$\chi^2 = \frac{\sum_{i=1}^{n} \left(X_i - \bar{X} \right)^2}{\sigma_0^2}$$

which follows a chi-square distribution with *n-1* degrees of freedom. Create your own new function for the testing problems and compare it with the results given by var.test of the PairedData package.

With the testing problem of parameters of normal distribution in the case of one sample behind us, we will next focus on the important two-sample problem.

Tests based on normal distribution – two sample

The two-sample problem has data from two populations where $(X_1, X_2, ..., X_n)$ are n_1 observations from $N(\mu_1, \sigma_1^2)$ and $(Y_1, Y_2, ..., Y_{n_2})$ are n_2 observations from $N(\mu_2, \sigma_2^2)$. We assume that the samples within each population are independent of each other and further, that the samples across the two populations are also independent. Similar to the one-sample problem, we have the following set of recurring and interesting hypotheses testing problems:

- Mean comparison with known variances σ_1^2 and σ_2^2:
  - $H_0 : \mu_1 > \mu_2$ vs $H_1 : \mu_1 \le \mu_2$
  - $H_0 : \mu_1 < \mu_2$ vs $H_1 : \mu_1 \ge \mu_2$
  - $H_0 : \mu_1 = \mu_2$ vs $H_1 : \mu_1 \ne \mu_2$

- Mean comparison with unknown variances σ_1^2 and σ_2^2: the same set of hypotheses problems as before. We make an additional assumption here that the variances σ_1^2 and σ_2^2 are assumed to be equal, though unknown.
- The variances comparison:

  - $H_0 : \sigma_1 > \sigma_2$ vs $H_1 : \sigma_1 \le \sigma_2$
  - $H_0 : \sigma_1 < \sigma_2$ vs $H_1 : \sigma_1 \ge \sigma_2$
  - $H_0 : \sigma_1 = \sigma_2$ vs $H_1 : \sigma_1 \ne \sigma_2$

First define the sample means for the two populations with $\bar{X} = \sum_{i=1}^{n_1} X_i / n_1$ and $\bar{Y} = \sum_{i=1}^{n_2} X_i / n_2$. For the case of known variances σ_1^2 and σ_2^2, the test statistic is defined by:

$$Z = \frac{\bar{X} - \bar{Y} - (\mu_1 - \mu_2)}{\sqrt{\sigma_1^2 / n_1 + \sigma_2^2 / n_2}}$$

Under the null hypotheses, $Z = (\bar{X} - \bar{Y}) \big/ \sqrt{\sigma_1^2/n_1 + \sigma_2^2/n_2}$ follows a standard normal distribution. The test procedure for the problem $H_0 : \mu_1 > \mu_2$ vs $H_1 : \mu_1 \leq \mu_2$ is to reject H_0 if $Z < Z_\alpha$, and the procedure for $H_0 : \mu_1 < \mu_2$ vs $H_1 : \mu_1 \geq \mu_2$ is to reject if $Z \geq Z_\alpha$. As expected and on earlier intuitive lines, the test procedure for the hypotheses problem $H_0 : \mu_1 = \mu_2$ vs $H_1 : \mu_1 \neq \mu_2$ is to reject H_0 is $|Z| \geq Z_{\alpha/2}$.

Let us now consider the case when the variances σ_1^2 and σ_2^2 are not known and assumed (or known) to be equal. In this case, we can't use the Z-test any further and need to look at the estimator of the common variance. For this, we defined the **pooled variance estimator** as follows:

$$S_p^2 = \frac{n_1 - 1}{n_1 + n_2 - 2} S_x^2 + \frac{n_2 - 1}{n_1 + n_2 - 2} S_y^2$$

where S_x^2 and S_y^2 are the sampling variance of the two populations. Define the t-statistic as follows:

$$t = \frac{\bar{X} - \bar{Y}}{\sqrt{S_p^2 \left(1/n_1 + 1/n_2\right)}}$$

The test procedure for the set of the three hypotheses testing problems is then to respectively reject the null hypotheses if $t < t_{n_1 + n_2 - 2, \alpha}$, $t > t_{n_1 + n_2 - 2, \alpha}$, or $|t| < t_{n_1 + n_2 - 2, \alpha/2}$.

Finally, we focus on the problem of testing variances across two samples. Here, the test statistic is given by:

$$F = \frac{S_x^2}{S_y^2}$$

The test procedures would be to respectively reject the null hypotheses of the testing problems $H_0 : \sigma_1 > \sigma_2$ vs $H_1 : \sigma_1 \leq \sigma_2$, $H_0 : \sigma_1 < \sigma_2$ vs $H_1 : \sigma_1 \geq \sigma_2$, and $H_0 : \sigma_1 = \sigma_2$ vs $H_1 : \sigma_1 \neq \sigma_2$ if $F < F_{n_1 - 1, n_2 - 1, \alpha}$, $F > F_{n_1 - 1, n_2 - 1, \alpha}$, $F < F_{n_1 - 1, n_2 - 1, \alpha/2}$.

Let us now consider some scenarios where we have the previously listed hypotheses testing problems.

Test examples: Let us consider some situations where the preceding set of hypotheses arises in a natural way:

- In continuation of the chemical experiment problem, let us assume that the chemists have come up with a new method of obtaining the same solution as discussed in the previous section. For the new technique, the standard deviation continues to be 0.05, and 12 observations for the new method yield the following measurements: 8.78, 8.85, 8.74, 8.83, 8.82, 8.79, 8.82, 8.74, 8.84, 8.78, 8.75, 8.81. Now, this new solution is acceptable if its mean is greater than the earlier one. Thus, the hypotheses testing problem is now $H_0 : \mu_{NEW} > \mu_{OLD}$ vs $H_1 : \mu_{NEW} \leq \mu_{OLD}$.

- Ross (2008), page 451. Precision of instruments in metal cutting is a very serious business and the cut pieces can't be significantly less than the target nor be greater than it. Two machines are used to cut 10 pieces of steel, and their measurements are respectively given in 122.4, 123.12, 122.51, 123.12, 122.55, 121.76, 122.31, 123.2, 122.48, 121.96, and 122.36, 121.88, 122.2, 122.88, 123.43, 122.4, 122.12, 121.78, 122.85, 123.04. The standard deviation of the length of a cut is known to be equal to 0.5. We need to test if the average cut length is the same for the two machines.

- For both the preceding problems, assume that though the variances are equal, they are not known. Complete the hypotheses testing problems using `t.test`.

- Freund and Wilson (2003), page 199. The monitoring of the amount of peanuts being put in the jars is an important issue from a quality control viewpoint. The consistency of the weights is of prime importance and the manufacturer has been introduced to a new machine, which is supposed to give more accuracy in the weights of the peanuts put in the jars. With the new device, 11 jars were tested for their weights and found to be 8.06, 8.64, 7.97, 7.81, 7.93, 8.57, 8.39, 8.46, 8.28, 8.02, 8.39, whereas a sample of nine jars from the previous machine weighed at 7.99, 8.12, 8.34, 8.17, 8.11, 8.03, 8.14, 8.14, 7.87. Now, the task is to test $H_0 : \sigma_{NEW} = \sigma_{OLD}$ vs $H_1 : \sigma_{NEW} \geq \sigma_{OLD}$.

Let us do the tests for the preceding four problems in R.

Time for action – testing two-sample hypotheses

For the problem of testing hypotheses for the means arising from two populations, we will be using the functions `z.test` and `t.test`:

1. As earlier, load the `library(PASWR)` library.

2. Carry out the Z-test using `z.test` and the options `x`, `y`, `sigma.x`, and `sigma.y`:

```
pH_Data = c(8.30, 8.42, 8.44, 8.32, 8.43, 8.41, 8.42,
8.46, 8.37, 8.42)
pH_New = c(8.78, 8.85, 8.74, 8.83, 8.82, 8.79, 8.82,
8.74, 8.84, 8.78, 8.75, 8.81)
z.test(x=pH_Data,y=pH_New,sigma.x=sigma.y=0.05,alternative="less")
```

The p-value is very small (`2.2e-16`) indicating that we reject the null hypothesis that $H_0 : \sigma_{NEW} > \sigma_{OLD}$.

3. For the steel length cut data problem, run the following code:

```
length_M1 = c(122.4, 123.12, 122.51, 123.12, 122.55,
121.76, 122.31, 123.2, 122.48, 121.96)
length_M2 = c(122.36, 121.88, 122.2, 122.88, 123.43,
122.4, 122.12, 121.78, 122.85, 123.04)
z.test(x=length_M1,y=length_M2,sigma.x=0.5,sigma.y=0.5)
```

The display of `p-value = 0.8335` shows that the machines do not cut the steel in different ways.

4. If the variances are equal but not known, we need to use `t.test` instead of the `z.test`:

```
t.test(x=pH_Data,y=pH_New,alternative="less")
t.test(x=length_M1,y=length_M2)
```

The p-values for the two hypotheses problems are `p-value = 3.95e-13` and `p-value = 0.8397`. We leave the interpretation aspect to the reader.

5. For the fourth problem, we have the following R program:

```
machine_new = c(8.06, 8.64, 7.97, 7.81, 7.93, 8.57, 8.39, 8.46,
8.28, 8.02, 8.39)
machine_old = c(7.99, 8.12, 8.34, 8.17, 8.11, 8.03, 8.14, 8.14,
7.87)
t.test(machine_new,machine_old, alternative="greater")
```

Again, we have p-value = 0.1005!

What just happened?

The functions `t.test` and `z.test` were simply extensions from the one-sample case to the two-sample test.

Have a go hero

In the one sample case you used `var.test` for the same datasets, which needed a comparison of means with some known standard deviation. Now, test for the variance in the two-sample case using `var.test` using appropriate hypotheses for them. For example, test whether the variances are equal for `pH_Data` and `pH_New`. Find more details of the test with `?var.test`.

Doing it in Python

We will now show how to perform the statistical tests in Python. The important packages here are `scipy` and `statsmodels`. However, we carry out the Z-test by defining two new functions:

1. The function `binom_test` from the `scipy.stats` module is useful to carry out the binomial test:

```
In [15]:  n_lcd = 893; x_lcd = 39; p_lcd = 0.04
          from scipy.stats import binom_test
          binom_test(x=x_lcd,n=n_lcd,p=p_lcd)

Out[15]:  0.54977099798723161
```

2. The proportion test `proportions_chisquare` is available in the `statmodels.stats.proportion` module. We use it to carry out the proportion test as follows:

```
In [17]:  Male_Admit = [512, 353, 120, 138,  53,  22]
          Male_Applied = [825, 560, 325, 417, 191, 373]
          Female_Prop = np.array([0.824, 0.680, 0.341, 0.349, 0.239, 0.070])
          from statsmodels.stats.proportion import proportions_chisquare
          proportions_chisquare(count = Male_Admit, nobs=Male_Applied,value=Female_Prop)

Out[17]:  (245.68193179139814, 3.4322059672585922e-50, (array([[512, 313],
                  [353, 207],
                  [120, 205],
                  [138, 279],
                  [ 53, 138],
                  [ 22, 351]]), array([[ 679.8  ,  145.2  ],
                  [ 380.8  ,  179.2  ],
                  [ 110.825,  214.175],
                  [ 145.533,  271.467],
                  [  45.649,  145.351],
                  [  26.11 ,  346.89 ]]))))
```

3. The first two entries of the output are the chi-square value and the p-value. The rest of the arrays contain the observed and expected frequencies.

4. Since the z-test is not available in Python packages, to the best of the authors survey and online searches, we create a new function as follows:

```
In [19]:  def z_test(x,mu,sd,alternative):
              import scipy
              xmean = x.mean(); n = len(x)
              ztest = np.sqrt(n)*(xmean-mu)/sd
              if alternative=="less":
                  pvalue = scipy.stats.norm.cdf(ztest)
              if alternative=="greater":
                  pvalue = 1-scipy.stats.norm.cdf(ztest)
              if alternative=="two.sided":
                  pvalue = 2*(1-scipy.stats.norm.cdf(ztest))
              print("The Z-test Value is :",ztest)
              print("The p-value is :",pvalue)
```

5. This function calculates the Z-statistic and returns the p-value. We apply it to the three problems at hand.

6. The z-test is now applied for the three problems: pH_Data, LCD_Data, and peanuts. The results are in agreement with the tests performed in R.

```
In [20]:  pH_Data = np.array([8.30,8.42,8.44,8.32,8.43,8.41,8.42,8.46,8.37,8.42])
          z_test(x=pH_Data,mu=8.4,sd=0.05,alternative="less")

          The Z-test Value is : -0.0632455532034
          The p-value is : 0.474785485576

In [21]:  LCD_Data = np.array([13.37, 10.96, 12.06, 13.82, 12.96, 10.47,10.55,
                              16.28, 12.94, 11.43, 14.51, 12.63, 13.50, 11.50, 12.87])
          z_test(x=LCD_Data,mu =12, sd =2,alternative="greater")

          The Z-test Value is : 1.271629532
          The p-value is : 0.101752389402

In [22]:  peanuts = np.array([8.08, 7.71, 7.89, 7.72, 8.00, 7.90, 7.77, 7.81,
                             8.33, 7.67, 7.79, 7.79, 7.94, 7.84, 8.17, 7.87])
          z_test(x=peanuts,mu=8,sd=0.03,alternative="two.sided")

          The Z-test Value is : -14.3333333333
          The p-value is : 2.0
```

7. We next define the z-test for two-sample problems.

8. The two-sample `z-test` is defined in Python as follows:

```
In [20]:   pH_Data = np.array([8.30,8.42,8.44,8.32,8.43,8.41,8.42,8.46,8.37,8.42])
           z_test(x=pH_Data,mu=8.4,sd=0.05,alternative="less")

           The Z-test Value is : -0.0632455532034
           The p-value is : 0.474785485576

In [21]:   LCD_Data = np.array([13.37, 10.96, 12.06, 13.82, 12.96, 10.47,10.55,
                                16.28, 12.94, 11.43, 14.51, 12.63, 13.50, 11.50, 12.87])
           z_test(x=LCD_Data,mu =12, sd =2,alternative="greater")

           The Z-test Value is : 1.271629532
           The p-value is : 0.101752389402

In [22]:   peanuts = np.array([8.08, 7.71, 7.89, 7.72, 8.00, 7.90, 7.77, 7.81,
                               8.33, 7.67, 7.79, 7.79, 7.94, 7.84, 8.17, 7.87])
           z_test(x=peanuts,mu=8,sd=0.03,alternative="two.sided")

           The Z-test Value is : -14.3333333333
           The p-value is : 2.0
```

9. It is now time to apply this defined test.

10. We compare two samples `pH_Data` and `pH_New`, and then compare `length_M1` and `length_M2`:

```
In [25]:   pH_Data = np.array([8.30, 8.42, 8.44, 8.32, 8.43, 8.41,
                               8.42, 8.46, 8.37, 8.42])
           pH_New = np.array([8.78, 8.85, 8.74, 8.83, 8.82, 8.79,
                              8.82, 8.74, 8.84, 8.78, 8.75, 8.81])
           z_test_two_samples(x1=pH_Data,x2=pH_New,s1=0.05,s2=0.05,
                              alternative="less",delta=0)

           The Z-test Value is : -18.5360598605
           The p-value is : 5.28434370461e-77
           The pooled variance is: 0.0214087209644

In [26]:   length_M1 = np.array([122.4, 123.12, 122.51, 123.12, 122.55,
                                 121.76, 122.31, 123.2, 122.48, 121.96])
           length_M2 = np.array([122.36, 121.88, 122.2, 122.88, 123.43,
                                 122.4, 122.12, 121.78, 122.85, 123.04])
           z_test_two_samples(x1=length_M1,x2=length_M2,s1=0.5,s2=0.5,
                              alternative="two.sided",delta=0)

           The Z-test Value is : 0.210190389885
           The p-value is : 0.833519079794
           The pooled variance is: 0.22360679775
```

Summary

In this chapter, we have introduced "statistical inference", which is a common usage term that consists of three parts: estimation, confidence intervals, and hypotheses testing. We began the chapter with the importance of likelihood and to obtain the MLE in many of the standard probability distributions using inbuilt modules. Later, simply to maintain the order of concepts, we defined functions exclusively for obtaining the confidence intervals. Finally, the chapter considered important families of tests that are useful across many important stochastic experiments.

In the next chapter, we will introduce the linear regression model, which more formally constitutes the applied face of the subject. We saw that the code development and application in Python is easier too, as we defined new tests as required and did not depend on an existing setup on the web.

6

Linear Regression Analysis

In the *Visualization techniques for continuous variable data* section of *Chapter 3, Data Visualization*, we saw different data visualization techniques that help in understanding data variables (boxplot and histograms) and their interrelationships (matrix of scatter plots).

We saw in *Example 4.6.1. Resistant line for the IO-CPU time*, an illustration of the resistant line, where CPU_Time depends linearly on the No_of_IO variable. The pair function's output in *Example 3.2.9. Octane rating of gasoline blends* indicated that the mileage of a car has strong correlations with the engine-related characteristics, such as displacement, horsepower, torque, the number of transmission speeds, and the type of transmission being manual or automatic. Further, the mileage of a car also strongly depends on the vehicle dimensions, such as its length, width, and weight.

The question addressed in this chapter is meant to further these initial findings through a more appropriate model. Now we take the next step forward and build linear regression models for the problems. Thus, in this chapter, we will provide more concrete answers for the mileage problem. At the end of this chapter, you will be able to build a regression model through the following steps:

- Building a linear regression model and their interpretation
- Validating the model assumptions
- Identifying the effect of every single observation, covariates, as well as the output
- Fixing the problem of dependent covariates
- Selecting the optimal linear regression model

Packages and settings - R and Python

The core R packages help us with most of the analysis, and we need only the additional package `faraway`. We first set the path and load the R packages followed by Python essentials:

1. Set the working directory:

   ```
   setwd("MyPath/R/Chapter_06")
   ```

2. Load the required R package:

   ```
   library(aplpack)
   ```

3. Complete the Python settings, actually Jupyter notebook (also, refer to *Chapter 6, Linear Regression Analysis*, ipynb):

   ```
   In [2]:  import os
            os.chdir("MyPath/Python/Chapter_06")
            import matplotlib.pyplot as plt
            import pandas as pd
            import numpy as np
            import statsmodels.api as sm
            import statsmodels.formula.api as smf
            from statsmodels.formula.api import ols
            from statsmodels.regression.linear_model import OLS
            import scipy.stats as st
   ```

The essence of regression

The first linear regression model was built by sir Francis Galton in 1908. The word regression implies towards the center. The covariates, also known as independent variables, features, or regressors, have a regressive effect on the output, also called dependent or regressand variable. Since the covariates are allowed and assumed to affect the output in linear increments, we call the model the **linear regression** model. The linear regression models provide an answer for the correlation between the regressand and the regressors and, as such, do not really establish causation.

As will be seen later in the chapter, using data, we will be able to understand the mileage of a car as a linear function of the car-related dynamics. From a purely scientific point of view, the mileage should really depend on complicated formulas of the car's speed, road conditions, climate, and so on.

However, it will be seen that linear models work just fine for the problem despite not really going into the technical details. However, there will also be a price to pay, in the sense that most regression models work well when the range of the variables is well defined and that an attempt to extrapolate the results does not usually result in satisfactory answers.

We will begin with the simple linear regression model where we have one dependent variable and one covariate.

The simple linear regression model

In *Example 4.6.1. Resistant line for the IO-CPU time* of *Chapter 4, Exploratory Analysis,* we built a resistant line for CPU_Time as a function of the No_of_IO processes. The results were satisfactory in the sense that the fitted line was very close to covering all the data points (refer to the *Resistant line for CPU_Time* figure of *Chapter 4, Exploratory Analysis*). However, we need more statistical validation of the estimated values of the slope and intercept terms. Here, we take a different approach and state the linear regression model in more technical details.

The simple linear regression model is given by $Y = \beta_0 + \beta_1 X + \varepsilon$, where X is the covariate/independent variable, Y is the regressand/dependent variable, and ε is the unobservable error term. The parameters of the linear model are specified by β_0 and β_1. Here, β_0 is the intercept term and corresponds to the value of Y when $x = 0$. The slope term, β_1, reflects the change in the Y value for a unit change in X. It is also common to refer to the β_0 and β_1 values as regression coefficients. To understand the regression model, we begin with n pairs of observations $(Y_1, X_1), \ldots, (Y_n, X_n)$, with each pair being completely independent of the other. We make an assumption of **normal** and **independent and identically distributed (iid)** for the error term ε, specifically $\varepsilon \sim N(0, \sigma^2)$, where σ^2 is the variance of the errors. The core assumptions of the model are as follows:

- All the observations are independent
- The regressand depends linearly on the regressors
- The errors are normally distributed, that is $\varepsilon \sim N(0, \sigma^2)$

We need to find all the unknown parameters in β_0, β_1, and σ^2. Suppose we have n independent observations. Statistical inference for the required parameters may be carried out using the `maximum likelihood` function as described in the *Maximum likelihood estimator* section of *Chapter 5, Statistical Inference*. The popular technique for the linear regression model is the `least squares` method, which identifies the parameters by minimizing the error sum of squares for the model and under the assumptions made thus far, agrees with the MLE. Let $\tilde{\beta}_0$ and $\tilde{\beta}_1$ be a choice of parameters. Then the residuals, the distance between the actual points and the model predictions, made using the proposed choice of $\left(\tilde{\beta}_0, \tilde{\beta}_1\right)$ on the i-th pair of observation $\left(Y_i, X_i\right)$ is defined by the following equation:

$$e_i = Y_i - \tilde{\beta}_0 + \tilde{\beta}_1 X_i, i = 1, 2, \ldots, n$$

Let's now specify different values for the pair (β_0, β_1) and visualize the residuals for them.

What happens to the arbitrary choice of parameters?

For the `IO_Time` dataset, the scatter plot suggests that the intercept term is about *0.05*. Further, the resistant line gives an estimate of the slope at about 0.04. We will have three pairs of guesses for (β_0, β_1) as *(0.05, 0.05)*, *(0.1, 0.04)*, and *(0.15, 0.03)*. We will now plot the data and see the different residuals for the three pairs of guesses.

Time for action - the arbitrary choice of parameters

1. We begin with reasonable guesses for the slope and intercept terms for a simple linear regression model. The idea is to inspect the difference between the fitted line and the actual observations. Invoke the graphics windows using `par(mfrow=c(3,1))`.

2. Obtain the scatter plot of `CPU_Time` against `No_of_IO` with the following:

    ```
    plot(No_of_IO,CPU_Time,xlab="Number of Processes",ylab="CPU Time",
    ylim=c(0,0.6),xlim=c(0,11))
    ```

3. For the guessed regression line with the values of (β_0, β_1) being *(0.05, 0.05)*, plot a line on the scatter plot with `abline(a=0.05,b=0.05,col= "blue")`.

4. Define a function that will find the `y` value for the guess of the pair *(0.05, 0.05)* using `myline1 = function(x) 0.05*x+0.05`.

5. Plot the error (residuals) made due to the choice of the pair *(0.05, 0.05)* from the actual points using the following loop, and give a title for the first pair of guesses:

```
for(i in 1:length(No_of_IO)){
   lines(c(No_of_IO[i], No_of_IO[i]), c(CPU_Time[i],
myline1(No_of_IO[i])),col="blue", pch=10)
        }
title("Residuals for the First Guess")
```

6. Repeat the preceding exercise for the last two pairs of guesses for the regression coefficients (β_0, β_1).

The complete R program is given as follows:

```
data(IO_Time)
par(mfrow=c(3,1))
plot(IO_Time$No_of_IO,IO_Time$CPU_Time,
     xlab="Number of Processes",ylab="CPU Time",
     ylim=c(0,0.6),xlim=c(0,11))
abline(a=0.05,b=0.05,col="blue")
myline1 = function(x) 0.05*x+0.05
for(i in 1:length(IO_Time$No_of_IO)) {
     lines(c(IO_Time$No_of_IO[i],IO_Time$No_of_IO[i]),
           c(IO_Time$CPU_Time[i],myline1(IO_Time$No_of_IO[i])),
           col="blue",pch=10)
        }
title("Residuals for the First Guess")
plot(IO_Time$No_of_IO,IO_Time$CPU_Time,
     xlab="Number of Processes",ylab="CPU Time",
     ylim=c(0,0.6),xlim=c(0,11))
abline(a=0.1,b=0.04,col="green")
myline2 = function(x) 0.04*x+0.1
for(i in 1:length(IO_Time$No_of_IO)) {
     lines(c(IO_Time$No_of_IO[i],IO_Time$No_of_IO[i]),
           c(IO_Time$CPU_Time[i],myline2(IO_Time$No_of_IO[i])),
           col="green",pch=10)
        }
title("Residuals for the Second Guess")
plot(IO_Time$No_of_IO,IO_Time$CPU_Time,
     xlab="Number of Processes",ylab="CPU Time",
     ylim=c(0,0.6),xlim=c(0,11))
abline(a=0.15,b=0.03,col="yellow")
myline3 = function(x) 0.03*x+0.15
for(i in 1:length(IO_Time$No_of_IO)) {
     lines(c(IO_Time$No_of_IO[i],IO_Time$No_of_IO[i]),
           c(IO_Time$CPU_Time[i],myline3(IO_Time$No_of_IO[i])),
           col="yellow",pch=10)
        }
title("Residuals for the Third Guess")
```

The output of the preceding R program is given as follows:

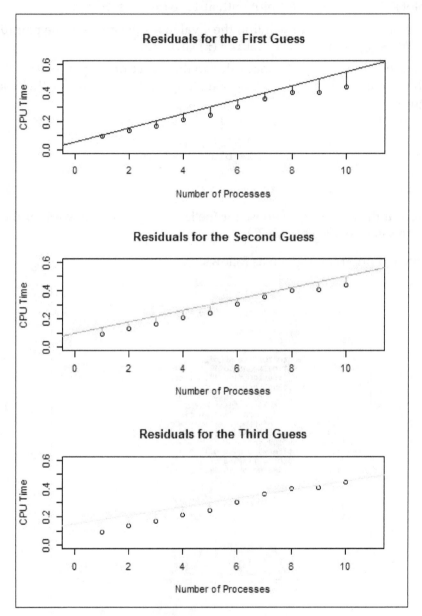

Residuals for the three choices of regression coefficients

What just happened?

We just executed an R program that displays the residuals of arbitrary choices for the regression parameters. The displayed result is shown in the preceding screenshot.

In the preceding R program, we first plot CPU_Time against No_of_IO. The first choice of the line is plotted using the abline function, and we specify the required intercept and slope through $a = 0.05$ and $b = 0.05$. From this straight line (color blue), we need to obtain the magnitude of error through perpendicular lines from the original points to the line. This is achieved through the for loop, where the lines function joins the points and the line.

For the pair *(0.05, 0.05)* as a guess of (β_0, β_1), we see that there is a progression in the residual values as x increases, and it is the other way for the guess of *(0.15, 0.03)*. In either of the cases, we are making huge mistakes (residuals) for certain x values. The middle plot for the guess *(0.1, 0.04)* does not seem to have large residual values. This choice may be better than the other two choices. Thus, we need to define a criterion that enables us to find the best values of (β_0, β_1) in some sense. The criterion is to minimize the sum of squared errors:

$$\min_{(\beta_0, \beta_1)} \sum_{i=1}^{n} e_i^2$$

Here, the following equation gives the sum of squared errors:

$$\sum_{i=1}^{n} e_i^2 = \sum_{i=1}^{n} \left\{ y_i - \left(\beta_0 + \beta_1 x_i \right) \right\}^2$$

Here, the summation is over all the observed pairs $(y_i, x_i), i = 1, 2, \ldots, n$. The technique of minimizing the error sum of squares is known as the method of least squares, and for the simple linear regression model, the values of (β_0, β_1) that meet the criterion are given by the following:

$$\hat{\beta_1} = \frac{S_{xy}}{S_{xx}}, \quad \hat{\beta_0} = \bar{y} - \hat{\beta_1}\bar{x}$$

Where:

$$\bar{x} = \frac{\sum_{i=1}^{n} x_i}{n}, and \, \bar{y} = \frac{\sum_{i=1}^{n} y_i}{n}$$

And:

$$S_{xx} = \sum_{i=1}^{n} (x_i - \bar{x})^2, and \, S_{xx} = \sum_{i=1}^{n} y_i (x_i - \bar{x})$$

We will now learn how to use R for building a simple linear regression model.

Building a simple linear regression model

We will use the R function `lm` for the required construction. The `lm` function creates an object of class `lm`, which consists of an ensemble of the fitted regression model. Through the following exercise, you will learn the following:

- The basic construction of an `lm` object
- The criterion that signifies the model significance
- The criterion that signifies the variable significance
- The variation of the output explained by the inputs

The relationship is specified by a formula in R, and the details related to the generic form may be obtained by entering `?formula` in the R console. That is, the `lm` function accepts a formula object for the model that we are attempting to build. `data.frame` may also be explicitly specified, which consists of the required data. We need to model `CPU_Time` as a function of `No_of_IO`, and this is carried out by specifying `CPU_Time ~ No_of_IO`. The `lm` function is wrapped around the formula to obtain our first linear regression model.

Time for action - building a simple linear regression model

We will build a simple linear regression model using the `lm` function with its useful arguments:

1. Create a simple linear regression model for `CPU_Time` as a function of `No_of_IO` by keying in `IO_lm <- lm(CPU_Time ~ No_of_IO, data=IO_Time)`.

2. Verify that `IO_lm` is of the `lm` class with `class(IO_lm)`.

3. Find the details of the fitted regression model using the `summary` function: `summary(IO_lm)`.

The output is given in the following screenshot:

```
> IO_lm <- lm(CPU_Time ~ No_of_IO,data=IO_Time)
> class(IO_lm)
[1] "lm"
> summary(IO_lm)

Call:
lm(formula = CPU_Time ~ No_of_IO, data = IO_Time)

Residuals:
      Min        1Q    Median        3Q       Max
 -0.01651  -0.01159  -0.00133   0.00528   0.02401

Coefficients:
             Estimate Std. Error t value Pr(>|t|)
(Intercept)   0.05093    0.01003    5.08  0.00096 ***
No_of_IO      0.04076    0.00162   25.21  6.6e-09 ***
---
Signif. codes:  0 '***' 0.001 '**' 0.01 '*' 0.05 '.' 0.1 ' ' 1

Residual standard error: 0.0147 on 8 degrees of freedom
Multiple R-squared: 0.988,      Adjusted R-squared: 0.986
F-statistic:  635 on 1 and 8 DF,  p-value: 6.57e-09
```

Building the first simple linear regression model

The first question the reader should ask himself is, "Is the model significant overall?". The answer is provided by the **p-value** of the **F-statistic** for the overall model. This appears in the final line of `summary(IO_lm)`. If the **p-value** is closer to 0, it implies that the model is useful. A rule of thumb for the significance of the model is that it should be less than 0.05. The general rule is that if you need the model significance at a certain percentage, say **P**, then the **p-value** of the **F-statistic** should be less than $(1-P/100)$.

Now that we know that the model is useful, we can ask whether the independent variable as well as the intercept term are significant or not. The answer to this question is provided by **Pr(>|t|)** for the variables in the summary.

R has a general way of displaying the highest significance level of a term using *******, ******, *****, and **.** in the **Signif. codes:**. This display may be easily compared with the review of a movie or a book! Just as with general ratings, where more stars indicate a better product, in our context, the higher the number of stars, the more significant the variables for the built model. In our linear model, we find No_of_IO to be highly significant. The estimate value of No_of_IO is given as **0.04076**. This coefficient has the interpretation that for a unit increase in the number of IOs, CPU_Time is expected to increase by **0.04076**.

Now that we know that the model as well as the independent variable are significant, we need to know how much of the variability in CPU_Time is explained by No_of_IO. The answer to this question is provided by the measure R_2, not to be confused with the letter R for the software, which when multiplied by 100 gives the percentage of variation in the regressand explained by the regressor. The term R_2 is also called the **coefficient of determination**.

In our example, 98.76 percent of the variation in CPU_Time is explained by No_of_IO, see the value associated with **Multiple R-squared** in summary(IO_lm). The R_2 measure does not consider the number of parameters estimated or the number of observations n in a model. A more robust explanation, which takes into consideration the number of parameters and observations, is provided by **Adjusted R-squared**, which is 98.6 percent.

We have thus far not commented on the first numerical display as a result of using the summary function. This relates to the residuals, and the display is about the basic summary of the residual values. The residuals vary from **-0.016509** to **0.024006**, which are not very large in comparison with the CPU_Time values, check with summary(CPU_Time) for instance. Also, the median of the residual values is very close to zero, and this is an important criterion as the median of the standard normal distribution is *0*.

What just happened?

You fitted a simple linear regression model where the independent variable is No_of_IO and the dependent variable (output) is CPU_Time. The important quantities to look for the model significance, the regression coefficients, and so on have been clearly illustrated.

Have a go hero

Load the `anscombe` dataset from the datasets package. The `anscombe` dataset has four pairs of datasets in `x1`, `x2`, `x3`, `x4`, `y1`, `y2`, `y3`, and `y4`. Fit a simple regression model for all four pairs and obtain the summary for each pair. Make your comments on the summaries. Pay careful attention to the details of the `summary` function. If you need further help, simply try out `example(anscombe)`.

We will next look at the **Analysis of Variance (ANOVA)** method for the regression model and obtain the confidence intervals for the model parameters.

ANOVA and the confidence intervals

The `summary` function of the `lm` object specifies the **p-value** for each variable in the model, including the intercept term. Technically, the hypothesis problem is testing $H_0^j : \beta_j = 0, j = 0,1$ against the corresponding alternative hypothesis, $H_1^j : \beta_j \neq 0, j = 0,1$. This testing problem is technically different from the simultaneous hypothesis testing, $H_0 : \beta_0 = \beta_1 = 0$ against the alternative that at least one of the regression coefficients is different from 0. The ANOVA technique gives the answer to the latter null hypothesis of interest.

> For more details about the ANOVA technique, you may refer to
> http://en.wikipedia.org/wiki/Analysis_of_variance.

Using the `anova` function, it is very simple in R to obtain the ANOVA table for a linear regression model. Let's apply it to our `IO_lm` linear regression model.

Time for action - ANOVA and the confidence intervals

The R functions--`anova` and `confint`--respectively help obtain the ANOVA table and confidence intervals from the `lm` objects. Here, we use them for the `IO_lm` regression object:

1. Use the `anova` function on the `IO_lm` object to obtain the ANOVA table by `IO_anova <- anova(IO_lm)`.

2. Display the ANOVA table by keying in `IO_anova` in the console.

3. The 95 percent confidence intervals for the intercept and the `No_of_IO` variable are obtained by `confint(IO_lm)`.

The output in R is as follows:

```
> IO_anova <- anova(IO_lm)
> IO_anova
Analysis of Variance Table

Response: CPU_Time
          Df Sum Sq Mean Sq F value  Pr(>F)
No_of_IO   1 0.1370  0.1370     635 6.6e-09 ***
Residuals  8 0.0017  0.0002
---
Signif. codes:  0 '***' 0.001 '**' 0.01 '*' 0.05 '.' 0.1 ' ' 1
> confint(IO_lm)
              2.5 %   97.5 %
(Intercept) 0.02780 0.07407
No_of_IO    0.03703 0.04449
```

ANOVA and the confidence intervals for the simple linear regression model

The ANOVA table confirms that the No_of_IO variable is indeed significant. Note the difference in the criteria for confirming this with respect to summary(IO_lm). In the former case, the significance was arrived at using the *t*-statistics, and here, we have used the *F*-statistic. Precisely, we check for the variance significance of the input variable. We now provide the tool for obtaining confidence intervals.

Check whether or not the estimated values of the parameters fall within the 95 percent confidence intervals. The preceding results show that we indeed have a very good linear regression model. However, we also made a host of assumptions in the beginning of the section, and a good practice is to ask how valid they are in the experiment. We next consider the problem of validation of the assumptions.

What just happened?

The ANOVA table is a very fundamental block for a regression model, and it gives the split of the sum of squares for the variable(s) and the error term. The difference between ANOVA and the summary of the linear model object is in the respective *p*-values reported by them as **Pr(>F)** and **Pr(>|t|)**. You also found a method for obtaining the confidence intervals for the independent variables of the regression model.

Model validation

The violations of the assumptions may arise in more than one way. Tattar, et. al. (2012), Kutner, et. al. (2005) discuss the numerous ways in which the assumptions are violated, and an adaption of the methods mentioned there is now considered:

- **The regression function is not linear**: In this case, we expect the residuals to have a pattern that is not linear when viewed against the regressors. Thus, a plot of the residuals against the regressors is expected to indicate whether this assumption is violated.

- **The error terms do not have constant variance**: Note that we made an assumption stating that $\varepsilon \sim N(0, \sigma^2)$, that is the magnitude of errors does not depend on the corresponding x or y value. Thus, we expect the plot of the residuals against the predicted y values to reveal whether this assumption is violated.

- **The error terms are not independent:** A plot of the residuals against the serial number of the observations indicates whether the error terms are independent or not. We typically expect this plot to exhibit a random walk if the errors are independent. If any systematic pattern is observed, we conclude that the errors are not independent.

- **The model fits all but one or a few outlier observations**: Outliers are a huge concern in any analytical study as even a single outlier tends to destabilize the entire model. A simple boxplot of the residuals indicates the presence of an outlier. If any outlier is present, such observations need to be removed and the model needs to be rebuilt. The current step of model validation needs to be repeated for the rebuilt model. In fact, the process needs to be iterated until there are no more outliers.

  However, we need to caution the reader that if the subject experts feel that such outliers are indeed expected values, it may convey that some appropriate variables are missing in the regression model.

- **The error terms are not normally distributed**: This is one of the most crucial assumptions of the linear regression model. The violation of this assumption is verified using the normal probability plot in which the predicted values (actually cumulative probabilities) are plotted against the observed values. If the values fall along a straight line, the normality assumption for errors holds true. The model is to be rejected if this assumption is violated.

The next section shows how to obtain the residual plots for model validation.

Time for action - residual plots for model validation

The R functions `resid` and `fitted` can be used to extract residuals and fitted values from an `lm` object through the following steps:

1. Find the residuals of the fitted regression model using the `resid` function--
   `IO_lm_resid <- resid(IO_lm)`.

2. We need six plots, and hence, we invoke the graphics editor with `par(mfrow = c(3,2))`.

3. Sketch the plot of residuals against the predictor variable with `plot(No_of_IO, IO_lm_resid)`.

4. To check whether the regression model is linear or not, obtain the plots of absolute residual values against the predictor variable and also that of squared residual values against the predictor variable respectively with `plot(No_of_IO, abs(IO_lm_resid),...)` and `plot(No_of_IO, IO_lm_resid^2,...)`.

5. The assumption that errors have constant variance may be verified by the plot of residuals against the fitted values of the regressand. The required plot is obtained by `plot(IO_lm$fitted.values,IO_lm_resid)`.

6. The assumption that the errors are independent of each other may be verified plotting the residuals against their index numbers--`plot.ts(IO_lm_resid)`.

7. Finally, the presence of outliers is investigated by the boxplot of the residuals--`boxplot(IO_lm_resid)`.

8. Finally, the assumption of normality for the error terms is verified through the normal probability plot. This plot is on a new graphics editor.

The complete R program is as follows:

```
attach(IO_Time)
IO_lm_resid=resid(IO_lm)
par(mfrow=c(3,2))
plot(No_of_IO, IO_lm_resid,main="Plot of Residuals Vs Predictor Variable",
     ylab="Residuals",xlab="Predictor Variable")
plot(No_of_IO, abs(IO_lm_resid), main=
     "Plot of Absolute Residual Values Vs Predictor Variable",
     ylab="Absolute Residuals", xlab="Predictor Variable")
# Equivalently
plot(No_of_IO, IO_lm_resid^2,main=
     "Plot of Squared Residual Values Vs Predictor Variable",
     ylab="Squared Residuals", xlab="Predictor Variable")
plot(IO_lm$fitted.values,IO_lm_resid, main=
     "Plot of Residuals Vs Fitted Values",
     ylab="Residuals", xlab="Fitted Values")
plot.ts(IO_lm_resid, main="Sequence Plot of the Residuals")
boxplot(IO_lm_resid,main="Box Plot of the Residuals")
rpanova = anova(IO_lm)
IO_lm_resid_rank=rank(IO_lm_resid)
tc_mse=rpanova$Mean[2]
IO_lm_resid_expected=sqrt(tc_mse)*qnorm((IO_lm_resid_rank-0.375)/
                                        (length(CPU_Time)+0.25))
plot(IO_lm_resid,IO_lm_resid_expected,xlab="Expected",
     ylab="Residuals",main="The Normal Probability Plot")
abline(0,1)
```

The resulting plot for the model validation plot is given next. If you run the preceding R program up to the `rpanova` code, you will find the plot looks like the following:

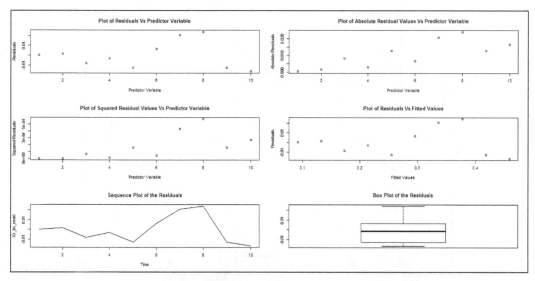

Checking for violations of assumptions of IO_lm

We have used the `resid` function to extract the residuals out of the `lm` object. The first plot of residuals against the predictor variable `No_of_IO` shows that the higher the number of IO processes, the larger the residual value, as is also confirmed by **Plot of Absolute Residual Values Vs Predictor Variable** and **Plot of Squared Residual Values Vs Predictor Variable**. However, there is no clear non-linear pattern suggested here.

The **Plot of Residuals Vs Fitted Values** is similar to the first plot of residuals against the predictor. The time series plot of residuals does not indicate a strict deterministic trend and appears a bit similar to the random walk. Thus, these plots do not give evidence of any kind of dependence among the observations. The boxplot does not indicate any presence of an outlier.

The Normal Probability Plot for the residuals is given next:

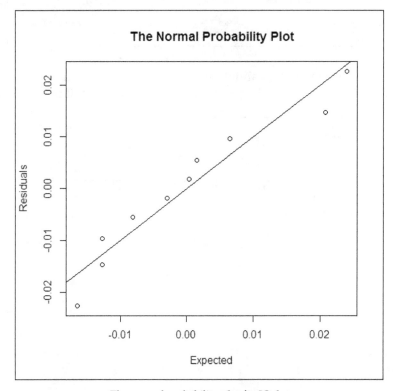

The normal probability plot for IO_lm

As all the points fall closer to the straight line, the normality assumption for the errors does not appear to be violated.

What just happened?

The R program given earlier gives various residual plots, which help in the validation of the model. It is important that these plots are always checked whenever a linear regression model is built. For CPU_Time as a function of No_of_IO, the linear regression model is a good model.

Doing it in Python

We will simply give the working of the essential Python program here:

1. For the IO_Time data, we first load and then plot the scatterplot:

```
In [4]:   IOT = pd.read_csv("Data/IO_Time.csv",delimiter=',')
          IO = IOT.No_of_IO
          CPUT = IOT.CPU_Time
          plt.plot(IO,CPUT)
          plt.xlabel("No of IO"); plt.ylabel("CPU Time")
          plt.show()
```

The output is not displayed here as it is a repeat of the R exercise. We use the statsmodels package for building the regression model.

2. We append the `IO` vector with the constant 1 and then use `OLS` from `statsmodels` to fit the linear regression model:

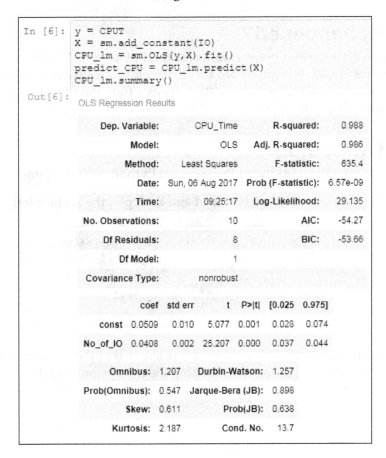

```
In [6]:  y = CPUT
         X = sm.add_constant(IO)
         CPU_lm = sm.OLS(y,X).fit()
         predict_CPU = CPU_lm.predict(X)
         CPU_lm.summary()
```

Out[6]:

OLS Regression Results

Dep. Variable:	CPU_Time	R-squared:	0.988
Model:	OLS	Adj. R-squared:	0.986
Method:	Least Squares	F-statistic:	635.4
Date:	Sun, 06 Aug 2017	Prob (F-statistic):	6.57e-09
Time:	09:25:17	Log-Likelihood:	29.135
No. Observations:	10	AIC:	-54.27
Df Residuals:	8	BIC:	-53.66
Df Model:	1		
Covariance Type:	nonrobust		

	coef	std err	t	P>|t|	[0.025	0.975]
const	0.0509	0.010	5.077	0.001	0.028	0.074
No_of_IO	0.0408	0.002	25.207	0.000	0.037	0.044

Omnibus:	1.207	Durbin-Watson:	1.257
Prob(Omnibus):	0.547	Jarque-Bera (JB):	0.898
Skew:	0.611	Prob(JB):	0.638
Kurtosis:	2.187	Cond. No.	13.7

Of course, we don't have different answers here. In fact, we are only giving the Python implementation. Fitting of the no-intercept model is given in the companion .ipynb file following the preceding code block. Next, we look at the ANOVA and confidence intervals.

To obtain the ANOVA table, we again fit the linear model using `ols` from the `statsmodels.formula.api` module and then apply `anova_lm` from the `stats` package:

```
In [9]:  CPU_lm2 = ols('CPU_Time~No_of_IO',data=IOT).fit()
         print(sm.stats.anova_lm(CPU_lm2,typ=2))

                    sum_sq    df          F        PR(>F)
         No_of_IO  0.137047  1.0  635.378763  6.569355e-09
         Residual  0.001726  8.0         NaN           NaN

In [10]:  print(CPU_lm.conf_int(0.05))

                        0         1
         const    0.027798  0.074069
         No_of_IO 0.037029  0.044486
```

The `conf_int` extraction gives the desired confidence intervals for the slope and intercept terms. Residual plots are considered next.

3. Six important residual plots for the validation are now built paralleling the previous R implementation. The codes are obvious and do not need further explanation:

```
In [12]:  CPU_Resid = CPU_lm.resid
          plt.subplot(3,2,1)
          plt.plot(IO,CPU_Resid)
          plt.xlabel("Predictor Variable")
          plt.ylabel("Residuals")
          plt.title("Plot of Residuals Vs Predictor Variable")
          plt.subplot(3,2,2)
          plt.plot(IO,abs(CPU_Resid))
          plt.xlabel("Predictor Variable")
          plt.ylabel("Absolute Residuals")
          plt.title("Plot of Absolute Residual Values Vs Predictor Variable")
          plt.subplot(3,2,3)
          plt.plot(IO,CPU_Resid**2)
          plt.xlabel("Predictor Variable")
          plt.ylabel("Squared Residuals")
          plt.title("Plot of Squared Residual Values Vs Predictor Variable")
          plt.subplot(3,2,4)
          plt.plot(predict_CPU,CPU_Resid)
          plt.xlabel("Fitted Values")
          plt.ylabel("Residuals")
          plt.title("Plot of Residuals Vs Predicted Values")
          plt.subplot(3,2,5)
          plt.plot(np.arange(1,len(CPU_Resid)+1),CPU_Resid)
          plt.xlabel("Sequence Number")
          plt.ylabel("Residuals")
          plt.title("Sequence Plot of the Residuals")
          plt.subplot(3,2,6)
          plt.boxplot(CPU_Resid)
          plt.title("Box Plot of the Residuals")
          plt.show()
```

The output of the preceding code block is chunked. Moreover, it is available in the companion `ipynb` file for reference.

Have a go hero

From a theoretical perspective and the author's experience, the seven plots obtained earlier were found to be very useful. However, R, by default, also gives a very useful set of residual plots for an `lm` object. For example, `plot(my_lm)` generates a powerful set of model validation plots. Explore the same for `IO_lm` with `plot(IO_lm)`. You can explore more about `plot` and `lm` with the `plot.lm` function.

We will next consider the general multiple linear regression model for the gasoline problem considered in the *Chapter 3, Data Visualization*, and *Chapter 4, Exploratory Analysis.*

Multiple linear regression model

In the *The simple linear regression model* section, we considered an almost (un)realistic problem of having only one predictor. We need to extend the model for the practical problems when one has more than a single predictor. In *Example 3.2.9. Octane rating of gasoline blends*, we had a graphical study of mileage as a function of various vehicle variables. In this section, we will build a multiple linear regression model for the mileage.

If we have X_1, X_2, ..., X_p independent sets of variables that have a linear effect on the dependent variable Y, the *multiple linear regression model* is given by the following equation:

$$Y = \beta_0 + \beta_1 X_1 + \beta_2 X_2 + \cdots + \beta_p X_p + \varepsilon$$

This model is similar to the simple linear regression model, and we have the same interpretation as earlier. Here, we have additional independent variables in X_1, ..., X_p and their effect on the regressand Y respectively through the additional regression parameters $\beta_2, ..., \beta_p$. Now suppose we have n pairs of random observations $(Y_1, X_1), ..., (Y_n, X_n)$ for understanding the multiple linear regression model, here $X_i = (X_{i1}, ..., X_{ip}), i = 1, ..., n$. A matrix form representation of the multiple linear regression model is useful in the understanding of the estimator for the vector of regression coefficients.

We define the following quantities:

$$Y = (Y_1, \ldots, Y_n)'$$

$$\varepsilon = (\varepsilon_1, \ldots, \varepsilon_n)'$$

$$\beta = (\beta_0, \beta_1, \ldots, \beta_p)', \text{ and}$$

$$X = \begin{bmatrix} 1 & X_{11} & X_{12} & \cdots & X_{1p} \\ 1 & X_{21} & X_{22} & \cdots & X_{2p} \\ \vdots & & \vdots & & \vdots \\ 1 & X_{n1} & X_{n2} & \cdots & X_{np} \end{bmatrix}$$

The multiple linear regression model for n observations can be written in a compact matrix form, as follows:

$$Y = X'\beta + \varepsilon$$

The `least squares` method estimate of β is given by the following equation:

$$\hat{\beta} = (X'X)^{-1} X'Y$$

Let's fit a multiple linear regression model for the gasoline mileage data considered earlier.

Averaging k simple linear regression models or a multiple linear regression model

We already know how to build a simple linear regression model. Why should we learn another theory when an extension is possible in a certain manner? Intuitively, we can build k models consisting of the kth variable and then simply average out over the k models. Such an averaging can also be considered for the univariate case.

Here, we may divide the covariate over distinct intervals, then build the simple linear regression model over the intervals, and finally average over the different models. Montgomery, et. al. (2001) highlights the drawback of such an approach, pages 120-122. Typically, the simple linear regression model may indicate the wrong sign for the regression coefficients. The wrong sign of such a naïve approach may arise from multiple reasons: restricting the range of some regressors, critical regressors may have been omitted from the model building, or some computational errors may have crept in.

To drive home the point, we consider an example from Montgomery, et. al.

Time for action - averaging k simple linear regression models

We build three models here. We have a vector of regressand `y` and two covariates `x1` and `x2`:

1. Enter the dependent variable and the independent variables with `y = c(1, 5,3,8,5,3,10,7)`, `x1 = c(2,4,5,6,8,10,11,13)`, and `x2 = c(1,2, 2,4,4,4,6,6)`.

2. Visualize the relationships among the variables with the following:

   ```
   par(mfrow=c(1,3))
   plot(x1,y)

   plot(x2,y)

   plot(x1,x2)
   ```

3. Build the individual simple linear regression model and our first multiple regression model with the following:

   ```
   summary(lm(y~x1))

   summary(lm(y~x2))

   summary(lm(y~x1+x2)) # Our first multiple regression model
   ```

```
> summary(lm(y~x1))
Call:
lm(formula = y ~ x1)
Residuals:
   Min    1Q Median     3Q    Max
-3.466 -1.303 -0.697  1.753  3.387
Coefficients:
            Estimate Std. Error t value Pr(>|t|)
(Intercept)    1.835      2.115    0.87     0.42
x1             0.463      0.259    1.79     0.12
Residual standard error: 2.58 on 6 degrees of freedom
Multiple R-squared: 0.348,     Adjusted R-squared: 0.24
F-statistic: 3.21 on 1 and 6 DF,  p-value: 0.124
> summary(lm(y~x2))
Call:
lm(formula = y ~ x2)

Residuals:
   Min    1Q Median     3Q    Max
-2.733 -0.979 -0.445  1.729  2.267
Coefficients:
            Estimate Std. Error t value Pr(>|t|)
(Intercept)    0.581      1.570    0.37    0.724
x2             1.288      0.391    3.29    0.017 *
---
Signif. codes:  0 '***' 0.001 '**' 0.01 '*' 0.05 '.' 0.1 ' ' 1
Residual standard error: 1.91 on 6 degrees of freedom
Multiple R-squared: 0.644,     Adjusted R-squared: 0.585
F-statistic: 10.9 on 1 and 6 DF,  p-value: 0.0165
> summary(lm(y~x1+x2))
Call:
lm(formula = y ~ x1 + x2)
Residuals:
      1      2      3      4      5      6      7      8
-1.2403 1.5550 0.7772 -0.2991 -0.8546 -0.4100 0.5136 -0.0418
Coefficients:
            Estimate Std. Error t value Pr(>|t|)
(Intercept)    1.036      0.895    1.16   0.2993
x1            -1.222      0.329   -3.72   0.0137 *
x2             3.649      0.672    5.43   0.0029 **
---
Signif. codes:  0 '***' 0.001 '**' 0.01 '*' 0.05 '.' 0.1 ' ' 1
Residual standard error: 1.08 on 5 degrees of freedom
Multiple R-squared: 0.905,     Adjusted R-squared: 0.868
F-statistic: 23.9 on 2 and 5 DF,  p-value: 0.00275
```

Averaging k simple linear regression models

What just happened?

The visual plot (the preceding screenshot) indicates that both x_1 and x_2 have a positive impact on y, and this is also captured in `lm(y~x1)` and `lm(y~x2)` (refer to the next R output display). We have omitted the scatter plot, but you should be able to see the same on your screen after running the R code after step 2 in the next section. However, both the models are under the assumption that the information contained in x_1 and x_2 is complete. The variables are also seen to have a significant effect on the output. However, the metrics such as multiple R-squared and adjusted R-squared are very poor for both the simple (linear) regression models.

This is one of the indications that we need to collect more information, and thus, we include both the variables and build our first multiple linear regression model (refer to the next section for more details). There are two important changes worth registering now. First, the sign of the regression coefficient x_1 now becomes negative, which is now contradicting the intuition. The second observation is the great increase in the R-squared metric value.

To summarize our observations here, it suffices to say that the sum of the parts may sometimes fall way short of the entire picture.

Building a multiple linear regression model

The R function `lm` remains the same as earlier. We will continue with *Example 3.2.9. Octane rating of gasoline blends* from the *Visualization techniques for continuous variable data* section of *Chapter 3, Data Visualization*. Recall that the variables--independent and dependent--are stored in the `Gasoline` dataset in the `RSADBE` package.

Now we tell R that y, which is the mileage, is the dependent variable, and we need to build a multiple linear regression model that includes all other variables of the `Gasoline` object. Thus, the formula is specified by y~., indicating that all other variables from the `Gasoline` object need to be treated as the independent variables. We proceed as earlier to obtain the summary of the fitted multiple linear regression model.

Time for action - building a multiple linear regression model

The method of building a multiple linear regression model remains the same as earlier. If all the variables in data.frame are to be used, we use the formula y ~ .. However, if we need specific variables, say x1 and x3, the formula would be y ~ x1 + x3:

1. Build the multiple linear regression model with gasoline_lm <- lm(y~., data=Gasoline). Here, the formula y~. considers the variable y as the dependent variable and all the remaining variables in the Gasoline data frame as independent variables.

2. Get the details of the fitted multiple linear regression model with summary(gasoline_lm).

The R screen then appears as follows:

```
> gasoline_lm <- lm(y~., data=Gasoline)
> summary(gasoline_lm)
Call:
lm(formula = y ~ ., data = Gasoline)
Residuals:
    Min      1Q Median      3Q     Max
 -3.582  -1.527  -0.007   1.729   4.270
Coefficients:
              Estimate Std. Error t value Pr(>|t|)
(Intercept)  -2.62e+02   2.39e+02   -1.10    0.295
x1           -1.39e-01   6.00e-02   -2.31    0.039 *
x2           -6.64e-02   8.80e-02   -0.75    0.465
x3            2.09e-01   1.07e-01    1.95    0.075 .
x4            2.44e+02   2.68e+02    0.91    0.380
x5            8.15e+01   5.94e+01    1.37    0.195
x6            1.28e+00   1.39e+00    0.92    0.374
x7           -2.66e+00   2.90e+00   -0.92    0.377
x8            2.60e-01   1.48e-01    1.75    0.105
x9            4.14e-02   3.85e-01    0.11    0.916
x10          -1.10e-02   7.11e-03   -1.54    0.149
x11M         -2.66e+00   3.03e+00   -0.88    0.398
---
Signif. codes:  0 '***' 0.001 '**' 0.01 '*' 0.05 '.' 0.1 ' ' 1
Residual standard error: 2.99 on 12 degrees of freedom
  (1 observation deleted due to missingness)
Multiple R-squared: 0.895,      Adjusted R-squared: 0.798
F-statistic: 9.27 on 11 and 12 DF,  p-value: 0.000281
```

Building the multiple linear regression model

As with the simple model, we need to first check whether the overall model is significant by looking at the p-value of the F-statistics, which appears as the last line of the summary output. Here, the value 0.0003 being much closer to zero, the overall model is significant. Of the 11 variables specified for modeling, only x_1 and x_3, that is the engine displacement and torque, are found to have a meaningful linear effect on the mileage. The estimated regression coefficient values indicate that the engine displacement has a negative impact on the mileage, whereas the torque impacts positively. These results are in confirmation with the basic science of the mileage issues.

We have a tricky output for the eleventh independent variable, which, for some strange reason, R has renamed `x11M`. We need to explain this. The reader should verify the output as a consequence of running `sapply(Gasoline,class)` on the console.

Now, the x_{11} variable is a factor variable assuming two possible values `A` and `M`, which stand for the transmission box being `Automatic` or `Manual`. As the categorical variables are of special nature, they need to be handled differently. The user may be tempted to skip this as the variable is seen to be insignificant in this case. However, the interpretation is very useful and the "skip" part may prove expensive later. For computational purposes, an m-level factor variable is used to create m-1 new different variables. If the variable assumes the level l, the lth variable takes value 1, else 0, for $l = 1, 2, …, m$-1. If the variable assumes level m, all the $(m$-1) new variables take the value 0.

Now, R takes the lth factor level and names that vector by concatenating the variable name and the factor level. Hence, we have `x11M` as the variable name in the output. Here, we found the factor variable to be insignificant. If in certain experiments, we find some factor levels to be significant at certain p-value, we can't ignore the other factor levels even if their p-values suggest them as insignificant.

What just happened?

The building of a multiple linear regression model is a straightforward extension of the simple linear regression model. The interpretation is where one must be more careful with the multiple linear regression model.

We will now look at the ANOVA and confidence intervals for the multiple linear regression model. It is to be noted that the usage is not different from the simple linear regression model as we are still dealing with the lm object.

The ANOVA and confidence intervals for the multiple linear regression model

Again, we use the anova and confint functions to obtain the required results. Here, the null hypothesis of interest is whether all the regression coefficients equal 0, that is $H_0 : \beta_0 = \beta_1 = ... = \beta_p = 0$ against the alternative that at least one of the regression coefficients is different from 0, that is $H_1 : \beta_j \neq 0$ for at least one $j = 0, 1, ..., p$.

Time for action - the ANOVA and confidence intervals for the multiple linear regression model

The use of anova and confint extend in a similar way as lm is used for simple and multiple linear regression models:

1. The ANOVA table for the multiple regression model is obtained in the same way as for the simple regression model; after all, we are dealing with the object of class lm: gasoline_anova<-anova(gasoline_lm).

2. The confidence intervals for the independent variables are obtained using `confint(gasoline_lm)`.

The R output is given as follows:

```
> gasoline_anova <- anova(gasoline_lm)
> gasoline_anova
Analysis of Variance Table
Response: y
          Df Sum Sq Mean Sq F value  Pr(>F)
x1         1    822     822   92.26 5.5e-07 ***
x2         1     10      10    1.08    0.32
x3         1      5       5    0.58    0.46
x4         1     15      15    1.64    0.22
x5         1      0       0    0.01    0.94
x6         1     15      15    1.67    0.22
x7         1     12      12    1.32    0.27
x8         1      3       3    0.39    0.54
x9         1      2       2    0.24    0.64
x10        1     18      18    2.05    0.18
x11        1      7       7    0.77    0.40
Residuals 12    107       9
---
Signif. codes:  0 '***' 0.001 '**' 0.01 '*' 0.05 '.' 0.1 ' ' 1
> confint(gasoline_lm)
                  2.5 %      97.5 %
(Intercept) -781.56833 258.535576
x1            -0.26958  -0.008064
x2            -0.25804   0.125315
x3            -0.02444   0.441848
x4          -339.18604 827.165428
x5           -47.88320 210.899288
x6            -1.74064   4.303165
x7            -8.96745   3.650417
x8            -0.06293   0.582128
x9            -0.79752   0.880287
x10           -0.02647   0.004523
x11M          -9.26003   3.947366
```

The ANOVA and confidence intervals for the multiple linear regression model

Note the difference between the `anova` and `summary` results. Now, we find only the first variable to be significant. The interpretation for the confidence intervals is left to you.

What just happened?

The extension from simple to multiple linear regression model in R, especially for the ANOVA and confidence intervals, is straightforward.

Have a go hero

The ANOVA table in the preceding screenshot and the summary of `gasoline_lm` in the screenshot given in step 2 of the *Time for action – building a multiple linear regression model* section build linear regression models using the significant variables only. Are you amused?

Useful residual plots

In the context of multiple linear regression models, modifications of the residuals have been found to be more useful than the residuals themselves. We have assumed the residuals to follow a normal distribution with mean zero and unknown variance. An estimator of the unknown variance is provided by the mean residual sum of squares. There are four useful types of residuals for the current model:

- **Standardized residuals**: We know that the residuals have zero mean. Thus, the standardized residuals are obtained by scaling the residuals with the estimator of the standard deviation, that is the square root of the mean residual sum of squares. The standardized residuals are defined by the following:

$$d_i = \frac{e_i}{\sqrt{MS_{Res}}}$$

Here, $MS_{Res} = \sum_{i=1}^{n} e_i^2 / (n-p)$, and p is the number of covariates in the model. The residual is expected to have mean 0, and MS_{Res} is an estimate of its variance. Hence, we expect the standardized residuals to have a standard normal distribution. This, in turn, helps us verify whether the normality assumption for the residuals is meaningful or not.

- **Semi-studentized residuals**: The semi-studentized residuals are defined by the following:

$$r_i = \frac{e_i}{\sqrt{MS_{Res}(1-h_{ii})}}, i = 1,\ldots,n$$

Here, *hii* is the *i*-th diagonal element of the matrix $H = X(X'X)^{-1}X'$.

The variance of a residual depends on the covariate value, and hence, a flat scaling by MS_{Res} is not appropriate. A correction is provided by $(1-h_{ii})$, and $MS_{Res}(1-h_{ii})$ turns out to be an estimate of the variance of e_i. This is the motivation for the semi-studentized residual r_i.

- **PRESS residuals**: The predicted residual, PRESS, for observation *i* is the difference between the actual value y_i and the value predicted for it, using a regression model based on the remaining *(n-1)* observations. Now let $\hat{\beta}_{(i)}$ be the estimator of regression coefficients based on the *(n-1)* observations (not including the ith observations). Then, PRESS for observations *i* is given by the following:

$$e_{(i)} = y_i - x_i\hat{\beta}_{(i)}, i = 1, \ldots, n$$

Here, the idea is that the estimate of residual for an observation is more appropriate when obtained from a model that is not influenced by its own value.

- **R-student residuals**: This residual is especially useful for the detection of outliers:

$$t_i = \frac{e_i}{\sqrt{MS_{Res(i)}(1-h_{ii})}}$$

Here, $MS_{Res(i)}$ is an estimator of the variance σ^2 based on the remaining *(n-1)* observations. The scaling change is on similar lines as with the studentized residuals.

The task of building n linear models may look daunting! However, there are very useful formulas in statistics and functions in R that save the day for us. It is appropriate that we use those functions and develop the residual plots for the Gasoline dataset. Let's set ourselves for some action.

Time for action - residual plots for the multiple linear regression model

R functions `resid`, `hatvalues`, `rstandard`, and `rstudent` are available, which can be applied on an `lm` object to obtain the required residuals:

1. Get the MSE of the regression model with `gasoline_lm_mse <- gasoline_anova$Mean[length(gasoline_anova$Mean)]`.

2. Extract the residuals with the `resid` function, and standardize the residuals using `stan_resid_gasoline <- resid(gasoline_lm)/sqrt( gasoline_lm_mse)`.

3. To obtain the semi-studentized residuals, we first need to get the h_{ii} elements, which are obtainable using the `hatvalues` function--`hatvalues(gasoline_lm)`. The remaining code is given at the end of this list.

4. The PRESS residuals are calculated using the `rstandard` function available in R.

5. The R-student residuals can be obtained using the `rstudent` function in R. The detailed code is as follows:

```
gasoline_lm_mse <- gasoline_anova$Mean[length(gasoline_anova$Mean)]
stan_resid_gasoline <- resid(gasoline_lm)/sqrt(gasoline_lm_mse)
#Standardizing the residuals
studentized_resid_gasoline <- resid(gasoline_lm)/
  (sqrt(gasoline_lm_mse*(1-hatvalues(gasoline_lm))))
#Studentizing the residuals
pred_resid_gasoline <- rstandard(gasoline_lm)
pred_student_resid_gasoline <- rstudent(gasoline_lm)
# returns the R-Student Prediction Residuals
par(mfrow=c(2,2))
plot(gasoline_fitted,stan_resid_gasoline,xlab="Fitted",
    ylab="Residuals")
title("Standardized Residual Plot")
plot(gasoline_fitted,studentized_resid_gasoline,xlab="Fitted",
    ylab="Residuals")
title("Studentized Residual Plot")
plot(gasoline_fitted,pred_resid_gasoline,xlab="Fitted",
    ylab="Residuals")
title("PRESS Plot")
plot(gasoline_fitted,pred_student_resid_gasoline,xlab="Fitted",
    ylab="Residuals")
title("R-Student Residual Plot")
```

All four residual plots in the screenshot given in the *Time for action – residual plots for model navigation* section look identical even though there is a difference in their y-scaling. It is apparent from the residual plots that there are no patterns that show the presence of non-linearity, that is the linearity assumption appears valid. In the standardized residual plot, all the observations are well within **-3** and **3**. Thus, it is correct to say that there are no outliers in the dataset:

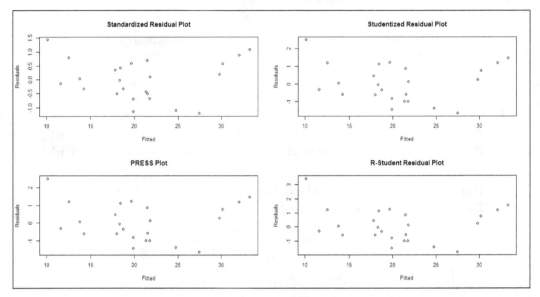

Residual plots for the multiple linear regression model

What just happened?

Using `resid`, `rstudent`, `rstandard`, and other functions, we have obtained useful residual plots for the multiple linear regression models.

Regression diagnostics

In the *Useful residual plots* subsection, we saw how outliers can be identified using the residual plots. If there are outliers, we need to ask the following questions:

- Is the observation an outlier due to an anomalous value in one or more covariate values?

- Is the observation an outlier due to an extreme output value?

- Is the observation an outlier because of both the covariate and output values being extreme values?

The distinction in the nature of an outlier is vital as one needs to be sure of its type. The techniques for an outlier identification are certainly different as is their impact. If the outlier is due to the covariate value, the observation is called a **leverage point**, and if it is due to the y value, we call it an **influential point**. The rest of the section is for the exact statistical technique for such an outlier identification.

Leverage points

As noted, a leverage point has an anomalous x value. The leverage points may be theoretically proved not to impact the estimates of the regression coefficients. However, these points are known to drastically affect the R^2 value. The question then is, how do we identify such points?

The answer is by looking at the diagonal elements of the hat matrix $H = X(X'X)^{-1}X'$. Note that the matrix H is of the order $n \times n$. The (i, i) element of the hat matrix h_{ii} may be interpreted as the **amount of leverage by the observation**, i, on the fitted value $\hat{y}_i$. The average size of a leverage is $\bar{h} = p/n$, where p is the number of covariates and n is the number of observations. It is better to leave out an observation as its leverage value is greater than double p/n, and we then conclude that the observation is a **leverage point**. Let's go back to the gasoline problem and see the leverage of all the observations. In R, we have a `hatvalues` function that readily extracts the diagonal elements of H. The R output is given in the next screenshot.

Clearly, we have 10 observations that are leverage points. This is indeed a matter of concern as we have only about 25 observations. Thus, the results of the linear model need to be interpreted with caution! Let's now identify the influential points for the gasoline linear model.

Influential points

An influential point tends to pull the regression line (plane) in its direction, and hence, it drastically affects the values of the regression coefficients. We want to identify the impact of an observation on the regression coefficients, and one approach is to consider how much the regression coefficient values change if the observation is not considered. The relevant mathematics for identification of influential points is beyond the scope of the book, and we simply help ourselves with the metric **cook's distance**, which finds the influential points. The R function, `cooks.distance`, returns the values of the Cook's distance for each observation, and the thumb rule is that if the distance is greater than 1, the observation is an influential point.

Let's use the R function and identify the influential points for the gasoline problem:

```
> hatvalues(gasoline_lm)
      Apollo          Nova       Monarch        Duster  Jenson Conv.       Skyhawk
      0.3996        0.2628        0.6177        0.8142        0.8122        0.3372
    Scirocco Corolla SR-5        Camaro        Datsun     Capri II         Pacer
      0.4381        0.4084        0.3709        0.4523        0.3731        0.8576
     Granada      Eldorado      Imperial       Nova LN      Starfire       Cordoba
      0.1740        0.6700        0.5556        0.2832        0.3637        0.7630
  Corolla E-S      Mark IV     Celica GT     Charger SE        Cougar      Corvette
      0.4247        0.6953        0.4682        0.5259        0.6314        0.3007
> which(hatvalues(gasoline_lm) > length(gasoline_lm$coefficients)/nrow(Gasoline))
     Monarch        Duster  Jenson Conv.         Pacer      Eldorado      Imperial
           3             4             5            12            14            15
     Cordoba       Mark IV    Charger SE        Cougar
          18            20            22            23
> cooks.distance(gasoline_lm)
      Apollo          Nova       Monarch        Duster  Jenson Conv.       Skyhawk
   0.0118387     0.0105139     0.0003984     0.3659401     0.0377396     0.0006086
    Scirocco Corolla SR-5        Camaro        Datsun      Capri II         Pacer
   0.0901897     0.0036403     0.1030566     0.1460417     0.0954345     0.6172658
     Granada      Eldorado      Imperial       Nova LN      Starfire       Cordoba
   0.0022775     1.0487993     0.1471334     0.0227722     0.0349818     0.3974417
  Corolla E-S      Mark IV     Celica GT     Charger SE        Cougar      Corvette
   0.0353443     0.0702832     0.1986185     0.0921016     0.0003173     0.0135121
```

Leverage and influential points of the gasoline_lm fitted model

For this dataset, we have only one influential point in **Eldorado**. The plot of cook's distance against the observation numbers and that of cook's distance against the leverages may be easily obtained with `plot(gasoline_lm,which=c(4,6))`.

DFFITS and DFBETAS

Belsley, Kuh, and Welsch (1980) proposed two additional metrics for finding the influential points. The DFBETAS metric indicates the change of regression coefficients (in standard deviation units) if the ith observation is removed. Similarly, DFFITS is a metric that gives the impact on the fitted values $\hat{y}_i$. The rule that indicates the presence of an influential point using the DFFITS is that $|DFFITS_i| > 2/\sqrt{p/n}$, where p is the number of covariates, and n is the number of observations.

Finally, an observation i is influential for regression coefficient j if $\left| DFBETAS_{j,i} \right| > 2/\sqrt{n}$:

```
> dffits(gasoline_lm)
      Apollo         Nova      Monarch       Duster Jenson Conv.      Skyhawk     Scirocco Corolla SR-5       Camaro       Datsun     Capri II
      0.3641      -0.3452      -0.0662      -2.0957      -0.6471       0.0819       1.0592       0.2006      -1.1721       1.3970      -1.1181
       Pacer      Granada     Eldorado      Imperial      Nova LN     Starfire      Cordoba  Corolla E-S      Mark IV    Celica GT   Charger SE
      2.7505      -0.1591       4.8852       1.3544      -0.5156       0.6402       2.2333       0.6390      -0.8931      -1.6796      -1.0511
      Cougar     Corvette
      0.0591      -0.3917
> dfbetas(gasoline_lm)
             (Intercept)      x1      x2      x3      x4      x5      x6      x7      x8      x9     x10    x11M
Apollo            0.2175  0.0260 -0.0580 -0.0153 -0.2027 -0.1580  0.2157  0.1351  0.0626  0.0596 -0.0486  0.0005
Nova              0.0893 -0.0421 -0.0245  0.0410 -0.0912 -0.0122  0.1477  0.0186 -0.0675  0.0608  0.0165  0.1309
Monarch          -0.0103 -0.0231  0.0162 -0.0179  0.0186 -0.0335  0.0252 -0.0060 -0.0440  0.0098  0.0476  0.0076
Duster            0.2674 -0.3548  0.0216  0.3503 -0.3865  0.3252  0.3406  0.7118  0.2488  0.2877 -0.3982 -1.7135
Jenson Conv.      0.1124 -0.0591 -0.1888  0.0629 -0.1318 -0.1333  0.3266  0.1408  0.2020  0.2841 -0.1214 -0.0980
Skyhawk           0.0256 -0.0093 -0.0100 -0.0017 -0.0177 -0.0235  0.0080  0.0086 -0.0125 -0.0274  0.0211 -0.0212
Scirocco          0.3159 -0.2133 -0.2525  0.3643 -0.4010  0.3298  0.3786 -0.2281  0.2773  0.2572 -0.3925  0.1658
Corolla SR-5     -0.0655  0.0171  0.0269 -0.0463  0.0695 -0.0414  0.0050  0.0692 -0.0442  0.0422  0.0318 -0.0351
Camaro            0.3309 -0.1080  0.0192  0.0433 -0.2654 -0.0729 -0.5407  0.1281 -0.1955 -0.5796  0.3874  0.2182
Datsun           -0.4268 -0.4806  0.1929  0.2934  0.3355  0.7955 -0.0617 -1.0030  0.3078 -0.3680 -0.1233  0.0930
Capri II         -0.5049 -0.1082 -0.1528  0.1230  0.4461  0.5657 -0.1581 -0.3797  0.1964 -0.4835  0.0699 -0.6351
Pacer             0.2486 -0.3881 -0.0187  0.0186 -0.1528 -0.6214  0.1217  0.4514 -1.6084  1.3906  0.5746 -0.4134
Granada          -0.0561 -0.0162  0.0214  0.0099  0.0646 -0.0532  0.0134  0.0122 -0.0277  0.0282 -0.0041  0.0416
Eldorado          0.2231  0.7241 -3.0073  1.0685 -0.1384 -0.7609  1.1596  1.5720 -0.4191  0.1038  0.0771  1.3467
Imperial          0.1250  0.2453  0.8371 -0.7487 -0.0933 -0.5135  0.1505  0.2159 -0.0221  0.4442  0.1691  0.1611
Nova LN           0.2006 -0.0198  0.0501 -0.0081 -0.1710 -0.1759 -0.1699  0.1979 -0.1112  0.0043  0.0876  0.1036
Starfire          0.1937 -0.0908 -0.0720 -0.0325 -0.1244 -0.1967  0.0687  0.0297 -0.1575 -0.2341  0.2351 -0.1491
Cordoba          -0.7548  0.0189  0.7866  0.2513  0.6745 -0.2380 -0.8743  0.3331  0.9407  0.7168 -1.2347 -0.4131
Corolla E-S      -0.2559  0.0370  0.0216 -0.0723  0.2614  0.0848 -0.1444  0.0533 -0.0514 -0.2339  0.1446 -0.1121
Mark IV          -0.1781  0.5921  0.1859 -0.4264  0.2075 -0.2833 -0.1978  0.2096  0.1094  0.1868 -0.2569  0.0046
Celica GT        -0.7780 -0.1488  0.2875 -0.1723  0.7891  0.2320  0.0376 -1.1038 -0.2111  0.0483  0.1902  0.0519
Charger SE        0.4018  0.7590  0.4270 -0.6002 -0.4070 -0.1473 -0.1398  0.2794  0.0439  0.2174 -0.2421  0.3203
Cougar            0.0070  0.0280  0.0248 -0.0371 -0.0090  0.0122 -0.0206 -0.0057  0.0015 -0.0076  0.0119  0.0014
Corvette          0.1493 -0.0665 -0.0904  0.0997 -0.1767  0.1076 -0.0543  0.0322  0.0952 -0.0250 -0.0224  0.0180
```

DFFITS and DFBETAS for the Gasoline problem

We have given the DFFITS and DFBETAS values for the `Gasoline` dataset. It is left as an exercise to the reader to identify the influential points from the preceding outputs.

The multicollinearity problem

One of the important assumptions of the multiple linear regression model is that the covariates are linearly independent. The linear independence here is the sense of linear algebra that a vector (covariate in our context) cannot be expressed as a linear combination of others. Mathematically, this assumption translates into an implication that $(X'X)^{-1}$ is nonsingular or that its determinant is non-zero. If this is not the case, we have one or more of the following problems:

- The estimated $\hat{\beta}$ will be unreliable, and there is a great chance of the regression coefficients having the wrong sign
- The relevant significant factors will not be identified by either the *t*-tests or the *F*-tests
- The importance of certain predictors will be undermined

Let's first obtain the correlation matrix for the predictors of the `Gasoline` dataset. We will exclude the final covariate as it is a factor variable:

```
> round(cor(Gasoline[,-c(1,12)],use="comp"),2)
       x1     x2     x3     x4     x5     x6     x7     x8     x9    x10
x1    1.00   0.95   0.99  -0.35  -0.68   0.66  -0.76   0.86   0.82   0.96
x2    0.95   1.00   0.97  -0.29  -0.58   0.76  -0.62   0.80   0.71   0.90
x3    0.99   0.97   1.00  -0.35  -0.68   0.66  -0.74   0.87   0.82   0.96
x4   -0.35  -0.29  -0.35   1.00   0.50   0.04   0.61  -0.27  -0.33  -0.32
x5   -0.68  -0.58  -0.68   0.50   1.00  -0.22   0.86  -0.62  -0.53  -0.63
x6    0.66   0.76   0.66   0.04  -0.22   1.00  -0.27   0.42   0.28   0.55
x7   -0.76  -0.62  -0.74   0.61   0.86  -0.27   1.00  -0.65  -0.69  -0.71
x8    0.86   0.80   0.87  -0.27  -0.62   0.42  -0.65   1.00   0.88   0.95
x9    0.82   0.71   0.82  -0.33  -0.53   0.28  -0.69   0.88   1.00   0.90
x10   0.96   0.90   0.96  -0.32  -0.63   0.55  -0.71   0.95   0.90   1.00
```

The correlation matrix of the Gasoline covariates

We can see that covariate x_1 is strongly correlated with all other predictors, except x4. Similarly, x_8 to x_{10} are also strongly correlated. This is a strong indication of the presence of the multicollinearity problem.

Define $C = (X'X)^{-1}$. Then it can be proved that (refer to Montgomery, et. al. (2003)) the j-th diagonal element of C can be written as $C_{jj} = (1 - R_j^2)^{-1}$, where R_j^2 is the coefficient of determination obtained by regressing all other covariates for x_j as the output. Now, the variable x_j is independent of all the other covariates; we expect the coefficient of determination to be zero and, hence, C_{jj} to be closer to unity. However, if the covariate depends on the others, we expect the coefficient of determination to be a high value and, hence, C_{jj} to be a large number. The quantity C_{jj} is also called the variance inflation factor, denoted by VIF_j. A general guideline for a covariate to be linearly independent of other covariates is that its VIF_j should be less than 5 or 10.

Time for action - addressing the multicollinearity problem for the gasoline data

The multicollinearity problem is addressed using the `vif` function, which is available from two libraries: `car` and `faraway`. We will use it from the `faraway` package.

1. Load the `faraway` package with `library(faraway)`.

2. We need to find the **variance inflation factor** (**VIF**) of the independent variables only. The covariate x_{11} is a character variable, and the first column of the Gasoline dataset is the regressand. Hence, run `vif(Gasoline[,-c(1,12)])` to find the VIF of the eligible independent variables.

3. The VIF for x_3 is the highest at 217.587. Hence, we remove it to find the VIF among the remaining variables with `vif(Gasoline[,-c(1,4,12)])`. Remember that x_3 is the fourth column in the Gasoline data frame.

4. In the previous step, we find `x10` having the maximum VIF at 77.810. Now, run `vif(Gasoline[,-c(1,4,11,12)])` to find whether all VIFs are less than 10.

5. For the first variable `x1` the VIF is 31.956, and we now remove it with `vif(Gasoline[,-c(1,2,4,11,12)])`.

6. At the end of the previous step, we have the VIF of `x1` at 10.383. Thus, run `vif(Gasoline[,-c(1,2,3,4,11,12)])`.

7. Now, all the independent variables have VIF less than 10. Hence, we stop at this step.

8. Removing all the independent variables with VIF greater than 10, we arrive at the final model, `summary(lm(y~x4+x5+x6+x7+x8+x9,data= Gasoline))`:

```
> library(faraway)
> vif(Gasoline[,-c(1,12)])
     x1      x2      x3      x4      x5      x6      x7      x8      x9     x10
132.806  42.959 217.587   2.024   7.883   6.032  10.641  26.701  13.380 128.087
> vif(Gasoline[,-c(1,4,12)])
     x1      x2      x4      x5      x6      x7      x8      x9     x10
 51.181  20.093   1.975   6.592   6.050   9.904  19.634  12.466  77.810
> vif(Gasoline[,-c(1,4,11,12)])
     x1      x2      x4      x5      x6      x7      x8      x9
 31.956  18.948   1.852   6.545   5.666   9.835   8.051  10.971
> vif(Gasoline[,-c(1,2,4,11,12)])
     x2      x4      x5      x6      x7      x8      x9
 10.383   1.845   6.488   5.123   8.678   7.996   9.304
> vif(Gasoline[,-c(1,2,3,4,11,12)])
    x4     x5     x6     x7     x8     x9
 1.612  5.654  1.407  8.161  7.798  7.871
```

Addressing the multicollinearity problem for the Gasoline dataset

What just happened?

We used the `vif` function from the `faraway` package to overcome the problem of multicollinearity in the multiple linear regression model. This helped reduce the number of independent variables from 10 to 6, which is a huge 40 percent reduction.

The function `vif` from the `faraway` package is applied to the set of covariates. Indeed, there is another function of the same name from the `car` package, which can be directly applied on an `lm` object.

Doing it in Python

Multiple linear regression analysis and its diagnostics are now done in Python:

1. We import the `Gasoline` file and fit our first multiple linear regression model using the `ols` function:

```
In [14]: Gasoline = pd.read_csv("Data/Gasoline.csv",delimiter=',')
         Mileage_lm = smf.ols(formula='y ~ x1 + x2 + x3 + x4 + x5 + x6 +
                              x7 + x8 + x9 + x10 + x11',data=Gasoline).fit()
         Mileage_lm.params

Out[14]: Intercept    -261.516375
         x11[T.M]       -2.656331
         x1             -0.138824
         x2             -0.066364
         x3              0.208705
         x4            243.989694
         x5             81.508041
         x6              1.281262
         x7             -2.658516
         x8              0.259600
         x9              0.041381
         x10            -0.010975
         dtype: float64
```

2. The model summary can be easily extracted as in the simple linear regression model:

```
In [15]: Mileage_lm.summary()

Out[15]:
         OLS Regression Results
```

Dep. Variable:	y	R-squared:	0.895
Model:	OLS	Adj. R-squared:	0.798
Method:	Least Squares	F-statistic:	9.274
Date:	Sun, 06 Aug 2017	Prob (F-statistic):	0.000281
Time:	09:25:44	Log-Likelihood:	-51.984
No. Observations:	24	AIC:	128.0
Df Residuals:	12	BIC:	142.1
Df Model:	11		

For brevity, the output is truncated.

3. The ANOVA table can be pulled earlier by running `print(sm.stats.anova_lm(Mileage_lm,typ=2))`.

4. The desired confidence intervals are obtained using the `conf_int` function--`print(Mileage_lm.conf_int(0.05))`

5. The residual plots follow the usual tricks, and we provide the implementation for the fitted gasoline linear model:

```
In [18]: plt.subplot(2,1,1)
         plt.plot(Mileage_lm.fittedvalues,Mileage_lm.resid,'.')
         plt.xlabel("Fitted Values")
         plt.ylabel("Residuals")
         plt.title("Plot of Residuals Vs Fitted Values")
         plt.subplot(2,1,2)
         plt.plot(Mileage_lm.fittedvalues,Mileage_lm.resid_pearson,'.')
         plt.xlabel("Fitted Values")
         plt.ylabel("Pearson Residuals")
         plt.title("Plot of Pearson Residuals Vs Fitted Values")
         plt.show()
```

The output can be found in the `Chapter_06_Linear_Regression_Analysis.ipynb` file.

6. We need to formally convert the categorical variable `x11` into a numeric vector form to obtain the `hatvalues`. Also, we have a missing observation in row 18, and that needs to be removed too. Unlike in R, we don't have a `hatvalues` function that can be directly applied; we define it first and then apply it:

```
In [20]: X = Gasoline[['x1', 'x2', 'x3', 'x4', 'x5', 'x6', 'x7', 'x8', 'x9', 'x10','x11']]
         X['x11'] = pd.Categorical(X.x11).codes
         y = Gasoline[['y']]
         X = sm.add_constant(X)
         X = X.drop(X.index[[18]])
         y = y.drop(y.index[[18]])
         Gasoline_lm = sm.OLS(y,X)

In [22]: def hatvalues(fitted_lm):
             X=fitted_lm.exog
             hat_mat = np.dot(X,np.dot(np.linalg.inv(np.dot(X.T,X)),X.T))
             hat_values = np.diagonal(hat_mat)
             return(hat_values)
         hatvalues(Gasoline_lm)

Out[22]: array([ 0.39960205,  0.26280906,  0.61765884,  0.81422573,  0.81218036,
                 0.33717959,  0.43814784,  0.40840887,  0.37085355,  0.45229869,
                 0.37311041,  0.85757222,  0.17400947,  0.66999631,  0.55562813,
                 0.28323158,  0.36373626,  0.76300789,  0.42472025,  0.69532943,
                 0.46822233,  0.52593567,  0.63141435,  0.30072114])
```

7. The cook's influence measures can be obtained by the extractor `get_` `influence()` and then `cooks_distance`:

```
In [24]:  Gasoline_lm_ols = smf.ols(formula='y~x1+x2+x3+x4+x5+x6+x7+x8+x9+x10+x11',data=Gasoline)
          Gasoline_fitted = Gasoline_lm_ols.fit()
          CD = Gasoline_fitted.get_influence()
          (cook,p) = CD.cooks_distance
          cook

Out[24]:  array([  1.18386769e-02,   1.05139203e-02,   3.98409216e-04,
                   3.65940145e-01,   3.77395763e-02,   6.08552314e-04,
                   9.01897236e-02,   3.64027880e-03,   1.03056580e-01,
                   1.46041690e-01,   9.54345413e-02,   6.17265807e-01,
                   2.27751292e-03,   1.04879933e+00,   1.47133426e-01,
                   2.27722033e-02,   3.49817984e-02,   3.97441718e-01,
                   3.53443340e-02,   7.02831892e-02,   1.98618471e-01,
                   9.21015791e-02,   3.17315775e-04,   1.35120737e-02])
```

8. The DFFITS and DFBETAS are obtained as follows:

```
In [25]:  (dffits,p) = CD.dffits
          dffits

Out[25]:  array([ 0.36412056, -0.34520663, -0.06620863, -2.09572122, -0.64714009,
                  0.08186631,  1.05916499,  0.20063732, -1.17209673,  1.396993  ,
                 -1.11814742,  2.75054881, -0.15914284,  4.88518347,  1.35436905,
                 -0.51557037,  0.64021958,  2.23328331,  0.63901189, -0.89312948,
                 -1.67964478, -1.0511131 ,  0.0590857 , -0.39173253])

In [26]:  CD.dfbetas
```

The output corresponding to the DFBETAS is not shown, again for brevity.

9. We delete the constant term before carrying out the VIF:

```
In [29]:  X2 = X
          del X2['const']
          from statsmodels.stats.outliers_influence import variance_inflation_factor
          vif = pd.DataFrame()
          vif["VIF Factor"] = [variance_inflation_factor(X2.values, i) for i in range(X2.shape[1])]
          vif["features"] = X2.columns
          vif.round(1)
```

Out[29]:

	VIF Factor	features
0	914.1	x1
1	403.3	x2
2	1652.3	x3
3	5352.3	x4
4	5025.6	x5
5	34.9	x6
6	212.9	x7
7	2194.3	x8
8	2004.7	x9
9	1898.1	x10
10	7.0	x11

Model selection

The method of removal of covariates in the *The multicollinearity problem* section depended solely on the covariates themselves. However, it may happen more often that the covariates in the final model are selected with respect to the output. Computational cost is almost a non-issue these days and especially for not-so-large datasets! The question that arises then is, can one retain all possible covariates in the model, or do we have any choice of covariates that meet certain regression metrics, say $R^2 > 60$ percent?

The problem is that having more covariates increases the variance of the model, while having less of them will have a large bias. The philosophical *Occam's Razor principle* applies here too, and the best model is the simplest model. In our context, the smallest model that fits the data is the best. There are two types of model selection: stepwise procedures and criterion-based procedures. In this section, we will consider both the procedures.

Stepwise procedures

There are three methods of selecting covariates for inclusion in the final model:

- Backward elimination
- Forward selection
- Stepwise regression.

We will first describe the backward elimination approach and develop the R function for it.

The backward elimination

In this model, one first begins with all the available covariates. Suppose we wish to retain all covariates for whom the *p*-value is at the most α. The value α is referred to as the **critical alpha**. Now, we first eliminate that covariate whose *p*-value is maximum among all the covariates having *p*-value greater than α. The model is refitted for the current covariates. We continue the process until we have all the covariates whose *p*-value is less than α. In summary, the backward elimination algorithm is as explained next:

1. Consider all the available covariates.
2. Remove the covariate with maximum *p*-value among all the covariates that have *p*-value greater than α.
3. Refit the model, and go to the first step.
4. Continue the process until all *p*-values are less than α.

Typically, the user investigates the *p*-values in the `summary` output and then carries out the preceding algorithm. Tattar, et. al. (2013) gives a function that executes the entire algorithm straight away; we adapt the same function here and apply it on the linear regression model `gasoline_lm`.

The forward selection

In the previous procedure, we started with all covariates. Here, we begin with an empty model and look forward for the most significant covariates with *p*-value lesser than α, that is, we build *k* new linear models with the *k*-th covariate for the *k*-th model.

Naturally, by "most significant", we mean that the *p*-value should be least among all the covariates whose *p*-value is lesser than α. Then we build the model with the selected covariate. A second covariate is selected by treating the previous model as the initial empty model. The model selection is continued until we fail to add any more covariate. This is summarized in the following algorithm:

1. Begin with an empty model.
2. For each covariate, obtain the p-value if it is added to the model. Select the covariates with the least *p* value among all the covariates whose *p* value is lesser than α.
3. Repeat the preceding step until no more covariates can be updated for the model.

We again use the function created in Tattar, et. al. (2013) and apply it to the gasoline problem.

The stepwise regression

There is yet another method of model selection. Here, we begin with the empty model:

1. We add a covariate as in the forward selection step and then perform a backward elimination to remove any unwanted covariate.
2. The forward and backward steps are continued until we can't either add a new covariate or remove an existing covariate.
3. Of course, the alpha critical values for forward and backward steps are specified distinctly.

This method is called **stepwise regression**. This method is, however, skipped for brevity.

Criterion-based procedures

A useful tool for the model selection problem is to evaluate all possible models and select one of them according to certain criteria. The **Akaike Information Criteria (AIC)** is one such criterion that can be used to select the best model. Let $\log\left(L\left(\hat{\beta}_0, \hat{\beta}_1, \ldots, \hat{\beta}_p, \hat{\sigma}^2 \mid y\right)\right)$ denote the log likelihood function of the fitted regression model. Define K = p + 2, which is the total number of estimated parameters.

The AIC for the fitted regression model is given by the following:

$$AIC = 2\left[-\log\left(L\left(\hat{\beta}_0, \hat{\beta}_1, \ldots, \hat{\beta}_p, \hat{\sigma}^2 \mid y \right) \right) + K \right]$$

Now, the model that has the least AIC among the candidate models is the best model. The `step` function available in R gets the job done for us, and we will close the chapter with the continued illustration of the gasoline problem.

Time for action - model selection using the backward, forward, and AIC criteria

For the forward and backward selection procedure under the stepwise procedures of the model selection problem, we first define two functions `backwardlm` and `forwardlm`. However, for the criteria-based model selection, say AIC, we use the `step` function that can be performed on the fitted linear models:

1. Create a function `pvalueslm` that extracts the *p*-values related to the covariates of an `lm` object:

```
pvalueslm <- function(lm) {summary(lm)$coefficients[-1,4]}
```

2. Create a `backwardlm` function defined as follows:

```
backwardlm <- function(lm,criticalalpha) {
  lm2=lm
  while(max(pvalueslm(lm2))>criticalalpha) {
    lm2=update(lm2,
               paste(".~.-",attr(lm2$terms,"term.labels")[
                 (which(pvalueslm(lm2)==max(pvalueslm(lm2))))]
                 ,sep=""))
  }
  return(lm2)
}
```

The code needs to be explained in more detail. There are two new functions created here for the implementation of the backward elimination procedure. Let's have a detailed look at them.

The `pvalueslm` function extracts the *p*-values related to the covariates of an `lm` object. The choice of `summary(lm)$coefficients[-1,4]` is vital as we are interested in the *p*-values of the covariates and not the intercept term. The *p*-values are available once the `summary` function is applied on the `lm` object.

Now, let's focus on the `backwardlm` function. Its arguments are the `lm` object and the value of critical α. Our goal is to carry out the iterations until we do not have any more covariates with *p*-value greater than α. Thus, we use the `while` function, which is typical of the algorithm, where the last step appears during the beginning of a function/program. We want our function to work for all the linear models and not just for `gasoline_lm`, and we need to get the names of the covariates that are specified in the `lm` object. Remember, we conveniently used the `lm(y~.)` formula, and this will try to haunt us! Thankfully, `attr(lm$terms, "term.labels")` extracts all the covariate names of an `lm` object.

The `[(which(pvalueslm(lm2)==max (pvalueslm (lm2))))]` argument identifies the covariate number that has the maximum *p*-value above α. Next, `paste(".~.-",attr(), sep="")` returns the formula that will remove the unwanted covariate. The explanation of the formula is lengthier than the function itself, which is not surprising as R is object-oriented and a few lines of code do more actions than detailed prose.

3. Obtain the efficient linear regression model by applying the `backwardlm` function, with critical alpha at `0.20` on the Gasoline `lm` object:

```
gasoline_lm_backward <- backwardlm(gasoline_lm,criticalalpha=0.20)
```

4. Find the details of the final model obtained in the previous step:

```
summary(gasoline_lm_backward)
```

The output obtained because of applying the backward selection algorithm is as follows:

```
> summary(gasoline_lm_backward)

Call:
lm(formula = y ~ x1 + x3 + x5 + x8 + x10, data = Gasoline)

Residuals:
   Min      1Q Median      3Q     Max
 -5.650  -1.311  0.037   1.495   4.564

Coefficients:
             Estimate Std. Error t value Pr(>|t|)
(Intercept) -25.95431   31.48358   -0.82    0.421
x1           -0.06575    0.04132   -1.59    0.129
x3            0.10188    0.05734    1.78    0.093 .
x5           45.42276   30.01164    1.51    0.148
x8            0.25577    0.12874    1.99    0.062 .
x10          -0.01103    0.00534   -2.07    0.053 .
---
Signif. codes:  0 '***' 0.001 '**' 0.01 '*' 0.05 '.' 0.1 ' ' 1

Residual standard error: 2.81 on 18 degrees of freedom
  (1 observation deleted due to missingness)
Multiple R-squared: 0.86,        Adjusted R-squared: 0.821
F-statistic: 22.1 on 5 and 18 DF,  p-value: 4.17e-07
```

The backward selection model for the Gasoline problem

5. The `forwardlm` function is given by the following:

```
forwardlm <- function(y,x,criticalalpha)  {
  yx = data.frame(y=Gasoline$y,Gasoline[,-1])
  mylm = lm(y~.,data=yx)
  avail_cov = attr(mylm$terms,"dataClasses")[-1]
  minpvalues=0
  while(minpvalues<criticalalpha) {
    pvalues_curr = NULL
    for(i in 1:length(avail_cov)) {
      templm = update(mylm,paste(".~.+",names(avail_cov[i])))
      mypvalues = summary(templm)$coefficients[,4]
      pvalues_curr = c(pvalues_curr,mypvalues[length(mypvalues)])
    }
    minpvalues = min(pvalues_curr)
    if(minpvalues<criticalalpha) {
      include_me_in = min(which(pvalues_curr<criticalalpha))
      mylm = update(mylm,paste(".~.+",names(avail_cov[include_me_in])))
      avail_cov = avail_cov[-include_me_in]
    }
  }
  return(mylm)
}
```

6. Apply the `forwardlm` function on the `Gasoline` dataset:

```
gasoline_lm_forward <- forwardlm(Gasoline$y,Gasoline[,-1],
criticalalpha=0.2)
```

7. Obtain the details of the finalized model with `summary( gasoline_lm_forward)`.

The output in R is as follows:

```
> summary(gasoline_lm_forward)

Call:
lm(formula = y ~ x1 + x6, data = yx)

Residuals:
   Min     1Q Median     3Q    Max
-4.812 -2.229  0.061  1.407  5.530

Coefficients:
            Estimate Std. Error t value Pr(>|t|)
(Intercept) 33.44911    1.57649   21.22  3.9e-16 ***
x1          -0.05435    0.00633   -8.59  1.8e-08 ***
x6           1.07822    0.69965    1.54     0.14
---
Signif. codes:  0 '***' 0.001 '**' 0.01 '*' 0.05 '.' 0.1 ' ' 1

Residual standard error: 2.83 on 22 degrees of freedom
Multiple R-squared: 0.829,     Adjusted R-squared: 0.813
F-statistic: 53.3 on 2 and 22 DF,  p-value: 3.66e-09
```

The forward selection model for the Gasoline dataset

Note that the forward selection and backward elimination have resulted in two different models. This is to be expected and should not be a surprise, and in such scenarios, one can pick up either of the models for further analysis/implementation. The understanding of the construction of the `forwardlm` function is left as an exercise to the reader.

8. The `step` function in R readily gives the best model using AIC:

```
step(gasoline_lm, direction="both")
```

```
> step(gasoline_lm,direction="both")
Start:  AIC=59.86
y ~ x1 + x2 + x3 + x4 + x5 + x6 + x7 + x8 + x9 + x10 + x11
        Df Sum of Sq RSS  AIC
- x9     1      0.1 107 57.9
- x2     1      5.1 112 59.0
- x11    1      6.8 114 59.3
- x4     1      7.4 114 59.5
- x7     1      7.5 114 59.5
- x6     1      7.6 114 59.5
<none>              107 59.9
- x5     1     16.8 124 61.4
- x10    1     21.2 128 62.2
- x8     1     27.4 134 63.3
- x3     1     33.9 141 64.5
- x1     1     47.7 155 66.7

Step:  AIC=57.88
y ~ x1 + x2 + x3 + x4 + x5 + x6 + x7 + x8 + x10 + x11
        Df Sum of Sq RSS  AIC
- x2     1      5.4 112 57.1
- x11    1      6.8 114 57.4
- x4     1      7.8 115 57.6
- x6     1      8.0 115 57.6
<none>              107 57.9
- x7     1     10.4 117 58.1
+ x9     1      0.1 107 59.9
- x5     1     22.9 130 60.5
- x10    1     23.4 130 60.6
- x8     1     27.4 134 61.4
- x3     1     34.8 142 62.6
- x1     1     48.8 156 64.9

Step:  AIC=57.06
y ~ x1 + x3 + x4 + x5 + x6 + x7 + x8 + x10 + x11
        Df Sum of Sq RSS  AIC
- x6     1      3.4 116 55.8
- x11    1      6.4 119 56.4
<none>              112 57.1
- x4     1     12.8 125 57.7
- x7     1     13.7 126 57.8
+ x2     1      5.4 107 57.9
+ x9     1      0.4 112 59.0
- x5     1     21.1 134 59.2
- x10    1     21.3 134 59.2
- x8     1     26.1 138 60.1
- x3     1     37.7 150 62.0
- x1     1     43.5 156 62.9
```

```
Step:  AIC=55.78
y ~ x1 + x3 + x4 + x5 + x7 + x8 + x10 + x11
        Df Sum of Sq RSS  AIC
- x11    1      6.5 122 55.1
<none>              116 55.8
- x7     1     11.8 128 56.1
- x4     1     15.5 131 56.8
+ x6     1      3.4 112 57.1
+ x2     1      0.8 115 57.6
+ x9     1      0.1 116 57.8
- x5     1     27.4 143 58.9
- x8     1     31.7 148 59.6
- x10    1     35.5 151 60.2
- x1     1     40.3 156 60.9
- x3     1     42.6 158 61.3

Step:  AIC=55.09
y ~ x1 + x3 + x4 + x5 + x7 + x8 + x10
        Df Sum of Sq RSS  AIC
<none>              122 55.1
- x4     1     13.3 136 55.6
+ x11    1      6.5 116 55.8
- x7     1     15.3 138 55.9
+ x6     1      3.5 119 56.4
+ x2     1      0.7 122 57.0
+ x9     1      0.2 122 57.1
- x5     1     22.7 145 57.2
- x8     1     27.9 150 58.0
- x10    1     31.8 154 58.6
- x1     1     34.3 157 59.0
- x3     1     36.7 159 59.4

Call:
lm(formula = y ~ x1 + x3 + x4 + x5 + x7 + x8 + x10, data = Gasoline)

Coefficients:
(Intercept)        x1        x3        x4        x5        x7
  -309.8881   -0.0973    0.1403  304.3762   78.6480   -3.2475
```

Stepwise AIC

Backward and forward selection can be easily performed using AIC with the `direction= "backward"` and `direction= "forward"` options.

What just happened?

We used two customized functions `backwardlm` and `forwardlm` for backward and forward selection criteria. The `step` function has been used for the model selection problem based on the AIC.

Have a go hero

The supervisor performance data is available in the SPD dataset from the RSADBE package. Here, Y (the regressand) represents the overall rating of the job done by a supervisor. The overall rating depends on six other inputs/regressors. Find more details about the dataset with ?SPD. First, visualize the dataset with the pairs function. Fit a multiple linear regression model for Y, and complete the necessary regression tasks, such as model validation, regression diagnostics, and model selection.

Summary

In this chapter, we learned how to build a linear regression model, check for violations in the model assumptions, fix the multicollinearity problem, and finally how to find the best model. Here, we were aided by two important assumptions: the output being a continuous variable and the normality assumption for the errors. The linear regression model provides the best footing for the general regression problems. However, when the output variable is discrete, binary, or multi-category data, the linear regression model lets us down. This is not actually a let down as it was never intended to solve this class of problems.

Thus, our next chapter will focus on the problem of regression models for binary data. Implementing the regression model and its diagnostics in both the software has been cleanly done throughout the chapter.

7
Logistic Regression Model

In this chapter, we will consider regression models when the regressand is dichotomous or binary in nature. The data is of the form $(Y_1, X_1), (Y_2, X_2), \ldots, (Y_n, X_n)$, where the dependent variable Y_i, $i = 1, \ldots, n$ are the observed binary output assumed to be independent (in the statistical sense) of each other, and the vector X_i, $i = 1, \ldots, n$, are the covariates (independent variables in the sense of a regression problem) associated with Y_i.

In the previous chapter, we considered linear regression models where the regressand was assumed to be continuous along with the assumption of normality for the error distribution. Here, we will consider a Gaussian (normal) model for the binary regression model, which is more widely known as the **probit model**. A more generic model has emerged during the past four decades in the form of **logistic regression model**. We will consider the logistic regression model for the rest of the chapter. The approach in this chapter will be on the following topics:

- The binary regression problem
- Probit regression model
- Logistic regression model
- Model validation and diagnostics
- Receiving operator curves
- Logistic regression for the German credit screening dataset

Packages and settings – R and Python

For R, we need `pscl` and `ROCR` packages. The path settings are dealt with to kick-off the chapter:

1. First set the working directory:

   ```
   setwd("MyPath/R/Chapter_07")
   ```

2. Load the required R packages:

   ```
   library(RSADBE)
   library(pscl)
   library(ROCR)
   ```

3. We have the published Python notebook file `Chapter_10_CART_and_Beyond.ipynb` in the output folder:

```
In [2]:  import os
         os.chdir("MyPath/Python/Chapter_07")
         import pandas as pd
         import matplotlib.pyplot as plt
         import numpy as np
         import statsmodels.formula.api as smfa
         import statsmodels.api as sm
         import pylab as pl
         import pysal
         from sklearn.metrics import roc_curve, auc
         from sklearn.cross_validation import train_test_split
         from sklearn.preprocessing import label_binarize
```

We are now set to begin the proceedings.

The binary regression problem

Consider the problem of modeling the completion of a stat course by students based on their Scholastic Assessment Test in the subject of mathematics SAT-M scores at the time of their admission. After the completion of the final exams we know which students successfully completed the course and which of them failed. Here, the output pass/fail may be represented by a binary number 1/0. It may be fairly said that the higher the SAT-M scores at the time of admission to the course, the more likelihood of the candidate completing the course. This problem has been discussed in detail in Johnson and Albert (1999) and Tattar, et. al. (2013).

Let us begin by denoting the pass/fail indicator by Y and the entry SAT-M score by X. Suppose that we have n pairs of observations on the students' scores and their course completion results. We can build the simple linear regression model for the probability of course completion $p_i = P(Y_i = 1)$ as a function of the SAT-M score with $p_i = \beta_0 + \beta_0 X_i + \varepsilon_i$. The data from page 77 of Johnson and Albert (1999) is available in the `sat` dataset of this book's *R package*. The columns that contain the data on the variables Y and X are named respectively `Pass` and `Sat`. To build a linear regression model for the probability of completing the course, we take *pi* as 1 if $Y_i = 1$, and 0 otherwise. A scatter plot of `Pass` against `Sat` indicates the students with higher SAT-M scores are more likely to complete the course. The SAT score varies from 463-649 and then we attempt to predict whether students with SAT scores of 400 and 700 would have successfully completed the course or not.

Time for action – limitation of linear regression model

A linear regression model is built for the dataset with a binary output. The model is used to predict the probabilities for some cases, which show the limitations:

1. Load the dataset from the RSADBE package with `data(sat)`.

2. Visualize the scatter plot of `Pass` against `Sat` with `plot(sat$Sat, sat$Pass,xlab="SAT Score", ylab = "Final Result")`.

3. Fit the simple linear regression model with `passlm <- lm(Pass~Sat, data=sat)` and obtain its summary by `summary(passlm)`. Add the fitted regression line to the scatter plot using `abline(passlm)`.

4.   Make a prediction for students with SAT-M scores of 400 and 700 by the R code `predict(passlm,newdata=list(Sat=400))` and `predict( passlm, newdata=list(Sat=700),interval="prediction")`:

```
> data(sat)
> plot(sat$Sat,sat$Pass,xlab="SAT Score", ylab = "Final Result")
> passlm<-lm(Pass~Sat,data=sat)
> summary(passlm)
Call:
lm(formula = Pass ~ Sat, data = sat)
Residuals:
    Min     1Q Median     3Q    Max
-0.869 -0.147  0.116  0.202  0.553
Coefficients:
             Estimate Std. Error t value Pr(>|t|)
(Intercept) -3.44224    0.96202   -3.58  0.00129 **
Sat          0.00741    0.00172    4.32  0.00018 ***
---
Signif. codes:  0 '***' 0.001 '**' 0.01 '*' 0.05 '.' 0.1 ' ' 1
Residual standard error: 0.368 on 28 degrees of freedom
Multiple R-squared:  0.4,        Adjusted R-squared: 0.378
F-statistic: 18.6 on 1 and 28 DF,  p-value: 0.000179
> abline(passlm)
> predict(passlm,newdata=list(Sat=400))
      1
-0.4793
> predict(passlm,newdata=list(Sat=700),interval="prediction")
    fit    lwr    upr
1 1.743 0.8315 2.654
```

Drawbacks of the linear regression model for the classification problem

The linear model is significant as seen by `p-value: 0.000179` associated with the `F-statistic`. Next, `Pr(>|t|)` associated with the `Sat` variable is `0.00018`, which is again significant. However, the predicted value for SAT-M marks at 400 and 700 are respectively seen as `-0.4793` and `1.743`. The problem with the model is that the predicted values can be negative as well as greater than 1. It is essentially these limitations that restrict the use of the linear regression model when the regressand is a binary outcome.

What just happened?

We used the simple linear regression model for the probability prediction of a binary outcome and observed that the probabilities are not bound in the unit interval [0,1] as they are expected to be. This shows that we need to have special/different statistical models for understanding the relationship between the covariates and the binary output.

We will use two regression models that are appropriate for binary regressand: probit regression and logistic regression. The former model will continue the use of normal distribution for the error through a **latent variable,** whereas the latter uses the binomial distribution and is a popular member of the more generic **generalized linear models (GLM).**

Probit regression model

The probit regression model is constructed as a **latent variable model.** Define a latent variable, also called an **auxiliary random variable,** Y^* as follows:

$$Y^* = X'\beta + \varepsilon$$

Which is the same at the earlier linear regression model with Y replaced by Y^*. The error term ε is assumed to follow a normal distribution $N(0, \sigma^2)$. Then Y can be considered 1 if the latent variable is positive, that is:

$$Y = \begin{cases} 1, & \text{if } Y^* > 0, \text{ equivalently } X'\beta > -\varepsilon \\ 0, & \text{otherwise} \end{cases}$$

Without loss of generality, we can assume that $\varepsilon \sim N(0,1)$. Then, the probit model is obtained by:

$$P(Y = 1 | X) = P(Y^* > 0) = P(\varepsilon > -X'\beta)$$
$$= P(\varepsilon < X'\beta) = \phi(X'\beta)$$

The method of **maximum likelihood estimation** is used to determine β. For a random sample of size n, the log likelihood function is given by:

$$\log L(\beta) = \sum_{i=1}^{n} \left(y_i \log \phi(x_i'\beta) + (1 - y_i) \log(1 - \phi(x_i'\beta)) \right)$$

Numerical optimization techniques can be deployed to find the MLE of β. Fortunately, we don't have to undertake this daunting task and R helps us out with the `glm` function. Let us fit the probit model for the `Sat` dataset seen earlier.

Time for action – understanding the constants

The probit regression model is built for the `Pass` variable as a function of the `Sat` score using the `glm` R function and the argument `binomial(probit)`:

1. Using the `glm` function and the `binomial(probit)` option we can fit the probit model for `Pass` as a function of the `Sat` score:

   ```
   pass_probit <- glm(Pass~Sat,data=sat,binomial(probit))
   ```

2. The details about the `pass_probit` `glm` object is fetched using `summary(pass_probit)`.

   The summary function does not give a measure of R^2, the coefficient of determination, as we obtained for the linear regression model. In general such a measure is not exactly available for the GLMs. However, certain pseudo-R2 measures are available and we will use the pR^2 function from the `pscl` package. This package has been developed at Political Science Computational Laboratory, Stanford University, which explains the name of the package as `pscl`.

3. Load the `pscl` package with `library(pscl)`, and apply the `pR2` function on `pass_probit` to obtain the measures of pseudo R2.

   Finally, we check how the probit model overcomes the problems posed by application of the linear regression model.

4. Find the probability of passing the course for students with SAT-M score of 400 and 700 with the code:

   ```
   predict(pass_probit,newdata=list(Sat=400),type = "response")
   predict(pass_probit,newdata=list(Sat=700),type = "response")
   ```

The following is a screenshot of R action:

```
> summary(pass_probit)
Call:
glm(formula = Pass ~ Sat, family = binomial(probit), data = sat)
Deviance Residuals:
    Min      1Q   Median      3Q      Max
 -2.298  -0.147    0.360   0.518    1.487
Coefficients:
             Estimate Std. Error z value Pr(>|z|)
(Intercept) -17.9611     6.6260   -2.71   0.0067 **
Sat           0.0334     0.0119    2.79   0.0052 **
---
Signif. codes:  0 '***' 0.001 '**' 0.01 '*' 0.05 '.' 0.1 ' ' 1
(Dispersion parameter for binomial family taken to be 1)
    Null deviance: 36.652  on 29  degrees of freedom
Residual deviance: 22.233  on 28  degrees of freedom
AIC: 26.23
Number of Fisher Scoring iterations: 6
> library(pscl)
> pR2(pass_probit)
      llh   llhNull         G2  McFadden      r2ML      r2CU
  -11.116   -18.326     14.419     0.393     0.382     0.541
> predict(pass_probit,newdata=list(Sat=400),type = "response")
        1
2.02e-06
> predict(pass_probit,newdata=list(Sat=700),type = "response")
1
1
```

The probit regression model for SAT problem

The $Pr(>|z|)$ for Sat is 0.0052, which shows that the variable has a significant say in explaining whether the student successfully completes the course or not. The regression coefficient value for the Sat variable indicates that if the Sat variable increases by one mark, the influence on the probit link increases by 0.0334. In easy words, the SAT-M variable has a positive impact on the probability of success for the student.

Next, the pseudo R^2 value of 0.3934 for the McFadden metric indicates that approximately 39.34 percent of the output is explained by the Sat variable. This appears to suggest that we need to collect more information about the students. That is, the experimenter may try to get information on how many hours the student spent exclusively for the course/examination, the students' attendance percentages, and so on. However, the SAT-M score that may have been obtained nearly two years before the final exam of the course continues to have a good explanatory power!

Finally, it may be seen that the probability of completing the course for students with SAT-M scores of 400 and 700 are respectively `2.019e-06` and `1`. It is important for the reader to note the importance of the `type = "response"` option. More details may be obtained running `?predict.glm` at the R terminal.

What just happened?

The probit regression model is appropriate for handling the binary outputs and is certainly much more appropriate than the simple linear regression model. The reader learnt how to build the probit model using the `glm` function, which is in fact more versatile as will be seen in the rest of the chapter. The prediction probabilities were also seen to be in the range of 0 to 1.

The `glm` function can be conveniently used for more than one covariate. In fact, the formula structure of `glm` remains the same as `lm`. Model-related issues have not been considered in full details until now. The reason being that there is more interest in the logistic regression model, as it will be the focus for the rest of the chapter, and the logic does not change. In fact we will return to the probit model diagnostics in parallel with the logistic regression model.

Doing it in Python

The `probit` regression model can be built in Python using the `Probit` module from `pysal.spreg.probit`. First, we import the necessary data using the `pandas` package:

1. Import the `Sat.csv` file from the `Data` folder and set up the y and x objects as required for fitting the `probit` regression model. We then fit the `probit` model using the `Probit` module and obtain the regression coefficients:

```
In [4]:  sat = pd.read_csv("Data/Sat.csv",delimiter=',')
         y = np.array(sat[["Pass"]]); X = np.array(sat[["Pass"]])
         pass_probit = pysal.spreg.probit.Probit(y,X)
         pass_probit.betas

Out[4]:  array([[-4.75670106],
                [ 9.66678352]])
```

2. The details of the fitted model are obtained by printing the summary:

```
In [5]:  print(pass_probit.summary)

         REGRESSION
         ----------
         SUMMARY OF OUTPUT: CLASSIC PROBIT ESTIMATOR
         ------------------------------------------
         Data set           :     unknown
         Weights matrix     :        None
         Dependent Variable :     dep_var          Number of Observations:          30
         % correctly predicted: 100.00
         Log-Likelihood     :  -0.0000
         LR test            :  36.6518
         LR test (p-value)  :   0.0000

         ------------------------------------------------------------------------------
                  Variable    Coefficient     Std.Error     z-Statistic    Probability
         ------------------------------------------------------------------------------
                  CONSTANT     -4.7567011    69.2435515     -0.0686952      0.9452322
                     var_1      9.6667835    94.7239852      0.1020521      0.9187153
         ------------------------------------------------------------------------------

         MARGINAL EFFECTS
         Method: Mean of individual marginal effects
         ------------------------------------------------------------------------------
                  Variable          Slope     Std.Error     z-Statistic    Probability
         ------------------------------------------------------------------------------
                     var_1      0.0000298     0.0029069      0.0102637      0.9918109

         ============================ END OF REPORT ============================
```

3. The probit regression model is available in Python and it can be easily fitted as seen in the preceding screenshot.

Logistic regression model

The binary outcomes may be easily viewed as failures or successes, and we have done the same on many earlier occasions. Typically, it is then common to assume that we have a binomial distribution for the probability of an observation to be successful. The logistic regression model specifies the linear effect of the covariates as a specific function of the probability of success. The probability of success for observation is denoted by $\pi(x) = P(Y = 1)$ and the model is specified through the logistic function:

$$\pi(x) = \frac{e^{\beta_0 + \beta_1 x_1 + \cdots + \beta_p x_p}}{1 + e^{\beta_0 + \beta_1 x_1 + \cdots + \beta_p x_p}}$$

The choice of this function is for fairly good reasons. Define $w = \beta_0 + \beta_1 x_1 + \cdots + \beta_p x_p$. Then, it may be easily seen that $\pi(x) = e^w / (1 + e^w) = 1 / (1 + e^{-w})$. Thus, as w decreases to negative of infinity, $\pi(x)$ approaches 0, and if w increases towards infinity, $\pi(x)$ reaches 1. For $w = 0$, $\pi(x)$ takes the value 0.5. The ratio of probability of success to that of failure is known as the **odds ratio**, denoted by OR, and following a simple arithmetic steps, it may be shown that:

$$OR = \frac{\pi(x)}{1 - \pi(x)} = e^{\beta_0 + \beta_1 x_1 + \cdots + \beta_p x_p}$$

And taking logarithm of the odds ration gets us:

$$\log OR = \log \left(\frac{\pi(x)}{1 - \pi(x)} \right) = \beta_0 + \beta_1 x_1 + \cdots + \beta_p x_p$$

And thus we finally see that the logarithm of the odds ratio as a linear function of the covariates. It is actually the second term $\log \left(\pi(x_i) / (1 - \pi(x_i)) \right)$, which is a form of `logit` function that this model derives its name from.

The log-likelihood function based on the data $(y_1, x_1), (y_2, x_2), \ldots, (y_n, x_n)$ is then:

$$Log\, L(\beta) = \sum_{i=1}^{n} \left(y_i \sum_{j=0}^{p} \beta_j x_{ij} \right) - \sum_{i=1}^{n} \log \left(1 + e^{\sum_{j=0}^{p} \beta_j x_{ij}} \right)$$

The preceding expression is indeed a bit complex in nature to obtain an explicit form for an estimate of β. Indeed, a specialized algorithm is required here and it is known as the **iterative reweighted least-squares (IRLS)** algorithm. We will not go into the details of the algorithm and refer the readers to an online paper by Scott A. Czepiel, available at `http://czep.net/stat/mlelr.pdf`. A raw R implementation of the IRLS is provided in *Chapter 19* of Tattar, et. al. (2013). For our purpose, we will be using the solution as provided from the `glm` function. Let us now fit the logistic regression model for the Sat-M dataset considered hitherto.

Time for action – fitting the logistic regression model

Logistic regression model is built using the `glm` function with the `family = 'binomial'` option. We will obtain the pseudo-R^2 values using the `pR2` function from the `pscl` package:

1. Fit the logistic regression model for the `Pass` as a function of the `Sat` using the option `family = 'binomial'` in the `glm` function:

    ```
    pass_logistic <- glm(Pass~Sat,data=sat,family = 'binomial')
    ```

2. The details of the fitted logistic regression model is obtained using the `summary` function: `summary(pass_logistic)`.

    In the summary, you will see two statistics called **Null deviance** and **Residual deviance**. In general, a deviance is a measure useful for assessing the goodness-of-fit, and for the logistic regression model it plays the analogous role of residual sum of squares for the linear regression model.

    The null deviance is the measure of a model that is built without using any information, such as `Sat`, and thus we would expect such a model to have a large value. If the `Sat` variable is influencing `Pass`, we expect the residuals of such a fitted model to be significantly lesser than the null deviance model. If the residual deviance is significantly smaller than the null deviance, we conclude that the covariates have significantly improved the model fit.

3. Find the pseudo-R^2 with `pR2(pass_logistic)` from the `pscl` package.

4. The overall model significance of the fitted logistic regression model is obtained with:

    ```
    with(pass_logistic, pchisq(null.deviance - deviance, df.null -
    df.residual, lower.tail = FALSE))
    ```

The p-value is `0.0001496`, which shows that the model is indeed significant. The p-values for the `Sat` covariate `Pr(>|z|)` is `0.011`, which means that this variable is indeed valuable for understanding the `Pass`. The estimated regression coefficient for `Sat` of `0.0578` indicates that for the increase of a single mark increases the odds of the candidate to pass the course by `0.0578`.

A brief explanation of this R code! It may be seen from the output following the `summary.glm(pass_logistic)` that we have all the terms `null.deviance`, `deviance`, `df.null`, and `df.residual`. So, the `with` function extracts all these terms from the `pass_logistic` object and finds the p-value using the `pchisq` function based on the difference between the deviances (`null.deviance - deviance`) and the correct degrees of freedom (`df.null - df.residual`).

```
> pass_logistic <- glm(Pass~Sat,data=sat,family = 'binomial')
> summary.glm(pass_logistic)
Call:
glm(formula = Pass ~ Sat, family = "binomial", data = sat)
Deviance Residuals:
   Min     1Q  Median     3Q     Max
-2.293  -0.193   0.366  0.503   1.505
Coefficients:
            Estimate Std. Error z value Pr(>|z|)
(Intercept) -31.1147    12.5596   -2.48    0.013 *
Sat           0.0578     0.0228    2.54    0.011 *
---
Signif. codes:  0 '***' 0.001 '**' 0.01 '*' 0.05 '.' 0.1 ' ' 1

(Dispersion parameter for binomial family taken to be 1)
    Null deviance: 36.652  on 29  degrees of freedom
Residual deviance: 22.274  on 28  degrees of freedom
AIC: 26.27
Number of Fisher Scoring iterations: 5
> pR2(pass_logistic)
      llh   llhNull        G2  McFadden      r2ML      r2CU
 -11.1370  -18.3259   14.3779    0.3923    0.3808    0.5399
> with(pass_logistic, pchisq(null.deviance - deviance, df.null
+ - df.residual, lower.tail = FALSE))
[1] 0.0001496
```

Logistic regression model for the Sat dataset

5. The confidence intervals, with default 95 percent requirement, for the parameters of the regression coefficients is extracted using the `confint` function: `confint(pass_logistic)`.

    The ranges of the 95 percent confidence intervals do not contain 0 among them, and hence we conclude that the intercept term and `Sat` variable are both significant.

6. The prediction for the unknown scores are obtained as in the probit regression model:

    ```
    predict.glm(pass_logistic,newdata=list(Sat=400),type = "response")
    predict.glm(pass_logistic,newdata=list(Sat=700),type = "response")
    ```

7. Let us compare the `logistic` and `probit` model. Consider a sequence of hypothetical SAT-M scores: `sat_x = seq(400,700, 10)`. For the new sequence `sat_x`, we predict the probability of course completion using both the `pass_logistic` and `pass_probit` models and visualize them if their predictions are vastly different:

    ```
    pred_l <- predict(pass_logistic,newdata=list(Sat=sat_x), type= "response")
    pred_p <- predict(pass_probit,newdata=list(Sat=sat_x), type= "response")
    plot(sat_x,pred_l,type="l",ylab="Probability",xlab="Sat_M")
    lines(sat_x,pred_p,lty=2)
    ```

The prediction says that a candidate with SAT-M score of 400 is very unlikely to complete the course successfully while the one with SAT-M score of 700 is almost guaranteed to complete it. The predictions with probabilities closer to 0 or 1 need to be taken with a bit of caution since we rarely have enough observations at the boundaries of the covariates.

```
> sat_x <- seq(400,700, 10)
> pred_l <- predict(pass_logistic,newdata=list(Sat=sat_x),type="response")
> pred_p <- predict(pass_probit,newdata=list(Sat=sat_x),type="response")
> plot(sat_x,pred_l,type="l",ylab="Probability",xlab="Sat_M",col=1)
> lines(sat_x,pred_p,lty=2,col=2)
> legend(600,0.4,c("Logistic","Probit"),col=c(1:2),pch="-")
```

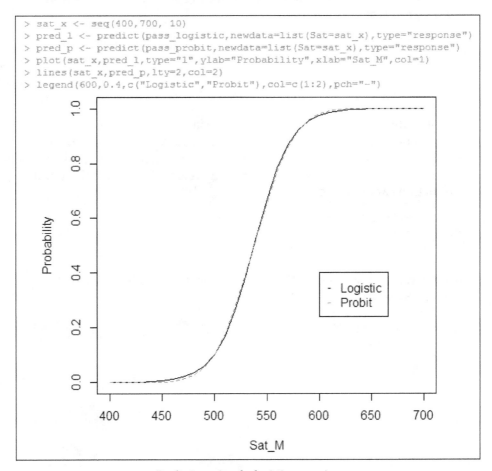

Prediction using the logistic regression

What just happened?

We fitted our first logistic regression model and viewed its various measures that tell us whether the fitted model is a good model or not. Next, we learnt how to interpret the estimated regression coefficients and also had a peek at the pseudo-R^2 value. The importance of confidence intervals is also emphasized. Finally, the model has been used to make prediction for some unobserved SAT-M scores too.

Doing it in Python

The logistic regression model can be built with the `Logit` module available in the `statsmodels` package:

1. Add an `Intercept` term to the `sat` data object. Invoke the `Logit` function from the `statsmodels` package. We create the structure of the logistic regression model in the second line of the Python block.

2. Fit the logistic regression model by running `Pass_logit.fit()`, and then obtain its details using the `summary` function.

```
In [7]: sat['Intercept'] = 1.0
        Pass_logit = sm.Logit(sat['Pass'],sat ['Intercept','Sat'] )
        PL_fit = Pass_logit.fit()
        print(PL_fit.summary())

        Optimization terminated successfully.
                 Current function value: 0.371233
                 Iterations 7
                             Logit Regression Results
        ==============================================================================
        Dep. Variable:               Pass    No. Observations:                  30
        Model:                       Logit    Df Residuals:                      28
        Method:                        MLE    Df Model:                           1
        Date:             Sun, 06 Aug 2017    Pseudo R-squ.:                 0.3923
        Time:                     11:16:58    Log-Likelihood:               -11.137
        converged:                    True    LL-Null:                      -18.326
                                              LLR p-value:               0.0001496
        ==============================================================================
                         coef    std err          z      P>|z|      [0.025      0.975]
        ------------------------------------------------------------------------------
        Intercept    -31.1147     12.562     -2.477      0.013     -55.735      -6.495
        Sat            0.0578      0.023      2.542      0.011       0.013       0.102
        ==============================================================================
```

3. Though the confidence intervals are provided in the summary details itself, we can extract the same as given by the next line of program:

```
In [8]:  PL_fit.conf_int()
Out[8]:
                        0          1

Intercept   -55.734779   -6.494572

      Sat     0.013241    0.102458
```

The residual analysis will be taken in a later section.

Hosmer-Lemeshow goodness-of-fit test statistic

We may be satisfied with the analysis thus far, and there is always a lot more that we can do. The testing hypothesis problem is of the form $H_0 : E(Y) = e^{\sum_{j=0}^{p} \beta_j x_{ij}} / \left(1 + e^{\sum_{j=0}^{p} \beta_j x_{ij}}\right)$ versus $H_1 : E(Y) \neq e^{\sum_{j=0}^{p} \beta_j x_{ij}} / \left(1 + e^{\sum_{j=0}^{p} \beta_j x_{ij}}\right)$. An answer to this hypothesis testing problem is provided by Hosmer-Lemeshow goodness-of-fit test statistic. The steps of the construction of this test statistic are first discussed:

1. Order the fitted values using sort and fitted functions.

2. Group the fitted values in to g classes, the preferred values of g vary between 6-10.

3. Find the observed and expected number in each group.

4. Perform a chi-square goodness-of-fit test on the previous groups. That is, denote Ojk for the number of observations of class k, $k = 0, 1$, in the group j, $j = 1, 2, ..., g$, and by E_{jk} the corresponding expected numbers. The chi-square test statistic is then given by:

$$\chi^2 = \sum_{j=1}^{g} \sum_{k=0,1} \frac{\left(O_{jk} - E_{jk}\right)^2}{E_{jk}}$$

and it may be proved that under the null-hypothesis $\chi^2 \sim \chi^2_{g-2}$.

We will use an R program available at http://sas-and-r.blogspot.in/2010/09/example-87-hosmer-and-lemeshow-goodness.html. It is important to note here that when we use the code available on the web we verify and understand that such code is indeed correct.

Time for action – Hosmer-Lemeshow goodness-of-fit statistic

The Hosmer-Lemeshow goodness-of-fit statistic for logistic regression is one of the very important metrics for evaluating a logistic regression model. The `hosmerlem` function from the preceding web link will be used for the `pass_logistic` regression model.

1. Extract the fitted values for the `pass_logistic` model with `pass_hat <- fitted(pass_logistic)`.

2. Create the function `hosmerlem` from the previously-mentioned URL:

```
hosmerlem <- function(y, yhat, g=10)          {
  cutyhat = cut(yhat,
     breaks = quantile(yhat, probs=seq(0,
       1, 1/g)), include.lowest=TRUE)
  obs = xtabs(cbind(1 - y, y) ~ cutyhat)
  expect = xtabs(cbind(1 - yhat, yhat) ~ cutyhat)
  chisq = sum((obs - expect)^2/expect)
  P = 1 - pchisq(chisq, g - 2)
  return(list(chisq=chisq,p.value=P))
}
```

What is the `hosmerlem` function exactly doing here? Obviously, it is a function of three variables, the real output values in `y`, the predicted (probabilities) in `yhat`, and the number of groups `g`. The `cutyhat` variable uses the `cut` function on the predicted probabilities among the ten groups and assigns them one of the 10 groups. The `obs` matrix obtains the count O_{jk} using the `xtabs` function and a similar action is repeated for E_{jk}. The code `chisq = sum((obs - expect)^2/expect)` then obtains the value of the Hosmer-Lemeshow chi-square test statistic, and using it we obtain the related p-value using `P = 1 - pchisq(chisq, g - 2)`. Finally, the required values are returned with `return(list(chisq=chisq,p.value=P))`.

3. Complete the computations of the Hosmer-Lemeshow goodness-of-fit test statistic for the fitted model `pass_logistic` with `hosmerlem( pass_logistic$y, pass_hat)`.

```
> pass_hat <- fitted(pass_logistic)
> hosmerlem <- function(y, yhat, g=10) {
+    cutyhat = cut(yhat,
+        breaks = quantile(yhat, probs=seq(0,
+            1, 1/g)), include.lowest=TRUE)
+    obs = xtabs(cbind(1 - y, y) ~ cutyhat)
+    expect = xtabs(cbind(1 - yhat, yhat) ~ cutyhat)
+    chisq = sum((obs - expect)^2/expect)
+    P = 1 - pchisq(chisq, g - 2)
+    return(list(chisq=chisq,p.value=P))
+ }
> hosmerlem(pass_logistic$y, pass_hat)
$chisq
[1] 4.653
$p.value
[1] 0.794
```

Hosmer-Lemeshow goodness-of-fit test

Since there is no significant difference between the observed and predicted y values, we concluded that the fitted model is a good fit. Now that we know that we got a good model on hand, it is time to investigate the validity of the model assumptions.

What just happened?

We used R code from the web and successfully adapted to the problem at hand! Particularly, the Hosmer-Lemeshow goodness-of-fit test is a vital metric for understanding the appropriateness of a logistic regression model.

Model validation and diagnostics

In the previous chapter, we saw the utility of residual techniques. A similar technique is also required for the logistic regression model and we will develop these methods for the logistic regression model in this section.

Residual plots for the GLM

In the case of linear regression model, we had explored the role of residuals for the purpose of model validation. In the context of logistic regression, actually GLM, we have five different types of residuals for the same purpose:

- **Response residual**: The difference between the actual values and the fitted values is the response residual, that is, $y_i - \hat{\pi}_i$, and in particular it is $1 - \hat{\pi}_i$ if $y_i = 1$ and $-\hat{\pi}_i$ for $y_i = 0$.

- **Deviance residual**: For an observation i, the deviance residual is the signed square root of the contribution of the observation to the sum of the model deviance. That is, it is given by:

$$r_i^{dev} = \pm \left\{ -2 \left[Y_i \log(\hat{\pi}_i) + (1 - Y_i) \log(1 - \hat{\pi}_i) \right] \right\}^{1/2}$$

Where the sign is positive if $Y_i \geq \hat{\pi}_i$, and negative otherwise, and $\hat{\pi}_i$ is the predicted probability of success.

- **Pearson residual**: The Pearson residual is defined by:

$$r_i^P = \frac{y_i - \hat{\pi}_i}{\sqrt{\hat{\pi}_i (1 - \hat{\pi}_i)}}$$

- **Partial residual**: The partial residual of the jth predictor, $j = 1, 2, \ldots, p$, for the ith observation is defined by:

$$r_{ij}^{part} = \hat{\beta}_j x_{ij} + \frac{y_i - \hat{\pi}_i}{\hat{\pi}_i (1 - \hat{\pi}_i)}, i = 1, \ldots, n, j = 1, \ldots, p$$

The partial residuals are very useful for identification of the type of transformation that needs to be performed on the covariates.

- **Working residual**: The working residual for the logistic regression model is given by:

$$r_i^W = \frac{y_i - \hat{\pi}_i}{\hat{\pi}_i \left(1 - \hat{\pi}_i\right)}$$

Each of the preceding residual variants is easily obtained using the residuals function, see ? `glm.summaries` for details. The residual variant is specified through the option type in the residuals function. We have not given the details related to probit regression model; however, the same functions for logistic regression apply here nevertheless. We will obtain the residual plots against the fitted values and examine the appropriateness of the logistic and probit regression models.

Time for action – residual plots for logistic regression model

The `residuals` and `fitted` functions will be used to obtain the residual plots from the probit and logistic regression models.

1. Initialize a graphics windows for three panels with `par(mfrow=c(1,3)`, `oma = c(0,0,3,0))`. The `oma` option ensures that we can appropriately title the grand output.

2. `Plot Response Residuals` against the `Fitted Values` of the `pass_logistic` model with:

   ```
   plot(fitted(pass_logistic), residuals(pass_logistic,"response"),
   col= "red", xlab="Fitted Values", ylab="Residuals",cex.axis=1.5,
   cex.lab=1.5)
   ```

   The reason for `xlab` and `ylab` has been explained in the earlier chapters.

3. For the purpose of comparison with the probit regression model, add their response residuals to the previous plot with:

   ```
   points(fitted(pass_probit), residuals(pass_probit,"response"),
   col= "green")
   ```

   and add a suitable legend and title as follows:

   ```
   legend(0.6,0,c("Logistic","Probit"),col=c("red","green"),pch="-")
   title("Response Residuals")
   ```

4. Add the horizontal line at 0 with `abline(h=0)`.

5. Repeat the preceding steps for deviance and `Pearson` residuals with:

```
plot(fitted(pass_logistic), residuals(pass_logistic,"deviance"),
col= "red", xlab="Fitted Values", ylab="Residuals",cex.axis=1.5,
cex.lab=1.5)
points(fitted(pass_probit), residuals(pass_probit,"deviance"),
col= "green")
legend(0.6,0,c("Logistic","Probit"),col=c("red","green"),pch="-")
abline(h=0)
title("Deviance Residuals")
plot(fitted(pass_logistic), residuals(pass_logistic,"pearson"),
col= "red",xlab="Fitted Values",ylab="Residuals",cex.axis=1.5,
cex.lab= 1.5)
points(fitted(pass_probit), residuals(pass_probit,"pearson"), col=
"green")
legend(0.6,0,c("Logistic","Probit"),col=c("red","green"),pch="-")
abline(h=0)
title("Pearson Residuals")
```

6. Give an appropriate title with `title(main="Response, Deviance, and Pearson Residuals Comparison for the Logistic and Probit Models",outer=TRUE, cex.main=1.5)`.

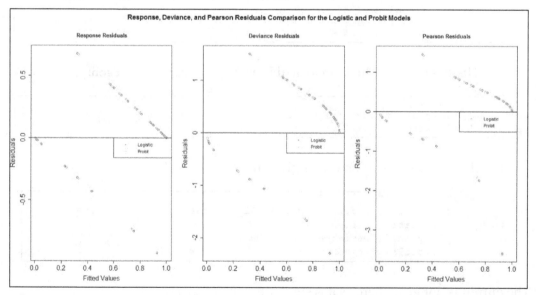

Residual plots for the logistic regression model

In each of the three preceding residual plots, we observe two trends of decreasing residuals whose slope is -1. The reason for such a trend is that the residuals take one of two values at a point X_i, either $1 - \hat{\pi}_i$ or $-\hat{\pi}_i$. Thus, in these residual plots we always get two linear trends with slope -1. Clearly, there is not much difference between the residuals of the logistic and probit models. The Pearson residual graph also indicates the presence of an outlier for the observation with residual value less than -3.

What just happened?

The `residuals` function along with the `type` option helps in model validation and identification of some residuals. A good thing is that the same function applies to logistic as well as the probit regression model.

Doing it in Python

This part will help in carrying out the residual analysis in Python.

1. The `PL_fit` object earlier also contains the fitted values as well as the residuals. The plot of fitted values against the actual residuals is given by

```
In [10]: plt.subplot(1,3,1)
         plt.plot(PL_fit.fittedvalues,PL_fit.resid_response,'.',color='red')
         plt.xlabel("Fitted Values")
         plt.ylabel("Residuals")
         plt.title("Fitted Vs Residuals Plot")
```

2. The `Pearson` residuals are available as `PL_fit.resid_pearson`:

```
plt.subplot(1,3,2)
plt.plot(PL_fit.fittedvalues,PL_fit.resid_pearson,'.',color='blue')
plt.xlabel("Fitted Values")
```

3. The residual deviation plot is given next:

```
plt.subplot(1,3,3)
plt.plot(PL_fit.fittedvalues,PL_fit.resid_dev,'.',color='green')
plt.xlabel("Fitted Values")
plt.ylabel("Deviance Residuals")
plt.title("Fitted Vs Deviance Residuals Plot")
```

The output is not given here as it is similar to the one produced in R.

Have a go hero

In the previous exercise, we have left out the investigation using partial and working type residuals. Obtain these plots!

Influence and leverage for the GLM

In the previous chapter, we saw how the influential and leverage points are identified in a linear regression model. It will be a bit difficult to go into the appropriate formulas and theory for the logistic regression model.

Time for action – diagnostics for the logistic regression

The influence and leverage points will be identified through the application of the functions, such as `hatvalues`, `cooks.distance`, `dffits`, and `dfbetas` for the `pass_logistic` fitted model.

1. The high leverage points of a logistic regression model is obtained with `hatvalues(pass_logistic)` while the Cooks distance is fetched with `cooks.distance(pass_logistic)`. The DFFITS and DFBETAS measures of influence are obtained by running `dfbetas(pass_logistic)` and `dffits(pass_logistic)`.

2. The influence and leverage measures are put together using the `cbind` function:

   ```
   cbind(hatvalues(pass_logistic),cooks.distance(pass_
   logistic),dfbetas(pass_logistic),dffits(pass_logistic))
   ```

The output is given in the following screenshot:

```
> cbind(hatvalues(pass_logistic),cooks.distance(pass_logistic),
+ dfbetas(pass_logistic),dffits(pass_logistic))
                                (Intercept)        Sat
1   0.141456 4.561e-02   -0.336338  0.324323 -0.434298
2   0.113253 5.438e-02   -0.296360  0.281300 -0.456390
3   0.073744 2.843e-02    0.101341 -0.087705  0.333571
4   0.051649 3.691e-01    0.534736 -0.553371 -0.698034
5   0.052064 2.388e-03   -0.079998  0.082880  0.105874
6   0.053571 3.291e-03   -0.085639  0.089363  0.123660
7   0.054146 4.198e-03   -0.086968  0.091506  0.138922
8   0.031671 2.755e-04   -0.033108  0.033726  0.036430
9   0.055572 9.167e-03   -0.053218  0.061379  0.199857
10  0.079014 3.459e-02    0.137099 -0.122598  0.364143
11  0.053571 3.291e-03   -0.085639  0.089363  0.123660
12  0.141456 2.019e-01    0.598747 -0.577358  0.773136
13  0.053920 3.722e-03   -0.086748  0.090863  0.131171
14  0.051649 2.234e-03   -0.078513  0.081249  0.102490
15  0.053920 3.722e-03   -0.086748  0.090863  0.131171
16  0.072974 8.878e-04   -0.063433  0.062708 -0.065336
17  0.043368 8.689e-04   -0.055349  0.056704  0.064432
18  0.056499 9.605e-02    0.094231 -0.114945 -0.497087
19  0.056499 9.605e-02    0.094231 -0.114945 -0.497087
20  0.050708 1.949e-03   -0.075304  0.077767  0.095904
21  0.040110 6.333e-04   -0.048302  0.049387  0.055090
22  0.159512 3.379e-02   -0.325941  0.316995 -0.383973
23  0.008398 6.888e-06   -0.005554  0.005616  0.005777
24  0.050708 1.949e-03   -0.075304  0.077767  0.095904
25  0.055624 4.105e-04   -0.043448  0.042999 -0.044495
26  0.046386 1.179e-03   -0.062710  0.064399  0.074907
27  0.118833 4.278e-03   -0.135563  0.133573 -0.142466
28  0.054644 7.138e-03   -0.071867  0.078748  0.178154
29  0.059734 1.407e-02   -0.006042  0.016384  0.242863
30  0.065344 1.963e-02    0.040723 -0.028778  0.282371
```

Influence measures for the logistic regression model

It is time to interpret these measures.

3. If the `hatvalues` associated with an observation is greater than $2(p+1)/n$, where p is the number of covariates considered in the model and n is the number of observations, it is considered as a high leverage point. For the `pass_logistic` object, we find the high leverage points with:

```
hatvalues(pass_logistic)>2*(length(pass_logistic$coefficients)-1)/
length(pass_logistic$y)
```

4. An observation is considered to have *great influence* on the parameter estimates if the Cooks distance, as given by `cooks.distance`, if the distance is greater than 10 percent quantile of the $F_{(P+1), n-(P+1)}$ distribution, and it is considered *highly influential* if it exceeds 50 percent quantile of the same distribution. In terms of R program, we need to execute:

```
cooks.distance(pass_logistic)>qf(0.1,length(pass_logistic$
coefficients),length(pass_logistic$y)-length(pass_logistic$
coefficients))
cooks.distance(pass_logistic)>qf(0.5,length(pass_logistic$
coefficients),length(pass_logistic$y)-length(pass_logistic$
coefficients))
```

```
> hatvalues(pass_logistic)>2*(length(pass_logistic$coefficients)-1
+ )/length(pass_logistic$y)
    1     2     3     4     5     6     7     8     9    10    11    12
 TRUE  TRUE  TRUE FALSE FALSE FALSE FALSE FALSE FALSE  TRUE FALSE  TRUE
   13    14    15    16    17    18    19    20    21    22    23    24
FALSE FALSE FALSE  TRUE FALSE FALSE FALSE FALSE FALSE  TRUE FALSE FALSE
   25    26    27    28    29    30
FALSE FALSE  TRUE FALSE FALSE FALSE
> cooks.distance(pass_logistic)>qf(0.1,length(pass_logistic$coefficients),
+ length(pass_logistic$y)-length(pass_logistic$coefficients))
    1     2     3     4     5     6     7     8     9    10    11    12
FALSE FALSE FALSE  TRUE FALSE FALSE FALSE FALSE FALSE FALSE FALSE  TRUE
   13    14    15    16    17    18    19    20    21    22    23    24
FALSE FALSE FALSE FALSE FALSE FALSE FALSE FALSE FALSE FALSE FALSE FALSE
   25    26    27    28    29    30
FALSE FALSE FALSE FALSE FALSE FALSE
> cooks.distance(pass_logistic)>qf(0.5,length(pass_logistic$coefficients),
+ length(pass_logistic$y)-length(pass_logistic$coefficients))
    1     2     3     4     5     6     7     8     9    10    11    12
FALSE FALSE FALSE FALSE FALSE FALSE FALSE FALSE FALSE FALSE FALSE FALSE
   13    14    15    16    17    18    19    20    21    22    23    24
FALSE FALSE FALSE FALSE FALSE FALSE FALSE FALSE FALSE FALSE FALSE FALSE
   25    26    27    28    29    30
FALSE FALSE FALSE FALSE FALSE FALSE
```

Identifying the outliers

The previous screenshot shows that there are eight high leverage points. We also see that at 10 percent quantile of the F-distribution we have two influential points whereas we don't have any highly influential point.

5. We define a function in Python to extract the `hatvalues`. The function is the same as in the case of linear regression model:

```
In [12]:  def hatvalues(fitted_lm):
              X=fitted_lm.exog
              hat_mat = np.dot(X,np.dot(np.linalg.inv(np.dot(X.T,X)),X.T))
              hat_values = np.diagonal(hat_mat)
              return(hat_values)
          hatvalues(Pass_logit)

Out[12]:  array([ 0.0588308 ,  0.04829732,  0.03772897,  0.04466554,  0.04369329,
                  0.039486  ,  0.03690495,  0.08739674,  0.03333421,  0.03905437,
                  0.039486  ,  0.0588308 ,  0.03810828,  0.04466554,  0.03810828,
                  0.20291618,  0.06127233,  0.03343884,  0.03343884,  0.04674084,
                  0.06786447,  0.0721546 ,  0.20912465,  0.04674084,  0.23507467,
                  0.05537777,  0.14384414,  0.03364812,  0.0341713 ,  0.03560134])
```

6. Use the `plot` function to identify the influential observations suggested by the `DFFITS` and `DFBETAS` measure:

```
par(mfrow=c(1,3))
plot(dfbetas(pass_logistic)[,1],ylab="DFBETAS - INTERCEPT")
plot(dfbetas(pass_logistic)[,2],ylab="DFBETAS - SAT")
plot(dffits(pass_logistic),ylab="DFFITS")
```

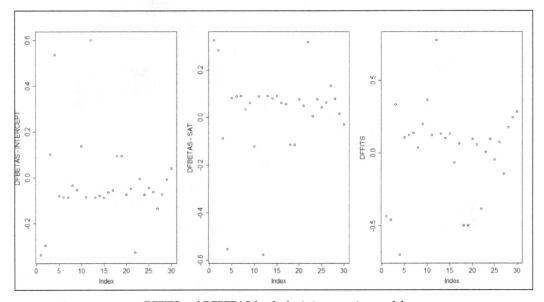

DFFITS and DFBETAS for the logistic regression model

As with the linear regression model, the DFFITS and DFBETAS are measures of influence of the observations on the regression coefficients. The thumb rule for the DFBETAS is that if their absolute value exceeds 1, the observations are having significant influence on the covariates. In our case, it is not the case and we conclude that we do not have influential observations. The interpretation of DFFITS is left as an exercise.

What just happened?

We adapted the influential measures in the context of generalized linear models, and especially in the context of logistic regression.

Have a go hero

The influence and leverage measures were executed on the logistic regression model, the pass_logistic object in particular. You also have pass_probit object! Repeat the entire exercise of hatvalues, cooks.distance, dffits, and dfbetas on pass_probit fitted probit model and draw your inference.

Receiving operator curves

In the binary classification problem, we have certain scenarios where the comparison between the predicted and actual class is of great importance. For example, there is genuine problem in the banking industry for identifying fraudulent transactions against the non-fraudulent transactions. There is another problem of sanctioning loans to customers who may successfully repay the entire loan and the customers who will default at some stage during the loan tenure. Given the historical data, we will build a classification model, for example the logistic regression model.

Now with the logistic regression model, or any other classification model for that matter, if the predicted probability is greater than 0.5, the observation is predicted as a successful observation, and a failure otherwise. We remind ourselves again that success/failure is defined according to the experiment. At least with the data on hand, we know the true labels of the observations and hence a comparison of the true labels with the predicted label makes a lot of sense.

In an ideal scenario we expect the predicted labels to match perfectly with the actual labels, that is, whenever the true label stands for success/failure, the predicted label is also success/failure. However, in the real scenario it is rarely the case. This means that there are some observations which are predicted as success/failure when the true labels are actually failure/success. In other words, we make mistakes! It is possible to put these notes in the form of a table widely known as the confusion matrix.

		Observed	
		Success	**Failure**
Predicted	**Success**	True Positive (TP)	False Positive (FP)
	Failure	False Negative (FN)	True Negative (TN)

The confusion matrix

The number in parenthesis is the count of the cases. It may be seen from the preceding table that the cells colored in green are the correct predictions made by the model whereas the red colored are the ones with mistakes. The following metrics may be considered for comparison across multiple models:

- **Accuracy:** $\dfrac{TP+TN}{TP+TN+FP+FN}$
- **Precision:** $\dfrac{TP}{TP+FP}$
- **Recall:** $\dfrac{TP}{TP+FN}$

However, it is known that these metrics have a lot of limitations and more robust steps are required. The answer is provided by **receiver operator characteristic (ROC)** curve. We need two important metrics towards the construction of an ROC. The **true positive rate (tpr)** and **false positive rate (fpr)** are respectively defined by:

$$tpr = \frac{TP}{TP+FN}, \; fpr = \frac{FP}{TN+FP}$$

The ROC graphs are constructed by plotting the `tpr` against the `fpr`. We will now explain this in detail. Our approach will be explaining the algorithm in an Action framework.

Time for action – ROC construction

A simple dataset is considered and the ROC construction is explained in a very simple step-by-step approach:

1. Suppose that the predicted probabilities of *n = 10* observations are 0.32, 0.62, 0.19, 0.75, 0.18, 0.18, 0.95, 0.79, 0.24, 0.59. Create a vector of it as follows:

   ```
   pred_prob<-c(0.32, 0.62, 0.19, 0.75, 0.18, 0.18, 0.95, 0.79, 0.24, 0.59)
   ```

2. Sort the predicted probabilities in a decreasing order:

   ```
   > (pred_prob=sort(pred_prob,decreasing=TRUE))
    [1] 0.95 0.79 0.75 0.62 0.59 0.32 0.24 0.19 0.18 0.18
   ```

3. Normalize the predicted probabilities in the preceding step to the unit interval:

   ```
   > pred_prob<-(pred_prob-min(pred_prob))/(max(pred_prob)-min(pred_prob))
   > pred_prob
    [1] 1.00000 0.79221 0.74026 0.57143 0.53247 0.18182 0.07792
   0.01299 0.00000 0.00000
   ```

   Now, at each percentage of the above sorted probability, we commit false positives as well as false negatives. Thus, we want to check at each part of our prediction percentiles, the quantum of `tpr` and `fpr`. Since ten points are much less, we now consider a dataset of predicted probabilities and the true labels.

4. Load the illustrative dataset from RSADBE package with `data(simpledata)`.

5. Set up the threshold vector `threshold <- seq(1,0,-0.01)`.

6. Find the number of positive (success) and negative (failure) cases in the dataset `P <- sum(simpledata$Label==1)` and `N <- sum(simpledata$Label ==0)`.

7. Initialize the `fpr` and `tpr` with `tpr <- fpr <- threshold*0`.

8. Set up the following loop which computes tpr and fpr at each point of the threshold vector:

   ```
   for(i in 1:length(threshold))  {
        FP=TP=0
        for(j in 1:nrow(simpledata))  {
        if(simpledata$Predictions[j]>=threshold[i]) {
        if(simpledata$Label[j]==1) TP=TP+1 else FP=FP+1
             }
          }
   ```

```
tpr[i]=TP/P
fpr[i]=FP/N
    }
```

9. Plot the `tpr` against the `fpr` with:

```
plot(fpr,tpr,"l",xlab="False Positive Rate", ylab="True Positive
Rate",col="red")
abline(a=0,b=1)
```

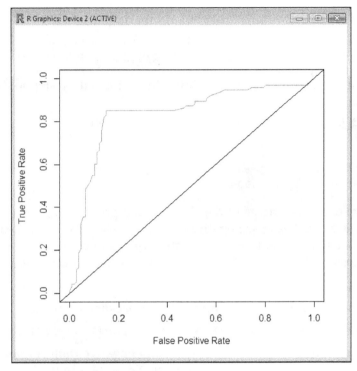

An ROC illustration

The diagonal line is about the performance of a random classifier in that it simply says yes or no without looking at any characteristic of an observation. Any good classifier must sit, rather be displayed, above this line. The classifier, albeit an unknown one, seems a much better classifier than the random classifier. The ROC curve is useful in comparison to competitive classifiers in the sense that if one classifier is always above another, we select the former.

What just happened?

The construction of ROC has been demystified! The preceding program is very primitive one. In the later chapters, we will use ROCR package for construction of ROC.

The ROC implementation in Python is taken up now.

Doing it in Python

The sklearn package gives many functions useful in every data analyses projects. Here, it gives us the required roc_curve function which helps to calculate the tpr and fpr.

1. First, we store the predicted values by adding it to the original data frame/ object. Using the roc_curve function, the tpr and fpr are calculated. Using the empirical tpr and fpr, we are then able to compute the area-under-curve of the ROC.

```
In [14]:  sat['pred'] = PL_fit.predict(sat[['Intercept','Sat']])
          fpr, tpr, thresholds = roc_curve(sat['Pass'], sat['pred'])
          roc_auc = auc fpr, tpr
          print("Area under the ROC Curve is : %f" % roc_auc)

          Area under the ROC Curve is : 0.867725
```

2. We now make use of the available tpr and fpr to plot the ROC curve:

```
In [15]:  plt.plot(fpr,tpr,color='red',lw=2,label='ROC Curve')
          plt.plot([0,1],[0,1],color='blue',lw=2,linestyle='--')
          plt.xlabel('FPR')
          plt.ylabel('TPR')
          plt.title('ROC Curve')
          plt.show()
```

With the important aspects of the logistic regression model with us, we now look at a complex problem.

We will next look at a real world problem.

Logistic regression for the German credit screening dataset

Millions of applications are made to a bank for a variety of loans! The loan may be a personal loan, home loan, car loan, and so forth. From a bank perspective, loans are an asset for them as obviously the customer pays them interest and over a period of time the bank makes profit. If all the customers promptly pay back their loan amount, all their tenure **equated monthly installment (EMI)** or the complete amount on preclosure of the principal amount, there is only money to be made.

Unfortunately, it is not always the case that the customers pay back the entire amount. In fact, the fraction of people who do not complete the loan duration may also be very small, say about five percent. However, a bad customer may take away the profits of may be 20 or more customers. In this hypothetical case, the bank eventually makes more losses than profit and this may eventually lead to its own bankruptcy.

Now, a loan application form seeks a lot of details about the applicant. The data from these details in the application can help the bank build appropriate classifiers, such as a logistic regression model, and make prediction about which customers are most likely to turn up as fraudulent. The customers who have been predicted to default in the future are then declined the loan. A real dataset about 1,000 customers who had borrowed loan from a bank is available on the web at `http://www.stat.auckland.ac.nz/~reilly/credit-g.arff` and `http://archive.ics.uci.edu/ml/datasets/Statlog+(German+Credit+Data)`. This data has been made available by Prof. Hofmann and it contains details on 20 variables related to the customer. It is also known whether the customers defaulted or not. The variables are described in the following table:

A detailed analysis of the dataset using R has been done by Sharma and his very useful document can be downloaded from `cran.r-project.org/doc/contrib/Sharma-CreditScoring.pdf`.

No	Variable	Characteristic	Description	No	Variable	Characteristic	Description
1	checking	integer	Status of existing checking account	12	property	factor	Property
2	duration	integer	Duration in month	13	age	numeric	Age in years
3	history	integer	Credit history	14	other	integer	Other installment plans
4	purpose	factor	Purpose	15	housing	integer	Housing
5	amount	numeric	Credit amount	16	existcr	integer	Number of existing credits at this bank
6	savings	integer	Savings account/ bonds	17	job	integer	Job
7	employed	integer	Present employment since	18	depends	integer	Number of people being liable to provide maintenance for
8	installp	integer	Installment rate in percentage of disposable income	19	telephon	integer	Telephone
9	marital	integer	Personal status and sex	20	foreign	integer	Foreign worker
10	coapp	integer	Other debtors/ guarantors	21	good_bad	factor	Loan defaulter
11	resident	integer	Present residence since	22	default	integer	good_bad in numeric

We have the German credit dataset with us in the GC data from the RSADBE package. Let us build a classifier for identifying the good customers apart from the bad ones.

Time for action – logistic regression for the German credit dataset

Logistic regression model will be built for credit card application scoring model and an ROC curve fit to evaluate the fit of the model.

1. Invoke the ROCR library with `library(ROCR)`.

2. Get the German credit dataset in your current session with `data(GC)`.

3. Build the logistic regression model for `good_bad` with `GC_LR <- glm(good_bad~.,data=GC,family=binomial())`.

4. Run `summary(GC_LR)` and identify the significant variables. Also answer the question of whether the model is significant.

5. Get the predictions using the `predict` function:

   ```
   LR_Pred <- predict( GC_LR,type='response')
   ```

6. Use the prediction function from ROCR package to set up a `prediction` object:

   ```
   GC_pred <- prediction(LR_Pred,GC$good_bad)
   ```

   The function `prediction` sets up different manipulations and computations as required for constructing the ROC curve. Get more details related to it with `?prediction`.

7. Set up the performance vector required to obtain the ROC curve with `GC_perf <- performance(GC_pred,"tpr","fpr")`.

   The `performance` function uses the prediction object to set up the ROC curve.

8. Finally, visualize the ROC curve with `plot(GC_perf)`.

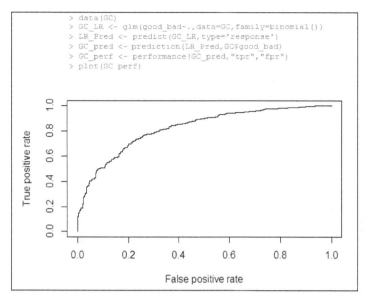

Logistic regression model for the German credit data

The ROC curve shows that the logistic regression is indeed effective in identifying fraudulent customers.

What just happened?

Now, we have considered a real-world problem with enough data points. The fitted logistic regression model gives a good explanation of the fraudulent customers in terms of the data that is collected about them.

Fitting of the logistic regression model to the German credit data is now carried out in Python.

Doing it in Python

Here, we use the `train_test_split` function from the `sklearn.cross_validation` module to partition the data by following the given steps:

1. Import the German credit data in Python using the function `pd.read_csv`.

2. Extract the covariates in X and the dependent variable `good_bad` in y.

3. `Binarize` the variable Y using `label_binarize` function.

4. Partition the data into training and test by using the `train_test_split` function.

5. The logistic regression is fitted using the method used earlier.

```
In [16]:  GC = pd.read_csv("Data/GC2.csv",delimiter=',')
          y = GC[['good_bad']]
          X = GC.iloc[:,0:20]
          y = label_binarize(y, classes=[0, 1])
          n_classes = y.shape[1]
          X_train, X_test, y_train, y_test = train_test_split(X, y, test_size=.2)
          Pass_logit = sm.Logit(y_train,X_train)
          PL_fit = Pass_logit.fit()

          Optimization terminated successfully.
                  Current function value: 0.485875
```

6. Using the fitted model, we obtain predicted values for the training as well as test partitions of the data. Applying the `roc_curve` function, we calculate the TPR and FPR's and then obtain the Area-under-curve.

```
In [17]:  y_train_pred = PL_fit.predict(X_train)
          y_test_pred = PL_fit.predict(X_test)
          fpr_train, tpr_train, thresholds = roc_curve(y_train,y_train_pred)
          fpr_test, tpr_test, thresholds = roc_curve(y_test,y_test_pred)
          roc_auc_train = auc(fpr_train,tpr_train)
          roc_auc_test = auc(fpr_test,tpr_test)
          print("Area under the ROC Curve for Train Data is : %f" % roc_auc_train)
          print("Area under the ROC Curve for Test Data is : %f" % roc_auc_test)

          Area under the ROC Curve for Train Data is : 0.793281
          Area under the ROC Curve for Test Data is : 0.788214
```

7. The ROC curves is now obtained using the `plot` function:

```
In [18]:  plt.plot(fpr_train,tpr_train,color='red',lw=2,label='ROC Curve')
          plt.plot(fpr_test,tpr_test,color='green',lw=2)
          plt.plot([0,1],[0,1],color='blue',lw=2,linestyle='--')
          plt.show()
```

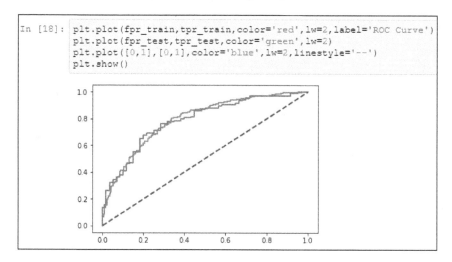

Have a go hero

For `simpledata`, a raw program was written to draw the ROC curve. Redo the exercise with a *red* color for the curve. Using the `prediction` and `performance` functions from the ROCR package, add the curve for `simpledata` obtained in the previous step with a *green* color. What do you expect?

Summary

We started with a simple linear regression model for the binary classification problem and saw t how limited it was. The probit regression model, which is an adaption of the linear regression model through a latent variable, overcomes the drawbacks of the straightforward linear regression model.

The versatile logistic regression model has been considered in detail and we considered the various kinds of residuals that help in the model validation. The influential and leverage point detection has been discussed too, which helps us build a better model by removing the outliers. A metric in the form of ROC helps us in understanding the performance of a classifier. Finally, we concluded the chapter with an application to the important problem of identifying good customers from the bad ones.

Despite the advantages of linearity, we still have many drawbacks with either the linear regression model or the logistic regression model. The next chapter begins with the family of polynomial regression models and later considers the impact of regularization.

8
Regression Models with Regularization

In *Chapter 6, Linear Regression Analysis*, and *Chapter 7, Logistic Regression Model*, we focused on the linear and logistic regression models. In the model selection issues with the linear regression model, we found that a **covariate** is either selected or not, depending on the associated p-value. However, the rejected covariates are not given any kind of consideration once the p-value is less than the threshold. This may lead to discarding the covariates, even if they have some influence on the regressand. In particular, the final model may thus lead to overfitting of the data, and this problem needs to be addressed.

We will first consider fitting a polynomial regression model, without the technical details, and see how higher order polynomials give a very good fit, which comes with a higher price. A more general framework of B-splines is considered next. This approach leads us to the smooth spline models, which are actually ridge regression models. The chapter concludes with an extension of the ridge regression for the linear and logistic regression models. For more details of the coverage, refer to *Chapter 2* of *Berk (2008)* and *Chapter 5* of *Hastie, et. al. (2008)*. This chapter will address the following topics:

- The problem of overfitting in a general regression model
- The use of regression splines for certain special cases
- Improving estimators of the regression coefficients, and overcoming the problem of overfitting with ridge regression for linear and logistic models
- The framework of train, validate, and test for regression models

Packages and settings – R and Python

We will need four R packages in ridge, DAAG, splines, and MASS. The required Python packages are matplotlib, pandas, numpy, pylab, statsmodels, and sklearn:

1. First set the working directory in R:

   ```
   setwd("MyPath/R/Chapter_06")
   ```

2. Load the essential R packages:

   ```
   > library(RSADBE)
   > library(ridge)
   > library(DAAG)
   > library(splines)
   > library(MASS)
   ```

3. Set the working directory and required packages and functions in Python now:

   ```
   In [2]:  import os
            os.chdir("MyPath/Python/Chapter_08")
            import matplotlib.pyplot as plt
            import pandas as pd
            import numpy as np
            import pylab
            import statsmodels.formula.api as smf
            from sklearn.linear_model import LogisticRegression
            from sklearn.preprocessing import PolynomialFeatures
            from sklearn.linear_model import Ridge
   ```

Using these packages and functions, we will be able to carry out the computations required in the rest of the chapter.

The overfitting problem

The limitation of the linear regression model is best understood through an example. I have created a hypothetical dataset for understanding the problem of overfitting. A scatterplot of the dataset is shown in the figure, *A non-linear relationship displayed by scatter plot.*

It appears from the scatterplot that, for *x*-values up to 6, there is a linear increase in y, and an eye-bird estimate of the slope is `(50 - 10) / (5.5 - 1.75) = 10.67`. This slope may be because of a linear term or even a quadratic term. On the other hand, the decline in *y*-values for *x*-values greater than 6 is very steep, approximately `(10 - 50) / (10 - 6) = -10`.

Now, looking at the complete picture, it appears that the output Y depends upon the higher order of the covariate X. Let us fit polynomial curves of various degrees and understand the behavior of the different linear regression models. A polynomial regression model of degree k is defined as follows:

$$Y = \beta_0 + \beta_1 X + \beta_2 X^2 + \cdots + \beta_k X^k + \varepsilon$$

Here, the terms $X, X^2, \ldots, X^k$ are treated as distinct variables, in the sense that one may compare the preceding model with the one introduced in the multiple linear regression model of *Chapter 6, Linear Regression Analysis*, by defining $X_1 = X, X_2 = X^2, \ldots, X_k = X^k$. The inference for the polynomial regression model proceeds in the same way as the multiple linear regression with k terms:

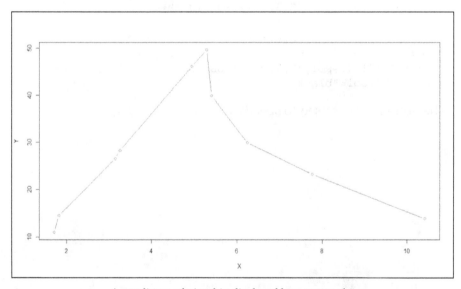

A non-linear relationship displayed by a scatter plot

The data for figure, *A non-linear relationship displayed by scatter plot* is available in the dataset OF from RSADBE. The option poly is used in the right side of the formula of the lm function for fitting the polynomial regression models.

Time for action – understanding overfitting

Polynomial regression models are built using the lm function, as we saw earlier, with the option poly:

1. Read the hypothetical dataset into R by using data(OF).

2. Plot Y against X by using:

    ```
    plot(OF$X, OF$Y,"b",col="red",xlab="X", ylab="Y").
    ```

3. Fit polynomial regression models of orders 1, 2, 3, 6, and 9, and add their fitted lines against the covariates X with the following code:

    ```
    lines(OF$X,lm(Y~poly(X,1,raw=TRUE),data=OF)$fitted.
    values,"b",col="green")
    lines(OF$X,lm(Y~poly(X,2,raw=TRUE),data=OF)$fitted.
    values,"b",col="wheat")
    lines(OF$X,lm(Y~poly(X,3,raw=TRUE),data=OF)$fitted.
    values,"b",col="yellow")
    lines(OF$X,lm(Y~poly(X,6,raw=TRUE),data=OF)$fitted.
    values,"b",col="orange")
    lines(OF$X,lm(Y~poly(X,9,raw=TRUE),data=OF)$fitted.
    values,"b",col="black")
    ```

    The option poly is used to specify the polynomial degree:

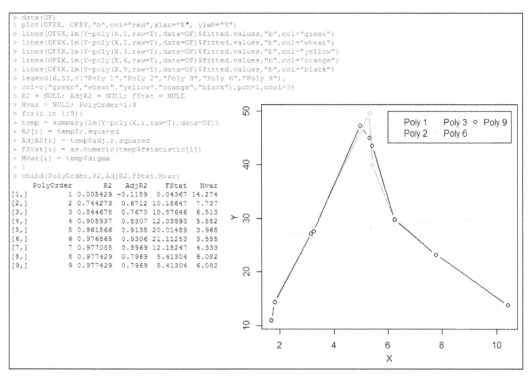

```
> data(OF)
> plot(OF$X, OF$Y,"b",col="red",xlab="X", ylab="Y")
> lines(OF$X,lm(Y~poly(X,1,raw=T),data=OF)$fitted.values,"b",col="green")
> lines(OF$X,lm(Y~poly(X,2,raw=T),data=OF)$fitted.values,"b",col="wheat")
> lines(OF$X,lm(Y~poly(X,3,raw=T),data=OF)$fitted.values,"b",col="yellow")
> lines(OF$X,lm(Y~poly(X,6,raw=T),data=OF)$fitted.values,"b",col="orange")
> lines(OF$X,lm(Y~poly(X,9,raw=T),data=OF)$fitted.values,"b",col="black")
> legend(6,50,c("Poly 1","Poly 2","Poly 3","Poly 6","Poly 9"),
+ col=c("green","wheat","yellow","orange","black"),pch=1,ncol=3)
> R2 = NULL; AdjR2 = NULL; FStat = NULL
> Mvar = NULL; PolyOrder=1:9
> for(i in 1:9){
+ temp = summary(lm(Y~poly(X,i,raw=T),data=OF))
+ R2[i] = temp$r.squared
+ AdjR2[i] = temp$adj.r.squared
+ FStat[i] = as.numeric(temp$fstatistic[1])
+ Mvar[i] = temp$sigma
+ }
> cbind(PolyOrder,R2,AdjR2,FStat,Mvar)
      PolyOrder       R2    AdjR2     FStat    Mvar
[1,]          1 0.005429 -0.1189  0.04367  14.274
[2,]          2 0.744273  0.6712 10.18647   7.737
[3,]          3 0.844678  0.7670 10.87646   6.513
[4,]          4 0.905937  0.8307 12.03893   5.552
[5,]          5 0.961566  0.9135 20.01489   3.968
[6,]          6 0.976865  0.9306 21.11253   3.555
[7,]          7 0.977085  0.8969 12.18247   4.333
[8,]          8 0.977429  0.7969  5.41304   6.082
[9,]          9 0.977429  0.7969  5.41304   6.082
```

Fitting higher-order polynomial terms in a regression model

4. Enhance the graph with a suitable legend:

```
legend(6,50,c("Poly 1","Poly 2","Poly 3","Poly 6","Poly 9"),
col=c("green","wheat","yellow","orange","black"),pch=1,ncol=3)
```

5. Initialize the following vectors:

```
R2 <- NULL; AdjR2 <- NULL; FStat <- NULL
Mvar <- NULL; PolyOrder<-1:9
```

6. Now, fit the regression models beginning with order 1 up to order 9 (since we only have 10 points) and extract their R2, AdjR2, FStat value, and model variability:

```
for(i in 1:9)  {
   temp <- summary(lm(Y~poly(X,i,raw=T),data=OF))
   R2[i] <- temp$r.squared
   AdjR2[i] <- temp$adj.r.squared
   FStat[i] <- as.numeric(temp$fstatistic[1])
   Mvar[i] <- temp$sigma
      }
cbind(PolyOrder,R2,AdjR2,FStat,Mvar)
```

We will more formally define polynomial regression models in the next section. The output is given in the figure *Fitting higher-order polynomial terms in a regression model*.

7. Let us also look at the magnitude of the regression coefficients:

```
as.numeric(lm(Y~poly(X,1,raw=T),data=OF)$coefficients)
as.numeric(lm(Y~poly(X,2,raw=T),data=OF)$coefficients)
as.numeric(lm(Y~poly(X,3,raw=T),data=OF)$coefficients)
as.numeric(lm(Y~poly(X,4,raw=T),data=OF)$coefficients)
as.numeric(lm(Y~poly(X,5,raw=T),data=OF)$coefficients)
as.numeric(lm(Y~poly(X,6,raw=T),data=OF)$coefficients)
as.numeric(lm(Y~poly(X,7,raw=T),data=OF)$coefficients)
as.numeric(lm(Y~poly(X,8,raw=T),data=OF)$coefficients)
```

The following screenshot shows the large size of the regression coefficients, particularly, as the degree of the polynomial increases, so does the coefficient magnitude. This is a problem! As the complexity of a model increases, the interpretability becomes very difficult. In the next section, we will discuss various techniques in polynomial regression.

```
> as.numeric(lm(Y~poly(X,1,raw=T),data=OF)$coefficients)
[1] 26.476  0.367
> as.numeric(lm(Y~poly(X,2,raw=T),data=OF)$coefficients)
[1] -11.75  17.27  -1.46
> as.numeric(lm(Y~poly(X,3,raw=T),data=OF)$coefficients)
[1] -45.73  42.50  -6.46   0.28
> as.numeric(lm(Y~poly(X,4,raw=T),data=OF)$coefficients)
[1]  18.742 -22.155  14.239  -2.328   0.112
> as.numeric(lm(Y~poly(X,5,raw=T),data=OF)$coefficients)
[1]  316.150 -402.854  187.601  -38.002    3.477   -0.118
> as.numeric(lm(Y~poly(X,6,raw=T),data=OF)$coefficients)
[1] -415.3037  677.6462 -420.9797  131.6922  -21.4927   1.7339   -0.0543
> as.numeric(lm(Y~poly(X,7,raw=T),data=OF)$coefficients)
[1] -6.01e+02  1.03e+03 -6.96e+02  2.42e+02 -4.64e+01  4.92e+00 -2.68e-01  5.81e-03
> as.numeric(lm(Y~poly(X,8,raw=T),data=OF)$coefficients)
[1]  1.13e+03 -2.80e+03  2.81e+03 -1.49e+03  4.57e+02 -8.42e+01  9.14e+00 -5.37e-01  1.31e-02
```

Regression coefficients of polynomial regression models

What just happened?

The scatter plot indicated that a polynomial regression model may be appropriate. Fitting higher order polynomial curves gives a closer approximation of the fit. The regression coefficients have been observed to increase with the degree of the polynomial fit.

In the next section, we consider the more general regression spline model.

Doing it in Python

For the same over-fitting data, OF as used in R, we can examine the impact of higher polynomials on the regression coefficients:

1. Import the OF.csv data using the pandas package.

2. Extract the dependent and independent variables as separate objects:

   ```
   X,Y = OF.X,OF.Y
   ```

3. Using the general format code `polyfit(X,Y,i)`, we fit an ith order polynomial degree. Here, i =1, 2, …, 9. Nine models are built now:

```
In [4]:  OF = pd.read_csv("Data/OF.csv",delimiter=',')
         X,Y = OF.X,OF.Y

In [5]:  m1 = np.polyfit(X,Y,1)
         m2 = np.polyfit(X,Y,2)
         m3 = np.polyfit(X,Y,3)
         m4 = np.polyfit(X,Y,4)
         m5 = np.polyfit(X,Y,5)
         m6 = np.polyfit(X,Y,6)
         m7 = np.polyfit(X,Y,7)
         m8 = np.polyfit(X,Y,8)
         m9 = np.polyfit(X,Y,9)
```

As we can see, the order of polynomial increases from 1 to 9. What happens to their coefficients?

4. The coefficients of the fitted polynomial regression models are extracted and rounded to fourth decimal accuracy.

5. As we can see in the output, the sign and magnitude of the coefficients are very large to make any practical sense.

```
         np.round(m1,4)
Out[5]:  array([  0.3667,   26.4764])

In [6]:  np.round(m2,4)
Out[6]:  array([ -1.4638,   17.2673,  -11.7487])

In [7]:  np.round(m3,4)
Out[7]:  array([  0.28  ,   -6.456 ,   42.5007,  -45.7319])

In [8]:  np.round(m4,4)
Out[8]:  array([  0.1115,   -2.3284,   14.2389,  -22.1551,   18.7418])

In [9]:  np.round(m5,4)
Out[9]:  array([ -1.17800000e-01,    3.47740000e+00,   -3.80018000e+01,
                 1.87601100e+02,   -4.02853700e+02,    3.16150300e+02])

In [10]:  np.round(m6,4)
Out[10]:  array([ -5.43000000e-02,    1.73390000e+00,   -2.14927000e+01,
                  1.31692200e+02,   -4.20979700e+02,    6.77646200e+02,
                 -4.15303700e+02])

In [11]:  np.round(m7,4)
Out[11]:  array([  5.80000000e-03,   -2.67700000e-01,    4.91640000e+00,
                 -4.64198000e+01,    2.41989700e+02,   -6.95699300e+02,
                  1.03371660e+03,   -6.00822100e+02])

In [12]:  np.round(m8,4)
Out[12]:  array([  1.31000000e-02,   -5.36600000e-01,    9.13730000e+00,
                 -8.42005000e+01,    4.56812700e+02,   -1.48561380e+03,
                  2.81081170e+03,   -2.80046260e+03,    1.12791030e+03])

In [13]:  np.round(m9,4)
Out[13]:  array([  3.18100000e-01,   -1.42172000e+01,    2.71921200e+02,
                 -2.91938830e+03,    1.93700290e+04,   -8.22599431e+04,
                  2.23263092e+05,   -3.72875993e+05,    3.47296294e+05,
                 -1.37395154e+05])
```

Have a go hero

The R2 value for `gasoline_lm` is at 0.895; see the figure *Building Multiple Linear Regression Model*, of *Chapter 6, Linear Regression Analysis*. Add higher order terms for the covariates and try to reach an R2 value of 0.95.

Regression spline

In this section, we will consider various enhancements/generalizations of the linear regression model. We will begin with a piecewise linear regression model and then consider the polynomial regression extension.

The term `spline` refers to a thin strip of wood that can be easily bent along a curved line.

Basis functions

In the previous section, we made multiple transformations of the input variable x with $X_1 = X, X_2 = X^2, ..., X_k = X^k$. In the *Data Re-expression* section of *Chapter 4, Exploratory Analysis,* we saw how a useful log transformation gave a better stem-and-leaf display than the original variable itself.

In many applications, it has been found that the transformed variables are more important than the original variable itself. Thus, we need a more generic framework to consider the transformations of the variables. Such a framework is provided by the basis functions.

For a single covariate X, the set of transformations may be defined as follows:

$$f(X) = \sum_{m=1}^{M} \beta_m h_m(X)$$

Here, $h_m(X)$ is the m th transformation of X, and β_m is the associated regression coefficient. In the case of a simple linear regression model, we have $h_1(X) = 1$ and $h_2(X) = X$. For the polynomial regression model, we have $h_m(X) = X^m, m = 1, 2, ..., k$, and for the logarithmic transformation $h(X) = \log X$. In general, for the p multiple linear regression model, we have the basis transformation as follows:

$$f(X_1, ..., X_p) = \sum_{i=1}^{p} \sum_{m=1}^{M_j} \beta_{jm} h_{jm}(X_j)$$

For the multiple linear regression model, we have $h_{j1}(X_j) = X_j, j = 1,...,p$. In general, the transformation includes functions such as sine, cosine, exponentiation, and indicator functions.

Piecewise linear regression model

Consider the scatter plot of the dataset, which is available in the dataset, PWR_Illus, in the next screenshot. We see a slanted letter N in the figure, *Scatterplot of a dataset (A) and the fitted values using piecewise linear regression model (B)*, where in the beginning, Y increases with X up to the point, approximately, 15, then there is a steep decline, or negative relationship, until 30, and finally there is an increase in the *y*-values beyond that.

In a certain way, we can imagine the *x*-values of 15 and 30 as break-down points. It is apparent from the scatterplot display that a linear relationship between the *x* and *y* values over the real line intervals less than 15, between 15 to 30, and greater than 30 is appropriate. The question then is, how do we build a regression model for such a phenomenon? The answer is provided by the piecewise linear regression model. In this case, we have a two-piece linear regression model.

In general, let x_a and x_b denote the two points, where we believe the linear regression model has the breakpoints. Furthermore, we denote an indicator function by I_a to represent that it equals 1when the *x* value is greater than x_a and takes the value 0 in other cases. Similarly, the second breakpoint indicator Ib is defined. The piecewise linear regression model is defined as follows:

$$Y = \beta_0 + \beta_1 X + \beta_2 (X - x_a) I_a + \beta_3 (X - x_b) I_b + \beta_3 (X - x_b) I_b + \varepsilon$$

In this piecewise linear regression model, we have four transformations, including $h_1(X) = 1$, $h_2(X) = X$, $h_3(X) = (X - x_a) I_a$, and $h_4(X) = (X - x_b) I_b$. The regression model needs to be interpreted with a bit of care. If the *x*-value is less than *xa*, the average Y value would be $\beta_0 + \beta_1 X$. For the *x*-value greater than *xa* but less than *xb*, the average of Y is $(\beta_0 + \beta_2 x_a) + (\beta_1 - \beta_2) X$. Finally, for values greater than *xb*, it will be $(\beta_0 + \beta_2 x_a - \beta_3 x_b) + (\beta_0 - \beta_2 + \beta_3) X$. The intercept term in these intervals will be β_0, $(\beta_0 - \beta_2 x_a)$, and $(\beta_0 - \beta_2 x_a - \beta_3 x_b)$, respectively, whereas the slopes are β_1, $(\beta_1 + \beta_2)$ and $(\beta_1 + \beta_2 + \beta_3)$. Of course, we are now concerned about fitting the piecewise linear regression model in R. Let us set ourselves up for this task!

Time for action – fitting piecewise linear regression models

A piecewise linear regression model can easily be fitted in R by using the same `lm` function and a bit of caution. A loop is used to find the points at which the model is supposed to have changed its trajectory:

1. Read the dataset into R with `data(PW_Illus)`.

2. For a matter convenience, attach the variables in the `PW_Illus` object by using `attach(PW_Illus)`.

3. To be on the safer side, we will select a range of the *x* values, which may be either of the breakpoints:

   ```
   break1 <- X[which(X>=12 & X<=18)]

   break2 <- X[which(X>=27 & X<=33)]
   ```

4. Get the number of points, which are candidates for being the breakpoints with `n1 <- length(break1)` and `n2 <- length(break2)`.

   We do not have a clear defining criterion to select one of the n1 or n2 *x* values to be the breakpoints. Hence, we will run various linear regression models and select that pair of points (*xa,xb*) to be the breakpoints, which return the least mean residual sum of squares. Towards this, we set up a matrix, which will have three columns with the first two columns for the possible potential pair of breakpoints, and the third column will contain the mean residual sum of squares. The choice of points, which corresponds to the least mean residual sum of squares, will be selected as the best model in the current case.

5. Set up the required matrix, build all the possible regression models with the pair of potential breakpoints, and note their mean residual sum of squares through the following program:

   ```
   MSE_MAT <- matrix(nrow=(n1*n2), ncol=3)
   colnames(MSE_MAT) = c("Break_1","Break_2","MSE")
   curriter=0
   for(i in 1:n1){
     for(j in 1:n2)   {
     curriter=curriter+1
     MSE_MAT[curriter,1]<-break1[i]
     MSE_MAT[curriter,2]<-break2[j]
     piecewise1 <- lm(Y ~ X*(X<break1[i])+X*(X>=break1[i] &
   X<break2[j])+X*(X>=break2[j]))
     MSE_MAT[curriter,3] <- as.numeric(summary(piecewise1)[6])
                 }
               }
   ```

Note the use of the formula ~ in specification of the piecewise linear regression model.

6. The time has arrived to find the pair of breakpoints:

```
MSE_MAT[which(MSE_MAT[,3]==min(MSE_MAT[,3])),]
```

The pair of breakpoints is hence (14.000, 30.000). Let us now look how good the model fit is!

7. First, re-obtain the scatter plot with `plot(PW_Illus)`. Fit the piecewise linear regression model with breakpoints at (14,30) with `pw_final <- lm(Y ~ X*(X<14)+X*(X>=14 & X<30)+X*(X>=30))`. Add the fitted values to the scatter plot with `points(PW_Illus$X,pw_final$fitted.values,col ="red")`.

Note that the fitted values are a very good reflection of the original data values, (refer the following figure part (B)). The fact that linear models can be extended to such different scenarios makes it very promising to study the same in even more detail as will be seen in the later part of this section.

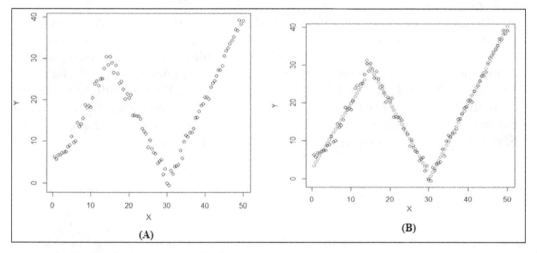

Scatterplot of a dataset (A) and the fitted values using piecewise linear regression model (B)

What just happened?

The piecewise linear regression model has been explored for a hypothetical scenario, and we investigated how to identify breakpoints by using the criterion of mean residual sum of squares.

The piecewise linear regression model shows a useful flexibility, and it is indeed a very useful model when there is a genuine reason to believe that there are certain breakpoints in the model. This has some advantages and certain limitations too.

From a technical perspective, the model is not continuous, whereas from an applied perspective, the model possesses problems in making guesses about the breakpoint values and the problem of extensions to multi-dimensional cases. It is thus necessary to look for a more general framework, where we need not be bothered about these issues. Some answers are provided in the following topics.

Natural cubic splines and the general B-splines

We will first consider the polynomial regression splines model. As noted in the previous discussion, we have a lot of discontinuity in the piecewise regression model. In some sense, "greater continuity" can be achieved by using cubic functions of x and then constructing regression splines in what are known as "piecewise cubic", (see *Berk (2008) Section 2.2*). Suppose that there are K data points at which we require the knots. Suppose that the knots are located at the points $(\xi_1, \xi_2, ..., \xi_k)$, which are between the boundary points ξ_0 *and* ξ_{k+1}, such that $\xi_0 < \xi_1 < \xi_2 < \cdots < \xi_k < \xi_{k+1}$. The piecewise cubic polynomial regression model is given as follows:

$$Y = \beta_0 + \beta_1 X + \beta_2 X^2 + \sum_{i=1}^{k} \theta_j \left(X - \xi_1 \right)_+^3 + \varepsilon$$

Here, the function $(\cdot)_+^3$ represents that the positive values from the argument are accepted and then the cube power performed on it; that is:

$$\left(X - \xi_j \right)_+^3 = \begin{cases} \left(X - \xi_j \right)^3, & if \ X > \xi_j \\ 0, & otherwise \end{cases}$$

For this model, the *K+4* basis functions are as follows:

$$h_1(X) = 1, \; h_2(X) = X, h_3(X) = X^2, h_4(X) = X^3, h_{j+4}(X) = (X - \xi_j)^3_+, j = 1, \ldots, k$$

We will now consider an example from *Montgomery, et. al. (2005)*, pages 231-3. It is known that the battery voltage drop in a guided missile motor has a different behavior as a function of time. The screenshot *Voltage drop data - scatter plot and a cubic polynomial regression model*, in the section, *Time for action – fitting the spline regression models*, displays the scatterplot of the battery voltage drop for different time points; see ?VD from the RSADBE package.

We need to build a piecewise cubic regression spline for this dataset with knots at time *t-6.5* and *t-13* seconds since it is known that the missile changes its course at these points. If we denote the battery voltage drop by *Y* and the time by *t*, the model for this problem is then given as follows:

$$Y = \beta_0 + \beta_1 t + \beta_2 t^2 + \beta_3 t^3 + \theta_1 (t - 6.5)^3_+ + \theta_2 (t - 13)^3_+ + \varepsilon$$

It is not possible with the math scope of this book to look into the details related to the natural cubic spline regression models or the B-spline regression models. However, we can fit them by using the ns and bs options in the formula of the lm function, along with the knots at the appropriate places. These models will be built and their fit will be visualized too.

Let us now fit the models!

Time for action – fitting the spline regression models

A natural cubic spline regression model will be fitted for the voltage drop problem:

1. Read the required dataset into R by using data(VD).
2. Invoke the graphics editor by using par(mfrow=c(1,2)).
3. Plot the data and provide an appropriate title:

```
plot(VD)
title(main="Scatter Plot for the Voltage Drop")
```

4. Build the piecewise cubic polynomial regression model by using the `lm` function and related options:

```
VD_PRS<-lm(Voltage_Drop~Time+I(Time^2)+I(Time^3)+I(((Ti
me-6.5)^3)*(sign(Time-6.5)==1))+I(((Time-13)^3)*(sign(Time-
13)==1)),data=VD)
```

The `sign` function returns the sign of a numeric vector as `1`, `0`, and `-1`, accordingly, according as the arguments are positive, zero, and negative respectively. The operator `I` is an inhibit interpretator operator, in that the argument will be taken in an as is format, check `?I`. This operator is especially useful in `data.frame` and the formula program of R.

5. To obtain the fitted plot along with the scatterplot, run the following code:

```
plot(VD)
```

```
points(VD$Time,fitted(VD_PRS),col="red","l")
```

```
title("Piecewise Cubic Polynomial Regression Model")
```

The following screenshot displays the scatterplot of the battery voltage drop for different time points:

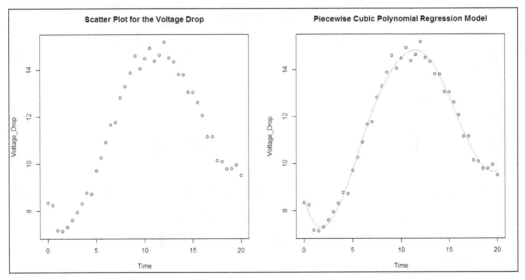

Voltage drop data - scatter plot and a cubic polynomial regression model

6. Obtain the details of the fitted model with `summary(VD_PRS)`.

The R output is given in the next screenshot. The `summary` output shows that each of the basis functions is indeed significant here.

```
> data(VD)
> par(mfrow=c(1,2))
> plot(VD)
> title(main="Scatter Plot for the Voltage Drop")
> VD_PRS = lm(Voltage_Drop~Time+I(Time^2)+I(Time^3)+I(((Time-6.5)^3)*(sign(Time-6.5)==1))
+ +I(((Time-13)^3)*(sign(Time-13)==1)),data=VD)
> plot(VD)
> points(VD$Time,fitted(VD_PRS),col="red","l")
> title("Piecewise Cubic Polynomial Regression Model")
> summary(VD_PRS)
Call:
lm(formula = Voltage_Drop ~ Time + I(Time^2) + I(Time^3) + I(((Time -
    6.5)^3) * (sign(Time - 6.5) == 1)) + I(((Time - 13)^3) *
    (sign(Time - 13) == 1)), data = VD)
Residuals:
    Min      1Q  Median      3Q     Max
-0.4517 -0.1850 -0.0355  0.2058  0.6169
Coefficients:
                                                      Estimate Std. Error t value Pr(>|t|)
(Intercept)                                            8.46568    0.20052   42.22  < 2e-16 ***
Time                                                  -1.45312    0.18159   -8.00  2.0e-09 ***
I(Time^2)                                             0.48989    0.04302   11.39  2.5e-13 ***
I(Time^3)                                            -0.02947    0.00285  -10.35  3.4e-12 ***
I(((Time - 6.5)^3) * (sign(Time - 6.5) == 1))  0.02471    0.00404    6.12  5.4e-07 ***
I(((Time - 13)^3) * (sign(Time - 13) == 1))    0.02711    0.00358    7.58  7.0e-09 ***
---
Signif. codes:  0 '***' 0.001 '**' 0.01 '*' 0.05 '.' 0.1 ' ' 1

Residual standard error: 0.268 on 35 degrees of freedom
Multiple R-squared: 0.99,        Adjusted R-squared: 0.989
F-statistic:  726 on 5 and 35 DF,  p-value: <2e-16
```

Details of the fitted piecewise cubic polynomial regression model

7. Fit the natural cubic spline regression model using the `ns` option:

```
VD_NCS <-lm(Voltage_Drop~ns(Time,knots=c(6.5,13),intercept= TRUE,
degree=3), data=VD)
```

8. Obtain the fitted plot as follows:

```
par(mfrow=c(1,2))
plot(VD)
points(VD$Time,fitted(VD_NCS),col="green","l")
title("Natural Cubic Regression Model")
```

Obtain the details related to VD_NCS with the `summary` function `summary(VD_NCS)`; see figure, *A first look at the linear ridge regression*.

9. Fit the B-spline regression model by using the `bs` option:

```
VD_BS <- lm(Voltage_Drop~bs(Time,knots=c(6.5,13),intercept=TRUE,
degree=3), data=VD)
```

10. Obtain the fitted plot for `VD_BS` with the R program:

```
plot(VD)
points(VD$Time,fitted(VD_BS),col="brown","l")

title("B-Spline Regression Model")
```

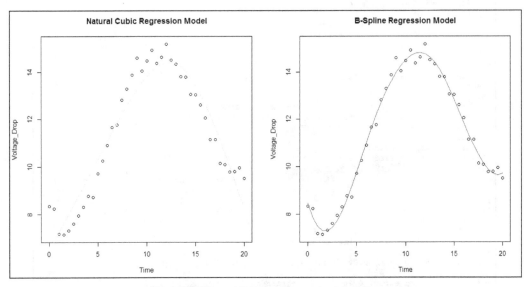

Natural Cubic and B-Spline Regression Modeling

11. Finally, get the details of the fitted B-spline regression model by using `summary(VD_BS)`.

The main purpose of the B-spline regression model is to illustrate that the splines are smooth at the boundary points in contrast with the natural cubic regression model. This can be clearly seen in the figure, *Details of the natural cubic and B-spline regression models.*

Both the models, `VD_NCS` and `VD_BS`, have good summary statistics and have really modeled the data well.

```
> VD_NCS <- lm(Voltage_Drop~ns(Time,knots=c(6.5,13),intercept=TRUE),data=VD)
> par(mfrow=c(1,2))
> plot(VD)
> points(VD$Time,fitted(VD_NCS),col="green","l")
> title("Natural Cubic Regression Model")
> summary(VD_NCS)
Call:
lm(formula = Voltage_Drop ~ ns(Time, knots = c(6.5, 13), intercept = TRUE),
    data = VD)
Residuals:
    Min     1Q Median     3Q     Max
-1.226 -0.588 -0.179  0.579  1.868
Coefficients: (1 not defined because of singularities)
                                                 Estimate Std. Error t value Pr(>|t|)
(Intercept)                                         10.78       2.44    4.41 8.5e-05 ***
ns(Time, knots = c(6.5, 13), intercept = TRUE)1      1.46       1.87    0.78 0.44212
ns(Time, knots = c(6.5, 13), intercept = TRUE)2      7.12       1.65    4.31 0.00011 ***
ns(Time, knots = c(6.5, 13), intercept = TRUE)3     -3.68       5.47   -0.67 0.50549
ns(Time, knots = c(6.5, 13), intercept = TRUE)4        NA         NA      NA      NA
---
Signif. codes:  0 '***' 0.001 '**' 0.01 '*' 0.05 '.' 0.1 ' ' 1

Residual standard error: 0.803 on 37 degrees of freedom
Multiple R-squared: 0.909,    Adjusted R-squared: 0.902
F-statistic:  123 on 3 and 37 DF,  p-value: <2e-16
> VD_BS <- lm(Voltage_Drop~bs(Time,knots=c(6.5,13),intercept=TRUE,degree=3),data=VD)
> plot(VD)
> points(VD$Time,fitted(VD_BS),col="brown","l")
> title("B-Spline Regression Model")
> summary(VD_BS)
Call:
lm(formula = Voltage_Drop ~ bs(Time, knots = c(6.5, 13), intercept = TRUE,
    degree = 3), data = VD)
Residuals:
    Min     1Q  Median     3Q     Max
-0.4517 -0.1850 -0.0355  0.2058  0.6169
Coefficients: (1 not defined because of singularities)
                                                           Estimate Std. Error t value Pr(>|t|)
(Intercept)                                                   9.707      0.197   49.31 < 2e-16 ***
bs(Time, knots = c(6.5, 13), intercept = TRUE, degree = 3)1  -1.241      0.287   -4.32 0.00012 ***
bs(Time, knots = c(6.5, 13), intercept = TRUE, degree = 3)2  -4.390      0.302  -14.53 < 2e-16 ***
bs(Time, knots = c(6.5, 13), intercept = TRUE, degree = 3)3   3.112      0.364    8.55 4.3e-10 ***
bs(Time, knots = c(6.5, 13), intercept = TRUE, degree = 3)4   7.310      0.284   25.74 < 2e-16 ***
bs(Time, knots = c(6.5, 13), intercept = TRUE, degree = 3)5  -0.642      0.394   -1.63 0.11171
bs(Time, knots = c(6.5, 13), intercept = TRUE, degree = 3)6      NA         NA      NA      NA
---
Signif. codes:  0 '***' 0.001 '**' 0.01 '*' 0.05 '.' 0.1 ' ' 1

Residual standard error: 0.268 on 35 degrees of freedom
Multiple R-squared: 0.99,    Adjusted R-squared: 0.989
F-statistic:  726 on 5 and 35 DF,  p-value: <2e-16
```

Details of the natural cubic and B-spline regression models

What just happened?

We began with the fitting of a piecewise polynomial regression model and then had a look at the natural cubic spline regression and B-spline regression models. All three models provide a very good fit to the actual data. Thus, with a good guess or experimental/ theoretical evidence, the linear regression model can be extended in an effective way.

Ridge regression for linear models

In the figure *Regression coefficients of polynomial regression models*, we saw that the magnitude of the regression coefficients increase in a drastic manner as the polynomial degree increases. The right tweaking of the linear regression model, as seen in the previous section, gives us the right results.

However, the models considered in the previous section had just one covariate and the problem of identifying the knots in the multiple regression model becomes an overtly complex issue. That is, if we have a problem where there are large numbers of covariates, there may naturally be some dependency among them, which cannot be investigated for certain reasons.

In such problems, it may happen that certain covariates dominate other covariates in terms of the magnitude of their regression coefficients, and this may mar the overall usefulness of the model. Furthermore, even in the univariate case, we have the problem that the choice of the number of knots, their placements, and the polynomial degree may be manipulated by the analyzer. We have an alternative to this problem in the way we minimize the residual sum of squares, $\min_{\beta} \sum_{i=1}^{n} e_i^2$. The least-squares solution leads to an estimator of β:

$$\hat{\beta} = \left(X'X \right)^{-1} X'Y$$

Protecting against overfitting

We had seen in *Chapter 6, Linear Regression Analysis*, how to guard ourselves against the outliers, the measures of model fit, and model selection techniques. However, these methods are in action after the construction of the model; therefore, although they offer protection in a certain sense to the problem of overfitting, we need more robust methods.

The question that arises is can we guard ourselves against overfitting when building the model itself? This will go a long way towards addressing the problem. The answer is obviously an affirmative, and we will check out this technique.

The least-squares solution is the optimal solution when we have the squared loss function. The idea then is to modify this loss function by incorporating a penalty term, which will give us additional protection against the overfitting problem.

Mathematically, we add the penalty term for the size of the regression coefficients in fact, the constraint would be to ensure that the sum of squares of the regression coefficients is minimized. Formally, the goal would be to obtain an optimal solution of the following problem:

$$\min_{\beta} \left[\sum_{i=1}^{n} e_i^2 + \lambda \sum_{j=1}^{p} \beta_j^2 \right]$$

Here, $\lambda > 0$ is the control factor, also known as the tuning parameter, and $\sum_{j=1}^{p} \beta_j^2$ is the penalty. If λ value is zero, we get the earlier least squares solution. Note that the intercept has been deliberately kept out of the penalty term!

Now, for the large values of $\sum_{j=1}^{p} \beta_j^2$, the residual sum of squares will be large. Thus, loosely speaking, for the minimum value of $\sum_{i=1}^{n} e_i^2 + \lambda \sum_{j=1}^{p} \beta_j^2$, we will require $\sum_{j=1}^{p} \beta_j^2$ to be at a minimum value too. The optimal solution for the preceding minimization problem is given as follows:

$$\hat{\beta}_{Ridge} = \left(X'X + \lambda I \right)^{-1} X'Y$$

The choice of λ is a critical one. There are multiple options to obtain it:

- Find the value of λ by using the cross-validation technique (discussed in the last section of this chapter)
- Find the value of a semi-automated method as described at `http://arxiv.org/pdf/1205.0686.pdf` for the value of λ

For the first technique, we can use the function `lm.ridge` from the MASS package, and the second method of semi-automatic detection can be obtained from the `linearRidge` function of the `ridge` package.

In the following R session, we use the functions `lm.ridge` and `linearRidge`.

Time for action – ridge regression for the linear regression model

The `linearRidge` function from the `ridge` package and `lm.ridge` from the `MASS` package are two good options for developing the ridge regression models:

1. Though the `OF` object may still be there in your session, let us again load it by using `data(OF)`.

2. Load the `MASS` and `ridge` package by using `library(MASS)`, and `library(ridge)`.

3. For a polynomial regression model of degree 3 and various values of lambda, including `0`, `0.5`, `1`, `1.5`, `2`, `5`, `10`, and `30`, obtain the ridge regression coefficients with the single line R code:

```
LR <-linearRidge(Y~poly(X,3),data=as.data.frame(OF),lambda =c(0,
0.5,1,1.5,2,5,10,30))
LR
```

   The function `linearRidge` from the `ridge` package performs the ridge regression for a linear model. We have two options. First, we specify the values of lambda, which may either be a scalar or a vector. In the case of a scalar lambda, it will simply return the set of (ridge) regression coefficients. If it is a vector, it returns the related set of regression coefficients.

4. Compute the value of $\sum_{j=1}^{p} \beta_j^2$ for different lambda values:

```
LR_Coef <- LR$coef
colSums(LR_Coef^2)
```

   Note that as lambda value increases, the value of $\sum_{j=1}^{p} \beta_j^2$ decreases. However, this is not to say that a higher lambda value is preferable, since the sum $\sum_{j=1}^{p} \beta_j^2$ will decrease to `0`, and eventually none of the variables will have a significant explanatory power about the output. The choice of selection of the lambda value will be discussed in the last section.

5. The `linearRidge` function also finds the "best" lambda value:

```
linearRidge(Y~poly(X,3),data=as.data.
frame(OF),lambda="automatic").
```

6. Fetch the details of the "best" ridge regression model with the following line of code:

```
summary(linearRidge(Y~poly(X,3),data=as.data.
frame(OF),lambda="automatic")).
```

The summary shows that the value of lambda is chosen at `0.07881`, and that it used three PCs. Now, what is a PC? **PC** is an abbreviation of **principal component**, and unfortunately we can't really go into the details of this aspect. Enthusiastic readers may refer to *Chapter 17* of *Tattar, et. al. (2013)*. Compare these results with those in the first section.

7. For the same choice of different lambda values, use the `lm.ridge` function from the MASS package:

```
LM <-lm.ridge(Y~poly(X,3),data = as.data.frame(OF),lambda
=c(0,0.5,1,1.5,2,5,10,30))
LM
```

The `lm.ridge` function obviously works a bit differently from `linearRidge`. The results are given in the following screenshot. Comparison of the results is left as an exercise to the reader. As with the `linearRidge` model, let us compute the value of $\sum_{j=1}^{p} \beta_j^2$ for `lm.ridge` fitted models too.

8. Use the `colSums` function to get the required result:

```
LM_Coef <- LM$coef
colSums(LM_Coef^2)
```

```
> data(OF)
> library(MASS); library(ridge)
> LR <- linearRidge(Y~poly(X,3),data=as.data.frame(OF),lambda=c(0,0.5,1,1.5,2,5,10,30))
> LR
Call:
linearRidge(formula = Y ~ poly(X, 3), data = as.data.frame(OF),
    lambda = c(0, 0.5, 1, 1.5, 2, 5, 10, 30))
           (Intercept) poly(X, 3)1 poly(X, 3)2 poly(X, 3)3
lambda=0        28.31       2.98271     -34.796     12.8273
lambda=0.5      28.31       1.98848     -23.198      8.5515
lambda=1        28.31       1.49136     -17.398      6.4137
lambda=1.5      28.31       1.19309     -13.919      5.1309
lambda=2        28.31       0.99424     -11.599      4.2758
lambda=5        28.31       0.49712      -5.799      2.1379
lambda=10       28.31       0.27116      -3.163      1.1661
lambda=30       28.31       0.09622      -1.122      0.4138
> LR_Coef <- LR$coef
> colSums(LR_Coef^2)
  lambda=0 lambda=0.5   lambda=1 lambda=1.5    lambda=2    lambda=5   lambda=10  lambda=30
   1384.23     615.21     346.06     221.48      153.80       38.45       11.44       1.44
> summary(linearRidge(Y~poly(X,3),data=as.data.frame(OF),lambda="automatic"))
Call:
linearRidge(formula = Y ~ poly(X, 3), data = as.data.frame(OF),
    lambda = "automatic")
Coefficients:
            Estimate Scaled estimate Std. Error (scaled) t value (scaled) Pr(>|t|)
(Intercept)    28.31              NA                  NA              NA       NA
poly(X, 3)1     2.76            2.76                5.66            0.49    0.625
poly(X, 3)2   -32.25          -32.25                5.66            5.69 1.2e-08 ***
poly(X, 3)3    11.89           11.89                5.66            2.10   0.036 *
---
Signif. codes:  0 '***' 0.001 '**' 0.01 '*' 0.05 '.' 0.1 ' ' 1
Ridge parameter: 0.07881, chosen automatically, computed using 3 PCs
Degrees of freedom: model 2.78 , variance 2.58 , residual 2.98
> LM <- lm.ridge(Y~poly(X,3),data=as.data.frame(OF),lambda=c(0,0.5,1,1.5,2,5,10,30))
> LM
            poly(X, 3)1 poly(X, 3)2 poly(X, 3)3
 0.0 28.31      2.9827     -34.796      12.827
 0.5 28.31      2.8407     -33.139      12.216
 1.0 28.31      2.7116     -31.633      11.661
 1.5 28.31      2.5937     -30.258      11.154
 2.0 28.31      2.4856     -28.997      10.689
 5.0 28.31      1.9885     -23.198       8.552
10.0 28.31      1.4914     -17.398       6.414
30.0 28.31      0.7457      -8.699       3.207
> LM_Coef <- LM$coef
> colSums(LM_Coef^2)
     0.0     0.5     1.0     1.5     2.0     5.0    10.0    30.0
 138.423 125.554 114.399 104.668  96.127  61.521  34.606   8.651
```

A first look at the linear ridge regression

So far, we are still working with a single covariate only.

However, we need to consider the multiple linear regression models and see how ridge regression helps us. Towards this, we will return to the gasoline mileage considered in *Chapter 6, Linear Regression Analysis*:

1. Read the Gasoline data into R by using `data(Gasoline)`.

2. Fit the ridge regression model (and the multiple linear regression model again) for the mileage as a function of other variables:

   ```
   gasoline_lm <- lm(y~., data=Gasoline)
   gasoline_rlm <- linearRidge(y~., data=Gasoline,lambda=
   "automatic")
   ```

3. Compare the `lm` coefficients with the `linearRidge` coefficients:

   ```
   sum(coef(gasoline_lm)[-1]^2)-sum(coef(gasoline_rlm)[-1]^2)
   ```

4. Look at the summary of the fitted ridge linear regression model by using `summary(gasoline_rlm)`.

   The difference between the sum of squares of the regression coefficients for the linear and ridge linear model is indeed very large. Furthermore, the `gasoline_rlm` details reveal that there are four variables, which have significant explanatory power for the mileage of the car.

   Note that the `gasoline_lm` model had only one significant variable for the cars mileage. The output is given in the figure ridge regression with the logistic regression model.

```
> data(Gasoline)
> gasoline_lm <- lm(y~., data=Gasoline)
> gasoline_rlm <- linearRidge(y~., data=Gasoline,lambda="automatic")
> sum(coef(gasoline_lm)[-1]^2)-sum(coef(gasoline_rlm)[-1]^2)
[1] 34779
> summary(gasoline_rlm)
Call:
linearRidge(formula = y ~ ., data = Gasoline, lambda = "automatic")
Coefficients:
            Estimate Scaled estimate Std. Error (scaled) t value (scaled) Pr(>|t|)
(Intercept) -1.28e+02              NA                  NA              NA       NA
x1          -1.07e-02           -6.37e+00            1.33e+00            4.77 1.8e-06 ***
x2          -1.54e-02           -3.43e+00            1.93e+00            1.78 0.07457 .
x3          -1.05e-02           -4.41e+00            1.27e+00            3.46 0.00055 ***
x4           1.77e+02            2.82e+00            2.66e+00            1.06 0.28876
x5           1.14e+01            1.65e+00            2.58e+00            0.64 0.52413
x6          -1.38e-01           -7.30e-01            2.47e+00            0.30 0.76758
x7           4.22e-01            1.44e+00            2.41e+00            0.60 0.55095
x8          -1.98e-03           -2.10e-01            2.34e+00            0.09 0.92859
x9          -1.04e-01           -2.95e+00            2.32e+00            1.27 0.20254
x10         -9.92e-04           -4.76e+00            1.22e+00            3.91 9.1e-05 ***
x11M         1.01e+00            2.25e+00            2.73e+00            0.82 0.41170
---
Signif. codes:  0 '***' 0.001 '**' 0.01 '*' 0.05 '.' 0.1 ' ' 1
Ridge parameter: 0.3112, chosen automatically, computed using 3 PCs
Degrees of freedom: model 4.29 , variance 2.82 , residual 5.76
```

Ridge regression for the gasoline mileage problem

What just happened?

We made use of two functions, namely `lm.ridge` and `linearRidge`, for fitting ridge regression models for the linear regression model. It is observed that the ridge regression models may sometimes reveal more significant variables.

In the next section, we will consider the ridge penalty for the logistic regression model.

Doing it in Python

Data preparation is required to get the higher order degrees:

1. Create higher order terms using the operator `**` and append them in the OF object:

```
In [15]: OF['X2'] = OF.X**2
         OF['X3'] = OF.X**3
         OF['X4'] = OF.X**4
         OF['X5'] = OF.X**5
         OF['X6'] = OF.X**6
         OF['X7'] = OF.X**7
         OF['X8'] = OF.X**8
         X = OF[['X','X2','X3','X4','X5','X6','X7','X8']]
         Y = OF.Y
```

2. We now obtain the regression coefficients for different ridge parameters. The lambda of R becomes alpha here. For large ridge penalty terms, the regression coefficients should become smaller and smaller and when the penalty term is near zero, we should get the earlier OLS solution.

This is realized in the following program for penalty values of 50, 5, 0.5, 0.05, 0.0005, and 0:

```
In [16]: rid = Ridge(alpha=50)
         M2 = rid.fit(X,Y)
         M2.intercept_,M2.coef_

Out[16]: (10.471940675126167,
          array([ 0.00101222,  0.00543543,  0.0250102 ,  0.08639525,  0.16578931,
                 -0.06980278,  0.00887011, -0.00036244]))

In [17]: rid = Ridge(alpha=5)
         M2 = rid.fit(X,Y)
         M2.intercept_,M2.coef_

Out[17]: (10.538480427197715,
          array([ 0.00563967,  0.0097609 ,  0.01785317,  0.06931315,  0.17771001,
                 -0.07258423,  0.00914475, -0.00037221]))

In [18]: rid = Ridge(alpha=0.5)
         M2 = rid.fit(X,Y)
         M2.intercept_,M2.coef_

Out[18]: (10.302591982260925,
          array([ 0.06538089,  0.10140446,  0.04923191,  0.00067073,  0.20516377,
                 -0.07739837,  0.00954014, -0.00038459]))

In [19]: rid = Ridge(alpha=0.05)
         M2 = rid.fit(X,Y)
         M2.intercept_,M2.coef_

Out[19]: (8.2475619511785005,
          array([ 5.78314963e-01,  8.46719469e-01,  2.63401016e-01,
                 -4.93498157e-01,  3.98757263e-01, -1.10603429e-01,
                  1.22139730e-02, -4.66919940e-04]))

In [20]: rid = Ridge(alpha=0.0005)
         M2 = rid.fit(X,Y)
         M2.intercept_,M2.coef_

Out[20]: (-25.020026438298668,
          array([ 2.23858711e+01,  1.52836561e+01, -1.74494285e+01,
                  6.29345545e+00, -9.08414296e-01,  2.58468060e-02,
                  4.86603915e-03, -3.07263458e-04]))

In [21]: rid = Ridge(alpha=0.0)
         M2 = rid.fit(X,Y)
         M2.intercept_,M2.coef_

Out[21]: (1148.4695952624731,
          array([ -2.84612769e+03,  2.85263189e+03, -1.50624463e+03,
                  4.62829538e+02, -8.52672137e+01,  9.24994515e+00,
                 -5.43094846e-01,  1.32726163e-02]))
```

As expected, we see that decreasing the penalty term impacts the size of the regression coefficients and approaches the OLS solution.

Ridge regression for logistic regression models

We will not be able to go into the math of the ridge regression for the logistic regression model, though we will happily make good use of the `logisticRidge` function from the `ridge` package, to illustrate how to build the "ridge regression for logistic regression model".

 For more details, we refer to the research paper of *Cule and De Iorio (2012)* available at http://arxiv.org/pdf/1205.0686.pdf.

In the previous section, we saw that `gasoline_rlm` found more significant variables than `gasoline_lm`. Now, in *Chapter 7, Logistic Regression Model*, we fit a logistic regression model for the German credit data problem in `GC_LR`. The question that arises is if we obtain a ridge regression model of the related logistic regression model, say `GC_RLR`, can we expect to find more significant variables?

Time for action – ridge regression for the logistic regression model

We will use the `logisticRidge` function here, from the `ridge` package to fit the ridge regression, and check if we can obtain more significant variables:

1. Load the German credit dataset with `data(German)`.

2. Use the `logisticRidge` function to obtain `GC_RLR`, a small manipulation required here, by using the following line of code:

   ```
   GC_RLR<-logisticRidge(as.numeric(good_bad)-1~.,data= as.data.
   frame(GC), lambda = "automatic")
   ```

3. Obtain the summaries of `GC_LR` and `GC_RLR` by using `summary(GC_LR)` and `summary(GC_RLR)`.

The detailed summary output is given in the following screenshot:

```
> summary(GC_LR); summary(GC_RLR)
Call:                                               Call:
glm(formula = good_bad ~ ., family = binomial(), data = GC)    logisticRidge(formula = as.numeric(good_bad) - 1 ~ ., data = as.data.frame(GC),
Deviance Residuals:                                     lambda = "automatic")
    Min      1Q   Median      3Q      Max          Coefficients:
 -2.586  -0.731   0.399   0.700    2.017                       Estimate Scaled estimate Std. Error (scaled) t value (scaled) Pr(>|t|)
Coefficients:                                       (Intercept) -3.39e+00              NA                  NA               NA       NA
             Estimate Std. Error z value Pr(>|z|)   checking     4.32e-01        1.72e+01             1.95e+00             8.79  < 2e-16 ***
(Intercept) -5.40e+00   1.11e+00   -4.85  1.2e-06 *** duration    -2.16e-02       -8.25e+00             1.95e+00            -4.24  2.2e-05 ***
checking     5.66e-01   7.28e-02    7.78  7.2e-15 *** history      2.88e-01        9.87e+00             1.95e+00             5.05  4.4e-07 ***
duration    -2.64e-02   8.96e-03   -2.95  0.00320 **  purpose1     8.68e-01        8.34e+00             2.01e+00             4.15  3.4e-05 ***
history      3.97e-01   8.92e-02    4.45  8.5e-06 *** purpose2     2.88e-01        3.51e+00             1.89e+00             1.85  0.06370 .
purpose1     1.61e+00   3.61e-01    4.47  7.8e-06 *** purpose3     4.24e-01        6.02e+00             1.96e+00             3.08  0.00210 **
purpose2     7.48e-01   2.53e-01    2.96  0.00310 **  purpose4     1.58e-01        5.45e-01             1.85e+00             0.29  0.76856
purpose3     8.26e-01   2.41e-01    3.43  0.00060 *** purpose5    -6.93e-02       -3.21e-01             1.84e+00            -0.17  0.86116
purpose4     5.45e-01   7.48e-01    0.73  0.46662     purpose6    -3.12e-01       -2.15e+00             1.85e+00            -1.16  0.24409
purpose5     2.19e-01   5.52e-01    0.40  0.69148     purpose8     8.88e-01        2.65e+00             2.06e+00             1.29  0.19717
purpose6    -7.17e-02   3.92e-01   -0.18  0.85473     purpose9     2.24e-01        2.10e+00             1.88e+00             1.12  0.26465
purpose8     1.67e+00   1.15e+00    1.45  0.14769     purposeX     5.35e-01        1.84e+00             1.80e+00             1.02  0.30688
purpose9     7.01e-01   3.20e-01    2.19  0.02854 *   amount      -7.14e-05       -6.37e+00             1.96e+00            -3.24  0.00118 **
purposeX     1.20e+00   7.27e-01    1.65  0.09967 .   savings      1.75e-01        8.74e+00             1.99e+00             4.40  1.1e-05 ***
amount      -1.13e-04   4.21e-05   -2.69  0.00722 **  employed     1.14e-01        4.36e+00             1.93e+00             2.26  0.02381 *
savings      2.51e-01   6.06e-02    4.15  3.4e-05 *** installp    -1.86e-01       -6.59e+00             1.93e+00            -3.42  0.00063 ***
employed     1.39e-01   7.40e-02    1.87  0.06128 .   marital      1.79e-01        4.01e+00             1.89e+00             2.12  0.03400 *
installp    -3.03e-01   8.52e-02   -3.55  0.00038 *** coapp        2.21e-01        3.34e+00             1.92e+00             1.74  0.08153 .
marital      2.42e-01   1.20e-01    2.02  0.04348 *   resident    -1.79e-02       -6.23e-01             1.91e+00            -0.33  0.74467
coapp        3.35e-01   1.84e-01    1.82  0.06932 .   property2   -1.03e-01       -1.38e+00             1.92e+00            -0.72  0.47423
resident    -1.64e-02   8.12e-02   -0.20  0.83954     property3   -8.06e-02       -1.20e+00             1.94e+00            -0.62  0.53488
property2   -2.17e-01   2.44e-01   -0.89  0.37443     property4   -5.13e-01       -5.86e+00             1.96e+00            -2.99  0.00277 **
property3   -1.53e-01   2.30e-01   -0.67  0.50560     age          1.01e-02        3.64e+00             1.98e+00             1.84  0.06577 .
property4   -8.17e-01   3.29e-01   -2.49  0.01293 *   other        2.40e-01        5.34e+00             1.84e+00             2.91  0.00367 **
age          1.34e-02   8.56e-03    1.57  0.11646     housing      2.09e-01        3.84e+00             1.94e+00             1.98  0.04789 *
other        3.39e-01   1.14e-01    2.98  0.00286 **  existcr     -9.86e-02       -1.80e+00             1.95e+00            -0.92  0.35598
housing      4.20e-01   1.87e-01    2.24  0.02489 *   job         -4.46e-02       -9.21e-01             1.93e+00            -0.48  0.63368
existcr     -2.20e-01   1.65e-01   -1.34  0.18186     depends     -7.38e-02       -8.45e-01             1.91e+00            -0.44  0.65910
job         -5.35e-02   1.42e-01   -0.38  0.70621     telephon     2.09e-01        3.24e+00             1.96e+00             1.65  0.09818 .
depends     -1.07e-01   2.38e-01   -0.45  0.65216     foreign      8.28e-01        4.94e+00             2.10e+00             2.36  0.01851 *
telephon     3.31e-01   1.94e-01    1.70  0.08829 .   ---
foreign      1.44e+00   6.18e-01    2.33  0.01993 *   Signif. codes:  0 '***' 0.001 '**' 0.01 '*' 0.05 '.' 0.1 ' ' 1
---                                                 Ridge paramter: 0.02438, chosen automatically, computed using 19 PCs
Signif. codes:  0 '***' 0.001 '**' 0.01 '*' 0.05 '.' 0.1 ' ' 1  Degrees of freedom: model 23.1 , variance 20
(Dispersion parameter for binomial family taken to be 1)
    Null deviance: 1221.73  on 999  degrees of freedom
Residual deviance:  916.12  on 969  degrees of freedom
AIC: 978.1
Number of Fisher Scoring iterations: 5
```

Ridge regression with the logistic regression model

The ridge regression model offers a very slight improvement over the standard logistic regression model.

What just happened?

The ridge regression concept has been applied to the important family of the logistic regression model. Although, in the case of the German credit data problem, we found a slight improvement in identification of the significant variables, it is vital that we should always be on the lookout to fit better models, as in sensitiveness to outliers, and the `logisticRidge` function appears as a good alternative to the `glm` function.

Another look at model assessment

In the previous two sections, we used the automatic option for obtaining the optimum λ values, as discussed in the work of *Cule and De Iorio (2012)*. There is an iterative technique for finding the penalty factor λ. This technique is especially useful when we do not have sufficient well-developed theory for regression models beyond the linear and logistic regression model. Neural networks, support vector machines, and so on, are some very useful regression models, where the theory may not have been well developed; well at least to the best known practice of the author. Hence, we will use the iterative method in this section.

For both the `linearRidge` and `lm.ridge` fitted models in *Section 3, Ridge regression for linear models*, we saw that for an increasing value of λ, the sum of squares of regression coefficients $\sum_{j=1}^{p} \beta_j^2$ decreases. The question then is how to select the "best" λ value. A popular technique in the data mining community is to split the dataset into three parts, namely train, validate, and test part. There are no definitive answers for what needs to be the split percentage for the three parts and some of the common practice is to split them into either 60:20:20 percentages or 50:25:25 percentages. Let us now understand this process:

- **Training dataset**: The models are built on the data available in this data part.
- **Validation dataset**: For this part of the data, we pretend as though we do not know the output values and make predictions based upon the covariate values. This step is to ensure that overfitting is minimized.

  The errors (residual squares for regression model and accuracy percentages for classification model) are then compared with respect to the counterpart errors in the training part. If the errors decrease in the training set while they remain the same for validation part, it means that we are overfitting the data. A threshold, after which this is observed, may be chosen as the better lambda value.

- **Testing dataset**: In practice, these are really unobserved cases for which the model is applied for forecasting purposes.

For the gasoline mileage problem, we will split the data into three parts and use the training and validation part to select the λ value.

Time for action – selecting λ iteratively and other topics

Iterative selection of the penalty parameter for ridge regression is considered. The useful framework of train + validate + test is also considered for the German credit data problem:

1. For the sake of simplicity, we will remove the character variable of the dataset by using `Gasoline <- Gasoline[,-12]`.

2. Set the random seed by using `set.seed(1234567)`. This step is to ensure that the user can validate the results of the program.

3. Randomize the observations to enable the splitting part:

   ```
   data_part_label = c("Train","Validate","Test")

   indv_label=sample(data_part_label,size=nrow(Gasoline),replace=TRUE
   ,prob=c(0.6,0.2,0.2))
   ```

4. Now, split the `gasoline` dataset:

   ```
   G_Train <- Gasoline[indv_label=="Train",]
   G_Validate <- Gasoline[indv_label=="Validate",]
   G_Test <- Gasoline[indv_label=="Test",]
   ```

5. Define the λ vector with `lambda <- seq(0,10,0.2)`.

6. Initialize the training and validation errors:

   ```
   Train_Errors <- vector("numeric",length=length(lambda))
   Val_Errors <- vector("numeric",length=length(lambda))
   ```

7. Run the following loop to get the required errors:

```
for(i in 1:length(lambda))        {
     GT_rlm <- lm.ridge(y~.,data=G_Train,lambda=lambda[i])
     GT_rlm_coef <- coef(GT_rlm)
     predicted_Train <- vector("numeric",length=nrow(G_Train))
     for(j in 1:nrow(G_Train))        {
          predicted_Train[j]<- GT_rlm_coef[1]+sum(GT_rlm_coef[-1]*G_Train[j,-1])
          }
     Train_Errors[i] <- sum((predicted_Train-G_Train[,1])^2,na.rm=TRUE)
     predicted <- vector("numeric",length=nrow(G_Validate))
     for(j in 1:nrow(G_Validate))     {
          predicted[j]<- GT_rlm_coef[1]+sum(GT_rlm_coef[-1]*G_Validate[j,-1])
          }
     Val_Errors[i] <- sum((predicted-G_Validate[,1])^2)
          }
```

8. Plot the training and validation errors:

```
plot(lambda,Val_Errors,"l",col="red",xlab=expression(lambda),ylab=
"Training and Validation Errors",ylim=c(0,600))
points(lambda,Train_Errors,"l",col="green")
legend(6,500,c("Training Errors","Validation Errors"),col=c(
"green","red"),pch="-")
```

The final output will be the following diagram:

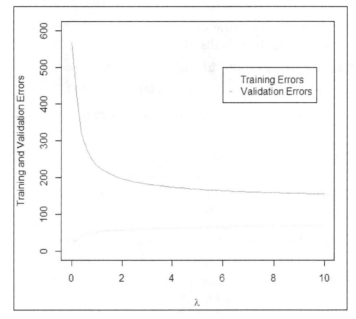

Training and validation errors

The preceding plot suggests that the lambda value is between 0.5 and 1.5. Why? The technique of train, validate, and test is not simply restricted to selecting the lambda value. In fact, for any regression/classification model, we can try to understand if the selected model really generalizes or not. For the German credit data problem in the previous chapter, we will make an attempt to see what the current technique suggests.

9. The program and its output (ROC curves) is displayed afterwards:

```
set.seed(1234567)
GC = read.csv("GermanCredit.csv", header=TRUE)
GC$property <-as.factor(GC$ property)
GC$age <-as.numeric(GC$age)
GC$amount<-as.double(GC$amount)
GC = GC[,-22]
data_part_label = c("Train","Validate","Test")
indv_label = sample(data_part_label,size=nrow(GC),replace=TRUE,prob=c(0.6,0.2,0.2))
GC_Train <- GC[indv_label=="Train",]
GC_Validate <- GC[indv_label=="Validate",]
GC_Test <- GC[indv_label=="Test",]
GC_glm <- glm(as.numeric(good_bad)~.,data=GC_Train)
Pred_Train_Class <- predict(GC_glm,type='response')
Pred_Train_Prob <-predict(GC_glm,type='response')
Train_Pred <- prediction(Pred_Train_Prob,as.numeric(GC_Train$good_bad))
Perf_Train <- performance(Train_Pred,"tpr","fpr")
plot(Perf_Train,col="green",lty=2)
Pred_Validate_Class <- predict(GC_glm,newdata = GC_Validate[,-21],type='response')
Pred_Validate_Prob <-predict(GC_glm,newdata = GC_Validate[,-21],type='response')
Validate_Pred <- prediction(Pred_Validate_Prob,as.numeric(GC_Validate$good_bad))
Perf_Validate <- performance(Validate_Pred,"tpr","fpr")
plot(Perf_Validate,col="yellow",lty=2,add=TRUE)
Pred_Test_Class <- predict(GC_glm,newdata = GC_Test[,-21],type='response')
Pred_Test_Prob <-predict(GC_glm,newdata = GC_Test[,-21],type='response')
Test_Pred <- prediction(Pred_Test_Prob,GC_Test$good_bad)
Perf_Test <- performance(Test_Pred,"tpr","fpr")
plot(Perf_Test,col="red",lty=2,add=TRUE)
legend(0.6,0.5,c("Train Curve","Validate Curve","Test Curve"),col=c("green","yellow","red"),pch="-")
```

10. The ROC plot is given in the following figure:

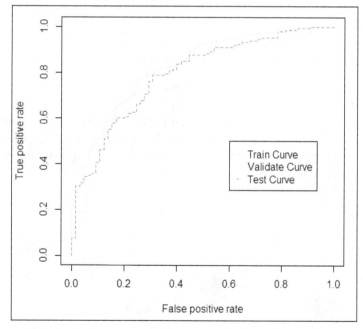

ROC plot for the train + validate + test partition of the German data

We will close the chapter with a short discussion. In the train, validate, and test partitioning, we had one technique of avoiding overfitting. A generalization of this technique is the well-known cross-validation method. In an *n*-fold cross-validation approach, the data is randomly partitioned into n divisions:

1. In the first step, the first part is held for `validation` and the model is built using the remaining n-1 parts, and the accuracy percentage is calculated.

2. Next, the second part is treated as the `validation` dataset and the remaining 1, 3, ..., n-1, n parts are used to build the model and then tested for accuracy on the second part.

3. This process is then repeated for the remaining n-2 parts.

4. Finally, an overall accuracy metric is reported. At the surface, this process is complex enough and hence we will resort to the well-defined functions available in the DAAG package.

11. As the `cross-validation` function itself carries out the *n*-fold partitioning, we build it over the entire dataset:

```
library(DAAG)
data(VD) CVlm(df=VD,form.lm=formula(Voltage_Drop~Time+I(Time^2)+I(
Time^3)+I(((Time-6.5)^3)*(sign(Time-6.5)==1))
+I(((Time-13)^3)*(sign(Time-13)==1))),m=10,plotit="Observed")
```

The VD data frame has 41 observations, and the output in the following figure, *Cross-validation for the voltage-drop problem*, shows that the 10-fold cross-validation has 10 partitions with fold 2 containing five observations and the rest of them having four each. Now, for each fold, the cubic polynomial regression model fits the model by using the data in the remaining folds.

```
> library(DAAG)
> data(VD)
> CVlm(df=VD,form.lm=formula(Voltage_Drop~Time+I(Time^2)+I(Time^3)+I(((Time-6.5)^3)
+ *(sign(Time-6.5)==1))+I(((Time-13)^3)*(sign(Time-13)==1))),m=10,plotit="Observed"
Analysis of Variance Table
Response: Voltage_Drop
                                          Df Sum Sq Mean Sq F value  Pr(>F)
Time                                       1   48.2   48.2   671.5  < 2e-16 ***
I(Time^2)                                  1  170.5  170.5  2377.2  < 2e-16 ***
I(Time^3)                                  1   11.8   11.8   164.4 8.8e-15 ***
I(((Time - 6.5)^3) * (sign(Time - 6.5) == 1))  1   25.6   25.6   357.2  < 2e-16 ***
I(((Time - 13)^3) * (sign(Time - 13) == 1))    1    4.1    4.1    57.4 7.0e-09 ***
Residuals                                 35    2.5    0.1
---
Signif. codes:  0 '***' 0.001 '**' 0.01 '*' 0.05 '.' 0.1 ' ' 1

fold 1
Observations in test set: 4
                2      8     19     38
Predicted   7.858  8.117 13.973  9.875
cvpred      7.715  8.106 13.911  9.894
Voltage_Drop 8.230 8.300 14.590  9.780
CV residual 0.515  0.194  0.679 -0.114
Sum of squares = 0.78    Mean square = 0.19    n = 4
fold 2
Observations in test set: 5
                3     11     25     33     36
Predicted   7.473  9.764 14.763 11.844 10.493
cvpred      7.524  9.788 14.694 11.867 10.546
Voltage_Drop 7.170 9.710 15.180 12.050 10.400
CV residual -0.354 -0.078 0.486  0.183 -0.406
Sum of squares = 0.57    Mean square = 0.11    n = 5
. . . .
fold 10
Observations in test set: 4
                7     13     15     23
Predicted   7.720 11.018 12.194 14.788
cvpred      7.678 11.086 12.286 14.844
Voltage_Drop 7.940 10.910 11.760 14.370
CV residual 0.262 -0.176 -0.526 -0.474
Sum of squares = 0.6     Mean square = 0.15    n = 4
Overall (Sum over all 4 folds)
     ms
0.0888
Warning message:
In CVlm(df = VD, form.lm = formula(Voltage_Drop ~ Time + I(Time^2) +  :
 As there is >1 explanatory variable, cross-validation
 predicted values for a fold are not a linear function
 of corresponding overall predicted values. Lines that
 are shown for the different folds are approximate
```

Cross-validation for the voltage-drop problem

Using the fitted polynomial regression model, prediction is made for the units in the fold. The observed versus predicted regressand values plot is given in the figure *Predicted versus observed plot using the cross-validation technique*. A close examination of the numerical predicted values and the plot indicate that we have a very good model for the voltage drop phenomenon.

The **generalized cross-validation (GCV)** errors are also given with the details of a `lm.ridge` fit model. We can use this information to arrive at the better λ value for the ridge regression models:

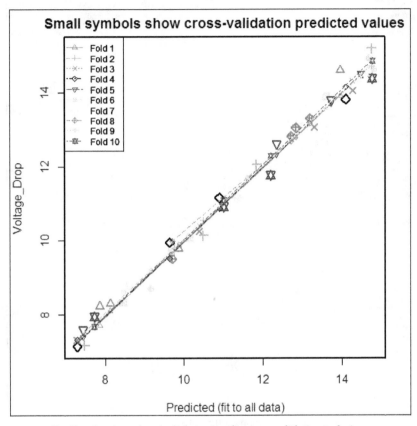

Predicted versus observed plot using the cross-validation technique

12. For the `OF` and `G_Train` data frames, use the `lm.ridge` function to obtain the GCV errors:

```
> LM_OF <- lm.ridge(Y~poly(X,3),data=as.data.frame(OF),
+ lambda=c(0,0.5,1,1.5,2,5,10,30))
> LM_OF$GCV
  0.0   0.5   1.0   1.5   2.0   5.0  10.0  30.0
 5.19  5.05  5.03  5.09  5.21  6.38  8.31 12.07
> LM_GT <- lm.ridge(y~.,data=G_Train,lambda=seq(0,10,0.2))
> LM_GT$GCV
```

0.0	0.2	0.4	0.6	0.8	1.0	1.2	1.4	1.6	1.8
1.777	0.798	0.869	0.889	0.891	0.886	0.877	0.868	0.858	0.848
2.0	2.2	2.4	2.6	2.8	3.0	3.2	3.4	3.6	3.8
0.838	0.830	0.821	0.813	0.806	0.798	0.792	0.786	0.780	0.774
4.0	4.2	4.4	4.6	4.8	5.0	5.2	5.4	5.6	5.8
0.769	0.764	0.760	0.755	0.751	0.748	0.744	0.740	0.737	0.734
6.0	6.2	6.4	6.6	6.8	7.0	7.2	7.4	7.6	7.8
0.731	0.729	0.726	0.723	0.721	0.719	0.717	0.715	0.713	0.711
8.0	8.2	8.4	8.6	8.8	9.0	9.2	9.4	9.6	9.8
0.710	0.708	0.707	0.705	0.704	0.703	0.701	0.700	0.699	0.698
10.0									
0.697									

For the OF data frame, the λ value appears to lie in the interval (1.0, 1.5). On the other hand for the GT data frame, the value appears in (0.2, 0.4).

What just happened?

The choice of the penalty factor λ is indeed very crucial for the success of a ridge regression model, and we saw different methods for obtaining the same. This step included the automatic choice of *Cule and De Iorio (2012)* and the cross-validation technique.

Furthermore, we also saw the application of the popular train, validate, and test approach. In practical applications, these methodologies will go a long way to obtain the best models.

Pop quiz

Here's a task for you:

- What do you expect as the results if you perform the model selection task step function on a polynomial regression model? That is, you are trying to select the variables for the polynomial model lm(Y~poly(X,9,raw=TRUE),data=OF), or say VD_PRS. Verify your intuition by completing the R programs.

- In the Python model, does the Logit function include the penalty term as a default choice? How do you change the penalty term to a number of your choice?

Summary

In this chapter, we began with a hypothetical dataset and highlighted the problem of overfitting. In case of a breakpoint, also known as knots, the extensions of the linear model in the piecewise linear regression model and the spline regression model were found to be very useful enhancements. The problem of overfitting can also sometimes be overcome by using the ridge regression. The ridge regression solution has been extended for the linear and logistic regression models. Finally, we saw a different approach of model assessment by using the train, validate, and test approach and the cross-validation approach.

In spite of the developments where we have intrinsically non-linear data, it becomes difficult for the models discussed in this chapter to emerge as useful solutions. The past two decades has witnessed a powerful alternative in the so-called **Classification and Regression Trees (CART)**. The next chapter discusses CART in greater depth, and the final chapter considers modern development related to it.

9
Classification and Regression Trees

In the previous chapters, we focused on regression models, and the majority of emphasis was on the linearity assumption. In what appears that the next extension must be non-linear models, we will instead deviate to recursive partitioning techniques, which are a bit more flexible than the non-linear generalization of the models considered in the earlier chapters. Of course, the recursive partitioning techniques, in most cases, may be viewed as non-linear models.

We will first introduce the notion of recursive partitions through a hypothetical dataset. It is apparent that the earlier approach of the linear models changes in an entirely different way with the functioning of the recursive partitions. Recursive partitioning depends upon the type of problem we have at hand. We develop a regression tree for the regression problem when the output is a continuous variable, as in the linear models. If the output is a binary variable, we develop a classification tree.

A regression tree is first created by using the `rpart` function from the `rpart` package. A very raw R program is created, which clearly explains the unfolding of a regression tree. A similar effort is repeated for the classification tree. In the final section of this chapter, a classification tree is created for the German credit data problem along with the use of ROC curves for understanding the model performance. The approach in this chapter will be on the following lines:

- Understanding the basis of recursive partitions and the general CART
- Construction of a regression tree
- Construction of a classification tree
- Application of a classification tree to the German credit data problem
- Finer aspects of CART

Packages and settings – R and Python

As the chapter reviews some of the techniques in the latter half of the book, we need a lot of packages and functions:

1. First set the working directory:

```
setwd("MyPath/R/Chapter_10")
```

2. Load the required R package:

```
library(RSADBE)
library(rpart)
library(rattle)
library(MASS)
library(ROCR)
```

3. A host of functions from `numpy`, `pandas`, `matplotlib`, and `sklearn` will be required for Python analyses:

```
In [1]:  import os
         os.chdir("MyPath/PyLab/Chapter09")
         import numpy as np
         import pandas as pd
         from sklearn.tree import DecisionTreeClassifier
         from sklearn.metrics import classification_report
         import sklearn.metrics
         from sklearn import tree
         from sklearn.cross_validation import train_test_split
         from sklearn.preprocessing import label_binarize
         from sklearn.metrics import roc_curve, auc
         import matplotlib.pyplot as plt
```

Understanding recursive partitions

The name of the library package `rpart`, shipped along with R, stands for **Recursive Partitioning**. The package was first created by Terry M Therneau and Beth Atkinson, and is currently maintained by Brian Ripley. We will first have a look at what recursive partitions means.

A complex and contrived relationship is generally not identifiable by linear models. In the previous chapter, we saw the extensions of the linear models in piecewise, polynomial, and spline regression models.

It is also well known that if the order of a model is larger than 4, then interpretation and usability of the model becomes more difficult. We will consider a hypothetical dataset, where we have two classes for the output Y and two explanatory variables in **X1** and **X2**. The two classes are indicated by filled-in green circles and red squares.

First, we will focus only on the left display of the following figure, *A complex classification dataset with partitions*, as it is the actual depiction of the data. At the outset, it is clear that a linear model is not appropriate, as there is quite an overlap of the green and red indicators. Now, there is a clear demarcation of the classification problem accordingly, as **X1** is greater than 6, or not.

In the area on the left side of X1=6, the mid-third region contains a majority of green circles and the rest are red squares. The red squares are pre-dominantly identifiable accordingly, as the **X2** values are either lesser than, or equal to 3, or greater than 6. The green circles are the majority values in the region of **X2** being greater than 3 and lesse than 6.

A similar story can be built for the points on the right side of **X1** greater than 6. Here, we first partitioned the data according to **X1** values first, and then, in each of the partitioned regions, we obtained partitions according to **X2** values. This is the act of recursive partitioning.

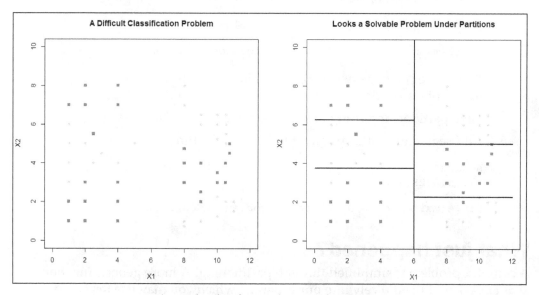

A complex classification dataset with partitions

Let us obtain the preceding plot in R.

Time for action – partitioning the display plot

We first visualize the CART_Dummy dataset and then look in the next subsection at how CART gets the patterns, which are believed to exist in the data:

1. Obtain the dataset CART_Dummy from the RSADBE package by using `data(CART_Dummy)`.

2. Convert the binary output Y as a factor variable, and attach the data frame with `CART_Dummy$Y <- as.factor(CART_Dummy$Y)`:

    ```
    attach(CART_Dummy)
    ```

    In the figure, *A complex classification dataset with partitions*, the red squares refer to 0 and green circles to 1.

3. Initialize the graphics windows for the three samples by using `par(mfrow=c(1,2))`.

4. Create a blank scatter plot:

    ```
    plot(c(0,12),c(0,10),type="n",xlab="X1",ylab="X2").
    ```

5. Plot the green circles and red squares:

    ```
    points(X1[Y==0],X2[Y==0],pch=15,col="red")

    points(X1[Y==1],X2[Y==1],pch=19,col="green")

    title(main="A Difficult Classification Problem")
    ```

6. Repeat the previous two steps to obtain the identical plot on the right side of the graphics window.

7. First, partition according to X1 values by using `abline(v=6,lwd=2)`.

8. Add segments on the graph with the `segment` function:

    ```
    segments(x0=c(0,0,6,6),y0=c(3.75,6.25,2.25,5),x1=c(6,6,12,12),y1=c(3.75,6.25,2.25,5),lwd=2)

    title(main="Looks a Solvable Problem Under Partitions")
    ```

What just happened?

A complex problem is simplified through partitioning! A more generic function, `segments`, has slipped nicely into our program, which you may use for many other scenarios.

Now, this approach of recursive partitioning is not feasible all the time! Why? We seldom deal with two or three explanatory variables and data points as less as in the preceding hypothetical example. The question is how one creates recursive partitioning of the dataset. *Breiman, et. al. (1984)* and *Quinlan (1988)* have invented tree building algorithms, and we will follow the *Breiman, et. al.* approach in the rest of book. The CART discussion in this book is heavily influenced by *Berk (2008)*.

Splitting the data

In the earlier discussion, we saw that partitioning the dataset can be of great benefit in reducing the noise in the data. The question is how does one begin with it? The explanatory variables can be discrete or continuous. We will begin with the continuous (numeric objects in R) variables.

For a continuous variable, the task is a bit simpler. First, identify the unique distinct values of the numeric object. Let us say, for example, that the distinct values of a numeric object, say height in cms, are 160, 165, 170, 175, and 180. The data partitions are then obtained as follows:

- `data[Height<=160,]`, `data[Height>160,]`
- `data[Height<=165,]`, `data[Height>165,]`
- `data[Height<=170,]`, `data[Height>170,]`
- `data[Height<=175,]`, `data[Height>175,]`

The reader should try to understand the rationale behind the code, and certainly this is just an indicative one.

Now, we consider the discrete variables. Here, we have two types of variables, namely **categorical** and **ordinal**. In the case of ordinal variables, we have an order among the distinct values.

For example, in the case of an economic status variable, the order may be among the classes very poor, poor, average, rich, and very rich. Here, the splits are similar to the case of a continuous variable, and if there are m distinct orders, we consider m-1 distinct splits of the overall data. In the case of a categorical variable with m categories, for example the departments A to F of the UCBAdmissions dataset, the number of possible splits becomes $2^{m-1}-1$. However, the benefits of using software like R are that we do not have to worry about these issues.

Now, we'll be studying the approaches used for setting up a classification and regression tree.

The first tree

In the CART_Dummy dataset, we can easily visualize the partitions for Y as a function of the inputs X1 and X2. Obviously, we have a classification problem, and hence we will build the classification tree. The approach illustrated here explicitly demonstrates each and every computation done for setting up a classification and regression tree. However, this illustration is entirely in R, and the Python functions, modules, and packages are used for direct setup of the CART.

> If the reader is interested to replicate the R approach in Python, a very good source on the web that accomplishes this is available at http://machinelearningmastery.com/implement-decision-tree-algorithm-scratch-python/.

Time for action – building our first tree

The rpart function from library rpart will be used to obtain the first classification tree. The tree will be visualized by using the plot options of rpart, and we will follow this up by extracting the rules of a tree by using the asRules function from the rattle package:

1.   Load the rpart package by using library(rpart).

2.   Create the classification tree with CART_Dummy_rpart <- rpart(Y~ X1+X2,data=CART_Dummy).

3.   Visualize the tree with appropriate text labels by using plot(CART_Dummy_rpart); text(CART_Dummy_rpart).

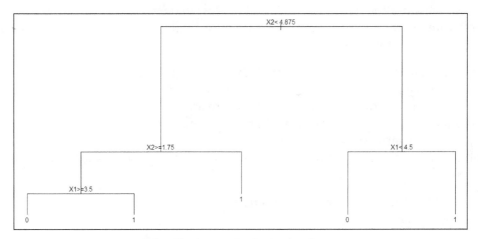

A classification tree for the dummy dataset

Now, the classification tree flows as follows. Obviously, the tree using the `rpart` function does not partition as simply as we did in *Figure 1: A complex classification dataset with partitions*, the working of which will be dealt in the third section of this chapter.

First, we check if the value of second variable **X2** is less than 4.875. If the answer is an affirmation, we move to the left side of the tree, but the right side in the other case. Let us move to the right side. A second question asked is whether **X1** is less than 4.5 or not, and then, depending upon the answer being yes it is identified as a red square, and otherwise a green circle. You are now asked to interpret the left side of the first node. Let us look at the summary of CART_Dummy_rpart.

4. Apply the summary, an S3 method, for the classification tree with `summary(CART_Dummy_rpart)`.

That is a lot of output!

```
> summary(CART_Dummy_rpart)
Call:
rpart(formula = Y ~ X1 + X2, data = CART_Dummy)
  n= 54

       CP nsplit rel error xerror   xstd
1 0.23077      0    1.0000 1.269 0.1378
2 0.11538      1    0.7692 1.115 0.1409
3 0.07692      2    0.6538 1.038 0.1413
4 0.03846      3    0.5769 1.077 0.1412
5 0.01000      4    0.5385 1.038 0.1413

Node number 1: 54 observations,    complexity param=0.2308
  predicted class=1  expected loss=0.4815
    class counts:    26    28
   probabilities: 0.481 0.519
  left son=2 (32 obs) right son=3 (22 obs)
  Primary splits:
      X2 < 4.875 to the left,  improve=1.980, (0 missing)
      X1 < 4.5   to the left,  improve=1.781, (0 missing)

Node number 2: 32 observations,    complexity param=0.07692
  predicted class=0  expected loss=0.4062
    class counts:    19    13
   probabilities: 0.594 0.406
  left son=4 (24 obs) right son=5 (8 obs)
  Primary splits:
      X2 < 1.75  to the right, improve=1.0210, (0 missing)
      X1 < 2.25  to the left,  improve=0.2604, (0 missing)

Node number 3: 22 observations,    complexity param=0.1154
  predicted class=1  expected loss=0.3182
    class counts:     7    15
   probabilities: 0.318 0.682
  left son=6 (9 obs) right son=7 (13 obs)
  Primary splits:
      X1 < 4.5   to the left,  improve=3.699, (0 missing)
      X2 < 6.75  to the right, improve=3.222, (0 missing)
  Surrogate splits:
      X2 < 6.75  to the right, agree=0.727, adj=0.333, (0 split)

Node number 4: 24 observations,    complexity param=0.03846
  predicted class=0  expected loss=0.3333
    class counts:    16     8
   probabilities: 0.667 0.333
  left son=8 (17 obs) right son=9 (7 obs)
  Primary splits:
      X1 < 3.5   to the right, improve=1.1200, (0 missing)
      X2 < 3.75  to the left,  improve=0.3556, (0 missing)

Node number 5: 8 observations
  predicted class=1  expected loss=0.375
    class counts:     3     5
   probabilities: 0.375 0.625

Node number 6: 9 observations
  predicted class=0  expected loss=0.3333
    class counts:     6     3
   probabilities: 0.667 0.333

Node number 7: 13 observations
  predicted class=1  expected loss=0.07692
    class counts:     1    12
   probabilities: 0.077 0.923

Node number 8: 17 observations
  predicted class=0  expected loss=0.2353
    class counts:    13     4
   probabilities: 0.765 0.235

Node number 9: 7 observations
  predicted class=1  expected loss=0.4286
    class counts:     3     4
   probabilities: 0.429 0.571
```

Summary of a classification tree

Our interests are in the nodes numbered 5 to 9! Why? The terminal nodes, of course! A terminal node is one in which we can't split the data any further, and for the classification problem, we arrive at a class assignment as the class that has majority count at the node. The summary shows that there are, indeed, some misclassifications too. Now, won't it be great if R gives the terminal nodes asRules. The function asRules from the rattle package extracts the rules from an rpart object. Let us do it!

5. Invoke the rattle package library(rattle) and, using the asRules function, extract the rules from the terminal nodes with asRules(CART_ Dummy_rpart).

The result is the following set of rules:

```
> library(rattle)
> asRules(CART_Dummy_rpart)

 Rule number:  7 [Y=1 cover=13 (24%) prob=0.92]
    X2>=4.875
    X1>=4.5
 Rule number:  5 [Y=1 cover=8 (15%) prob=0.62]
    X2< 4.875
    X2< 1.75
 Rule number:  9 [Y=1 cover=7 (13%) prob=0.57]
    X2< 4.875
    X2>=1.75
    X1< 3.5
 Rule number:  6 [Y=0 cover=9 (17%) prob=0.33]
    X2>=4.875
    X1< 4.5
 Rule number:  8 [Y=0 cover=17 (31%) prob=0.24]
    X2< 4.875
    X2>=1.75
    X1>=3.5
```

Extracting "rules" from a tree!

We can see that the classification tree is not, according to our "eye-bird", partitioning. However, as a final aspect of our initial understanding, let us plot the segments using the naïve way. That is, we will partition the data display according to the terminal nodes of the CART_Dummy_rpart tree.

6. The R code is given right away, though you should make an effort to find the logic behind it. Of course, it is very likely that, by now, you need to run some of the earlier code that was given earlier:

```
abline(h=4.875,lwd=2)
segments(x0=4.5,y0=4.875,x1=4.5,y1=10,lwd=2)
abline(h=1.75,lwd=2)
segments(x0=3.5,y0=1.75,x1=3.5,y1=4.875,lwd=2)
title(main="Classification Tree on the Data Display")
```

It can be easily seen from the following diagram that `rpart` works really well:

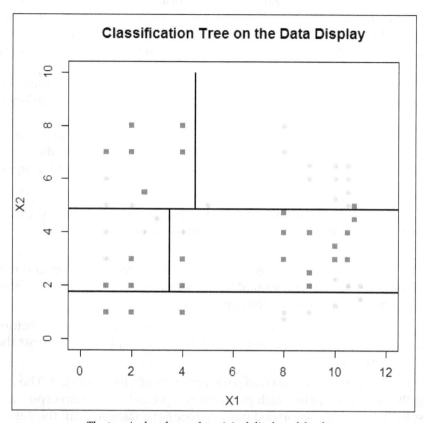

The terminal nodes on the original display of the data

What just happened?

We obtained our first classification tree, which is a good thing. Given the actual data display, the classification tree gives satisfactory answers.

We have understood the "how" part of a classification tree. The "why" aspect is absolutely vital in science, and the next section explains the science behind the construction of a regression tree: it will be followed later by a detailed explanation of the working of a classification tree.

Constructing a regression tree

In the CART_Dummy dataset, the output is a categorical variable, and we had built a classification tree for it. In *Chapter 6, Linear Regression Analysis,* the linear regression models were built for a continuous random variable, while in *Chapter 7, Logistic Regression Model,* we built a logistic regression model for a binary random variable. The same distinction is required in CART, and, thus , we build classification trees for binary random variables, where regression trees are for continuous random variables. Recall the rationale behind the estimation of regression coefficients for the linear regression model. The main goal was to find the estimates of the regression coefficients, which minimize the error sum of squares between the actual regressand values and the fitted values. A similar approach is followed here, in the sense that we need to split the data at the points that keep the residual sum of squares to a minimum:

1. For each unique value of a predictor, which is a candidate for the node value, we find the sum of squares of y's within each partition of the data, and then add them up.

2. This step is performed for each unique value of the predictor, and the value, which leads to the least sum of squares among all the candidates, is selected as the **best split point** for that predictor.

3. In the next step, we find the best split points for each of the predictors, and then the best split is selected across the best split points across the predictors. Easy!

Now, the data is partitioned into two parts according to the best split. The process of finding the best split within each partition is repeated in the same spirit as for the first split. This process is carried out in a recursive fashion until the data can't be partitioned any further. What is happening here? The residual sum of squares at each child node will be less than that in the parent node.

1. At the outset, we record that the rpart function does the exact same thing.

2. However, as a part of a clearer understanding of the regression tree, we will write raw R codes and ensure that there is no ambiguity in the process of understanding CART.

3. We will begin with a simple example of a regression tree, and use the rpart function to plot the regression function.

4. Then, we will first define a function, which will extract the best split given by the covariate and dependent variable.

   This action will be repeated for all the available covariates, and then we find the best overall split. This will be verified with the regression tree.

5. The data will then be partitioned by using the best overall split, and then the best split will be identified for each of the partitioned data.

The process will be repeated until we reach the end of the complete regression tree given by the `rpart`. First, the experiment!

The `cpus` dataset available in the `MASS` package contains the relative performance measure of 209 CPUs in the `perf` variable. It is known that the performance of a CPU depends on factors such as the cycle time in nanoseconds (`syct`), minimum and maximum main memory in kilobytes (`mmin` and `mmax`), cache size in kilobytes (`cach`), and minimum and maximum number of channels (`chmin` and `chmax`). The task on hand is to model the `perf` as a function of `syct`, `mmin`, `mmax`, `cach`, `chmin`, and `chmax`. The histogram of `perf` — try `hist(cpus$perf)` — will show a highly skewed distribution, and hence we will build a regression tree for the logarithm transformation `log10(perf)`.

Time for action – the construction of a regression tree

A regression tree is first built by using the `rpart` function. The `getNode` function is introduced, which helps in identifying the split node at each stage, and using it we build a regression tree and verify that we had the same tree as returned by the `rpart` function:

1. Load the `MASS` library by using `library(MASS)`.

2. Create the regression tree for logarithm (to the base 10) of `perf` as a function of the covariates explained earlier, and display the regression tree:

   ```
   cpus.ltrpart <- rpart(log10(perf)~syct+mmin+mmax+cach+chmin+chmax,
   data=cpus)
   ```

   ```
   plot(cpus.ltrpart); text(cpus.ltrpart)
   ```

The regression tree will be indicated as follows:

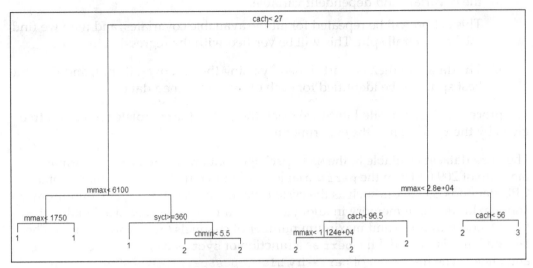

Regression tree for the "perf" of a CPU

We will now define the getNode function. Given the regressand and the covariate, we need to find the best split in the sense of sum of squares criterion. The evaluation needs to be done for every distinct value of the covariate. If there are *m* distinct points, we need *m*-1 evaluations. At each distinct point, the regressand needs to be partitioned accordingly, and the sum of squares should be obtained for each partition. The two sums of squares (in each part) are then added to obtain the reduced sum of squares. Thus, we create the required function to meet all these requirements.

3. Create the getNode function in R by running the following code:

```
getNode <- function(x,y)  {
    xu <- sort(unique(x),decreasing=TRUE)
    ss <- numeric(length(xu)-1)
    for(i in 1:length(ss))  {
    partR <- y[x>xu[i]]
    partL <- y[x<=xu[i]]
    partRSS <- sum((partR-mean(partR))^2)
    partLSS <- sum((partL-mean(partL))^2)
    ss[i]<-partRSS + partLSS
        }
return(list(xnode=xu[which(ss==min(ss,na.rm=TRUE))],
    minss = min(ss,na.rm=TRUE),ss,xu))

    }
```

The getNode function gives the best split for a given covariate. It returns a list consisting of four objects:

° xnode, which is a datum of the covariate x that gives the minimum residual sum of squares for the regressand y

° The value of the minimum residual sum of squares

° The vector of the residual sum of squares for the distinct points of the vector x

° The vector of distinct x values

We will run this function for each of the six covariates, and find the best overall split. The argument na.rm=TRUE is required, as at the maximum value of x we won't get a numeric value.

4. We will first execute the getNode function on the syct covariate, and look at the output we get as a result:

```
> getNode(cpus$syct,log10(cpus$perf))$xnode
[1] 48
> getNode(cpus$syct,log10(cpus$perf))$minss
[1] 24.72
> getNode(cpus$syct,log10(cpus$perf))[[3]]
  [1] 43.12 42.42 41.23 39.93 39.44 37.54 37.23 36.87 36.51 36.52
35.92 34.91
 [13] 34.96 35.10 35.03 33.65 33.28 33.49 33.23 32.75 32.96 31.59
31.26 30.86
 [25] 30.83 30.62 29.85 30.90 31.15 31.51 31.40 31.50 31.23 30.41
30.55 28.98
 [37] 27.68 27.55 27.44 26.80 25.98 27.45 28.05 28.11 28.66 29.11
29.81 30.67
 [49] 28.22 28.50 24.72 25.22 26.37 28.28 29.10 33.02 34.39 39.05
39.29
> getNode(cpus$syct,log10(cpus$perf))[[4]]
  [1] 1500 1100  900  810  800  700  600  480  400  350  330  320
300  250  240
 [16]  225  220  203  200  185  180  175  167  160  150  143  140
133  125  124
 [31]  116  115  112  110  105  100   98   92   90   84   75   72
70   64   60
 [46]   59   57   56   52   50   48   40   38   35   30   29   26
25   23   17
```

The least sum of squares at a split for the best split value of the syct variable is 24.72, and it occurs at a value of syct greater than 48. The third and fourth list objects given by getNode, respectively, contain the details of the sum of squares for the potential candidates and the unique values of syct. The values of interest are highlighted. Thus, we will first look at the second object from the list output for all the six covariates to find the best split among the best split of each of the variables, by the residual sum of squares criteria.

5. Now, run the getNode function for the remaining five covariates:

```
getNode(cpus$syct,log10(cpus$perf))[[2]]
getNode(cpus$mmin,log10(cpus$perf))[[2]]
getNode(cpus$mmax,log10(cpus$perf))[[2]]
getNode(cpus$cach,log10(cpus$perf))[[2]]
getNode(cpus$chmin,log10(cpus$perf))[[2]]
getNode(cpus$chmax,log10(cpus$perf))[[2]]
getNode(cpus$cach,log10(cpus$perf))[[1]]
sort(getNode(cpus$cach,log10(cpus$perf))[[4]],decreasing=FALSE)
```

The output is as follows:

```
> getNode(cpus$syct,log10(cpus$perf))[[2]]
[1] 24.72
> getNode(cpus$mmin,log10(cpus$perf))[[2]]
[1] 24.08
> getNode(cpus$mmax,log10(cpus$perf))[[2]]
[1] 21.81
> getNode(cpus$cach,log10(cpus$perf))[[2]]
[1] 19.43
> getNode(cpus$chmin,log10(cpus$perf))[[2]]
[1] 22.33
> getNode(cpus$chmax,log10(cpus$perf))[[2]]
[1] 28.53
> getNode(cpus$cach,log10(cpus$perf))[[1]]
[1] 24
> sort(getNode(cpus$cach,log10(cpus$perf))[[4]],decreasing=FALSE)
 [1]   0   1   2   4   6   8   9  12  16  24  30  32  48  64  65
[16]  96 112 128 131 142 160 256
```

Obtaining the best "first split" of regression tree

The sum of squares for cach is least, and hence we need to find the best split associated with it, which is 24. However, the regression tree shows that the best split is for the cach value of 27. The getNode function says that the best split occurs at a point greater than 24, and hence we take the average of 24 and the next unique point at 30. Having obtained the best overall split, we next obtain the first partition of the dataset.

6. Partition the data by using the best overall split point:

```
cpus_FS_R <- cpus[cpus$cach>=27,]

cpus_FS_L <- cpus[cpus$cach<27,]
```

The new names of the data objects are clear with _FS_R indicating the dataset obtained on the right side for the first split, and _FS_L indicating the left side. In the rest of the section, the nomenclature won't be explained further.

7. Identify the best split in each of the partitioned datasets:

```
getNode(cpus_FS_R$syct,log10(cpus_FS_R$perf))[[2]]
getNode(cpus_FS_R$mmin,log10(cpus_FS_R$perf))[[2]]
getNode(cpus_FS_R$mmax,log10(cpus_FS_R$perf))[[2]]
getNode(cpus_FS_R$cach,log10(cpus_FS_R$perf))[[2]]
getNode(cpus_FS_R$chmin,log10(cpus_FS_R$perf))[[2]]
getNode(cpus_FS_R$chmax,log10(cpus_FS_R$perf))[[2]]
getNode(cpus_FS_R$mmax,log10(cpus_FS_R$perf))[[1]]
sort(getNode(cpus_FS_R$mmax,log10(cpus_FS_R$perf))[[4]],
decreasing=FALSE)
getNode(cpus_FS_L$syct,log10(cpus_FS_L$perf))[[2]]
getNode(cpus_FS_L$mmin,log10(cpus_FS_L$perf))[[2]]
getNode(cpus_FS_L$mmax,log10(cpus_FS_L$perf))[[2]]
getNode(cpus_FS_L$cach,log10(cpus_FS_L$perf))[[2]]
getNode(cpus_FS_L$chmin,log10(cpus_FS_L$perf))[[2]]
getNode(cpus_FS_L$chmax,log10(cpus_FS_L$perf))[[2]]
getNode(cpus_FS_L$mmax,log10(cpus_FS_L$perf))[[1]]
sort(getNode(cpus_FS_L$mmax,log10(cpus_FS_L$perf))[[4]],
decreasing=FALSE)
```

The following screenshot gives the results of running the preceding R code:

```
> cpus_FS_R <- cpus[cpus$cach>=27,]
> cpus_FS_L <- cpus[cpus$cach<27,]
> getNode(cpus_FS_R$syct,log10(cpus_FS_R$perf))[[2]]
[1] 4.672
> getNode(cpus_FS_R$mmin,log10(cpus_FS_R$perf))[[2]]
[1] 4.796
> getNode(cpus_FS_R$mmax,log10(cpus_FS_R$perf))[[2]]
[1] 3.864
> getNode(cpus_FS_R$cach,log10(cpus_FS_R$perf))[[2]]
[1] 5.584
> getNode(cpus_FS_R$chmin,log10(cpus_FS_R$perf))[[2]]
[1] 5.104
> getNode(cpus_FS_R$chmax,log10(cpus_FS_R$perf))[[2]]
[1] 5.512
> getNode(cpus_FS_R$mmax,log10(cpus_FS_R$perf))[[1]]
[1] 24000
> sort(getNode(cpus_FS_R$mmax,log10(cpus_FS_R$perf))[[4]],
+ decreasing=FALSE)
 [1]  2620  5000  6000  8000 10480 12000 16000 20970 24000 32000
[11] 64000
> getNode(cpus_FS_L$syct,log10(cpus_FS_L$perf))[[2]]
[1] 9.139
> getNode(cpus_FS_L$mmin,log10(cpus_FS_L$perf))[[2]]
[1] 8.907
> getNode(cpus_FS_L$mmax,log10(cpus_FS_L$perf))[[2]]
[1] 7.939
> getNode(cpus_FS_L$cach,log10(cpus_FS_L$perf))[[2]]
[1] 9.88
> getNode(cpus_FS_L$chmin,log10(cpus_FS_L$perf))[[2]]
[1] 9.968
> getNode(cpus_FS_L$chmax,log10(cpus_FS_L$perf))[[2]]
[1] 9.016
> getNode(cpus_FS_L$mmax,log10(cpus_FS_L$perf))[[1]]
[1] 6000
> sort(getNode(cpus_FS_L$mmax,log10(cpus_FS_L$perf))[[4]],
+ decreasing=FALSE)
 [1]    64   512   768  1000  1500  2000  3000  3500  4000  4500
[11]  5000  6000  6200  6300  8000 12000 16000 32000
```

Obtaining the next two splits

Thus, for the first right partitioned data, the best split is for the mmax value as the mid-point between 24000 and 32000; that is, at mmax = 28000. Similarly, for the first left-partitioned data, the best split is the average value of 6000 and 6200, which is 6100, for the same mmax covariate. Note the important step here. Even though we used cach as the criteria for the first partition, it is still used with the two partitioned data. The results are consistent with the display given by the regression tree, in the figure, *Regression tree for the "perf" of a CPU*. The next R program will take care of the entire first split's right side's future partitions.

8. Partition the first right part cpus_FS_R as follows:

```
cpus_FS_R_SS_R <- cpus_FS_R[cpus_FS_R$mmax>=28000,]

cpus_FS_R_SS_L <- cpus_FS_R[cpus_FS_R$mmax<28000,]
```

Obtain the best split for cpus_FS_R_SS_R and cpus_FS_R_SS_L by running the following code:

```
cpus_FS_R_SS_R <- cpus_FS_R[cpus_FS_R$mmax>=28000,]
cpus_FS_R_SS_L <- cpus_FS_R[cpus_FS_R$mmax<28000,]
getNode(cpus_FS_R_SS_R$syct,log10(cpus_FS_R_SS_R$perf))[[2]]
getNode(cpus_FS_R_SS_R$mmin,log10(cpus_FS_R_SS_R$perf))[[2]]
getNode(cpus_FS_R_SS_R$mmax,log10(cpus_FS_R_SS_R$perf))[[2]]
getNode(cpus_FS_R_SS_R$cach,log10(cpus_FS_R_SS_R$perf))[[2]]
getNode(cpus_FS_R_SS_R$chmin,log10(cpus_FS_R_SS_R$perf))[[2]]
getNode(cpus_FS_R_SS_R$chmax,log10(cpus_FS_R_SS_R$perf))[[2]]
getNode(cpus_FS_R_SS_R$cach,log10(cpus_FS_R_SS_R$perf))[[1]]
sort(getNode(cpus_FS_R_SS_R$cach,log10(cpus_FS_R_SS_R$perf))[[4]],
decreasing=FALSE)
getNode(cpus_FS_R_SS_L$syct,log10(cpus_FS_R_SS_L$perf))[[2]]
getNode(cpus_FS_R_SS_L$mmin,log10(cpus_FS_R_SS_L$perf))[[2]]
getNode(cpus_FS_R_SS_L$mmax,log10(cpus_FS_R_SS_L$perf))[[2]]
getNode(cpus_FS_R_SS_L$cach,log10(cpus_FS_R_SS_L$perf))[[2]]
getNode(cpus_FS_R_SS_L$chmin,log10(cpus_FS_R_SS_L$perf))[[2]]
getNode(cpus_FS_R_SS_L$chmax,log10(cpus_FS_R_SS_L$perf))[[2]]
getNode(cpus_FS_R_SS_L$cach,log10(cpus_FS_R_SS_L$perf))[[1]]
sort(getNode(cpus_FS_R_SS_L$cach,log10(cpus_FS_R_SS_L$perf))
[[4]],decreasing=FALSE)
```

For the cpus_FS_R_SS_R part, the final division is according to cach being greater than 56 or not (average of 48 and 64). If the cach value in this partition is greater than 56, then perf (actually log10(perf)) ends in the terminal leaf 3, else 2. However, for the region cpus_FS_R_SS_L, we partition the data further by the cach value being greater than 96.5 (average of 65 and 128). In the right side of the region, log10(perf) is found as 2, and a third level split is required for cpus_FS_R_SS_L with cpus_FS_R_SS_L_TS_L.

Note that though the final terminal leaves of the `cpus_FS_R_SS_L_TS_L` region shows the same 2 as the final `log10(perf)`, this may actually result in a significant variability reduction of the difference between the predicted and the actual `log10(perf)` values. We will now focus on the first main split's left side.

```
> cpus_FS_R_SS_R <- cpus_FS_R[cpus_FS_R$mmax>=28000,]
> cpus_FS_R_SS_L <- cpus_FS_R[cpus_FS_R$mmax<28000,]
> getNode(cpus_FS_R_SS_R$syct,log10(cpus_FS_R_SS_R$perf))[[2]]
[1] 1.054
> getNode(cpus_FS_R_SS_R$mmin,log10(cpus_FS_R_SS_R$perf))[[2]]
[1] 1.108
> getNode(cpus_FS_R_SS_R$mmax,log10(cpus_FS_R_SS_R$perf))[[2]]
[1] 1.523
> getNode(cpus_FS_R_SS_R$cach,log10(cpus_FS_R_SS_R$perf))[[2]]
[1] 0.7228
> getNode(cpus_FS_R_SS_R$chmin,log10(cpus_FS_R_SS_R$perf))[[2]]
[1] 0.9653
> getNode(cpus_FS_R_SS_R$chmax,log10(cpus_FS_R_SS_R$perf))[[2]]
[1] 1.04
> getNode(cpus_FS_R_SS_R$cach,log10(cpus_FS_R_SS_R$perf))[[1]]
[1] 48
> sort(getNode(cpus_FS_R_SS_R$cach,log10(cpus_FS_R_SS_R$perf))[[4]],
+ decreasing=FALSE)
[1]   32   48   64   96  112  128  256
> getNode(cpus_FS_R_SS_L$syct,log10(cpus_FS_R_SS_L$perf))[[2]]
[1] 1.879
> getNode(cpus_FS_R_SS_L$mmin,log10(cpus_FS_R_SS_L$perf))[[2]]
[1] 2.096
> getNode(cpus_FS_R_SS_L$mmax,log10(cpus_FS_R_SS_L$perf))[[2]]
[1] 1.878
> getNode(cpus_FS_R_SS_L$cach,log10(cpus_FS_R_SS_L$perf))[[2]]
[1] 1.764
> getNode(cpus_FS_R_SS_L$chmin,log10(cpus_FS_R_SS_L$perf))[[2]]
[1] 1.994
> getNode(cpus_FS_R_SS_L$chmax,log10(cpus_FS_R_SS_L$perf))[[2]]
[1] 1.846
> getNode(cpus_FS_R_SS_L$cach,log10(cpus_FS_R_SS_L$perf))[[1]]
[1] 65
> sort(getNode(cpus_FS_R_SS_L$cach,log10(cpus_FS_R_SS_L$perf))[[4]],
+ decreasing=FALSE)
 [1]   30   32   48   64   65  128  131  142  160  256
> cpus_FS_R_SS_L_TS_L <- cpus_FS_R_SS_L[cpus_FS_R_SS_L$cach<96.5,]
> getNode(cpus_FS_R_SS_L_TS_L$syct,log10(cpus_FS_R_SS_L_TS_L$perf))[[2]]
[1] 1.125
> getNode(cpus_FS_R_SS_L_TS_L$mmin,log10(cpus_FS_R_SS_L_TS_L$perf))[[2]]
[1] 0.9578
> getNode(cpus_FS_R_SS_L_TS_L$mmax,log10(cpus_FS_R_SS_L_TS_L$perf))[[2]]
[1] 0.808
> getNode(cpus_FS_R_SS_L_TS_L$cach,log10(cpus_FS_R_SS_L_TS_L$perf))[[2]]
[1] 1.523
> getNode(cpus_FS_R_SS_L_TS_L$chmin,log10(cpus_FS_R_SS_L_TS_L$perf))[[2]]
[1] 1.391
> getNode(cpus_FS_R_SS_L_TS_L$chmax,log10(cpus_FS_R_SS_L_TS_L$perf))[[2]]
[1] 1.273
> getNode(cpus_FS_R_SS_L_TS_L$mmax,log10(cpus_FS_R_SS_L_TS_L$perf))[[1]]
[1] 10480
> sort(getNode(cpus_FS_R_SS_L_TS_L$mmax,log10(cpus_FS_R_SS_L_TS_L$perf))[[4]],
+ decreasing=FALSE)
[1]   8000 10480 12000 16000 20970 24000
```

Partitioning the right partition after the first main split

9. Partition cpus_FS_L accordingly, as the mmax value being greater than 6100 or otherwise:

```
cpus_FS_L_SS_R <- cpus_FS_L[cpus_FS_L$mmax>=6100,]

cpus_FS_L_SS_L <- cpus_FS_L[cpus_FS_L$mmax<6100,]
```

The rest of the partition for cpus_FS_L is given next.

10. The details will be skipped and the R program is given right away:

```
cpus_FS_L_SS_R <- cpus_FS_L[cpus_FS_L$mmax>=6100,]
cpus_FS_L_SS_L <- cpus_FS_L[cpus_FS_L$mmax<6100,]
getNode(cpus_FS_L_SS_R$syct,log10(cpus_FS_L_SS_R$perf))[[2]]
getNode(cpus_FS_L_SS_R$mmin,log10(cpus_FS_L_SS_R$perf))[[2]]
getNode(cpus_FS_L_SS_R$mmax,log10(cpus_FS_L_SS_R$perf))[[2]]
getNode(cpus_FS_L_SS_R$cach,log10(cpus_FS_L_SS_R$perf))[[2]]
getNode(cpus_FS_L_SS_R$chmin,log10(cpus_FS_L_SS_R$perf))[[2]]
getNode(cpus_FS_L_SS_R$chmax,log10(cpus_FS_L_SS_R$perf))[[2]]
getNode(cpus_FS_L_SS_R$syct,log10(cpus_FS_L_SS_R$perf))[[1]]
sort(getNode(cpus_FS_L_SS_R$syct,log10(cpus_FS_L_SS_R$perf))[[4]],
decreasing=FALSE)
getNode(cpus_FS_L_SS_L$syct,log10(cpus_FS_L_SS_L$perf))[[2]]
getNode(cpus_FS_L_SS_L$mmin,log10(cpus_FS_L_SS_L$perf))[[2]]
getNode(cpus_FS_L_SS_L$mmax,log10(cpus_FS_L_SS_L$perf))[[2]]
getNode(cpus_FS_L_SS_L$cach,log10(cpus_FS_L_SS_L$perf))[[2]]
getNode(cpus_FS_L_SS_L$chmin,log10(cpus_FS_L_SS_L$perf))[[2]]
getNode(cpus_FS_L_SS_L$chmax,log10(cpus_FS_L_SS_L$perf))[[2]]
getNode(cpus_FS_L_SS_L$mmax,log10(cpus_FS_L_SS_L$perf))[[1]]
sort(getNode(cpus_FS_L_SS_L$mmax,log10(cpus_FS_L_SS_L$perf))
[[4]],decreasing=FALSE)
cpus_FS_L_SS_R_TS_R <- cpus_FS_L_SS_R[cpus_FS_L_SS_R$syct<360,]
getNode(cpus_FS_L_SS_R_TS_R$syct,log10(cpus_FS_L_SS_R_TS_R$
perf))[[2]]
getNode(cpus_FS_L_SS_R_TS_R$mmin,log10(cpus_FS_L_SS_R_TS_R$
perf))[[2]]
getNode(cpus_FS_L_SS_R_TS_R$mmax,log10(cpus_FS_L_SS_R_TS_R$
perf))[[2]]
getNode(cpus_FS_L_SS_R_TS_R$cach,log10(cpus_FS_L_SS_R_TS_R$
perf))[[2]]
getNode(cpus_FS_L_SS_R_TS_R$chmin,log10(cpus_FS_L_SS_R_TS_R$
perf))[[2]]
getNode(cpus_FS_L_SS_R_TS_R$chmax,log10(cpus_FS_L_SS_R_TS_R$
perf))[[2]]
```

```
getNode(cpus_FS_L_SS_R_TS_R$chmin,log10(cpus_FS_L_SS_R_TS_R$
perf))[[1]]
sort(getNode(cpus_FS_L_SS_R_TS_R$chmin,log10(cpus_FS_L_SS_R_TS_
R$perf))[[4]],decreasing=FALSE)
```

We will now see how the preceding R code gets us closer to the regression tree:

```
> cpus_FS_L_SS_R <- cpus_FS_L[cpus_FS_L$mmax>=6100,]
> cpus_FS_L_SS_L <- cpus_FS_L[cpus_FS_L$mmax<6100,]
> getNode(cpus_FS_L_SS_R$syct,log10(cpus_FS_L_SS_R$perf))[[2]]
[1] 2.63
> getNode(cpus_FS_L_SS_R$mmin,log10(cpus_FS_L_SS_R$perf))[[2]]
[1] 2.831
> getNode(cpus_FS_L_SS_R$mmax,log10(cpus_FS_L_SS_R$perf))[[2]]
[1] 3.087
> getNode(cpus_FS_L_SS_R$cach,log10(cpus_FS_L_SS_R$perf))[[2]]
[1] 3.459
> getNode(cpus_FS_L_SS_R$chmin,log10(cpus_FS_L_SS_R$perf))[[2]]
[1] 2.972
> getNode(cpus_FS_L_SS_R$chmax,log10(cpus_FS_L_SS_R$perf))[[2]]
[1] 3.452
> getNode(cpus_FS_L_SS_R$syct,log10(cpus_FS_L_SS_R$perf))[[1]]
[1] 320
> sort(getNode(cpus_FS_L_SS_R$syct,log10(cpus_FS_L_SS_R$perf))[[4]],
+ decreasing=FALSE)
 [1]  17  25  26  50  56  57  70  72  75  92 100 105 110 115 124 125 133 140 143
[20] 160 180 185 200 220 250 300 320 400 700 800
> getNode(cpus_FS_L_SS_L$syct,log10(cpus_FS_L_SS_L$perf))[[2]]
[1] 3.37
> getNode(cpus_FS_L_SS_L$mmin,log10(cpus_FS_L_SS_L$perf))[[2]]
[1] 3.409
> getNode(cpus_FS_L_SS_L$mmax,log10(cpus_FS_L_SS_L$perf))[[2]]
[1] 2.733
> getNode(cpus_FS_L_SS_L$cach,log10(cpus_FS_L_SS_L$perf))[[2]]
[1] 3.664
> getNode(cpus_FS_L_SS_L$chmin,log10(cpus_FS_L_SS_L$perf))[[2]]
[1] 3.429
> getNode(cpus_FS_L_SS_L$chmax,log10(cpus_FS_L_SS_L$perf))[[2]]
[1] 2.91
> getNode(cpus_FS_L_SS_L$mmax,log10(cpus_FS_L_SS_L$perf))[[1]]
[1] 1500
> sort(getNode(cpus_FS_L_SS_L$mmax,log10(cpus_FS_L_SS_L$perf))[[4]],
+ decreasing=FALSE)
 [1]   64  512  768 1000 1500 2000 3000 3500 4000 4500 5000 6000
> cpus_FS_L_SS_R_TS_R = cpus_FS_L_SS_R[cpus_FS_L_SS_R$syct<360,]
> getNode(cpus_FS_L_SS_R_TS_R$syct,log10(cpus_FS_L_SS_R_TS_R$perf))[[2]]
[1] 2.047
> getNode(cpus_FS_L_SS_R_TS_R$mmin,log10(cpus_FS_L_SS_R_TS_R$perf))[[2]]
[1] 1.758
> getNode(cpus_FS_L_SS_R_TS_R$mmax,log10(cpus_FS_L_SS_R_TS_R$perf))[[2]]
[1] 1.996
> getNode(cpus_FS_L_SS_R_TS_R$cach,log10(cpus_FS_L_SS_R_TS_R$perf))[[2]]
[1] 2.404
> getNode(cpus_FS_L_SS_R_TS_R$chmin,log10(cpus_FS_L_SS_R_TS_R$perf))[[2]]
[1] 1.758
> getNode(cpus_FS_L_SS_R_TS_R$chmax,log10(cpus_FS_L_SS_R_TS_R$perf))[[2]]
[1] 2.307
> getNode(cpus_FS_L_SS_R_TS_R$chmin,log10(cpus_FS_L_SS_R_TS_R$perf))[[1]]
[1] 6
> sort(getNode(cpus_FS_L_SS_R_TS_R$chmin,log10(cpus_FS_L_SS_R_TS_R$perf))[[4]],
+ decreasing=FALSE)
[1] 1 2 3 4 5 6 8
```

Partitioning the left partition after the first main split

We leave it to you to interpret the output arising from the previous action.

What just happened?

Using the `rpart` function from the `rpart` library we first built the regression tree for `log10(perf)`. Then, we explored the basic definitions underlying the construction of a regression tree and defined the `getNode` function to obtain the best split for a pair of regressand and a covariate. This function is then applied for all the covariates, and the best overall split is obtained; using the same, we get our first partition of the data, which will be in agreement with the tree given by the `rpart` function. We then recursively partitioned the data by using the `getNode` function and verified that all the best splits in each partitioned data is in agreement with the one provided by the `rpart` function.

The reader may wonder if the preceding tedious task was really essential. However, it has been the experience of the author that the users/readers seldom remember the rationale behind using direct code/functions for any software after some time. Moreover, CART is a difficult concept and it is imperative that we clearly understand our first tree, and return to the preceding program whenever the understanding of a science behind CART is forgotten.

The construction of a classification tree uses entirely different metrics, and hence its working is also explained in considerable depth in the next section.

Constructing a classification tree

We first need to set up the splitting criteria for a classification tree. In the case of a regression tree, we saw the sum of squares as the splitting criteria. For identifying the split for a classification tree, we need to define certain measures known as **impurity** measures. The three popular measures of impurity are:

- Bayes error
- The cross-entropy function
- Gini index

Let p denote the percentage of success in a dataset of size n. The formulae of these impurity measures are given in the following table:

Measure	Formula
Bayes error	$\varphi_B(p) = \min(p, 1-p)$
The cross-entropy measure	$\varphi_{CE}(p) = -p\log p - (1-p)\log(1-p)$
Gini index	$\varphi_G(p) = p(1-p)$

We will write a short program to understand the shape of these impurity measures as a function of p:

```
p <- seq(0.01,0.99,0.01)
plot(p,pmin(p,1-p),"l",col="red",xlab="p",xlim=c(0,1),ylim=c(0,1),
ylab="Impurity Measures")
points(p,-p*log(p)-(1-p)*log(1-p),"l",col="green")
points(p,p*(1-p),"l",col="blue")
title(main="Impurity Measures")
legend(0.6,1,c("Bayes Error","Cross-Entropy","Gini Index"),col=c("red"
,"green","blue"),pch="-")
```

The preceding R code when executed in an R session gives the following output:

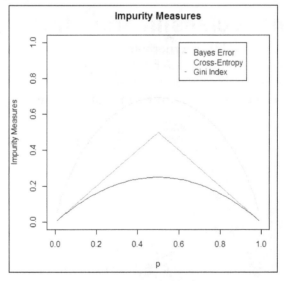

Impurity metrics – Bayes error, cross-entropy, and Gini index

Basically, we have these three choices of impurity metrics as a building block of a classification tree. The popular choice is the Gini index, and there are detailed discussions about the reason in the literature; see *Breiman, et. al. (1984)*. However, we will delve into this aspect and, for the development in this section; we will be using the `cross-entropy` function.

Now, for a given predictor, assume that we have a node denoted by A. In the initial stage, where there are no partitions, the impurity is based on the proportion p. The impurity of node A is taken to be a non-negative function of the probability $y = 1$, and is mathematically written as $p(y=1|A)$. The impurity of node A is defined as follows:

$$I(A) = \varphi \left[p(y=1|A) \right]$$

Here φ is one of the three impurity measures. When A is one of the internal nodes, the tree gets bifurcated to a left- and right- side; that is, we now have left daughter A_L and a right daughter A_R. For the moment, we will take the split according to the predictor variable x; that is, if $x \le c$, the observation moves to A_L, otherwise to A_R. Then, according to the split criteria, we have the following table; this is the same as *Table 3.2 of Berk (2008)*:

Split criteria	Failure (0)	Success (1)	Total
AL $x \le c$	n11	n12	n1.
ARx > c	n21	n22	n2.
$x \le c$	n.1	n.2	n..

Using the frequencies in the preceding table, the impurity for the daughter nodes A_L and A_R, based on the `cross-entropy` metric, are given as follows:

$$I(A_L) = -\frac{n_{11}}{n_1} \log\left(\frac{n_{11}}{n_1}\right) - \frac{n_{12}}{n_1} \log\left(\frac{n_{12}}{n_1}\right)$$

and:

$$I(A_R) = -\frac{n_{21}}{n_2} \log\left(\frac{n_{21}}{n_2}\right) - \frac{n_{22}}{n_2} \log\left(\frac{n_{22}}{n_2}\right)$$

The probability of an observation falling in the left- and right- daughter nodes are respectively given by $p(A_L) = n_1/n$ and $p(A_R) = n_2/n$. Then, the benefit of using the node A is given as follows:

$$\Delta(A) = I(A) - p(A_L)I(A_L) - p(A_R)I(A_R).$$

Now, we capture $\Delta(A)$ for all unique values of a predictor, and choose that value as the best split for which $\Delta(A)$ is a maximum. This step is repeated across all the variables, and the best split is selected, which has maximum $\Delta(A)$. According to the best split, the data is partitioned, and, as seen earlier during the construction of the regression tree, a similar search is performed in each of the partitioned data. The process continues until the gain by the split reaches a threshold minimum in each of the partitioned data.

We will begin with the classification tree as delivered by the rpart function. The illustrative dataset kyphosis is selected from the rpart library itself. The data relates to children who had corrective spinal surgery. This medical problem is about the exaggerated outward curvature of the thoracic region of the spine, which results in a rounded upper back.

In this study, 81 children have undergone a spinal surgery and following the surgery, information is captured to know whether the children still have the kyphosis problem in the column named Kyphosis. The value of Kyphosis="absent" indicates that the child has been cured of the problem, and Kyphosis="present" means that the child has not been cured for kyphosis. The other information capture is related to the age of the children, the number of vertebrae involved, and the number of first (topmost) vertebrae operated on. The task for us is building a classification tree, which gives the Kyphosis status dependent on the described variables.

We will first build the classification tree for Kyphosis as a function of the three variables Age, Start, and Number. The tree will then be displayed and rules will be extracted from it. The getNode function will be defined based on the cross-entropy function, which will be applied on the raw data and the first overall optimal split obtained to partition the data. The process will be recursively repeated until we get the same tree as returned by the rpart function.

Time for action – the construction of a classification tree

The getNode function is now defined here to help us identify the best split for the classification problem. For the Kyphosis dataset from the rpart package, we plot the classification tree by using the rpart function. The tree is re-obtained by using the getNode function:

1. Using the option of split="information", construct a classification tree based on the cross-entropy information for the kyphosis data with the following code:

   ```
   ky_rpart <- rpart(Kyphosis ~ Age + Number + Start, data=kyphosis,p
   arms=list(split="information"))
   ```

2. Visualize the classification tree by using plot(ky_rpart); text(ky_rpart):

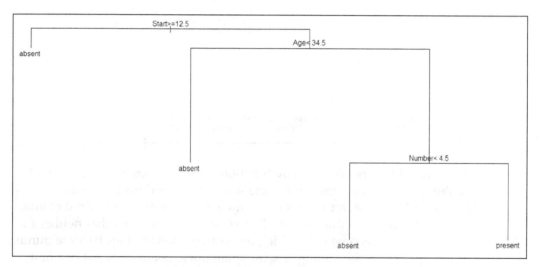

Classification tree for the kyphosis problem

3. Extract rules from ex_rpart by using asRules:

   ```
   > asRules(ky_rpart)
    Rule number: 15 [Kyphosis=present cover=13 (16%) prob=0.69]
      Start< 12.5
      Age>=34.5
      Number>=4.5
   ```

```
Rule number: 14 [Kyphosis=absent cover=12 (15%) prob=0.42]
 Start< 12.5
 Age>=34.5
 Number< 4.5
Rule number: 6 [Kyphosis=absent cover=10 (12%) prob=0.10]
 Start< 12.5
 Age< 34.5
Rule number: 2 [Kyphosis=absent cover=46 (57%) prob=0.04]
 Start>=12.5
```

4. Define the `getNode` function for the classification problem:

```
getNode <- function(x,y)          {
        xu = sort(unique(x),decreasing=FALSE)
        delta_ISA = numeric(length(xu)-1)
        for(i in 1:(length(xu)-1))           {
                partR = y[x>xu[i]]
                partL = y[x<=xu[i]]
                if((length(partR)>0) & (length(partL)>0))        {
                tt =  table(x>xu[i],y)
                IA_L = -(tt[1,1]/(tt[1,1]+tt[1,2]))*log(tt[1,1]/(tt[1,1]+tt[1,2]))
                        -(tt[1,2]/(tt[1,1]+tt[1,2]))*log(tt[1,2]/(tt[1,1]+tt[1,2]))
                IA_R = -(tt[2,1]/(tt[2,1]+tt[2,2]))*log(tt[2,1]/(tt[2,1]+tt[2,2]))
                        -(tt[2,2]/(tt[2,1]+tt[2,2]))*log(tt[2,2]/(tt[2,1]+tt[2,2]))
                pA_L = (tt[1,1]+tt[1,2])/sum(tt)
                pA_R = (tt[2,1]+tt[2,2])/sum(tt)
                pA = mean(y)
                IA = -pA*log(pA)-(1-pA)*log(1-pA)
                delta_ISA[i] = IA -pA_L*IA_L - pA_R*IA_R
                                                                }
                else delta_ISA[i]=0
                                      }
        return(list(xnode=xu[which(delta_ISA==max(delta_ISA,na.rm=T))],
        max_delta_ISA = max(delta_ISA,na.rm=T), delta_ISA,xu))
                        }
```

In the preceding function, the key functions would be `unique`, `table`, and `log`. We use `unique` to ensure that the search is carried for the distinct elements of the predictor values in the data. `table` gets the required counts as discussed earlier in this section. The `if` condition ensures that neither the p nor 1-p values become 0, in which respective cases the logs become minus infinity. The rest of the coding is self-explanatory. Let us now get our first best split.

5. We will need a few data manipulations to ensure that our R code works on the expected lines:

```
KYPHOSIS <- kyphosis
KYPHOSIS$Kyphosis_y <- (kyphosis$Kyphosis=="absent")*1
```

6. To find the first best split among the three variables, execute the following code; the output is given in a consolidated screenshot after all the iterations:

```
getNode(KYPHOSIS$Age,KYPHOSIS$Kyphosis_y)[[2]]
getNode(KYPHOSIS$Number,KYPHOSIS$Kyphosis_y)[[2]]
getNode(KYPHOSIS$Start,KYPHOSIS$Kyphosis_y)[[2]]
getNode(KYPHOSIS$Start,KYPHOSIS$Kyphosis_y)[[1]]
sort(getNode(KYPHOSIS$Start,KYPHOSIS$Kyphosis_y)[[4]],
decreasing=FALSE)
```

Now, getNode indicates that the best split occurs for the Start variable, and the point for the best split is 12. Keeping in line with the argument of the previous section, we split the data into two parts accordingly, as the Start value is greater than the average of 12 and 13. For the partitioned data, the search proceeds in a recursive fashion.

7. Partition the data accordingly, as the Start values are greater than 12.5, and find the best split for the right daughter node, as the tree display shows that a search in the left daughter node is not necessary:

```
KYPHOSIS_FS_R <- KYPHOSIS[KYPHOSIS$Start<12.5,]
KYPHOSIS_FS_L <- KYPHOSIS[KYPHOSIS$Start>=12.5,]
getNode(KYPHOSIS_FS_R$Age,KYPHOSIS_FS_R$Kyphosis_y)[[2]]
getNode(KYPHOSIS_FS_R$Number,KYPHOSIS_FS_R$Kyphosis_y)[[2]]
getNode(KYPHOSIS_FS_R$Start,KYPHOSIS_FS_R$Kyphosis_y)[[2]]
getNode(KYPHOSIS_FS_R$Age,KYPHOSIS_FS_R$Kyphosis_y)[[1]]
sort(getNode(KYPHOSIS_FS_R$Age,KYPHOSIS_FS_R$Kyphosis_y)[[4]],
decreasing=FALSE)
```

The maximum incremental value occurs for the predictor Age, and the split point is 27. Again, we take the average of the 27 and next highest value of 42, which turns out as 34.5. The (first) right daughter node region is then partitioned in two parts accordingly, as the Age values are greater than 34.5, and the search for next split continues in the current right daughter part.

8. The following code completes our search:

```
KYPHOSIS_FS_R_SS_R <- KYPHOSIS_FS_R[KYPHOSIS_FS_R$Age>=34.5,]
KYPHOSIS_FS_R_SS_L <- KYPHOSIS_FS_R[KYPHOSIS_FS_R$Age<34.5,]
getNode(KYPHOSIS_FS_R_SS_R$Age,KYPHOSIS_FS_R_SS_R$Kyphosis_y)[[2]]
getNode(KYPHOSIS_FS_R_SS_R$Number,KYPHOSIS_FS_R_SS_R$
Kyphosis_y)[[2]]
getNode(KYPHOSIS_FS_R_SS_R$Start,KYPHOSIS_FS_R_SS_R$
Kyphosis_y)[[2]]
```

```
getNode(KYPHOSIS_FS_R_SS_R$Number,KYPHOSIS_FS_R_SS_R$
Kyphosis_y)[[1]]
sort(getNode(KYPHOSIS_FS_R_SS_R$Number,KYPHOSIS_FS_R_SS_R$
Kyphosis_y)[[4]],
decreasing=FALSE)
```

We see that the final split occurs for the predictor `Number` and the split is 4, and we again stop at 4.5.

We see that results from our raw code completely agree with the `rpart` function. Thus, the efforts of writing a custom code for the classification tree have paid appropriate dividends. We now have enough clarity for the construction of the classification tree:

```
> KYPHOSIS <- kyphosis
> KYPHOSIS$Kyphosis_y <- (kyphosis$Kyphosis=="absent")*1
> getNode(KYPHOSIS$Age,KYPHOSIS$Kyphosis_y)[[2]]
[1] 12.31
> getNode(KYPHOSIS$Number,KYPHOSIS$Kyphosis_y)[[2]]
[1] 12
> getNode(KYPHOSIS$Start,KYPHOSIS$Kyphosis_y)[[2]]
[1] 10.05
> getNode(KYPHOSIS$Start,KYPHOSIS$Kyphosis_y)[[1]]
[1] 8
> sort(getNode(KYPHOSIS$Start,KYPHOSIS$Kyphosis_y)[[4]],
+ decreasing=FALSE)
 [1]  1  2  3  5  6  8  9 10 11 12 13 14 15 16 17 18
> KYPHOSIS_FS_R <- KYPHOSIS[KYPHOSIS$Start<12.5,]
> KYPHOSIS_FS_L <- KYPHOSIS[KYPHOSIS$Start>=12.5,]
> getNode(KYPHOSIS_FS_R$Age,KYPHOSIS_FS_R$Kyphosis_y)[[2]]
[1] 7.06
> getNode(KYPHOSIS_FS_R$Number,KYPHOSIS_FS_R$Kyphosis_y)[[2]]
[1] 7.729
> getNode(KYPHOSIS_FS_R$Start,KYPHOSIS_FS_R$Kyphosis_y)[[2]]
[1] 7.632
> getNode(KYPHOSIS_FS_R$Age,KYPHOSIS_FS_R$Kyphosis_y)[[1]]
[1] 27
> sort(getNode(KYPHOSIS_FS_R$Age,KYPHOSIS_FS_R$Kyphosis_y)[[4]],
+ decreasing=FALSE)
 [1]    1   2   8  15  17  18  20  27  42  51  52  59  61  68  71  73  81  91  96
[20] 105 114 120 121 125 127 128 130 131 139 140 143 206
> KYPHOSIS_FS_R_SS_R <- KYPHOSIS_FS_R[KYPHOSIS_FS_R$Age>=34.5,]
> KYPHOSIS_FS_R_SS_L <- KYPHOSIS_FS_R[KYPHOSIS_FS_R$Age<34.5,]
> getNode(KYPHOSIS_FS_R_SS_R$Age,KYPHOSIS_FS_R_SS_R$Kyphosis_y)[[2]]
[1] 5.091
> getNode(KYPHOSIS_FS_R_SS_R$Number,KYPHOSIS_FS_R_SS_R$Kyphosis_y)[[2]]
[1] 5.686
> getNode(KYPHOSIS_FS_R_SS_R$Start,KYPHOSIS_FS_R_SS_R$Kyphosis_y)[[2]]
[1] 5.733
> getNode(KYPHOSIS_FS_R_SS_R$Number,KYPHOSIS_FS_R_SS_R$Kyphosis_y)[[1]]
[1] 4
> sort(getNode(KYPHOSIS_FS_R_SS_R$Number,KYPHOSIS_FS_R_SS_R$Kyphosis_y)[[4]],
+ decreasing=FALSE)
[1]  2  3  4  5  6  7  9 10
```

Finding the best splits for the classification tree using the getnode function

What just happened?

A deliberate attempt has been made at demystifying the construction of a classification tree. As with the earlier attempt at understanding a regression tree, we first deployed the rpart function, and saw a display of the classification tree for the Kyphosis as a function of Age, Start, and Number, for the choice of the cross-entropy impurity metric. The getNode function is defined on the basis of the same impurity metric and in a very systematic fashion; we reproduced the same tree as obtained by the rpart function.

With the understanding of the basic construction behind us, we will now build the classification tree for the German credit data problem from *Chapter 7, Logistic Regression Model*.

We will now describe how to set up classification and regression trees in Python.

Doing it in Python

First, we try to replicate the classification tree for the CART_Dummy dataset:

1. Using the Pandas read_csv file, import the CART Dummy data. Also, separate the covariates and output too.

```
In [3]: CD = pd.read_csv("Data/CART_Dummy.csv",delimiter=',')
        CD = CD.dropna()

In [4]: CD_X = CD[['X1','X2']]
        CD_Y = CD[['Y']]
```

2. First invoke the required classifier function from the sklearn package in DecisionTreeClassifier, fit it on the data constituents, predict the y's, and then print the fitted object:

```
In [5]: classifier = DecisionTreeClassifier()
        treefit = classifier.fit(CD_X,CD_Y)
        tree_pred = treefit.predict(CD_X)

In [6]: print(treefit)

        DecisionTreeClassifier(class_weight=None, criterion='gini', max_depth=None,
                    max_features=None, max_leaf_nodes=None,
                    min_impurity_split=1e-07, min_samples_leaf=1,
                    min_samples_split=2, min_weight_fraction_leaf=0.0,
                    presort=False, random_state=None, splitter='best')
```

Clearly, the preceding print is nothing but the parameter specified while building the model. Since the `max_leaf_nodes` is unspecified, by default `DecisionTreeClassifier` keeps on splitting the tree until each observations is perfectly classified.

The fitted classification tree can be printed at the Notebook console itself by using a new function defined by an Python user "paulkernfeld" on the web `https://stackoverflow.com/questions/20224526/how-to-extract-the-decision-rules-from-scikit-learn-decision-tree`. We use the function to print the tree next.

3. Define a new function named as `tree_to_code` as created by Paulkernfeld, and then apply it to the fitted classifier:

```python
def tree_to_code(tree, feature_names):
    from sklearn.tree import _tree
    tree_ = tree.tree_
    feature_name = [
        feature_names[i] if i != _tree.TREE_UNDEFINED else "undefined!"
        for i in tree_.feature
    ]
    print("def tree({}):".format(", ".join(feature_names)))
    def recurse(node, depth):
        indent = "  " * depth
        if tree_.feature[node] != _tree.TREE_UNDEFINED:
            name = feature_name[node]
            threshold = tree_.threshold[node]
            print("{}if {} <= {}:".format(indent, name, threshold))
            recurse(tree_.children_left[node], depth + 1)
            print("{}else:  # if {} > {}".format(indent, name, threshold))
            recurse(tree_.children_right[node], depth + 1)
        else:
            print("{}return {}".format(indent, tree_.value[node]))
    recurse(0, 1)
```

```
In [8]: tree_to_code(treefit,['X1','X2'])

def tree(X1, X2):
  if X2 <= 4.875:
    if X1 <= 10.875:
      if X2 <= 0.875:
        return [[ 0.   1.]]


      if X1 <= 2.25:
        return [[ 0.   3.]]
      else:  # if X1 > 2.25
        return [[ 1.   0.]]
    else:  # if X2 > 6.5
      return [[ 5.   0.]]
  else:  # if X1 > 4.5
    if X1 <= 10.625:
      return [[ 0.   12.]]
    else:  # if X1 > 10.625
      return [[ 1.   0.]]
```

Note that we have curtailed the output and made it representative of the actual one. The reader can either run the codes in their Python session or refer to this chapter's notebook `Chapter_09_Classification_and_Regression_Trees.ipynb`.

Visualizing the classification tree is an important task. An open source like Python gives too many options to perform the same task.

In our approach, we will first export data related to the classification tree to a Microsoft Word format.

 A software program useful for visualizing the tree is `graphviz` and it can be downloaded from `http://www.graphviz.org/Download_windows.php`.

The user needs to download and install this software. For Ubuntu users, the procedure is similar, though we provide only Windows implementation. Please refer to the comments in cell 9 and 10 of `Chapter_09_Classification_and_Regression_Trees.ipynb`.

4. Extract the information in fitted tree and export it using the `tree.export_graphviz` function:

```
In [9]: tree.export_graphviz(treefit,out_file='tree1.doc')
```

The export process for a Windows doc file is:

1. The exported Word file `tree1.doc` would be found in the current working directory.

2. On executing and completing the installation of graphviz software in Windows, you would have an icon GVEdit in the list of installed software.

3. The reader should open it and then hit *Ctrl+O* and go to the current directory and load the `tree1.doc` file.

The action will result in the creation of a classification tree that looks as follows:

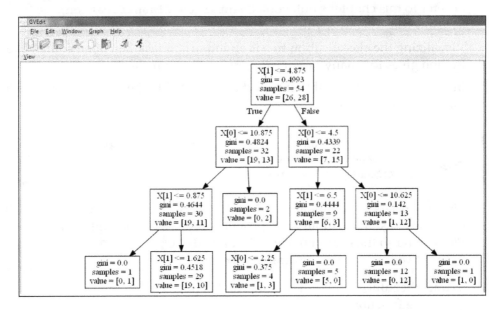

5. Of course, the tree is incomplete. Note that, by using the default settings, we will have 100% classification accuracy as the tree grows until each node has 100% accuracy. We next show how to plot the classification trees by exporting the file as a pdf file. The Python package `pydotplus` would be useful here. Following the installation of `graphviz` software, change the path settings as:

```
In [11]:  import os
          os.environ["PATH"] += os.pathsep + 'C:/Program Files (x86)/Graphviz2.38/bin/'
```

Note that the path might depend on your local settings.

6. The `pydotplus` package is central to setting the plots and exporting the tree to a pdf file:

```
import pydotplus
from sklearn.externals.six import StringIO
dot_data = StringIO()
tree.export_graphviz(treefit,out_file=dot_data)
graph = pydotplus.graph_from_dot_data(dot_data.getvalue())
graph.write_pdf("Output/CART_Illus.pdf")
```

The user may either refer to the file `CART_Illus.pdf`, or run the codes and generate the file.

7. Using the `DecisionTreeRegressor`, we can create regression trees in Python. The program syntax changes only slightly to accommodate the regression aspect, instead of the classification problem.

```
In [14]:  cpus = pd.read_csv("Data/cpus.csv",delimiter=',')
          perf10 = np.log10(cpus[['perf']])
          cpusX = cpus[['syct','mmin','mmax','cach','chmin','chmax']]

In [15]:  regressor = tree.DecisionTreeRegressor()
          cpus_fit = regressor.fit(cpusX,perf10)
          cpus_data = StringIO()
          tree.export_graphviz(cpus_fit,out_file=cpus_data,feature_names=list(cpusX))
          cpus_graph = pydotplus.graph_from_dot_data(cpus_data.getvalue())
          cpus_graph.write_pdf("Output/CPUS_Tree.pdf")

Out[15]:  True
```

The program is straightforward to explain. The regression tree growth is similar to that in its classification counterpart implementation. We will skip the illustration of the Kyphosis classification tree, though its program, notebook, and associated tree in PDF file are all available.

Classification tree for the German credit data

In *Chapter 7, Logistic Regression Model*, we constructed a logistic regression model, and, in the previous chapter, we obtained the ridge regression version for the German credit data problem. However, problems such as these and many others may have non-linearity built in them, and it is looking at the same problem by using a classification tree.

Also, we saw another model performance of the German credit data using the train, validate, and test approach. We will employ the following approach. First, we will partition the German dataset into three parts, namely `train`, `validate`, and `test`. The classification tree will be built by using the data in train set, and then it will be applied on the validate part. The corresponding ROC curves will be visualized, and, if we feel that the two curves are reasonably similar, we will apply it on the test region, and take the necessary action of sanctioning the customers, required loans.

Time for action – the construction of a classification tree

A classification tree is now built for the German credit data by using the rpart function. The approach of train, validate, and test is implemented, and the ROC curves are obtained too:

1. The following code has been used earlier in this book, so there won't be an explanation of it here:

```
set.seed(1234567)
data_part_label <- c("Train","Validate","Test")
indv_label = sample(data_part_label,size=1000,replace=TRUE,prob
=c(0.6,0.2,0.2))
library(ROCR)
data(GC)
GC_Train <- GC[indv_label=="Train",]
GC_Validate <- GC[indv_label=="Validate",]
GC_Test <- GC[indv_label=="Test",]
```

2. Create the classification tree for the German credit data, and visualize the tree. We will also extract the rules from this classification tree:

```
GC_rpart <- rpart(good_bad~.,data=GC_Train)
plot(GC_rpart); text(GC_rpart)
asRules(GC_rpart)
```

The classification tree for the German credit data appears as in the following screenshot:

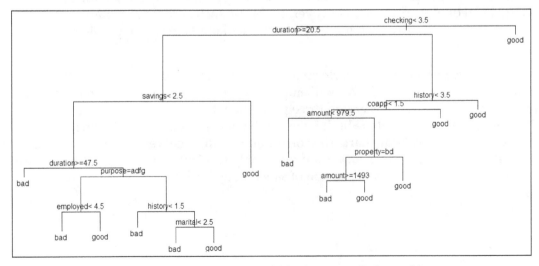

Classification tree for the test part of the German credit data problem

By now, we know how to find the rules of this tree. An edited version of the rules is given as follows:

```
Rule number: 21 [good_bad=good cover=20 (3%) prob=1.00]
  checking< 3.5
  duration< 20.5
  history< 3.5
  coapp>=1.5
Rule number: 3 [good_bad=good cover=244 (41%) prob=0.89]
  checking>=3.5
Rule number: 11 [good_bad=good cover=41 (7%) prob=0.88]
  checking< 3.5
  duration< 20.5
  history>=3.5
Rule number: 143 [good_bad=good cover=25 (4%) prob=0.84]
  checking< 3.5
  duration>=20.5
  savings< 2.5
  duration< 47.5
  purpose=1,2,9
  history>=1.5
  marital>=2.5
Rule number: 9 [good_bad=good cover=37 (6%) prob=0.73]
  checking< 3.5
  duration>=20.5
  savings>=2.5
Rule number: 69 [good_bad=good cover=11 (2%) prob=0.73]
  checking< 3.5
  duration>=20.5
  savings< 2.5
  duration< 47.5
  purpose=0,3,5,6
  employed>=4.5
Rule number: 83 [good_bad=good cover=69 (12%) prob=0.72]
  checking< 3.5
  duration< 20.5
  history< 3.5
  coapp< 1.5
  amount>=979.5
  property=1,3
Rule number: 165 [good_bad=good cover=11 (2%) prob=0.64]
  checking< 3.5
  duration< 20.5
  history< 3.5
  coapp< 1.5
  amount>=979.5
  property=2,4
  amount< 1493

Rule number: 142 [good_bad=bad cover=14 (2%) prob=0.36]
  checking< 3.5
  duration>=20.5
  savings< 2.5
  duration< 47.5
  purpose=1,2,9
  history>=1.5
  marital< 2.5
Rule number: 70 [good_bad=bad cover=12 (2%) prob=0.33]
  checking< 3.5
  duration>=20.5
  savings< 2.5
  duration< 47.5
  purpose=1,2,9
  history< 1.5
Rule number: 40 [good_bad=bad cover=28 (5%) prob=0.32]
  checking< 3.5
  duration< 20.5
  history< 3.5
  coapp< 1.5
  amount< 979.5
Rule number: 164 [good_bad=bad cover=19 (3%) prob=0.26]
  checking< 3.5
  duration< 20.5
  history< 3.5
  coapp< 1.5
  amount>=979.5
  property=2,4
  amount>=1493
Rule number: 68 [good_bad=bad cover=46 (8%) prob=0.17]
  checking< 3.5
  duration>=20.5
  savings< 2.5
  duration< 47.5
  purpose=0,3,5,6
  employed< 4.5
Rule number: 16 [good_bad=bad cover=22 (4%) prob=0.09]
  checking< 3.5
  duration>=20.5
  savings< 2.5
  duration>=47.5
```

Rules for the German credit data

3. We use the tree given in the previous step on the validate region, and plot the ROC for both the regions:

```
Pred_Train_Class <- predict(GC_rpart,type='class')
Pred_Train_Prob <- predict(GC_rpart,type='prob')
Train_Pred <- prediction(Pred_Train_Prob[,2],GC_Train$good_bad)
Perf_Train <- performance(Train_Pred,"tpr","fpr")
plot(Perf_Train,col="green",lty=2)
Pred_Validate_Class<-predict(GC_rpart,newdata=GC_Validate[,-
21],type='class')
Pred_Validate_Prob<-predict(GC_rpart,newdata=GC_Validate[,-
21],type='prob')
Validate_Pred<-prediction(Pred_Validate_Prob[,2], GC_
Validate$good_bad)
Perf_Validate <- performance(Validate_Pred,"tpr","fpr")
plot(Perf_Validate,col="yellow",lty=2,add=TRUE)
```

We will go ahead and predict for the test part too.

4. The necessary code is as follows:

```
Pred_Test_Class<-predict(GC_rpart,newdata=GC_Test[,-
21],type='class')
Pred_Test_Prob<-predict(GC_rpart,newdata=GC_Test[,-
21],type='prob')
Test_Pred<- prediction(Pred_Test_Prob[,2],GC_Test$good_bad)
Perf_Test<- performance(Test_Pred,"tpr","fpr")
plot(Perf_Test,col="red",lty=2,add=TRUE)
legend(0.6,0.5,c("Train Curve","ValidateCurve","Test Curve"),col=c
("green","yellow","red"),pch="-")
```

The final ROC curve looks like the following screenshot:

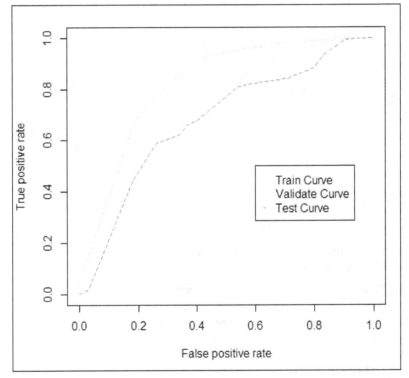

ROC Curves for German Credit Data

The performance of the classification tree is certainly not satisfactory with the validate group itself. The only solace here is that the test curve is a bit like the validate curve. We will look at more up-to-date ways of improving the basic classification tree in the next chapter.

The classification tree in the figure, *Classification tree for the test part of the German credit data problem*, is very large and complex, and we sometimes need to truncate the tree to make the classification method a bit simpler. Of course, one of the things that we should suspect whenever we look at very large trees, is that maybe we are again having the problem of overfitting. The final section deals with a simplistic method of overcoming the problem.

What just happened?

A classification tree has been built for the German credit dataset. The ROC curve shows that the tree does not perform well on the validate data part. In the next and concluding section, we look at the two ways of improving this tree.

Next, we provide the Python implementation for the German credit data problem.

Doing it in Python

The complete analysis of German credit data is now carried out in Python:

1. Using the Pandas `read_csv` file, import the German credit data. We separate the covariates and output too.

2. The dataset is partitioned into train and test parts using the test `train_test_split` function.

```
In [19]: GC = pd.read_csv("Data/GC2.csv",delimiter=',')
         y = GC[['good_bad']]
         X = GC.iloc[:,0:20]
         n_classes = y.shape[1]

In [20]: X_train, X_test, y_train, y_test = train_test_split(X, y, test_size=.2, random_state=0)
```

3. Using the `DecisionTreeClassifier` we build a decision tree based on `X_train` and `y_train`. The decision tree is exported as `GC_Tree.pdf` and the predictions based on `X_train` and `X_test` are obtained for setting up the ROC curves:

```
In [21]:  classifier = DecisionTreeClassifier(max_depth=7,min_samples_split=10)
          GC_Fit = classifier.fit(X_train, y_train)
          y_train_pred = GC_Fit.predict(X_train)
          y_test_pred = GC_Fit.predict(X_test)

In [22]:  GC_data = StringIO()
          tree.export_graphviz(GC_Fit,out_file=GC_data,feature_names = list(X))
          GC_graph = pydotplus.graph_from_dot_data(GC_data.getvalue())
          GC_graph.write_pdf("Output/GC_Tree.pdf")
```

Note the difference in specification of `DecisionTreeClassifier` here from the earlier instances. The purpose is to ensure that we don't have an over-fitted tree.

Using the `roc_curve` function, as earlier, the ROC curves are plotted as shown in the following figure:

```
In [23]:  fpr_train, tpr_train, thresholds = roc_curve(y_train,y_train_pred)
          fpr_test, tpr_test, thresholds = roc_curve(y_test,y_test_pred)
          roc_auc_train = auc(fpr_train,tpr_train)
          roc_auc_test = auc(fpr_test,tpr_test)
          print("Area under the ROC Curve for Train Data is : %f" % roc_auc_train)
          print("Area under the ROC Curve for Test Data is : %f" % roc_auc_test)

          Area under the ROC Curve for Train Data is : 0.805467
          Area under the ROC Curve for Test Data is : 0.620083

In [24]:  plt.plot(fpr_train,tpr_train,color='red',lw=2,label='ROC Curve')
          plt.plot(fpr_test,tpr_test,color='green',lw=2)
          plt.plot([0,1],[0,1],color='blue',lw=2,linestyle='--')
          plt.show()
```

Have a go hero

Using the `getNode` function, verify the first five splits of the classification tree for the German credit data.

Pruning and other finer aspects of a tree

Recall from the figure, *Classification tree for the test part of the German credit data problem*, in the *Time for action – the construction of a classification tree* section, that the rules numbered `21, 143, 69, 165, 142, 70, 40, 164,` and `16`, respectively, cover only `20, 25, 11, 11, 14, 12, 28, 19,` and `22`. If we look at the total number of observations, we have about 600, and individually these rules do not even cover about five percent of them.

This is one reason to suspect that maybe we overfit the data. Using the option of `minsplit`, we can restrict the minimum number of observations each rule should cover at the least.

Another technical way of reducing the complexity of a classification tree is by "pruning" the tree. Here, the least important splits are recursively snipped off according to the complexity parameter.

[For details, refer to *Breiman, et. al. (1984)*, or Section 3.6 of *Berk (2008)*.]

We will illustrate the action through the R program.

Time for action – pruning a classification tree

A CART is improved by using `minsplit` and `cp` arguments in the `rpart` function:

1. Invoke the graphics editor with `par(mfrow=c(1,2))`.

2. Specify `minsplit=30`, and re-do the ROC plots by using the new classification tree:

```
GC_rpart_minsplit<- rpart(good_bad~.,data=GC_Train, minsplit=30)
GC_rpart_minsplit <- prune(GC_rpart,cp=0.05)
Pred_Train_Class<- predict(GC_rpart_minsplit,type='class')
Pred_Train_Prob<-predict(GC_rpart_minsplit,type='prob')
Train_Pred<- prediction(Pred_Train_Prob[,2],GC_Train$good_bad)
Perf_Train<- performance(Train_Pred,"tpr","fpr")
```

```
plot(Perf_Train,col="green",lty=2)
Pred_Validate_Class<-predict(GC_rpart_minsplit,newdata=GC_
Validate[,-21],type='class')
Pred_Validate_Prob<-predict(GC_rpart_minsplit,newdata= GC_
Validate[,-21],type='prob')
Validate_Pred<- prediction(Pred_Validate_Prob[,2],GC_
Validate$good_bad)
Perf_Validate<- performance(Validate_Pred,"tpr","fpr")
plot(Perf_Validate,col="yellow",lty=2,add=TRUE)
Pred_Test_Class<- predict(GC_rpart_minsplit,newdata = GC_Test[,-
21],type='class')
Pred_Test_Prob<-predict(GC_rpart_minsplit,newdata = GC_Test[,-
21],type='prob')
Test_Pred<- prediction(Pred_Test_Prob[,2],GC_Test$good_bad)
Perf_Test<- performance(Test_Pred,"tpr","fpr")
plot(Perf_Test,col="red",lty=2,add=TRUE)
legend(0.6,0.5,c("Train Curve","ValidateCurve","Test Curve"),col=c
("green","yellow","red"),pch="-")
title(main="Improving a Classification Tree with "minsplit"")
```

3. For the pruning factor cp=0.02, repeat the ROC plot exercise:

```
GC_rpart_prune <- prune(GC_rpart,cp=0.02)
Pred_Train_Class<- predict(GC_rpart_prune,type='class')
Pred_Train_Prob<-predict(GC_rpart_prune,type='prob')
Train_Pred<- prediction(Pred_Train_Prob[,2],GC_Train$good_bad)
Perf_Train<- performance(Train_Pred,"tpr","fpr")
plot(Perf_Train,col="green",lty=2)
Pred_Validate_Class<-predict(GC_rpart_prune,newdata = GC_
Validate[,-21],type='class')
Pred_Validate_Prob<-predict(GC_rpart_prune,newdata = GC_
Validate[,-21],type='prob')
Validate_Pred<- prediction(Pred_Validate_Prob[,2],GC_
Validate$good_bad)
Perf_Validate<- performance(Validate_Pred,"tpr","fpr")
plot(Perf_Validate,col="yellow",lty=2,add=TRUE)
Pred_Test_Class<- predict(GC_rpart_prune,newdata = GC_Test[,-
21],type='class')
Pred_Test_Prob<-predict(GC_rpart_prune,newdata = GC_Test[,-
21],type='prob')
Test_Pred<- prediction(Pred_Test_Prob[,2],GC_Test$good_bad)
Perf_Test<- performance(Test_Pred,"tpr","fpr")
plot(Perf_Test,col="red",lty=2,add=TRUE)
legend(0.6,0.5,c("Train Curve","ValidateCurve","Test Curve"),col=c
("green","yellow","red"),pch="-")
title(main="Improving a Classification Tree with Pruning")
```

The choice of `cp=0.02` has been drawn from the plot of the complexity parameter and the relative error; try it yourselves with `plotcp(GC_rpart)`.

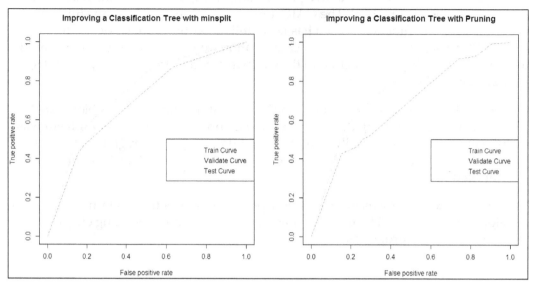

Pruning the CART

What just happened?

Using the `minsplit` and `cp` options, we have managed to obtain a reduced set of rules, and, in that sense, the fitted model does not appear to be an overfit. The ROC curves show that there has been considerable improvement in the performance of the validate region. Again, as earlier, the validate and test region have a similar ROC, and it is hence preferable to use `GC_rpart_prune` or `GC_rpart_minsplit` over `GC_rpart`.

Pop quiz

With the experience of model selection from the previous chapter, justify the choice of `cp=0.02` from the plot obtained as a result of running `plotcp(GC_rpart)`.

Summary

We began with the idea of recursive partitioning and gave a legitimate reason why such an approach is practical. The CART technique is completely demystified by using the getNode function, which has been defined appropriately, depending upon whether we require a regression or a classification tree. With the conviction behind us, we applied the rpart function to the German credit data, and with its results, we basically had two problems.

First, the fitted classification tree appeared to overfit the data. This problem can often be overcome by using the minsplit and cp options. The second problem was that the performance was really poor in the validate region. Though the reduced classification trees had slightly better performance as compared to the initial tree, we still need to improve the classification tree.

The next chapter will focus more on this aspect and discuss the modern development of CART. The user can now develop decision trees using either of the two software programs.

10
CART and Beyond

In the previous chapter, we studied CART as a powerful recursive partitioning method, useful for building (nonlinear) models. Despite the overall generality, CART does have certain limitations that necessitate some enhancements. It is these extensions that form the crux of the final chapter of the book. For technical reasons, we will focus solely on the classification trees in this chapter. We will also briefly look at some limitations of the CART tool.

One improvement of the CART is provided by the **bagging** technique. In this technique, we build multiple trees on the bootstrap samples drawn from the actual dataset. An observation is put through each of the trees and a prediction is made for its class, and, based on the majority prediction of its class, it is predicted to belong to the majority count class. A different approach is provided by **random forests**, where one compares a random pool of covariates against the observations. We finally consider another important enhancement of a CART by using **boosting algorithms**. The chapter will cover the following topics:

- Cross-validation errors for CART
- The bootstrap aggregation (bagging) technique for CART
- Extending the CART with random forests
- A consolidation of the applications developed from *Chapter 6, Linear Regression Analysis,* to *Chapter 10, CART and Beyond*

Packages and settings – R and Python

As this chapter reviews some of the techniques in the latter half of the book, we need lot of packages and functions:

1. First, set the working directory:

```
setwd("MyPath/R/Chapter_10")
```

Load the required R package:

```
library(boot)
library(RSADBE)
library(ipred)
library(randomForest)
library(rpart)
library(rattle)
```

We will only develop the bagging and random forest in Python.

2. A lot of functions are required to set up the bagging and random forest method in Python:

```
In [1]:  import os
         os.chdir("MyPath/Python/Chapter_10")
         import numpy as np
         import pandas as pd
         from sklearn.tree import DecisionTreeClassifier
         from sklearn.ensemble import BaggingClassifier
         from sklearn.ensemble import RandomForestClassifier
         from sklearn.metrics import classification_report
         import sklearn.metrics
         from sklearn import tree
         from sklearn.cross_validation import train_test_split
         from sklearn.preprocessing import label_binarize
         from sklearn.metrics import roc_curve, auc
         import matplotlib.pyplot as plt
         from sklearn.utils import column_or_1d
```

Improving the CART

In the *Another look at model assessment* section of *Chapter 8, Regression Models with Regularization*, we saw that the technique of train, validate, and test may be further enhanced by using the cross-validation technique. In the case of the linear regression model, we used the CVlm function from the DAAG package for the purpose of cross-validation of linear models. The cross-validation technique for the logistic regression models may be carried out by using the CVbinary function from the same package.

> Professors, *Therneau* and *Atkinson* have created the package
> rpart, and a detailed documentation of the entire rpart
> package is available on the web at https://cran.r-
> project.org/web/packages/rpart/vignettes/
> longintro.pdf.

Consider the slight improvement provided in the *Pruning and other finer aspects of a tree* section of the previous chapter. The two aspects considered there related to the complexity parameter cp and the minimum split criterion minsplit. Now the problem of overfitting with the CART may be reduced to an extent by using the cross-validation technique.

In the ridge regression model, we had the problem of selecting the penalty factor λ. Similarly, here we have the problem of selecting the complexity parameter, though not in an analogous way. That is, if the complexity parameter is a number between 0 and 1, then we need to obtain the predictions based on the cross-validation technique. This may lead to minor loss of accuracy; however, we will then have gained an advantage in looking at the generality.

An object of the rpart class has many summaries contained within, and the various complexity parameters are stored in the cptable matrix. This matrix has values for the following metrics: CP, nsplit, rel error, xerror, and xstd. Let us understand this matrix through the default example in the rpart package, which is example(xpred.rpart). See the following figure:

```
> example(xpred.rpart)
xprd.r> fit <- rpart(Mileage ~ Weight, car.test.frame)
xprd.r> xmat <- xpred.rpart(fit)
xprd.r> xerr <- (xmat - car.test.frame$Mileage)^2
xprd.r> apply(xerr, 2, sum)    # cross-validated error estimate
0.79767 0.28300 0.04154 0.01133
 1394.6   756.1   551.9   538.2
xprd.r> # approx same result as rel. error from printcp(fit)
xprd.r> apply(xerr, 2, sum)/var(car.test.frame$Mileage)
0.79767 0.28300 0.04154 0.01133
  60.74   32.93   24.04   23.44
xprd.r> printcp(fit)
Regression tree:
rpart(formula = Mileage ~ Weight, data = car.test.frame)
Variables actually used in tree construction:
[1] Weight
Root node error: 1355/60 = 23
n= 60
      CP nsplit rel error xerror  xstd
1 0.595      0      1.00   1.04 0.180
2 0.135      1      0.40   0.59 0.087
3 0.013      2      0.27   0.45 0.076
4 0.010      3      0.26   0.44 0.076
```

Understanding the example for xpred.rpart function

Here, the tree has the CP at four values, namely $0.595, 0.135, 0.013$, and 0.010. The corresponding nsplit numbers are $0, 1, 2$, and 3, and similarly, the relative error values xerror and xstd are given in the last part of the previous screenshot. The interpretation for the CP value is slightly different, the reason being that these have to be considered as ranges and not values, in the sense that the rest of the performance is not with respect to the CP values, as mentioned previously; rather, they are with respect to the intervals $[0.595, 1], [0.135, 0.595), [0.013, 0.135),$ and $[0.010, 0.013)$; see ?xpred.rpart for more information. Now, the function xpred.rpart returns the predictions based on the cross-validated technique.

Thus, we will use this function for the German data problem and for different CP values — or rather ranges — and obtain the accuracy of the cross-validation technique.

Time for action – cross-validation predictions

We use the xpred.rpart function from rpart for obtaining the cross-validation predictions from a rpart object:

1. Load the German dataset and the rpart package with data(GC); library(rpart).

2. Fit the classification tree with GC_Complete <- rpart(good_bad~., data=GC).

3. Check cptable with GC_Complete$cptable:

```
       CP nsplit rel error xerror    xstd
1 0.05167      0    1.0000 1.0000 0.04830
2 0.04667      3    0.8400 0.9833 0.04807
3 0.01833      4    0.7933 0.8900 0.04663
4 0.01667      6    0.7567 0.8933 0.04669
5 0.01556      8    0.7233 0.8800 0.04646
6 0.01000     11    0.6767 0.8833 0.04652
```

4. Obtain the cross-validation predictions with GC_CV_Pred <- xpred.rpart(GC_Complete).

5. Find the accuracy of the cross-validation predictions:

```
sum(diag(table(GC_CV_Pred[,2],GC$good_bad)))/1000
sum(diag(table(GC_CV_Pred[,3],GC$good_bad)))/1000
sum(diag(table(GC_CV_Pred[,4],GC$good_bad)))/1000
sum(diag(table(GC_CV_Pred[,5],GC$good_bad)))/1000
sum(diag(table(GC_CV_Pred[,6],GC$good_bad)))/1000
```

6. The accuracy output is as follows:

```
> sum(diag(table(GC_CV_Pred[,2],GC$good_bad)))/1000
[1] 0.71
> sum(diag(table(GC_CV_Pred[,3],GC$good_bad)))/1000
[1] 0.744
> sum(diag(table(GC_CV_Pred[,4],GC$good_bad)))/1000
[1] 0.734
> sum(diag(table(GC_CV_Pred[,5],GC$good_bad)))/1000
[1] 0.74
> sum(diag(table(GC_CV_Pred[,6],GC$good_bad)))/1000
[1] 0.741
```

It is natural that, when you execute the same code, you will most likely have a different output! Why? Also, you need to answer for yourselves why we did not check the accuracy of GC_CV_Pred[,1]. In general, for decreasing the CP range, we expect higher accuracy. We have checked the cross-validation predictions for various CP ranges. There are other techniques to enhance the performance of a CART.

What just happened?

We used the xpred.rpart function to obtain the cross-validation predictions for a range of the CP values. The accuracy of a prediction model has been assessed by using simple functions, such as table and diag.

However, the control actions of minsplit and cp are of a reactive nature after the splits have already been decided. In that sense, when we have a large number of covariates, the CART may lead to an overfit of the data and may try to capture all the local variations of the data, and thus lose sight of the overall generality. Thus, we need useful mechanisms to overcome this problem.

The classification and regression tree covered in the previous chapter is a single model. That is, we are seeking the opinion (prediction) of a single model. Wouldn't it be nice if we could extend this? Alternatively, we can seek multiple models instead of a single model. What does this mean? In the forthcoming sections, we will examine the use of multiple models for the same problem.

Understanding bagging

Bagging is an abbreviation for **bootstrap aggregation**. The important underlying concept here is the bootstrap, which was invented by the eminent scientist Bradley Efron. We will first digress here slightly from the CART technique and consider a very brief illustration of the bootstrap technique.

The bootstrap

Consider a random sample $X_1, ..., X_n$ of size n from $f(x, \theta)$. Let $T(X_1, ..., X_n)$ be an estimator of θ. To begin with, we first draw a random sample of size n from $X_1, ..., X_n$ with a replacement; that is, we obtain a random sample $X_1^*, X_2^*, ..., X_n^*$, where some of the observations from the original sample may have repetitions and some may not be present at all. There is no one-to-one correspondence between $X_1, ..., X_n$ and $X_1^*, X_2^*, ..., X_n^*$. Using $X_1^*, X_2^*, ..., X_n^*$, we compute $T^1(X_1^*, ..., X_n^*)$. Repeat this exercise several times, say B. The inference for θ is carried out by using the sampling distribution of the bootstrap samples $T^1(X_1^*, ..., X_n^*)$, ..., $T^B(X_1^*, ..., X_n^*)$.

Let us illustrate the concept of the bootstrap with the famous aspirin example; see *Chapter 8* of *Tattar, et. al. (2013)*. A surprising double-blind experiment conducted by the New York Times indicated that an aspirin consumed on alternate days significantly reduces the rate of heart attacks. In their experiment, 104 out of 11,034 healthy middle-aged men consuming the small doses of aspirin suffered a fatal or non-fatal heart attack, whereas 189 out of 11,037 individuals who were consuming a placebo had a heart attack. Thus, the odds ratio of the aspirin-to-placebo heart attack possibility is `(104 / 11034) / (189 / 11037) = 0.5504`. This indicates that only 55 percent of the number of heart attacks observed for the group taking the placebo is likely to be observed for men consuming small doses of aspirin. That is, the chances of having a heart attack if the person is taking aspirin are almost halved. Given that the experiment is scientific, the results look very promising.

However, we would like to obtain a confidence interval for the odds ratio of the heart attack. If we don't know the sampling distribution of the odds ratio, we can use the bootstrap technique to obtain it. There is another aspect of the aspirin study. It has been observed that the aspirin group had about 119 individuals who had strokes. The number of strokes for the placebo group is 98. Thus, the odds ratio of a stroke is `(114 / 11034) / (98 / 11037) = 1.164`. This is shocking! It says that though the aspirin reduces the possibility of a heart attack, about 16 percent more people are likely to have a stroke when compared to the placebo group.

Now, let's use the bootstrap technique to obtain the confidence intervals for the heart attack as well as the strokes.

Time for action – understanding the bootstrap technique

The boot package, which comes shipped along with R base, will be used for bootstrapping the odds ratio:

1. Get the `boot` package with `library(boot)`.

    The `boot` package is shipped along with the R software itself, and, thus, it does not require separate installation. The main components for the `boot` function will soon be explained.

2. Define the odds ratio function:
    ```
    OR <- function(data,i)    {
    x <- data[,1]; y <- data[,2]
    odds.ratio <- (sum(x[i]==1,na.rm=TRUE)/length(na.omit(x[i])))/
    (sum(y[i]==1,na.rm=TRUE)/length(na.omit(y[i])))
    return(odds.ratio)
                    }
    ```

    The `OR` name stands, of course, for odds-ratio. The data for this function consists of two columns, one of which may have more observations than the other. The option `na.rm` is used to ignore the `NA` data values, whereas the `na.omit` function will remove them. It is easier to see that the `odds.ratio` object does indeed, compute the odds ratio. Note that we have specified `i` as an input to the function `OR`, since this function will be used within boot. Thus, `i` is used to indicate that the odds ratio should be calculated for the ith bootstrap sample. Note that `x[i]` does not reflect the ith element of `x`.

3. Get the data for both the aspirin and placebo groups, and the heart attack and strokes data, with the following code:
    ```
    aspirin_hattack <- c(rep(1,104),rep(0,11037-104))
    placebo_hattack <- c(rep(1,189),rep(0,11034-189))
    aspirin_strokes <- c(rep(1,119),rep(0,11037-119))

    placebo_strokes <- c(rep(1,98),rep(0,11034-98))
    ```

4. Combine the data groups and run 1,000 bootstrap replicates, calculating the odds ratio for each of the bootstrap samples, by using the `boot` function:
    ```
    hattack <- cbind(aspirin_hattack,c(placebo_hattack,NA,NA,NA))
    hattack_boot <- boot(data=hattack,statistic=OR,R=1000)
    strokes <- cbind(aspirin_strokes,c(placebo_strokes,NA,NA,NA))
    strokes_boot <- boot(data=strokes,statistic=OR,R=1000)
    ```

We are using three options of the boot function, namely `data`, `statistic`, and `R`. The first option accepts the data frame of interest, the second one the statistic, either an existing R function or a function defined by the user, and the third option the number of bootstrap replications. The `boot` function creates an object of the `boot` class, and, in this case, we are obtaining the odds ratio for various bootstrap samples.

5. Using the bootstrap samples, and the odds ratio for the bootstrap samples, obtain a 95 percent confidence interval by using the `quantile` function:

    ```
    quantile(hattack_boot$t,c(0.025,0.975))
    quantile(strokes_boot$t,c(0.025,0.975))
    ```

    The 95 percent confidence interval for the odds ratio of the heart attack rate is given as (`0.4763, 0.6269`), while the odds ratio for the strokes is given as (`1.126, 1.333`). Since the point estimates lie in the 95 percent confidence intervals, we accept that the odds ratio of a heart attack for the aspirin tablet group indeed reduces by 55 percent in comparison with the placebo group.

What just happened?

We used the `boot` function from the `boot` package, and obtained bootstrap samples for the problem of the odds-ratio.

Now that we understand the bootstrap technique, let us check out how the bagging algorithm works.

How the bagging algorithm works

Breiman (1996) proposed the extension of CART in the following manner. Suppose that the values of the n random observations for the classification problem are $(y_1, x_1), (y_2, x_2), \ldots, (y_n, x_n)$. As with our setup, the dependent variables y_i are binary. As with the bootstrap technique explained earlier, we obtain a bootstrap sample of size n from the data with the replacement and build a tree. If we prune the tree, it is very likely that we may end up with the same tree on most occasions. Hence, pruning is not advisable here.

Now, using the tree based on the (first) bootstrap sample, a prediction is made for the class of the ith observation and the predicted value is noted. This process is repeated many times, say B. A general practice is to take $B = 100$. Thus, we have B number of predictions for every observation. The goal of the decision process is to classify the observation to the category that has the majority class predictions for it. That is, if more than 50 times out of $B = 100$ it has been predicted to belong to a particular class, we say that the observation is predicted to belong to that class.

Let us formally state the bagging algorithm:

1. Draw a sample of size n with the replacement from the data $(y_1, x_1), (y_2, x_2), \dots, (y_n, x_n)$, and denote the first bootstrap sample with $(y_1, x_1)^1, (y_2, x_2)^1, \dots, (y_i, x_n)^1$.

2. Create a classification tree with $(y_1, x_1)^1, (y_2, x_2)^1, \dots, (y_i, x_n)^1$. Do not prune the classification tree. Such a tree may be called a **bootstrapped tree**.

3. For each terminal node, assign a class, put each observation down the tree, and find its predicted class.

4. Repeat steps 1 to 3 many times, say B.

5. Find the number of times each observation is classified to a particular class out of the B bootstrapped trees. The bagging procedure classifies an observation to belong to a particular class that has the majority count.

6. Compute the confusion table from the predictions made in step 5.

The advantage of multiple trees is that the problem of overfitting, which happens in the case of a single tree, is overcome to a large extent, as we expect that resampling will ensure that the general features are captured and the impact on local features is minimized. Thus, if an observation is classified to belong to a particular class because of a local issue, it will not get repeated over in the other bootstrapped trees. Hence, with predictions based on many trees, it is expected that the final prediction of an observation really depends upon its general features and not on a local feature.

There are some measures that are important to consider with the bagging algorithm. A good classifier, a single tree, or a bunch of them, should be able to predict the class of an observation with more conviction. For example, we use a probability threshold of 0.5 and preceding as a prediction for success when using a logistic regression model. If the model can predict most observations in the neighborhood of either 0 or 1, we will have more confidence in the predictions. Therefore, we will be a bit hesitant to classify an observation as either a success or failure if the predicted probability is near 0.5. This precarious situation applies to the bagging algorithm too.

Suppose we choose $B = 100$ for the number of bagging trees. Assume that an observation belongs to a class `Yes`, and let the overall classes for the study be {`"Yes"`, `"No"`}. If many trees predict that an observation belongs to the `Yes` class, we are confident about the prediction, and that the observation has been classified according to the right class.

On the other hand, if approximately B/2 numbers of trees classify the observation to the Yes class, the decision gets swapped if a few more trees had predicted the observation to belong to the No class. Thus, we introduce a measure called **margin** to refer to the difference between the number of times an observation is correctly classified and the number of times it is incorrectly classified. If the bagging algorithm is a good model, we expect the average margin over all the observations to be a large number away from 0. If bagging is not appropriate, we expect the average margin to be near 0. Let us get ready for action. The bagging algorithm is available in ipred and the randomForests packages.

Time for action – the bagging algorithm

The bagging function from the ipred package will be used for bagging a CART. The options of coob=FALSE and nbagg=200 are used to specify the appropriate options:

1. Get the ipred package by using library(ipred).

2. Load the German credit data by using data(GC).

3. For *B*=200, fit the bagging procedure for the GC data:

```
GC_bagging <- bagging(good_bad~.,data=GC,coob=FALSE,
nbagg=200,keepX=T)
```

We know that we have fit *B*=200 number of trees. Would you like to see them? Fine; here we go.

4. The *B*=200 trees are stored in the mtrees list of classbagg GC_bagging. That is, GC_bagging$mtrees[[i]] gives us the ith bootstrapped tree, and plot(GC_bagging$mtrees[[i]]$btree) displays that tree. Adding text(GC_bagging$mtrees[[i]]$btree,pretty=1, use.n=T) is, of course, important.

Next, put the entire thing in a loop, execute it, and simply sit back and enjoy the display of the *B* number of trees:

```
for(i in 1:200) {
  plot(GC_bagging$mtrees[[i]]$btree);
  text(GC_bagging$mtrees[[i]]$btree,pretty=1,use.n=T)
    }
```

We hope that the reader understands that we can't publish all the 200 trees! The next goal is to obtain the margin of the bagging algorithm.

5. Predict the class probabilities of all the observations with the `predict.classbagg` function by using `GCB_Margin = round(predict( GC_bagging,type="prob")*200,0)`.

   Let us understand the preceding code. The `predict` function returns the probabilities of an observation as belonging to the good and bad classes. We have used `200` trees, and hence multiplying these probabilities with it gives us the expected number of times an observation is predicted to belong to these classes. The `round` function with the `0` argument completes the prediction to integers.

6. Check the first six predicted classes with `head(GCB_Margin)`:

   ```
       bad good
   [1,]  17 183
   [2,] 165  35
   [3,]  11 189
   [4,] 123  77
   [5,] 101  99
   [6,]  95 105
   ```

7. To obtain the overall margin of the bagging technique, use the R code `mean(pmax(GCB_Margin[,1],GCB_Margin[,2]) pmin(GCB_Margin[,1],GCB_Margin[,2]))/200`.

   The overall margin for the author's execution turns out to be `0.5279`. You may, however, get a different answer. Why?

   Thus far, the bagging technique made predictions for the observations from which it also built the model. In the earlier chapters, we championed the need of the validate group and cross-validation techniques. That is, we did not always rely on the model measures solely from the data on which it was built. There is always the possibility of a failure to generalize for unforeseen examples. Can the bagging technique be built to take care of the unforeseen observations?

   The answer is a definite yes, and this is well known as out-of-bag validation. In fact, such an option has been suppressed when building the bagging model in step 3 here (see the option `coob=FALSE`). coob stands for an out-of-bag estimate of the error rate. Rebuild the bagging model with the `coob=TRUE` option.

8. Build an out-of-bag bagging model with `GC_bagging_oob <-` `bagging(good_bad~.,data=GC,coob=TRUE,nbagg=200,keepX=T)`. Find the error-rate with `GC_bagging_oob$err`.

```
> GC_bagging_oob <- bagging(good_bad~.,data=GC,coob=TRUE,
nbagg=200,keepX=T)
> GC_bagging_oob$err
[1] 0.241
```

What just happened?

We have seen an important extension of the CART model in the bagging algorithm. To an extent, this enhancement is vital and vastly different compared with the improvements of earlier models. The bagging algorithm is different, in the sense that we rely on the predictions based on more than a single model. This ensures that the overfitting problem, which occurs due to local features, is almost eliminated.

It is important to note that the bagging technique is not without limitations. The reader may especially refer to *section 4.5 of Berk (2008)*. We now move to the final model of the book, which is an important technique for the CART school.

Doing it in Python

The German credit data should be first imported in Python:

1. Using the pandas `read_csv` file, we import the data:

```
In [3]: GC = pd.read_csv("Data/GC2.csv",delimiter=',')
        y = GC[['good_bad']]
        y = column_or_1d(y, warn=True)
        X = GC.iloc[:,0:20]
```

2. We will partition the German data as we did earlier for the training and test period. Using the classification tree as the base estimator, and with the number of bagging trees set at 500, we complete the bagging setup:

```
In [4]: X_train, X_test, y_train, y_test = train_test_split(X,
                                    y, test_size=.2, random_state=0)

In [5]: cart = DecisionTreeClassifier(max_depth=6,min_samples_leaf=10)
        num_trees = 500
        model = BaggingClassifier(base_estimator=cart,
                        n_estimators=num_trees).fit(X=X_train,y=y_train)
```

3. We next make predictions for the test dataset:

```
In [6]: model.predict(X_test)

Out[6]: array([0, 1, 1, 1, 1, 1, 1, 1, 1, 0, 0, 0, 1, 1, 0, 1, 1, 1, 1, 1, 1, 0, 0,
               1, 1, 0, 1, 1, 1, 0, 1, 1, 1, 1, 1, 0, 1, 1, 1, 1, 1, 0, 1, 1, 1, 0,
               1, 0, 1, 1, 1, 0, 1, 1, 0, 1, 0, 1, 1, 1, 0, 1, 0, 1, 1, 1, 1, 1, 0,
               1, 1, 1, 0, 1, 0, 1, 1, 1, 1, 1, 0, 1, 1, 1, 1, 1, 1, 0, 1, 1, 1, 1,
               1, 1, 1, 1, 0, 1, 1, 1, 1, 1, 1, 1, 0, 0, 0, 1, 1, 0, 0, 1, 1,
               1, 0, 1, 1, 1, 1, 1, 1, 0, 1, 1, 1, 1, 1, 1, 1, 1, 0, 1, 1, 1, 1, 1,
               1, 0, 0, 0, 1, 1, 1, 1, 1, 0, 1, 1, 1, 1, 1, 1, 1, 1, 1, 1, 1, 1, 1,
               1, 1, 1, 0, 0, 0, 1, 1, 1, 0, 1, 0, 1, 1, 0, 0, 1, 1, 1, 1, 0, 1, 0,
               1, 1, 1, 1, 1, 1, 1, 0, 1, 1, 1, 1, 1, 1, 1, 1], dtype=int64)
```

4. Using the `roc_curve` function, we set up the `roc_curves` for the test and training datasets while computing the `tpr` and `fpr` along the way:

```
In [7]: y_train_pred = model.predict(X_train)
        y_test_pred = model.predict(X_test)
        fpr_train, tpr_train, thresholds = roc_curve(y_train, y_train_pred)
        fpr_test, tpr_test, thresholds = roc_curve(y_test, y_test_pred)
        roc_auc_train = auc(fpr_train, tpr_train)
        roc_auc_test = auc(fpr_test, tpr_test)
        print("Area under the ROC Curve for Train Data is : %f" % roc_auc_train)
        print("Area under the ROC Curve for Test Data is : %f" % roc_auc_test)

        Area under the ROC Curve for Train Data is : 0.755902
        Area under the ROC Curve for Test Data is : 0.653715

In [8]: plt.plot(fpr_train,tpr_train,color='red',lw=2,label='ROC Curve')
        plt.plot(fpr_test,tpr_test,color='green',lw=2)
        plt.plot([0,1],[0,1],color='blue',lw=2,linestyle='--')
        plt.show()
```

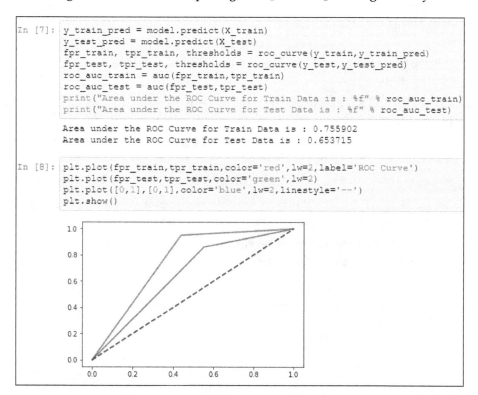

Thus, we are now able to handle the bagging of classification trees in Python.

Random forests

In the previous section, we built multiple models for the same classification problem. The bootstrapped trees were generated by using resamples of the observations. Breiman (2001) suggested an important variation—actually, there is more to it than just a variation—where a CART is built with the covariates (features) being resampled for each of the bootstrapped samples of the dataset. Since the final tree of each bootstrap sample has different covariates, the ensemble of the collective trees is called a **random forest**.

A formal algorithm is given here:

1. As with the bagging algorithm, draw a sample of size $n1$, $n2 < n$, with replacement from the data $(y_1, x_1), (y_2, x_2), ..., (y_n, x_n)$, and denote the first resampled data with $(y_1, x_1)', (y_2, x_2)', ..., (y_i, x_n)'$. The remaining n to $n1$ data forms the `out-of-bag` dataset.

2. Among the covariate vector x, select a random number of covariates without replacement. Note that the same covariates are selected for all the observations.

3. Create the CART tree from the data in steps 1 and 2, and, as earlier, do not prune the tree.

4. For each terminal node, assign a class. Put each out-of-bag data down the tree and find its predicted class.

5. Repeat steps 1 to 3 several times, say 200 or 500.

6. For each observation, count the number of times it is predicted to belong to a class only when it is a part of the out-of-bag dataset.

7. The majority count for the observation belonging to a particular class is considered as its predicted class.

Now, this is quite a complex algorithm, although, fortunately, it isn't really, as the `randomForest` package helps us out. We will continue with the German credit data problem.

Time for action – random forests for the German credit data

The function `randomForest` from the same named package will be used to build a random forest for the German credit data problem:

1. Get the `randomForest` package by using `library(randomForest)`.

2. Load the German credit data by using `data(GC)`.

3. Create a random forest with 500 trees:

    ```
    GC_RF <- randomForest(good_bad~.,data=GC,keep.forest=TRUE,
    ntree=500).
    ```

    It is very difficult to visualize a single tree of the random forest. A very ad-hoc approach can be seen at http://stats.stackexchange.com/questions/2344/best-way-to-present-a-random-forest-in-a-publication. Now, we reproduce the necessary function to get the trees, and, as the solution step is not exactly perfect, the reader may skip steps 4 and 5.

4. Define the `to.dendrogram` function:

    ```
    to.dendrogram <- function(dfrep,rownum=1,height.increment=0.1)  {
         if(dfrep[rownum,'status'] == -1)            {
              rval <- list()
              attr(rval,"members") <- 1
              attr(rval,"height") <- 0.0
              attr(rval,"label") <- dfrep[rownum,'prediction']
              attr(rval,"leaf") <- TRUE
                                          }
         else      {
              left <- to.dendrogram(dfrep,dfrep[rownum,'left daughter'],height.increment)
              right <- to.dendrogram(dfrep,dfrep[rownum,'right daughter'],height.increment)
              rval <- list(left,right)
              attr(rval,"members") <- attr(left,"members") + attr(right,"members")
              attr(rval,"height") <- max(attr(left,"height"),attr(right,"height")) + height.increment
              attr(rval,"leaf") <- FALSE
              attr(rval,"edgetext") <- dfrep[rownum,'split var']
              }
    class(rval) <- "dendrogram"
    return(rval)
                                          }
    ```

5. Use the `getTree` function, and with the `to.dendrogram` function defined previously, visualize the first 20 trees of the forest:

    ```
    for(i in 1:20)      {
     tree <- getTree(GC_RF,i,labelVar=T)
     d <- to.dendrogram(tree)
    plot(d,center=TRUE,leaflab='none',edgePar=list(t.cex=1,p.col=NA,p.
    lty=0))
            }
    ```

The error rate is of primary concern. As we increase the number of trees in the forest, we expect a decrease in the error rate. Let us investigate this for the GC_RF object.

6. Plot the out-of-bag error rate against the number of trees with
   `plot(1:500,GC_RF$err.rate[,1],"l",xlab="No.of.Trees",ylab="OOB Error Rate"):`

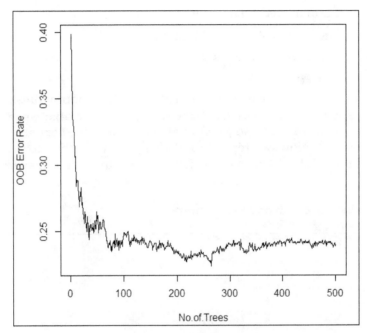

Performance of a random forest

The covariates (features) are selected differently for different trees. Now we need to know which variables are significant. The important variables are obtained using the `varImpPlot` function.

7. The function `varImpPlot` gives a display of the importance of the variables by using `varImpPlot(GC_RF)`:

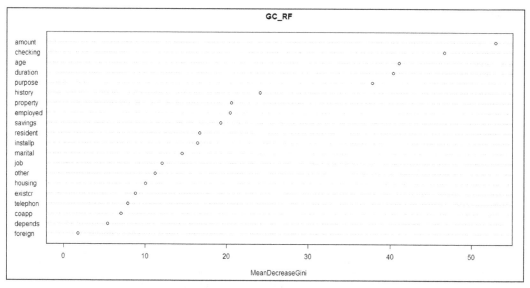

Important variables of German credit data problem

Thus, we can see which variables have more relevance over the others.

What just happened?

Random forests are a very important extension of the CART concept. In this technique, we need to know the error-rate distribution as the number of trees increases. This is expected to decrease with the increase in the number of trees. `varImpPlot` also gives a very important display of the importance of the covariates for classifying the customers as good or bad.

In conclusion, we will undertake a classification dataset and revise all the techniques seen in the book, especially those from *Chapter 6, Linear Regression Analysis* to *Chapter 10, CART and Beyond*. We will consider the problem of low birth weight among infants.

Doing it in Python

We already have the German credit data in our session. Now, we will go about carrying out the random forest analyses using Python:

1. Use the function `RandomForestClassifier` from the `sklearn.ensemble` module:

```
In [10]:  model = RandomForestClassifier(n_estimators=100,
                                  max_depth=6, min_samples_split=10)
          model_RF = model.fit(X_train,y_train)
```

2. Predicting the output for the training and test dataset, we now set up the ROC analyses:

```
In [11]:  y_train_pred = model_RF.predict(X_train)
          y_test_pred = model_RF.predict(X_test)
          fpr_train_RF, tpr_train_RF, thresholds_RF = roc_curve(y_train,y_train_pred)
          fpr_test_RF, tpr_test_RF, thresholds = roc_curve(y_test,y_test_pred)
          roc_auc_train_RF = auc(fpr_train_RF,tpr_train_RF)
          roc_auc_test_RF = auc(fpr_test_RF,tpr_test_RF)
          print("Area under the ROC Curve for Train Data is : %f" % roc_auc_train_RF)
          print("Area under the ROC Curve for Test Data is : %f" % roc_auc_test_RF)

          Area under the ROC Curve for Train Data is : 0.731057
          Area under the ROC Curve for Test Data is : 0.607819

In [12]:  plt.plot(fpr_train_RF,tpr_train_RF,color='red',lw=2,label='ROC Curve')
          plt.plot(fpr_test_RF,tpr_test_RF,color='green',lw=2)
          plt.plot([0,1],[0,1],color='blue',lw=2,linestyle='--')
          plt.show()
```

Python is an important instrument on a data scientist's computing machine. R has provided the conceptual development while Python implementation would be quite handy too.

The consolidation

The goal of this section is to quickly review all of the techniques learned in the latter half of the book. To this end, a dataset has been selected where we have ten variables, including the output. Low birth weight is a serious concern, and it needs to be understood as a factor of many other variables. If the weight at birth is lower than 2,500 grams, it is considered as a low birth weight. This problem has been studied in *Chapter 19* of *Tattar, et. al. (2013)*. The following table gives a description of the variables. Since the dataset may be studied as a regression problem (variable BWT), as well as a classification problem (LOW), the reader can choose any path(s) that they deem fit. Let the final action begin:

Serial number	Description	Abbreviation
1	Identification code	ID
2	Low birth weight	LOW
3	Age of mother	AGE
4	Weight of mother at last menstrual period	LWT
5	Race	RACE
6	Smoking status during pregnancy	SMOKE
7	History of premature labor	PTL
8	History of hypertension	HT
9	Presence of uterine irritability	UI
10	Number of physician visits during the first trimester	FTV
11	Birth weight	BWT

Time for action – random forests for the low birth weight data

The techniques learned from *Chapter 6, Linear Regression Analysis* to *Chapter 10, CART and Beyond* will now be put to the test. That is, we will use the linear regression model, logistic regression, as well as CART:

1. Read the dataset into R with `data(lowbwt)`.

2. Visualize the dataset using the options `diag.panel`, `lower.panel`, and `upper.panel`:

   ```
   pairs(lowbwt,diag.panel=panel.hist,lower.panel=panel.smooth,upper.
   panel=panel.cor)
   ```

   Interpret the matrix of scatter plots and decide which statistical model seems most appropriate:

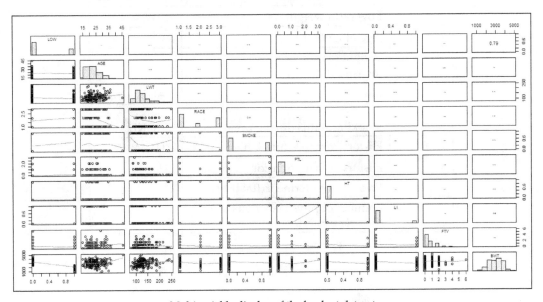

Multivariable display of the lowbwt dataset

As the correlations look weak, it seems that a regression model may not be appropriate. Let us check.

3. Create (sub) datasets for the regression and classification problems:

```
LOW <- lowbwt[,-10]
BWT <- lowbwt[,-1]
```

4. First, we will check whether a linear regression model is appropriate:

```
BWT_lm <- lm(BWT~., data=BWT)
summary(BWT_lm)
```

Interpret the output in light of the understanding of the linear regression model; refer to *Chapter 6, Linear Regression Analysis*, if necessary:

```
> BWT_lm <- lm(BWT~., data=BWT)
> summary(BWT_lm)
Call:
lm(formula = BWT ~ ., data = BWT)
Residuals:
    Min      1Q  Median      3Q     Max
-1817.4  -427.8    16.2   493.5  1655.5
Coefficients:
            Estimate Std. Error t value Pr(>|t|)
(Intercept) 3132.588    344.173    9.10  < 2e-16 ***
AGE           -0.345      9.593   -0.04  0.97131
LWT            3.435      1.700    2.02  0.04475 *
RACE        -189.478     57.722   -3.28  0.00124 **
SMOKE       -357.029    107.496   -3.32  0.00108 **
PTL          -51.590    102.980   -0.50  0.61701
HT          -600.632    204.305   -2.94  0.00371 **
UI          -510.098    140.251   -3.64  0.00036 ***
FTV          -15.550     46.926   -0.33  0.74075
---
Signif. codes:  0 '***' 0.001 '**' 0.01 '*' 0.05 '.' 0.1 ' ' 1
Residual standard error: 657 on 180 degrees of freedom
Multiple R-squared: 0.223,    Adjusted R-squared: 0.188
F-statistic: 6.45 on 8 and 180 DF,  p-value: 2.25e-07
```

Linear model for low birth weight

The low R^2 makes it difficult for us to use the model. Let us check out the logistic regression model.

5. Fit the logistic regression model with:

```
BWT_glm <- glm(BWT~., data=BWT)
summary(BWT_glm).
```

The summary of the model is given in the following screenshot:

```
> LOW_glm <- glm(LOW~.,data=LOW)
> summary(LOW_glm)
Call:
glm(formula = LOW ~ ., data = LOW)
Deviance Residuals:
    Min      1Q  Median      3Q     Max
 -0.841  -0.301  -0.153   0.422   0.913
Coefficients:
              Estimate Std. Error t value Pr(>|t|)
(Intercept)   0.42702    0.22905    1.86   0.0639 .
AGE          -0.00529    0.00638   -0.83   0.4088
LWT          -0.00211    0.00113   -1.86   0.0640 .
RACE          0.07743    0.03841    2.02   0.0453 *
SMOKE         0.16296    0.07154    2.28   0.0239 *
PTL           0.11712    0.06853    1.71   0.0892 .
HT            0.37013    0.13597    2.72   0.0071 **
UI            0.15424    0.09334    1.65   0.1002
FTV           0.00703    0.03123    0.23   0.8220
---
Signif. codes:  0 '***' 0.001 '**' 0.01 '*' 0.05 '.' 0.1 ' ' 1
(Dispersion parameter for gaussian family taken to be 0.1911)
    Null deviance: 40.582  on 188  degrees of freedom
Residual deviance: 34.392  on 180  degrees of freedom
AIC: 234.3
Number of Fisher Scoring iterations: 2
```

Logistic regression model for the low birth weight

6. The Hosmer–Lemeshow goodness-of-fit test for the logistic regression model is given by `hosmerlem(LOW_glm$y,fitted(LOW_glm))`.

   Now, the p-value obtained is `0.7813`, which shows that there is no significant difference between the fitted values and the observed values. Hence, we conclude that the logistic regression model is a good fit. However, we will go ahead and perform CART models for this problem.

Note that the estimated regression coefficients are not huge values, and hence we do not need to check out the ridge regression problem.

7. Fit a classification tree with the `rpart` function:

```
LOW_rpart <- rpart(LOW~.,data=LOW)
plot(LOW_rpart)
text(LOW_rpart,pretty=1)
```

Does the classification tree appear more appropriate than the logistic regression fitted earlier?

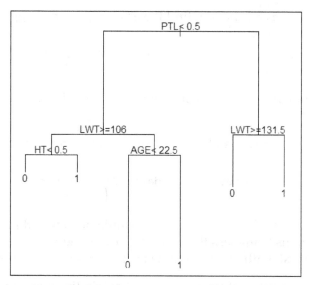

Classification tree for low birth weight

8. Get the rules of the classification tree by using `asRules(LOW_rpart)`:

```
Rule number: 11 [LOW=1 cover=10 (5%) prob=0.80]
    PTL< 0.5
    LWT< 106
    AGE>=22.5
Rule number: 7 [LOW=1 cover=21 (11%) prob=0.71]
    PTL>=0.5
    LWT< 131.5
Rule number: 9 [LOW=1 cover=9 (5%) prob=0.56]
    PTL< 0.5
    LWT>=106
    HT>=0.5
Rule number: 6 [LOW=0 cover=9 (5%) prob=0.33]
    PTL>=0.5
    LWT>=131.5
Rule number: 10 [LOW=0 cover=18 (10%) prob=0.28]
    PTL< 0.5
    LWT< 106
    AGE< 22.5
Rule number: 8 [LOW=0 cover=122 (65%) prob=0.19]
    PTL< 0.5
    LWT>=106
    HT< 0.5
```

Rules for the low birth weight problem

It appears that these rules are of great importance to the physician who does the operations. Let us check the bagging effect on the classification tree.

9. Using the `bagging` function, find the error rate of the bagging technique with the following code:

```
LOW_bagging <- bagging(LOW~., data=LOW,coob=TRUE,nbagg=50,keepX=T)
LOW_bagging$err
```

The error rate is `0.3228`, which seems very high. Let us see if random forests help us out.

10. Using the `randomForest` function, find the error rate for the out-of-bag problem:

```
LOW_RF <- randomForest(LOW~.,data=LOW,keep.forest=TRUE, ntree=50)
LOW_RF$err.rate
```

The error rate is still around `0.34`. The initial idea was that, with the number of observations being less than 200, we developed it with only `50` trees. Repeat the task with `150` trees and check whether the error rate decreases.

11. Increase the number of trees to `150` and obtain the error-rate plot:

```
LOW_RF <- randomForest(LOW~.,data=LOW,keep.forest=TRUE, ntree=150)
plot(1:150,LOW_RF$err.rate[,1],"l",xlab="No.of.Trees",ylab="OOB
Error Rate")
```

The error rate of about `0.32` appears as the best solution we can obtain for this problem.

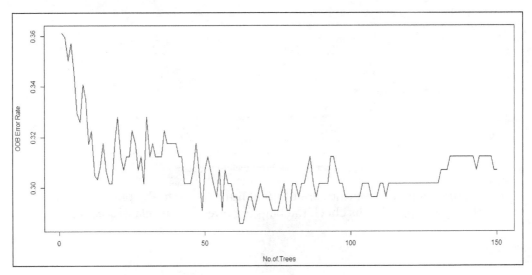

The error rate for the low birth weight problem

What just happened?

We did a very quick analysis of all the results using techniques from the last five chapters of the book.

Summary

The chapter began with two important variations of the CART technique, looking at the bagging technique and random forests. The random forest particularly is a very modern technique invented in 2001 by Breiman. The goal of the chapter was to familiarize the reader with these modern techniques.

Together with the German credit data and the complete revision of the techniques with the low birth weight problem, I hope that you benefitted a lot from the book, and have gained enough confidence to apply these tools to your analytical problems.

Index

Symbols

80-20 rule 126
4253H 157

A

abline function 102
actual probabilities 7
aes function 130
Akaike Information Criteria (AIC) 247
alternative hypothesis 182
Anaconda distribution
  reference 16
Analysis of Variance (ANOVA)
  about 215
  and confidence intervals 215, 216
  reference 215
and independent and identically
      distributed (iid) 207
ANOVA, and confidence intervals
  for multiple linear regression
      model 231-233
arbitrary choice of parameters 208-211
Automotive Research Association of
      India (ARAI) 4
auxiliary random variable 259

B

bagging 377
bagging algorithm
  working 380-384
bagplot
  about 150
  for Gasoline mileage problem 151
  reference 151

bagplot display
  for multivariate datasets 151, 152
bar chart
  about 87
  built-in examples, of R 87
  for bug metrics dataset 88
  for bug metrics of five software 88
  visualizing, in R 89-93
barchart function 87, 94
barplot function 87, 94
basic arithmetic 45
binary regression problem 256, 257
binomial distribution 23-27
binomial test 183
bins 114
bivariate boxplot 150
boot function 380
bootstrap aggregation 377
bootstrapped tree 381
bootstrap technique 378-380
box-and-whisker plot 107
boxplot
  about 107
  example 107
  for resistivity data 108
  in Python 111
  using 108-111
bwplot function 108

C

CART
  improving 374-376
categorical variable 20, 335
chi-square test 186